Christmas 1986

To Maurice

with

Ex Libris

Maurice

Green

Pen and Pencil Pictures

OF

Old Bradford.

Scene on the Bradford Canal.

Drawn by Chas Cousen

Engraved by J. C. Bentley

Bierley Hall.

PEN AND PENCIL PICTURES

OF

Old Bradford.

(W. R. YORKS.)

BY WILLIAM SCRUTON,
Author of "The Birthplace of Charlotte Brontë, etc.

[See page 245.]

WITH PLAN, PORTRAITS, AND OTHER ILLUSTRATIONS.

THE AMETHYST PRESS
ILKLEY ROAD
Otley, West Yorkshire

First edition published 1890,
Second edition published 1891

This paperback edition published in 1985 by

The Amethyst Press Limited
Ilkley Road
Otley
West Yorkshire LS21 3JP

ISBN. 0–904293–13–0

Printed and bound by
SMITH SETTLE
Ilkley Road, Otley,
West Yorkshire, LS21 3JP

WILLIAM SCRUTON 1840—1924

WILLIAM Scruton was born in Little Horton Green, Bradford, on 24 April 1840 and died at his daughter's home in Bradford on 31 January 1924. He was buried in Scholemoor Cemetery. He had lived in a period during which Bradford, once a relatively unimportant semi-rural township had become one of the great industrial and commercial cities of the world. The new institutions needed for its successful administration and development had been created. A way of life characteristic of the region of which Bradford was the focal point had emerged; it was this culture which had so impressed J.B. Priestley as a young man that he was prepared to bet that Bradford had produced more well-known people—musicians, writers, artists, painters, scientists and the like than any other place of comparable size in the United Kingdom.

After decades of social chaos spent in the pursuit of wealth and economic growth, Bradford's population was discovering by the late 1860s a new pattern of order and stability. The first signs of a Bradfordian civic consciousness were emerging and men and women wanted both a definition of the transformation they had shared, and an indication of where it all was taking them. "Men enter the future looking backwards, there is nowhere else to look", one eminent historian remarked some years ago. In Bradford from the mid-century onwards a lively interest in the process of historical change as it had affected the locality was developed. A number of men were stimulated to record what they could discover. In 1878 they founded the Bradford Historical and Antiquarian Society to push forward the work and most of them wrote up the products of their research in works of local history which still have very great value. Among them three men stand out —John James, William Cudworth and William Scruton.

To live in Little Horton Green as Scruton did in the nineteenth century was in itself something of a stimulus to a lively mind and an historical imagination. The Green, and there still was a Green, remained a rural enclave in the very centre of the new industrial city growing around it. To walk along the Green was to pass from the nineteenth century to the seventeenth and eighteenth centuries, for the proprietors of Horton Hall and Horton Old Hall, both located there amid a huddle of old-fashioned cottages, ensured that industrial encroachment was kept at bay. Contemporary records on Scruton also note that the father had a lot to do with the development of the son's historical interests. He was a man of lively mind and imagination and an unusual capacity for vivid description. He had lived through the excitements of revolution and change in the early part of the century and it delighted him to talk about his recollections of the period.

Scruton obtained the best part of his education at the Mechanics' Institute which in the middle of the nineteenth century fulfilled something of the function of a college of further education. It never achieved the role in the education of working men that its title suggested but for a sensible young man somewhat above the level of working class poverty it offered facilities for commercial training and general education not available elsewhere in the town. Scruton frequently acknowledged the debt. He was first employed by Robert Milligan and Henry Forbes as a warehouse clerk in the mercantile enterprise next door to St George's Hall. Later he moved to Messrs Herbert J. Jeffrey and Sons, Solicitors, Cheapside, and stayed there for 59 years, becoming the chief cashier.

He was a devout and devoted member of the Moravian Church in Little Horton all his life. Beyond this, his friends and companions were to be found in the literary, artistic and local history circles of the town. He was frequently to be found in Abraham Holroyd's shop in Westgate, for Holroyd, the *doyen* of Bradford's literary life, had organised there a sort of literary circle where Scruton and others of like mind could discuss their work together. He himself acknowledged a special debt of gratitude to William Cudworth for the help he had received when first starting to write. He was recognised as friendly and helpful to others but known as a sharp critic of plagiarists who made use of his work without giving him proper acknowledgement. He had considerable talent as an artist and spent a great deal of time recording views of buildings and scenes on the verge of disappearing—among them, the Old Corn Mill, the Old Piece Hall and the Quaker Chapel at Goodmansend. A good local historian, he spent many hours wandering around the district; on one such ramble he came across the ancient Baildon stocks embedded in the wall of a reservoir, and saw to it that they were restored and placed at the centre of the village.

The first article he published was an account of some of Bradford's oldest inns and public houses. It appeared in the *Bradford Observer*. By the late seventies he was a regular contributor to the local press; the *Bradford Observer*, the *Bradford Daily Telegraph*, the *Yorkshireman* and several of the Leeds papers, and for many years he wrote and lectured frequently for the Historical and Antiquarian Society. The most important article he wrote was a scholarly account of the great Bradford strike of 1825—still a work of reference for students of nineteenth century Labour history today. Articles on the Moravians of Little Horton; Benjamin Bartlett, the much respected Quaker apothecary who lived at the bottom of Bolton Lane; the schoolmaster Joseph Hinchcliffe, at whose establishment many of Bradford's early industrial leaders were educated, are three of the many articles which provided early accounts of aspects of Bradford's social history. In an introduction to an edition of *Abraham Holroyd's Collection of Yorkshire Ballads* he contributed a sketch of the life of that remarkable and redoubtable man. He also got together a considerable stock of blueprints, autographs and documents of all kinds relating to Bradford; on his death a good deal of it was dispersed to private hands and the rest deposited in the Bradford Central Reference Library. This has now been handed over to the West Yorkshire Archives Service, Bradford.

The most successful of the books he wrote was the one concerning the Bronte family, *The birthplace of Charlotte Bronte*; it went into three editions very quickly and was later reprinted in an amended version as *Thornton and the Brontes*. He also compiled a much used *Bradford Fifty Years Ago, a Jubilee memorial of the Bradford Corporation*, and the present volume *Pen and Pencil Pictures of Old Bradford*, his most important contribution to the history of the locality. In it he gathered a wealth of information about the leaders of Bradford society—their activities, their families, and their place in the pattern of the town's development.

It was one of the three or four books which established the foundations of the history and historiography of Bradford. John James' work on the worsted industry and the parish of Bradford took the story just beyond the middle of the nineteenth century. William Cudworth concentrated in the main on the work of the new Corporation of Bradford and on the old townships which went to make up the new Bradford. Scruton provides a more general picture and brings the story very nearly up to the last decade of the century. He is particularly concerned with recording what he sees as the most important changes in social life in the eighteenth and nineteenth centuries. The work is of course uncritical in its appraisements—the assumption of progress is more or less absolute. The working classes, about eighty per cent of the population, do not appear often except as recipients of some form of paternalistic charity. Nevertheless, the book's concentration on social activities of different kinds—churches and chapels, Sunday schools, educational institutions, inns and taverns, theatres, and music halls,—gives it its unique value.

The book starts with a short chronological survey, taking us briefly from earliest times through the middle ages into the nineteenth century. This chapter is really a reminder of the revolutionary nature of that century. Although the period between about 1400 and 1780 was eventful enough, until the Industrial Revolution very little happened to change the nature of society significantly. It is worth recalling that in 1800 there was still a good deal of medieval Bradford about. The open cattle fairs, for instance, those "living illustrations of the fifteenth century", as one *Bradford Observer* correspondent wrote, only disappeared in the 1870s.

The longest section of the book is devoted to the religious activities of the community. The devoutness of the Victorian age may well be exaggerated, but the evidence of the Ecclesiastical Census of 1851 is clear enough. In Bradford somewhere between a fifth and a third of the inhabitants were regular church or chapel goers and among them were almost all the acknowledged leaders of the community. The moral climate was determined by the churches and chapels. There is one chapter on the Anglican persuasion and two on the dissenter/non-conformist communities—a reasonable allocation since Bradford was pre-eminently a non-Anglican town. Dominated numerically at least by the non-conformists and dissenters it was one of the leading centres from which pressure was exerted on governments to reduce the age old privileges of the state-established church.

Scruton on the whole avoids painful controversy and concentrates on the building programmes and the ministries of the various divines. There is some justification for this for it describes a very important function; the mechanism by which the churches and chapels exercised their principal secular role of providing and maintaining a system of morality for a population which had grown from 13,000 to 103,000 in fifty years with little provision for effective social control.

In other areas also he avoids the controversies and relates the quieter story of the decay of old institutions and their replacement by the appropriate landmarks of an industrial-urban world; schools and adult educational facilities, law courts, banks, the Dispensary and Infirmary, the Exchange Building in Piccadilly and the Post Offices. He restricts his view of politics to the successive parliamentary elections and so avoids the fierce controversies of the working class struggle for the vote. Chartism barely appears. There is nothing at all about that remarkable day of Bradford's history in 1864, when thousands of working men greeted Lord Palmerston, the principal barrier at the time to the vote for working men, in absolute and devastating silence, when he appeared before a public gathering to lay the foundation stone of the new Wool Exchange in Market Street. In fact Scruton was responding to a public taste which he probably shared. Many Victorians believed that the act of 1867, which gave the vote to all male *householders* over 21 (but not all males over 21), had resolved the basic problems of democracy. In future, political differences could be ironed out quietly in Parliament and they assumed that the fierce political conflicts which had marked the years between 1830 and 1870 were best forgotten.

Of the various histories of Bradford written in the nineteenth century *Pen and Pencil Portraits of Old Bradford* is the most generally informative. It is very well illustrated both with Scruton's own work and with portraits and sketches done by other notable Bradfordians. We should also bear in mind that it was written amid all the difficulties which attend the preparation of pioneer material for public use. I can recommend it—it's been invaluable for me.

Jack Reynolds June 1985

PREFACE TO THE SECOND EDITION.

A YEAR has elapsed since the first edition of this work made its appearance. That edition met with so very favourable a reception, and was so soon disposed of, that I feel emboldened to embark upon another. I do so partly in compliance with the request of numerous friends, and partly because no effort has, as yet, been made to circulate the work beyond the limits of the town and neighbourhood of Bradford.

If it be true that "imitation is the sincerest form of flattery," perhaps I ought to feel flattered by the fact that the appearance of my work was immediately followed by others bearing nearly the same title, and making liberal, though I regret to say, unacknowledged use of the information and illustrations contained in mine. I must however, decline the compliment, if such it be, and leave my readers to form their own opinion upon it, merely remarking that while any *original* contribution to local historic lore may always rely upon a cordial welcome, the work of the plagiarist cannot be too strongly censured.

It is with feelings of unfeigned gratitude that I acknowledge the kindly welcome given to my work both by the Press and the Public. From friends and strangers alike I have received encouraging words, and generous help in making the book known.

Writing to me on the 11th of December last, the late kind and genial Edwin Waugh said "I have been reading your book ever since I got it. It is an admirable production, and I find it full of interest all through. I sincerely wish you success in all that you may do hereafter."

WILLIAM SCRUTON.

West Bowling,
Bradford,
December 1891.

THE RIGHT HONBLE. VISCOUNT CRANBROOK.
(*From a Photograph by* ALEXANDER BASSANO, *London*.)

To

THE RIGHT HONOURABLE

THE VISCOUNT CRANBROOK, G.C.S.I.

Lord President of the Privy Council,

This MEMORIAL of

HIS LORDSHIP'S NATIVE TOWN,

IS MOST RESPECTFULLY

Dedicated by

THE AUTHOR.

Bradford, *November 1889.*

ILLUSTRATIONS.

WHOLE PAGE PICTURES.

OTHER ILLUSTRATIONS.

PREFACE.

I HAVE no apology to make in submitting this work to my numerous subscribers and the public. That there is abundant scope for it, and that the proper time for its appearance has arrived, I am fully assured. That it will meet with a favourable reception I have very little doubt.

More than twenty years have elapsed since the publication of Mr. James' "History of Bradford with Additions and Continuation," and during that period so great a transformation has taken place, and the *old* has so completely given way to the *new* that anyone revisiting Bradford after an absence of a quarter of a century or so, would fail to recognise it, and would require the magic aid of Alladin's Lamp or Fortunatus' Cap in wandering through its labyrinth of newly-formed streets and thoroughfares. Few indeed are the relics of "Old Bradford" that remain to revive the "lingering memories" of its old inhabitants, or to awaken the curiosity of its "young and rising generation." The unceasing activity of a wealthy and enterprising Corporation in the work of "street improvements" has obliterated almost every trace of the old "nooks and corners" and the familiar landmarks that served as connecting links between Bradford as a small rural town, and Bradford as a large commercial metropolis. While this great change was being made, it occurred to me that unless an effort were made, and made speedily, to secure views of the principal objects of interest in the old streets, the opportunity of rescuing these from complete annihilation would be lost for ever. With such artistic ability as I possessed, and the aid of some knowledge of the history of the town, I succeeded in securing sketches of many places of great historic interest. These sketches, with some few exceptions, form the illustrations to the present work. It is far from my wish, however, to claim all the honour of having secured pictorial mementos of the Bradford that used to be. Mr. McArthur, a local artist of considerable ability, took several water-colour sketches of places of great interest, and was fortunate in securing views of such as the Union Passage, the Old Market House, the Woolpacks' Inn, the Old Butter Market, etc. Mr. Appleton, the photographer, has more recently brought out a fine set of photographic views of the principal public buildings of Bradford, while Mr. Bottomley, photographer, has been very successful in commemorating some recent public events, such as the ceremony of laying the foundation stone of the Town Hall; the uncovering of the Lister Statue, etc.

As to my qualifications for the task of producing such a work as this, I need, perhaps, only state that my tastes have always had a strong tendency towards local historical research, and that I have for several years past contributed sketches to the local press bearing upon the history of Bradford. Referring to a paper contributed by me to the "Bradford Antiquary"—the journal of the Bradford

Historical and Antiquarian Society—the *Bradford Observer* said: "Mr. Scruton has a proper reverence for old places, old families, and old associations, and in his remarks contrives to arouse a deep interest in the mind of the reader. He is a most entertaining *cicerone* through the regions of the local past."

As it was impossible to attempt anything like a complete history of Bradford within the limits of a work like the present, I have confined myself to subjects of the most general interest, and such as afforded the widest and best scope for pictorial illustration. With this end in view, I have substituted an intended chapter on "Early Bradford Wills" (kindly contributed by Mr. J. Horsfall Turner), and one on "Strikes and Riots" for others of a more interesting character. The reader will please note this explanation, as reference has been inadvertently made to these subjects in the letter-press, (see pages 29 and 114).

It will be seen at a glance that the illustrations form a very special feature of this book. No true book-lover can be insensible to the additional charm given to works of this character by the introduction of authentic and artistic pictures. The re-drawing of several sketches, and the making of the blocks of the illustrations have been entrusted to Mr. Alexander Shepherd of this town, the excellence of whose workmanship may be left to speak for itself. Among the names of other artists, whom I am proud to mention as associated with the pictorial adornment of these pages, are those of Angelina Geller, John Sowden, A.M., Arthur North ("Ant."), G. A. Gaskell, A. M'Arthur, Harold Furniss, J. W. Knight, H. Cragg, and S. Ward.

Foremost among those to whom I am indebted for generous and gratuitous help, I have to name my dear friend and antiquarian colleague, Mr. J. Horsfall Turner, of Idle. My thanks are also due to Miss Geller, Mr. Sowden, Mr. Joseph Margerison, and Mr. J. W. Knight, for artistic work most cheerfully given, and to Mr. W. Maw for the loan of two scarce pictures.

The excellent portraits of S. C. Lister, Esq. and Ald: Angus Holden are from the photographs by Mr. Albert Sachs; and that of the Right Hon. W. E. Forster is from the admirable photograph taken by Mr. Appleton, Manningham Lane.

I gratefully acknowledge my obligations to Mrs. Arthur Tempest, of Coleby Hall, Lincoln, for historic notes relating to the Tempest family.

Mr. William Cudworth has been to me a "Friend in Council." I cannot forget the words of encouragement received from him when making my first literary venture. "I hail with pleasure," he wrote, "your proposal to give something to the antiquarian world, as I feel sure you will not stop after your first essay."

Among those who have manifested their kindly interest in my project by inducing friends to become subscribers, I very gratefully mention the names of Mr. Lewis Hainsworth, Mr. William Glossop, Mr. Bennet Carter, Mr. John Braithwaite, Mr. John Schofield, Mr. S. E. Dean, and Mr. George Newboult.

W. S.

CONTENTS.

CHAPTER I.—Historical Survey.

CHAPTER II.—The Parish Church.

CHAPTER III.—Modern Churches.

CHAPTER IV.—The Dissenters.

PLAN OF BRADFORD.
IN
1800.
For the better identification of this Map several buildings are shewn that have been erected since 1800. The dates of their erection are given in the accompanying Reference.
OCTAGON CHAPEL
HALIFAX ROAD (HORTON ROAD).
HORTON LANE INDEPENDENT CHAPEL
HALIFAX ROAD (LITTLE HORTON LANE)
HUDDERSFIELD (MANCHESTER) ROAD
MILL RACE OF GOIT
BECK
TURLS
TOAD (CHAPEL) LANE
GOODMANS-END
BOWLING BECK
MARKET PLACE
IVE-GATE
SKINNER LANE
PIPERS' GRAVE
FOOTPATH
SITE OF PICCADILLY
Shepherd Bros Engd

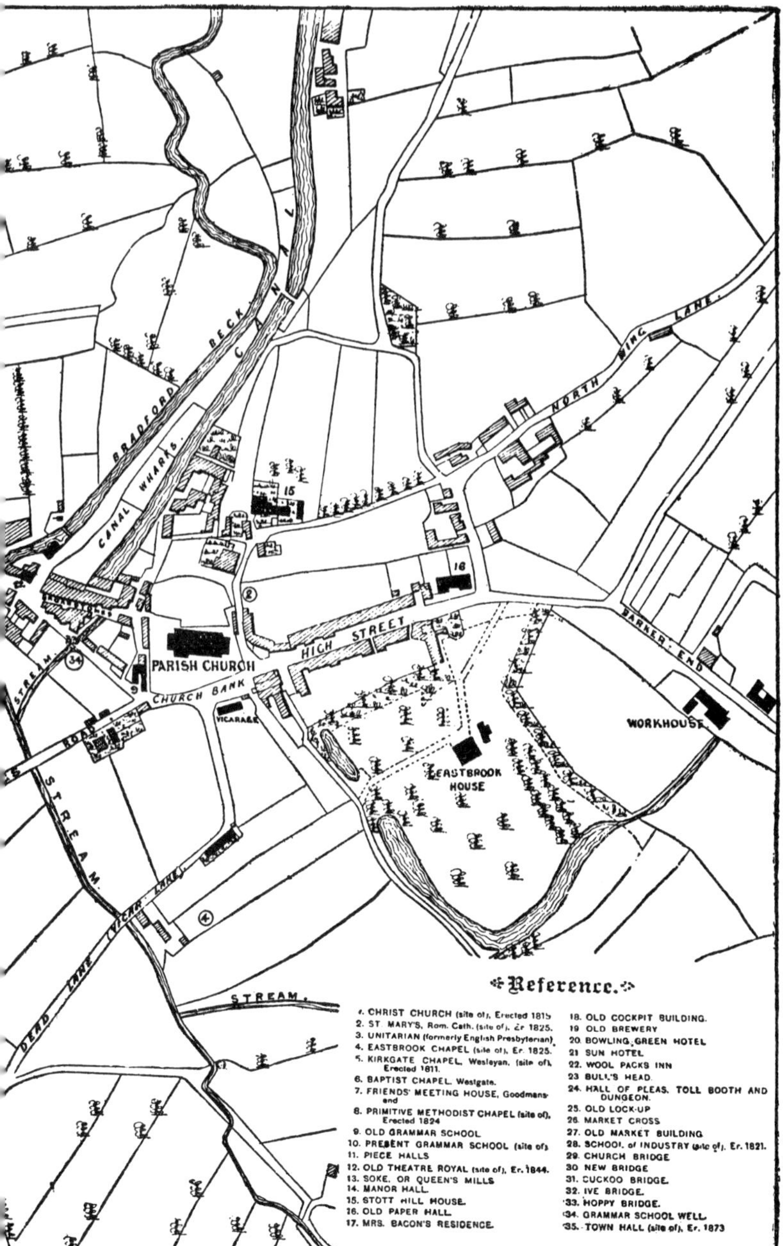
BRADFORD BECK
CANAL
CANAL WHARFS
NORTH WING LANE
HIGH STREET
BARKER END
WORKHOUSE
PARISH CHURCH
CHURCH BANK
VICARAGE
EASTBROOK HOUSE
STREAM
DEAD LANE (VICAR LANE)
STREAM
Reference.
1. CHRIST CHURCH (site of), Erected 1815
2. ST. MARY'S, Rom. Cath. (site of), Er 1825.
3. UNITARIAN (formerly English Presbyterian).
4. EASTBROOK CHAPEL (site of), Er. 1825.
5. KIRKGATE CHAPEL, Wesleyan, (site of), Erected 1811.
6. BAPTIST CHAPEL, Westgate.
7. FRIENDS' MEETING HOUSE, Goodmans-end
8. PRIMITIVE METHODIST CHAPEL (site of), Erected 1824
9. OLD GRAMMAR SCHOOL
10. PRESENT GRAMMAR SCHOOL (site of)
11. PIECE HALLS
12. OLD THEATRE ROYAL (site of), Er. 1844.
13. SOKE, OR QUEEN'S MILLS
14. MANOR HALL.
15. STOTT HILL HOUSE.
16. OLD PAPER HALL.
17. MRS. BACON'S RESIDENCE.
18. OLD COCKPIT BUILDING.
19. OLD BREWERY
20. BOWLING GREEN HOTEL
21. SUN HOTEL
22. WOOL PACKS INN
23. BULL'S HEAD.
24. HALL OF PLEAS, TOLL BOOTH AND DUNGEON.
25. OLD LOCK-UP
26. MARKET CROSS
27. OLD MARKET BUILDING
28. SCHOOL of INDUSTRY (site of). Er. 1821.
29. CHURCH BRIDGE
30. NEW BRIDGE
31. CUCKOO BRIDGE.
32. IVE BRIDGE.
33. HOPPY BRIDGE.
34. GRAMMAR SCHOOL WELL.
35. TOWN HALL (site of), Er. 1873

PEN AND PENCIL PICTURES

OF

OLD BRADFORD.

CHAPTER I.—Historical Survey.

IN attempting to tread "the long extent of backward time," in the study of history, it is better to be guided by the calendar of events rather than by the mere enumeration of years. It is easy to speak of five hundred years as so many round figures, but not so easy to form a just conception of the actual span of time represented by the same. Only by taking a glance at the more prominent features or landmarks of history can this be even fairly realised. Thus it will be necessary to look far beyond the days of the Commonwealth, the Spanish Armada, the Reformation, and even the Wars of the Red and White Roses, before we approach the time when the Plantagenet King, Edward III., sat upon the throne, and Chaucer wrote his "Canterbury Tales." Three hundred years of Feudal bondage takes us further back to the Norman Conquest, and well nigh the same period intervenes before Egbert subdues the seven Saxon Kingdoms, and under the name of "England" makes them into one, of which he was himself the first proud monarch. Then comes a long stretch of some eight hundred years ere we get back to the Roman invasion, at which point we take leave of the written page of history, and fall back upon the wide domain of conjecture and speculation.

But the scholarly Cæsar tells us of the painted and skin-clad Briton whom he found upon our shores, and of the priests or Druids who chanted the lays of the valorous deeds of their forefathers. He also tells us (but doubtless from hearsay) of the Brigantes—those fierce and warlike Britons of the hill-country, to conquer whom it took many long years of severe encounter and bitter struggle. But this sturdy race was eventually compelled to surrender before the disciplined and numerous troops that fought under the Eagle standard.

That Bradford occupies the site of what was once a Brigantian town is not at all improbable, although the place is destitute of any British remains sufficient to prove the fact. Dr. Whitaker the historian says, that in these northern parts the towns of the ancient Britons were generally in the hollows of the valleys, either upon the margin of one stream or the confluence of two, for the convenience of water, and security from winds. It may therefore be assumed that as Bradford answers pretty well to this description, it was "once upon a time" a Brigantian town, and consisted of a number of huts surrounded by a forest in which the bear, the wolf, the wild ox and other ferocious animals abounded. These huts, the dwelling-places of our remote ancestors the ancient Britons, were made in the form of pits from six to eight, or even sixteen to eighteen feet in diameter, and had for a top a conical roof made weatherproof by wattling—a covering of rushes and branches, matted together with hurdles and sods of turf. Of the people who inhabited these rude abodes, it is recorded that they lived on the wild fruit of the forest, and that their clothing was made from the skins of wild beasts, their shoes being made of untanned leather. They tipped their arrows with flint, used hammers made of stone; were not unacquainted with the use of bronze and iron, and traded with coins made of tin. They were tall of stature, had blue eyes and red hair, and by way of adding to these attractions they tattooed and stained their bodies with paint and coloured juices, and altogether appeared to live in pretty much the same style as did the wild and uncivilized tribes of the North American Indians of more recent times.

It is the common belief that Bradford derived its name from a *broad-ford* by which the stream at the foot of the Church hill was formerly crossed. Dr. Whitaker, however, contends, that the name is to be traced to the word *brae*, a hill;—*Bradford* thus meaning the *ford* at the foot of the hill.

In Domesday book, however, it is spelled *Bradeford*, but Mr. James, author of the "History of Bradford and its Parish," although favouring the derivation *Broadford*, found it difficult to get over the fact that the syllable *broad* could hardly be applied to a passage over such an inconsiderable stream as that known to Bradfordians of modern times. "Some old inhabitants," he says "call it *Brafforth* or *Bradforth*, but this is a mere corruption of no very old date." In this statement, however, Mr. James is not correct, for in the wills at York of former Bradford inhabitants, dating so far back as 1420, the name is invariably spelled *Bradforth*.

But it must be impossible to form, at this time of day, anything like a just conception of what the width of this stream would be eleven or twelve hundred years ago—the probable period when Bradford took its name. It is worth remembering that the old topographer, Leland, in his "Itinerary" (*temp* Henry VIII.) makes special mention of the "brokes" of the town in his reference to Bradford. It is also supposed that the "mill" of which he speaks, as well the ancient fulling mill referred to in the "Inquisition" of 1311 stood on the stream near the ford. There is the fact too, that the name

"Broadstones" was taken from the large flat stepping-stones by which the beck had formerly to be crossed.

The authentic history of England commences with the invasion of the Romans, B.C. 55, but so far as Bradford is concerned there is little evidence to lay hold of by which to link it with the Roman period. There are certainly traces of Roman roads not far away, one of which even passed through the town by way of Westgate and Whetley Hill, and forward to Colne (Colunio). Another, in close proximity to Bradford, was that running by way of Dudley Hill and Adwalton, known (to this day) as the "Street," from *Stratum* denoting a Roman way.

But unquestionably one of the most distinct traces of the Roman occupation of this district was that mentioned by the learned Dr. Richardson, of Bierley Hall, who in a letter to his friend Hearne, said "That iron was made in this neighbourhood (Bierley) in the time of the Romans, a late discovery sufficiently convinced me. Upon removing a heap of cinders to repair the roads with, a quantity of copper Roman coins was discovered, some of which I have in my possession. They were of the period of Constantine, Diocletian, and the usurper Carausius. This country abounds with such heaps of cinders, though we have not so much as any tradition that ever iron was made here."

For four hundred years the Romans were masters of Britain. The withdrawal of their Legions however, left all these northern parts at the mercy of the Picts and Scots. The Saxons, then a powerful and warlike people, were invited to come over to assist the Britons against their ferocious enemies. The invitation was accepted. They came over and drove out the foe, but only that they might in their turn become despoilers of the land and masters of the people. Alas! the poor Britons were in a pitiable plight. A new enemy now appeared in the shape of the savage and blood-thirsty Danes, and slaughter and rapine swept over the land. The story is too well known to need recapitulation. It is a stain upon the page of history; but happily history tells us that at length (A.D. 876) through the wisdom of the great and good King Alfred, a time of peace was brought about, and the inhabitants for many long years cultivated the land, and tended their flocks in uninterrupted quietness.

It would be difficult, perhaps, for the imagination to realise the appearance of Bradford at this early stage of its history, but Mr. James, a careful and accurate historian, and by no means given to painting fancy pictures, has left us the following sketch of what he believed would be its general aspect as a Saxon village.

"On the site of the lower part of Kirkgate stood a few huts, one story high, without chimneys, and thatched with straw or covered with sods; formed of mud, wattles or wood, according to the poverty or opulence of the inhabitants, placed at straggling distances, and without order. Around each hut was the homestead, or erection for the shelter of the cattle, enclosed by its toft or croft. On the summit of the hill where the church now stands, there was, enclosed with wood, probably a small chapel, or oratory of wood, in which the humble devotions of the inhabitants were offered up. The land around, which had been cleared for cultivation or pasturage, lay open and unenclosed and had no bound but the thicket or the brake! All the land would be in common as far as enclosures went. The inhabitants ploughed and reaped together, and divided the fruits of the earth according to their respective quantities of land or importance in the village."

In the famous survey, known as the "Domesday Book," which was begun in the year 1080, and was six years in completing, we are told that Bradford was the chief "vill." of the manor, and had six berewicks, or groups of houses dependent upon it, comprising fifteen carucates, or fifteen hundred acres of cultivated land, on which eight ploughs were employed. The manor was then in the possession of one Gamel, who appears to have been a person of some importance, as he was also owner of a great number of other manors in this part of the country. Soon after the Conquest, however, the Bradford manor fell into the hands of Ilbert de Lacy, one of the adventurers who came over from Normandy with William the Bastard; fought valiantly under his standard at the battle of Hastings, and for his pains had no less than 150 manors in the West Riding given to him. He was made Baron of Pontefract, and at Pontefract he built himself a castle in which he took up his quarters.

Barely a year had elapsed since the coronation of William, when a revolt, chiefly in Yorkshire, Northumberland, and Durham, took place, which so incensed the "Conqueror" that he swore "by the splendour of God" (his favourite oath) that he would not leave a soul alive in those counties. History has recorded how literally he carried out his threat. Simeon the Chronicler of Durham, says the country between York and Durham was so devastated that it lay waste for nine years, and that the inhabitants who escaped ate rats, mice, and other vermin, to sustain life. William of Malmesbury also records that there were destroyed and laid waste "such splendid towns, such lofty castles, and such beautiful pastures, that had a stranger viewed the scene he must have been moved with compassion."

Bradford, of course, shared in this widespread devastation, for says the Domesday record *Ilbert has it, and it is waste.* The thrifty Saxon village pictured by Mr. James would be completely transformed, for many of the inhabitants were massacred, and cattle, crops, and everything that could support human life were destroyed. One of the Norman chroniclers has left the sad record that not fewer than a hundred thousand persons perished in Yorkshire at this time, and that the whole country was made into a desert.

But it would seem as if nothing could crush the spirit of the people, for in course of time the population steadily increased; tracts of land were brought into a state of comparative cultivation, and various species of handicraft and trade were introduced.

Bradford eventually became one of the most valuable possessions of the Lacies, and it was to the interest of these feudal lords, who ruled over their manors as though they were kings, to obtain for the industrious inhabitants as many privileges as possible. Thus we find that Edmund de Lacy, who was in favour with the king, obtained several important grants, among which (in 1251) was a charter for holding a market at Bradford, and a grant of free warren in the manor. Passing on to 1277 when an "Inquisition" was taken, we get an interesting glimpse of how the people of Bradford were ruled in that remote period of its history. The Inquisition sets forth that "Henry de Lacy (Earl of Lincoln) hath many liberties in the town of *Bradeford;* to wit, a gallows, assize of bread and beer, a market-place, and a free court from ancient times."

The right of gallows was traced from the time of the Saxons, as express mention is made of it in the laws of Edward the Confessor. Mr. James believed that the Bradford gallows stood near to the present Bowling Foundry, because a certain field there is still known by the name of the "Gallows Close."

At the Free Court named in the Inquisition, fines could be imposed for unruly tempers, for gaming, card-playing at night, and other such trifling offences, while it had the power to inflict a fine of 10s. for an assault where blood was drawn, and 3s. 4d. for an assault where no blood was drawn. The assize of bread and beer was a right which the Lord of the Manor had of overlooking the weight and measure, and ascertaining the purity of those two articles. If any delinquencies were discovered the offenders were severely punished.

The Inquision also contains the curious item—"And they say that Nicholas de Burton, Steward of Henry de Lacy, had Evam, *weaver*, of Gomersal, in the prison at Bradeford, and took from him two cows, and him permitted to go without judgment." This is interesting as showing that weaving was carried on in or near to Bradford at so very early a date. We are kept in ignorance of the man's crime, but whatever it was, he paid the penalty of it by the loss of two cows.

It is also interesting to find that so early as 1287, *Frizinghall* is mentioned as belonging to Robert de Everingham, Lord of the Manor of Heaton. The name is of Flemish origin, and is believed to have been taken from certain cloths called *frieze* or *frize* for the making of which the Flemings were noted. Differences of opinion are held as to the correct derivation of the name *Frizinghall.* To those who give the preference to the termination *ley* over that of *hall*, we would simply state the fact that in the Manor Court Rolls of Bradford for 1348 a "Robert de Frizinghall" is mentioned; and in the Poll Tax for Manningham (1378) the name of a certain "Adam Ffrisynghall" occurs. A modern authority on local nomenclature maintains that *Frizinghall* was the *hall* in the *ing* where frieze was manufactured. Old inhabitants in the district, however, still cling to "*Frizingley.*"

Upon the death of Henry, Earl of Lincoln, who was the last Lacy who owned the Manor of Bradford, an Inquisition of all his lands and possessions was taken at Pontefract on the 3rd day of March, 1311. This document throws a flood of light upon the position held by Bradford in the earlier part of the fourteenth century. The following are some of the items mentioned in it—

"The Earl had at Bradford a Hall (Aulum) or Manor-house, with chambers, and it is nothing worth beyond necessary repairs, and there are forty acres in demesne, demised to divers tenants at will, and the value whereof yearly is (8d. an acre) £1. 6s. 8d.

And there is one Water-mill valued by the year at £10, and a Fulling mill which is worth yearly £1. And there is a certain Market every seventh day, upon the Lord's Day, the toll of which is worth yearly £3. And there is a certain Fair which is held annually upon the Feast of Saint Andrew the Apostle, the toll of which is worth yearly £3. And there are certain Villains who hold twenty-three ox-gangs of land in bondage, and render yearly, at the Feast of Saint Martin, (4s. for every oxgang) £4 16s. 0d. And the same Villains do work in autumn, which is worth yearly, for every oxgang 3d."

Commenting on the facts set out in this Inquisition, Dr. Whitaker says—"The Parish of Bradford is about fifteen miles in length, and at an average four in breadth; it contains therefore, forty thousand acres, more or less. Of these, little more than fifteen hundred appear to have been reclaimed at the time of the Inquisition. There were twenty-eight burgage-houses, a few free tenants at will, and a few in bondage, but from the smallness of their rents their numbers cannot have been considerable. If we suppose them to have equalled the burgesses it will perhaps give a fair estimate of the population of the town. The profits of the Corn mill amounted to more than one-fourth of all the lord's receipts for the parish. The soke must therefore have extended over the whole. From the existence of a Fulling mill I do not see how we can avoid inferring that the cloth manufactory had been commenced. The market was held on the Lord's-day, a concession (however inexcusable) to the circumstances of the greater part of the parish; for the church was situated at one extremity, and few, perhaps, would have resorted to it from the more distant quarters, who had not the additional inducement of purchasing and carrying home necessaries for their families. The glebe of the church was eight oxgangs, or one carucate, which, according to another survey, extended to ninety-six acres, so that the oxgang at Bradford equalled twelve acres."

Mr. James, while giving Dr. Whitaker credit for being "the best of all our topographers," at the same time takes exception to some of his conclusions, and especially his statement that the Soke must have extended over the whole parish. He maintains that there is every reason for believing that it merely extended over the same district as in recent times. He also differs from him in his estimate of the population of the town, and bases his own estimate upon the following figures. "Allowing ten acres of land for every family in the town, including bondmen, cotters, and the lowest rabble, the number of families would be one hundred. There were also twenty-nine burgage-houses, and reckoning one family to each, the whole number of families would be about 130, which, at five persons to a family, gives a population of 650 persons."

It seems pretty certain that Bradford could boast of a castle at this period of its history, which would be built by the Lacies as a halting place in their passage to and from Blackburnshire, and those portions of the south which they were occasionally in the habit of visiting, its probable locality being near the spot where the Bermondsey Hotel recently stood.

The precise time when the parish of Bradford was formed, and its first church erected, is involved in obscurity, but distinct mention is made of the existence of the latter in 1281, and from the Inquisition above mentioned we learn that its patrons, the Lacies, endowed it with ninety-six acres of land. As a recognition of its ancient dependence upon its mother church at Dewsbury it paid, and we believe still continues to pay to the latter, the sum of eight shillings per annum.

The very curious custom of holding the market on "Lord's Day," and in the church-yard, was not at all peculiar to Bradford. In the 13th Edward I., a statute was made forbidding the holding of fairs and markets in church-yards, but the law on this point seems to have been "more honoured in the breach than the observance," for the custom was continued for a long time afterwards in different parts of the country. Quarrels and fights were events of common occurrence at the monastic fairs in church-yards, and one authority states that when they were held within the precincts of a cathedral or a monastery, it was not uncommon to compel every one to take an oath at the gate, previous to his admission, that he would "neither lie, nor steal, nor cheat." So recently as the 7th year of Elizabeth's reign it was directed that at all fairs and common markets *falling upon Sunday*, "there be no shewing of any wares before the service be done."

From the Inquisition of 1311 we get an insight into the feudal system of classifying the inhabitants. These consisted of bondmen or villains, tenants at will, burgesses, free farmers, and free-holders. Of the villain class, Sir William Temple in his "Introduction to English History" says, they were "in a condition of downright servitude, used and employed in the most servile work, and belonging, both they, their children and effects, to the lord of the soil, like the rest of the cattle or stock upon it." So degraded was their condition that the Commons petitioned King Richard the Second that no villains should *put their children to school.* The tenants in bondage and tenants at will are said to have been the predecessors of our copy holders, and the burgesses were the handicraftsmen of the town to whom were committed the arts and mysteries of trades. They were regarded as a superior class to the tillers of the soil.

The Inquisition makes the following mention of the freeholders of Bradford—

"And there are certain freeholders who held their own tenements of the Earl, and tendered yearly the rents and services at the Feast of Saint Martin, according to the particulars thereof underwritten."

Then follow the names of thirty-two freeholders with the amounts which they severally paid. These freeholders were the most considerable men in the parish; and many of their descendants for centuries after were large owners of land in the same locality. The Pollards, the Balmes, the Thorntons, the Northrops, and others being examples.

The Manninghams were the custodians of the manorial records, and clerks or registrars of the proceedings of its courts. They appear to have been an important family in their time, but evidently they did not flourish long as their name has been lost sight of for many generations past.

A source of much profit to the Lord of the Manor was the Free Court at which all tenants were required to attend. There was also a Sheriff's Turn Court Leet for the whole of the parish, as there were no Justices of the Peace, and the Assizes were few and far between. This Court was worth £30 a year of our own money, and was a speedy and cheap way of redress. Among other privileges which the Lord of the Manor enjoyed was the gate toll, which was to keep cattle from straying in from the commons. These gates being placed at the head of what were then the three principal streets of the town, doubtless gave rise to the names by which they have so long been known—Kirk-gate, Ive-gate and West-gate.

The surveys of this period shew that the inhabited portion of the town was almost entirely on its north-western side, and extended from Barkerend, about the Parish Church, and in a more scattered form along Kirkgate and Westgate as far as White Abbey, down Millbank, into the Turles (near Tyrrel Street) and for a little way into Little Horton.

The social and domestic condition of the people at this time and for a long stretch into the fourteenth century was of a deplorable character. The huts or cottages of the poor consisted of one room, the fire being in the centre, and as there were no chimneys the smoke had to find its way out of the door or the roof. The people slept on straw pallets, with a log of wood for their pillow.

The well-to-do strewed their floors with rushes, which lay for months without being removed. The houses of the "lower orders" were either mud-walled, wattled, or of wood, the windows of which were mere loop-holes filled in with lattis work instead of glass. The food then in use consisted of bread of rye, barley, beans, peas, oats, and in times of famine, (then not uncommon) of acorns. Herds of pigs wandered about in the surrounding woods. These were slain and salted, and formed the chief flesh diet of the poor.

This portion of our subject may be fittingly concluded by quoting some curious items of cost from a scale of the average prices of certain articles about the year 1310, based upon Stow and other authorities of the period. "Wheat was 6s. a quarter; oats, 3s.; a cow, 12s. 6d.; a sheep, 1s. 2d.; a fat hog, 3s. 4d.; a fat goose, 2½d.; wine, 4d. a gallon; ale, 0½d. a gallon; a labourer's wages 1½d. a day, in harvest time 2d.; a journeyman carpenter, 2d. a day; a pair of shoes, 4d.; an English slave and his family were sold for 13s. 4d.; a Bible was worth £33 6s. 8d. The rule for reducing money of this period to that of our standard is (as laid down by Dr. Whitaker and other authorities) to multiply the former by fifteen.

By the male heirs of the Lacies becoming extinct, the manor of Bradford passed by marriage into the hands of the Earls of Lancaster.

In 1361, Henry, Duke of Lancaster, died and left two daughters, Maude and Blanche, as his heiresses; and the latter, who succeeded to the manor, married John of Gaunt, who eventually acquired the whole of the manorial estate. On his death Richard II. seized the estates, and thus the manor of Bradford became attached to the Crown. It is to the period of John of Gaunt's ownership that we have to trace the origin of that very singular tenure of horn-blowing, which has survived nearly to our own day. It is thus described by Gough in his *Britannia*.

"Bradford belonged to John of Gaunt, who granted to John Northrop, of Manningham, and his heirs, three messuages and six bovates of land, to come to Bradford on the blowing of a horn in winter, and to wait upon him and his heirs, on their way from Blackburn here, with a lance and hunting dog, for thirty days; to have for yeoman's board one penny for himself, and a half-penny for his dog. A descendant of this Northrop afterwards granted land to Rushworth, of Horton, to hold the lance while Northrop's man blew the horn. The name of Hornman or Hornblowing Land, was imposed upon the lands in question, and the custom is still kept up. A man comes into the market-place with a horn, halbert and a dog, and is there met by the owner of the lands in Horton. After the proclamation made, the former calls aloud, 'Heirs of Rushworth, come hold me my hound while I blow three blasts with my horn, to pay the rent due to our Sovereign lord the King.' He then delivers the string to the man from Horton, and winds his horn thrice. The original horn is still preserved though stripped of its original ornaments."

Tradition kindly steps in to complete the above narrative; and to a certain James Hartley, a schoolmaster, who flourished in Bradford about the middle of last century, we are indebted for the following version of it—

"A ravenous wild boar" says he, "of a most enormous size, haunted a certain place called the Cliffe Wood, and at times very much infested the town (Bradford) and the neighbouring inhabitants thereof; so that a reward was offered by the Government to any person or persons, who would bring the head of this boar; which much excited some to attempt it. Now the story runs thus: that this boar frequented a certain well in the aforesaid wood to drink, which to this day is called the 'Boar's well'; that he was watched by a certain person who shot him dead there, took his tongue out of his head, and immediately repaired to court to claim the promised reward. Presently after his departure from the well, another person came thither upon the same intention; and finding the beast dead, without any further examination, cuts off his head, and away he hastes towards the same place, and in expectation of the reward as the former, and there arrives before him. Being introduced into his Majesty's presence, the head was examined, but was found without a tongue, concerning which the man being interrogated could give no satisfactory account.

"Whilst this was held in suspense, the other man was introduced with the tongue, claimed the promised reward, and unfolded the riddle, by informing his majesty, how, and by what means he killed the beast; and thus received the following grant, namely, a certain piece or portion of land lying at Great Horton, known by the name of Hunt Yard, and for the tenure of which he, and his heirs for ever, should annually attend in the market-place at Bradford, on St. Martin's Day in the forenoon, and there, by the name of the heir of Rushforth, hold a dog of the hunting kind, whilst three blasts were blown on a Gelder's horn and these words ("Come, heir of Rushforth, etc.") expressed aloud."

This is the oldest bit of tradition of which Bradford can boast, and there is this to be said for it, that it gave rise to the town's crest or arms. The horn, one of our most ancient and interesting relics, after passing through many hands has at length found a resting-place in the public museum, Darley Street, where, we trust it may now remain undisturbed.

The span of history known as the "Plantagenet Period" might be very well passed over, so far as Bradford is concerned, but for the happening of certain events which seriously affected its progress.

The battle of Bannockburn (1314) was a tremendous blow to England, and especially to the North, which suffered severely from the incursions of the Scots, who plundered and devastated all before them. The cultivated districts of Craven-dale, we are told, were laid waste. Northallerton and Boroughbridge; and Scarborough and Skipton were reduced to ashes, and even Bradford shared in the wide-spread disasters.

The following figures are significant of how the town had sunk in wealth and status. In 1292 the living of the church was valued as follows:—

"Church of Bradford,	£53 6s. 8d.
Vicarage there,	£13 6s. 8d.

Re-valued in 1318 it stood thus:—

"Church of Bradford,	£28 0s. 0d.
Vicarage,	£5 0s. 0d.

But a worse enemy than even the savage Scot came in the shape of plague and famine. From the plague known as "the Black Death"—the most frightful scourge that England has ever known—none seemed to be exempt, for the York Registers of the time show that more than half the parish priests in the county were swept away by it. What then must the poorer classes have suffered? There is little or nothing to show to what extent Bradford was affected by this terrible visitation. Considerable light however, is thrown on the position of the town in the year 1378, by that wonderful document known as the Poll Tax of Richard II. This obnoxious tax was levied for the purpose of raising funds by which he might be the better able to carry on his wars. Lists were made of all persons above sixteen years of age, and the sums which, according to their station in life, they had to pay. An esquire was charged 20/-; an attorney, 6/8 (!); merchants, 13/4 to 20/-; tradesmen and artificers not gaining anything from land, from 6d. to 6/8; man and wife, not merchants, 4d.; and each single person, not a merchant, 4d. But following so soon on the heels of plague and famine, this impost came as a great hardship, especially to the poor, for although fourpence does not seem a large sum, it represented at that period at least four day's labour. The revolt which followed on the part of the peasantry, headed by Wat Tyler and Jack Straw, is matter of history, and need not be dwelt upon here.

Considered apart from its unhappy associations, however, this Poll Tax is of peculiar interest, giving, as it does, a faithful and accurate picture of the Bradford of five hundred years ago. The following are the lists for Bradford and Manningham:—

POLL TAX FOR BRADEFORTH.*

Willelmus Burges, *Hostiler*, & ux (wife) - *xijd.*
Johannes Leggard, *Hostiler*, & ux - - *xijd.*
Willelmus de Horneby, *Hostiler*, & ux - *xijd.*
Henricus Ouroune, *Cissor*, & ux - - *vjd.*
Thomas Walker, *Fullo*, & ux *vjd.*
Johannes Cote, *Sutor*, & ux *vjd.*
Willelmus filius Thorne, *sutor*, ux - *vjd.*
Johannes de Hetton, *cissor*, & ux - - *vjd.*
Willelmus Dynghale, *Cimentor*, & ux - - *vjd.*
Willelmus Harper, & ux *iiijd.*
Robertus del Syke, & ux *iiijd.*
Adam Nichelson, & ux *iiijd.*
Ricardus Walker, & ux *iiijd.*
Willelmus Ayell, & ux *iiijd.*
Johannes Elys, & ux *iiijd.*
Johannes de Preston, & ux *iiijd.*
Ricardus Barker, & ux *iiijd.*
Johannes Clerk, & ux *iiijd.*
Johannes Margaret, & ux *iiijd.*
Johannes Milner, & ux *iiijd.*
Gilbertus Chellawe, & ux *iiijd.*
Willelmus de Bulton, & ux *iiijd.*
Robertus filius Ricardi, & ux *ii jd.*
Willelmus filius Willelmi, & ux *iiijd.*
Hugo Nuttebroune, & ux *iiijd.*
Thomas Smyth, & ux *iiijd.*
Ricardus de Ourom *iiijd.*
Johanna Webster *iiijd.*

* From the Yorkshire Archæological Journal.

Alicia filia Roberti *iiijd.*
Celicia Sclater *iiijd.*
Alicia Scharpe *iiijd.*
Johanna Walker *iiijd.*
Willelmus Elys *iiijd.*
Alicia filia Walteri *iiijd.*
Johanna de Bynglay *iiijd.*
Isabella de Preston *iiijd.*
Dionisia de Horton *iiijd.*
Margareta relicta (widow) Ricardi *iiijd.*
Elizabetha Perkyn *iiijd.*
Adam Webster *iiijd.*
Margareta de Horneby *iiijd.*
Alicia relicta Rogeri *iiijd.*
Willelmus filius Johannis *iiijd.*
Christiana filia Johannis *iiijd.*
Margeria Manyngham *iiijd.*
Alicia filia Juliane *iiijd.*
Christiana, serviens (servant of) Willelmi *iiijd.*
Christiana filia Roberti *iiijd.*
Johannes Burges *iiijd.*
Alicia filia Willelmi *iiijd.*
Amicia Vttyngwyf *iiijd.*
Margaretta filia Walteri *iiijd.*
Johannes ffabe *iiijd.*
Robertus, serviens Johannis *iiijd.*
Thomas filius Willelmi *iiijd.*
Alicia filia Thorne *iiijd.*
Thomas Elys *iiijd.*
Johanna, serviens Willelmi *iiijd.*
Alicia filia Gilberti *iiijd.*
Alicia filia Johannis *iiijd.*

Summa *xxiijs.*

POLL TAX FOR MANYNGHAM.

Dionisius de Manyngham *iiijd.*
Johannes de Northorp & ux *iiijd.*
Johannes de Sthelwora & ux *iiijd.*
Adam atte Yate & ux *iiijd.*
Willelmus filius Ricardi & uxor *iiijd.*
Adam ffrisynghall & ux *iiijd.*
Robertus filius Willelmi & ux *iiijd.* *iiijd.*
Robertus atte Yate & ux *iiijd.*
Agnes, relicta Scerlonis *iiijd.*
Margeria Curtays *iiijd.*
Johannes filius Roberti *iiijd.*
Willelmus filius Ade *iiijd.*

Summa *iiijs. iiijd.*

Want of space precludes our setting out the names of those who paid the Poll Tax in the surrounding townships. They may be summarised as follows:—Horton; twenty-three persons paid 4d. each except "Thomas filius Rogeri," who was described as a *merchant*, and who was therefore mulcted in 12d. Bowling; nineteen paid 4d. each, and John Bowling 6/8. Thornton; twenty-one paid 4d. each, except William Leventhorp, who as a *franklin* (gentleman) had to pay 3/4. Allerton; forty at 4d. each. Clayton; twelve at 4d. North Bierley; twenty-four at 4d.; and Shipley, twenty-eight at 4d.

In contrast with certain other towns in the Riding, Bradford appears to have been put down at a very low figure. Thus, Pontefract paid £14 10s. 0d.; Doncaster, £11 13s. 4d.; Sheffield, £6 11s. 2d.; Selby, £6 6s. 0d.; and Wakefield, £4 15s. 8d. Of the neighbouring manufacturing towns of to-day, which were then of but little importance, we find Halifax paying 12/8; Morley, 11/4; Dewsbury, 13/4; Batley, 39/-; Gomersal, 17/-; and Heckmondwike 4/8.

Curiously interesting are many of the items that peep out of these taxation lists. Not only do they give the names of the inhabitants above sixteen years of age, but also their several callings and conditions in life.

Thus, we learn that in Bradford there were three innkeepers, (*hostilers*); two tailors (*cissors*); two shoemakers (*sutors*); one fuller, and one mason (*cimentor*). Why the innkeepers were taxed the highest of these is not shown.

There were then in Bradford twenty-six married couples; thirteen unmarried males and twenty females, of whom two were widows.

In Manningham there were seven married couples; two unmarried males and three females, one of whom was a widow.

Horton had seventeen married couples; two unmarried males and five females.

Bowling had thirteen married couples; four unmarried males and three females.

For Bolton there is the simple but sad record that "no one remains in this township, therefore nothing collected." Are we to assume that the terrible ravages of the Black Death, of some twenty years previous, had left the place destitute of inhabitants.

The population of Bradford five hundred years ago has been estimated at about 300. At the present time of writing it is over 220,000.

During the severe and long-protracted struggle between the houses of York and Lancaster, Bradford again came in for its share of suffering and depression. The inhabitants ranged themselves on the side of the Lancastrians (the Red Rose); but for all that Edward the Fourth (White Rose) was gracious enough to overlook the offence, and not only granted them exemption from toll, but gave them a grant for holding two annual fairs of three days each.

With the breaking down of the old feudal system came greater freedom for the people, and from this time right away to the unhappy contention between King Charles and his people, Bradford made rapid strides in prosperity, and greatly increased both in trade and population.

It was in the reign of Henry VIII. that Leland the topographer, made the following curious, and yet flattering remarks about Bradford in his famous "Itinerary"—"Bradforde, a praty quik market towne, *dimideo ant eo amplius, minus Wackfelda*. It hath one paroche churche, and a chapel of Saint Sitha. It standith much by clothing, and is distant vi. miles from Halifax and four from Christeal Abbay." He then adds,—"Ledis (Leeds) two miles lower than Christeal Abbay, in Aire Ryver, is a praty market, having one paroche churche reasonably well builded (that is, the town) and as large as Bradeforde, but not so quik."

Leeds must soon, however, have rapidly outstripped Bradford, for early in the seventeenth century it had increased so much in size as to have doubled the population of the latter town.

The Civil Wars dealt a tremendous blow at Bradford's progressive career. The "quik towne" that had got such a reputation for its "clothing," figured somewhat conspicuously in that sad conflict; more so indeed than was good for it, as it took well nigh a hundred years ere it fully recovered from its disastrous effects. The following figures, taken from the Parish Church Registers, tell their own tale.

YEAR.	BAPTISMS.	MARRIAGES.	DEATHS.
1639	209	61	183
1659	113	38	117
1739	182	94	134

Very soon after the rupture between the King and his Parliament, the former sent troops to be quartered here. Indeed it would seem that Bradford was the scene of the first civil conflict which took place in the Northern Counties, for Fairfax commences his Memoirs by saying,—"The first action we had was at Bradford." The conduct of the King's troops was hardly of a kind however, to encourage a spirit of loyalty among the inhabitants, for, according to Lister, in his "Genuine Account of the Sore Calamities that befel Bradford in the time of the Civil Wars," they threatened what they would do in the way of destroying the town by fire and sword, as soon as they received orders from head-quarters. "We therefore began," says Lister, "to think of putting ourselves in some position of defence; accordingly we called to our assistance the neighbouring villages, who willingly seconded our resolution."

The first attack upon Bradford was made on Sunday, December 18th, 1642. "When the enemy approached the town, a number of horsemen were at once despatched to Halifax, Bingley, and the small towns about, who came with all speed with such arms as they had, and did much service." One of such messengers went to Coley Church (the scene of the faithful labours of good Oliver Heywood), and the minister there exhorted his flock to such good purpose that brave Captain John Hodgson and many more at once "put their hands to the plough." Hodgson, with a well-armed body of Halifax men, arrived just as the Royalists were on the point of assaulting the Parish Church, in which the devout inhabitants were assembled for worship. He attacked them with great fury, and forced them to retreat to their battery; nor did he give them much time to recover from their surprise. He led on his brave handful of men, and they rushed into the ranks of the enemy fighting without any order, but resolutely, and hand to hand.

The hottest work was in Dead Lane, so called, it is said, from the large number that were found slain there. Late in the afternoon the Royalists drew off, and ignominiously retreated to Leeds.

Captain Hodgson and his gallant companions spent the night on guard, talking over the exploits of that memorable Sabbath day, and blessing God for his deliverance. If the Puritan cloth-workers of Bradford could pray and sing psalms, the Cavaliers were not long in finding out that they could fight too.

Sir Thomas Fairfax was at this time at Selby, but on hearing the position of affairs at Bradford, he lost no time in making his way here, in order to cast in his lot with its valiant defenders, The news of "fiery Tom's" arrival spread like wild-fire from village to village, up the vales of Aire and Wharfe, and round over the hills to Halifax and Dewsbury. Men armed with clubs, and scythes fastened to poles came crowding into Bradford, and Captain Hodgson, who was on the point of going home again to Halifax, changed his mind, and resolved to serve permanently under the banner of Fairfax.*

Church Steeple hung with Wool-packs.—facsimile of ancient print.

* Markham's Life of The Great Lord Fairfax.

The Earl of Newcastle becoming acquainted with this repulse, at once sent a more formidable force under the command of Sir William Savile, who on arriving, erected a battery in Barkerend, from which the principal objects of attack were the Church (which seems to have been improvised as a sort of fortress by the besieged), and the steeple, which was hung round with wool-packs. The Royalists also fired from the windows of two houses lying within a few yards of the church. "The largenesse of the church windows, and smallnesse of the houses, made their assault secure and our defence dangerous, which our men perceiving, resolved to win or lose all at once; watching an opportunity betwixt the discharge and charge of the enemy, they sallyed out of the church, and being seconded by those in the lanes, rushed in upon the houses, burst open the doors, slewe those that resisted, tooke those that yielded; the rest fled into the next field, whither some of ours followed, and in the field the skirmish was hotter than ever."

The fight lasted altogether eight hours, and was not brought to a close till the enemy had been driven back as far as Bradford Moor.

Such was what is known as the *first* siege of Bradford. The second was a much more serious matter. The Earl of Newcastle, after the battle on Adwalton Moor, in which the Roundheads had met with a most signal defeat, turned his force towards Bradford and took up his quarters at Bowling Hall. The commanding position of this spot had doubtless attracted his military eye: and from this standpoint he at once set about investing the town. He took three or four days in doing this, although there were no batteries to raise, as the hills surrounding Bradford were near enough to render such unnecessary. He placed his guns in two positions, and opened a heavy fire, which was returned by Sir Thomas Fairfax—who was defending the town—with volleys of musketry. But this time the odds were sadly against the Bradfordians, brave fighting men though they were. The church steeple was again hung with wool-packs, on the side facing the enemy; but the latter "presently began (says Lister) to play their cannon upon us with the greatest fury and indignation imaginable, so that their shot cut the cords whereon the sheets of wool hung, and down they fell, which the enemy perceiving, loudly huzza'd at their fall! but night approaching, the fire of their cannon in some measure ceased, and we in some sort repaired our breaches."

Reduced at length, to the extremity of possessing only one barrel of powder, *but no match*, Sir Thomas saw that he must either cut his way through the Royalists, or surrender with the town. He adopted the former course, and by this step all hope of saving Bradford from falling into the hands of the enemy was abandoned. He succeeded in getting safely to Leeds, but his wife, Lady Fairfax, was taken prisoner on horse-back at the spot in High Street where the "Cock and Bottle" now stands; but the Earl of Newcastle, with that manly and noble courtesy which distinguished the true Cavalier, sent her home in his own carriage.

The besieged at Bradford now found themselves in a most pitiable plight, for they were completely at the mercy of the enemy. "Oh! that dreadful and never-to-be-forgotten night, which was mostly spent in firing those deadly engines upon us! so that the blaze arising therefrom appeared like lightening from heaven, the elements being as it were on fire, and the loud roaring of the canon resembling the mighty thunders of the sky! . . . Oh! what a night was that in which Bradford was taken; what weeping and wringing of hands! none expecting to live any longer than till the enemy came into the town, the Earl of Newcastle having charged his men to kill all—man, woman, and child. Words cannot express, thoughts cannot imagine, nay, art itself is not able to paint out the calamities, and woeful distresses we are now overwhelmed withal! Every countenance overspread with sorrow; every house overwhelmed with grief; husbands lamenting over their families; women wringing their hands in despair; children shrieking, crying, and clinging to their parents; death, in all its dreadful forms and frightful aspects stalking in every street, and every corner! In short, horror! despair! and destruction! united their efforts to spread devastation, and compleat our ruin!"

It is pleasant to turn from this heartrending picture, and to find that after all the town was to be spared.

What courage and bravery had failed to do was accomplished by an *apparition*—the ever-memorable Bolling Hall Ghost! While the Earl was sleeping (so runs the tradition) in one of the rooms of the hall, (known as the "Ghost Room" even unto this day), on the eve of the day that was to witness the destruction of the town, a lady in white appeared, pulled the clothes off his bed several times, and cried out with a lamentable voice, "Pity poor Bradford!" on which he sent out orders that neither man, woman nor child should be killed; whereupon the apparition, which had so disturbed his slumbers, left him and went away.

Of course, in these days of Board Schools, and science lectures, a story like this has not the ghost of a chance of gaining credence; hence some will have it that in the carousals of the soldiers, in anticipation of the carnage to take place on the following day, the wine had flowed a little too freely, and that the Earl, in a restless, broken sleep had conjured up some weird unearthly shape in his dreams, which, in a superstitious age would readily be taken as some spectre from the spirit land. Others, again, have gone the length of regarding it as the clever performance of some Bradford lass, who, afraid lest anything should happen to her relations, or possibly her lover, boldly assumed this ghostly guise in order to frighten the Earl from his cruel purpose. For ourselves, we prefer to take the legend simply on its merits, and without offering any apology for it whatever. It is enough to know that the Earl gave final orders that Bradford should be spared and that he speedily withdrew his troops, to the no small joy and relief of many who were quaking with fear, believing that, verily they were in the jaws of death.

Bradford had to pay dearly for its zeal in the Parliamentary cause. Its trade, once so flourishing, was now utterly paralysed, and for many a long year the erstwhile "quik" town lay as if in a stupor. Even when the end of the century was reached, it was found that the annual value of its "stallages," tolls, etc., was less than when "bluff King Hal" sat upon the throne.

Facsimile of ancient print.

There is nothing on record to show with what feelings the news of the Restoration was received by the good Puritans of Bradford. Some of them were implicated in that foolish attempt at conspiracy known as the "Farnley Wood Plot," but somehow they contrived to escape

THE FIRST BRADFORD FACTORY. THE "HOLME," (THORNTON ROAD.)

(FROM A SCARCE OLD PRINT.)

the fate of the unfortunate ones who suffered the penalty of death for their pains. The inhabitants, however, had not a happy time of it during the reign of the so called "merrie monarch"—Charles II. During the terrible plague of 1665, the infection was accidentally brought to Bradford in a bundle of old clothes; the disorder spread rapidly, and many died from its effects. The roads were so infested with highwaymen that it was almost impossible to travel in safety from one town to another. Persecution for religious and political principles was rampant, and for very trifling offences people were thrust into prison, or incarcerated in the stocks or the pillory. It was at this time that John Wynn the pious Quaker of Bradford was bitterly persecuted for preaching the gospel, and was thrice stripped of all he possessed.

With the ascension of William and Mary a new era began—the dawn of a happier and more prosperous state of things. The woollen manufacture, for which Bradford had once been famous, having failed to revive after the Civil Wars, the inhabitants wisely (as the sequel showed) turned their attention to the making of worsted goods.

So rapid was the progress made in this industry, that although the hum of the spinning wheel could be heard in every house, the looms became so numerous that yarn could not be produced in sufficient quantities in the town to supply them, and the demand had to be met by supplies from Craven-dale and the northern valleys of Yorkshire.

It was surely a distinct evidence of recovery, that Bradford could now afford to interest itself in matters affecting the well-being of the nation, for when in 1782 rumours were current that an invasion of England was contemplated by France and Spain, and orders were issued by the Government, for the formation of armed bodies in all the *principal* towns of the kingdom, the inhabitants of Bradford at once responded to the summons, and held themselves in readiness to be called upon. Again in 1794, during the earlier stage of the French Revolutionary Wars, a Volunteer Corps was formed here, under the command of Col. Busfeild, their dress consisting of scarlet coats turned up with buff, white breeches, and black caps and bobtails. The Corps came to be known as the "Ready and Steady" from the circumstance of the men having these words inserted as a motto on their buttons.

Soon after the middle of the eighteenth century, unmistakeable signs of commercial prosperity appear, first, in the opening of a Bank (Leach, Pollard & Hardcastle's); then, in the erection of the Piece Hall (1773), followed soon after by the formation of the Bradford Canal—events big with importance to a town composed of not more than 4,200 inhabitants. The year 1790 saw the introduction of the first spinning-jenny into Bradford, this branch of industry having been hitherto done by hand, and the year 1798 will ever be memorable as the one in which the first Bradford factory was erected.

The census of 1801 shews that the population of the parish of Bradford was 29,794. Of this number, the inhabitants of the borough, which included the four townships, Bradford, Horton, Bowling and Manningham—comprised 13,624, the township of Bradford alone containing a population of 6,393 persons, out of which 1,290 were employed in trade or manufactures.

But with all its progress in trade and population, Bradford was, as yet, only a small rural town, surrounded by green fields and quiet country lanes, and composed chiefly of tradespeople—"clothiers, weavers, and husbandmen"—and a fair sprinkling of landed gentry. The town proper consisted of a cluster of buildings in the neighbourhoods of Kirkgate, Westgate, the Turls (Tyrrel street), Bridge street, New (now Market) street; and from this centre, straggling and irregular lines of buildings, chiefly houses, stretched out in the direction of Good-mans-end, Barker-end and Westgate. Beyond, all was open country, pleasantly diversified by trees and hedgerows (in modern times replaced by ugly walls), waving corn-fields, and here and there the quaint old homesteads or mansions of a race of gentry long since departed. We have it on indisputable authority that Bradford was at this time a really pleasant and picturesque spot; almost every dwelling had its bit of garden, or paddock, and charming walks and pathways abounded where now are granite pavements and noisy tramways.

The well-to-do people had their houses in Kirkgate, Westgate, the neighbourhood of the Parish Church, and at "Town-end." The last-named place was a cluster of good residences reaching from Chapel Lane to the bottom of Horton Road, and was then regarded as the very "West-end" of the town.

In the space between Kirkgate and the front of the Bowling Green Hotel a rookery flourished, and in Hall Ings there was a fine plantation of trees.

Indeed, we might point to many other evidences of the rural character of Bradford at this period. From the accompanying plan it will be seen that the Bradford beck and its tributary streams were quite uncovered, except by the bridges at the main crossings. These latter, by the way, were the Ive-bridge at the bottom of Ivegate; Cuckoo-bridge opposite the end of the present Leeds Road; New-bridge near Messrs. Brown & Muff's shop, and Church-bridge near Broad-stones. The old Cuckoo-bridge was one of the most interesting bits of old Bradford, and we regret that we have been unable to secure a sketch of it for this work.

For purposes of traffic the roads leading from Bradford were in a very unsatisfactory condition. There were only two roads by which to get to Manningham; one by way of Skinner Lane (Cheapside) and the other by Westgate and Northgate (then known as Fair-Gap). Manningham Lane lay between hedges, and was so narrow that Mr. E. C. Lister found it difficult to get along it with his carriage, and usually preferred driving round by Whetley Hill and Westgate.

The market was still held near the bottom of Westgate, but it was hardly worthy of the name, for it consisted of little more than a few straggling stalls and shambles running up each side of the street.

PARISH CHURCH, MIDDLE OF LAST CENTURY.
(FROM A SCARCE OLD PRINT.)

The town, as yet, could boast of only one church—the venerable St. Peter's, which was then, as it always had been, regarded as a grand and imposing structure for so insignificant a place. But it was not, as now, begrimed with smoke, or hidden from view by erections much more pretentious in style, but inferior in taste. The Wesleyans were still worshipping in their quaint little sanctuary in Horton Road—the Octagon Chapel. The Congregationalists (then better known as "Independents") had but recently taken possession of their spacious chapel in Little Horton Lane. The Baptists had entered upon a new phase of their history by the erection of a new chapel, which from its elevated position soon became known as the "Top o't taan Chapel." The Unitarians and Quakers were not apparently in haste to "arise and build," but were content to worship in peace and quietness in buildings that were growing hoary with age, and which had the history of "olden times" written on their very walls.

But perhaps the most convincing proof of the simple style of life of our forefathers, and how very little sufficed them in the way of "local government," is to be found in the fact that at the close of the century, the town had no other protection than what half a dozen watchmen could give, the said watchmen being entirely supported by voluntary subscriptions. The streets had no better light than what a few dismal oil lamps could impart, which with an eye to economy, were placed at considerable distances apart. That time-honoured functionary, the Parish Beadle, was still an important personage in Bradford, notwithstanding that his services were but poorly remunerated, for his stipend only amounted (exclusive of perquisites) to four pounds, and one suit of clothes per annum.

With the begining of a new century a new order of things began. The birth of the steam engine was the birth of a new life for the inhabitants of Bradford. From its long repose in the bosom of its peaceful valleys, the town shot upwards and outwards with the suddenness of the American aloe, which atones in a few weeks for the apparent rest of a century; and from the dimensions of a miniature country town it assumed the size and importance of a manufacturing capital. As the limits of the old town became too circumscribed for the rapidly increasing population, the outlying districts were invaded by capitalists and builders, and became absorbed into a general mass of stone and mortar, pretty much as one blue speck of sky after another becomes absorbed into the gathering thunder-cloud.

Tall chimneys, huge factories, costly warehouses and shops, and innumerable streets of houses were reared in all directions, swelling out into the vast proportions that make up the Bradford of to-day!

For a long time however, the social, intellectual, and municipal wants of the town, failed to keep pace with its increasing wealth and commercial importance. The streets, mostly unpaved and without footpaths, were miserably lighted, and many of the dwellings of the poorer classes were unfit for human habitation. The education and mental advancement of the labouring population were almost wholly neglected—indeed the long hours of toil left little time either for the cultivation of the mind or the recreation of the body. When the first half of the century had been reached it was said of Bradford that it was more backward in all that related to art and science than any town of half its size in the kingdom. Of private, money-making enterprise there was plenty, but of public, philanthropic spirit, alas! there was but too little. Happily there were *some* worthy citizens whose creed was not *self*, and who sought and laboured for the elevation of the people, and the true advancement of the town, from pure motives, and with untiring energy. All honour be to their memory! As the result of their disinterested and self-denying efforts, other buildings besides factories and shops, sprang into being,—churches, chapels, schools, scientific and literary institutions, and places set apart for recreation and amusement.

But, indeed, progressive strides have in recent times been made in all directions, and, looking around us at this present time of writing, we behold, in Bradford, a town to which we may well point with pride and satisfaction as one of the handsomest, healthiest, and best regulated in all Her Majesty's dominions.

In the chapters succeeding this brief "historical survey" we hope to be able to show how these good and desirable changes have been brought about; and how Bradford has gained the prominent and proud position which it now holds.

Old Gateway. Unitarian Chapel

Parish Church in the time of Vicar Crosse.

CHAPTER II.—The Parish Church.

THERE is a certain majesty in old historic buildings which impresses one, and this may truly be said of that venerated structure the Bradford Parish Church. Its antiquity is beyond question, for it has looked down upon the town from its commanding position for fully four centuries, the growth of which it has watched from earliest infancy to manhood.

One thinks of many things while gazing upon such a time-worn edifice as this. Of the far-away time, for example, when a scattered population composed of sturdy yeomen and farmers from Bradford-dale, and the wild hills and moors beyond, first gathered within its walls for "praise and prayer," astounded meanwhile at the magnificence of a structure, which to them, must have seemed a veritable Cathedral! Of stormy times when the steeple was turned into a fortress, and its walls had to be hung with wool-packs to protect them against the cannonading of Royalist soldiers; and of peaceful, prosperous times when Bradford could boast of its "gentry," whose mansions were in the very heart of the town, and who were driven to church in carriages bedecked with "armorial trappings"—old families that have long-ago given place to a generation who cared little for the "taint" of trade, or the turmoil of factory life, so long as fortunes were to be made or wealth easily acquired.

To do anything like justice to the history of the Bradford Parish Church, would require the proportions of a portly volume. There are certain points concerning very remote times upon which historians are not agreed, and, which, even if authenticated, would be of little interest to the general reader. These, if at all, must be but briefly alluded to, in order to give place to matter of a more reliable and interesting character.

The present church, dedicated to Saint Peter, was erected in the time of Henry VI., and was completed about the thirty-sixth year of that king's reign (1458), having taken twenty-seven years in building. The body of the church alone consumed twelve, and the steeple or tower, fifteen years in their erection, the latter, indeed, not being quite completed till fully fifty years after the church. "There can be little doubt," says Mr. James, "that the present structure, probably the *third* on the same site, occupies the ground where the old Anglo-Norman church—the "kirk in the wood" of olden times,—stood, surrounded by the remains of *Sylvia*, once covering the whole of the hill-side."

History records that there was considerable difficulty in those early times in raising heavy rates. This may possibly account for the long time that was occupied in rearing the church. With the exception of Haworth, there then existed no other place of worship in the parish, so that although the sanctuary at Bradford might be considered as somewhat in advance of its time, it had to do service for a very extensive district, and a widely scattered population.

The manor and the advowson, or church living of Bradford, kept each other company, as the joint property of the Lacy family, until the death of Henry, Earl of Lincoln, who settled the latter upon his daughter Alice, wife of Thomas, Earl of Lancaster. In 1322, the advowson was seized by Edward II., on the confiscation of the Lancaster estates. The manor and advowson afterwards became vested in Henry, Duke of Lancaster, and on the Inquisition taken upon his death in 1361 the advowson was stated to be worth £100 per annum. From this point they run together, and are in the same hands until the reign of Henry V., who by a grant dated 7th of November, 1416, gave the church of Bradford to the college of the Blessed Mary, commonly called the Newark, at Leicester. On the dissolution of this college the rectory and advowson became vested in the Crown when they were "leased out," Sir Richard Tempest, of Bolling Hall, being the "tenant" thereof in 1607.

King Charles the First greatly displeased the inhabitants of Bradford by selling both the manor and the rectory to the citizens of London. They, however, in turn, disposed of the latter to Sir Hugh Middleton, and he to Mary, wife of John Maynard of Tooting, Knight, and keeper of the Great Seal of Charles I. Maynard, in right of his wife, was absolute owner of the rectory, and for his steward, he had the stout-hearted Parliamentarian, John Sharp, of Horton Hall, father of the distinguished mathematician Abraham Sharp.

It is unnecessary to follow the vicissitudes of the rectory of the Parish Church further than to state that after passing, as a piece of family property, through a long succession of ownerships it eventually came by purchase into the possession of the Rev. John Crosse, who became vicar of Bradford in 1784. From him it passed, again by purchase, to Mr. Henry Thornton of Clapham, whose executors sold it to Mr. Richard Fawcett, father of the late Canon Fawcett of Low Moor. Subsequently it was conveyed to the Rev. Charles Simeon, vicar of Trinity Church, Leeds, in whose trustees the right of presentation to the living is now vested.

From a document of ancient date we glean some curious items concerning the vicarial dues of former times:—"The small tythes wherewith the vicarage of Bradford is endowed are these:—calves, milk, pigs, geese, turkeys, foals, bees, eggs, Easter offerings, etc." The several apportionments of these according to their "kind" are minutely set forth. The following are some of them. Concerning pigs, "if the sow hath six or more pigs, there is one pig due, the vicar paying to the owner as many pence as there wants of ten, and if she hath under six, there is a penny a pig due for so many as she hath. Geese are gathered in kind where the vicar pleaseth; where

PARISH CHURCH BEFORE RESTORATION.

they are not taken in kind, there is a penny a piece due for every goose the owner hath hatched and brought up in that year. There are few turkeys kept in the parish, but some there are, and they pay as geese do, one in six. Foals are not taken in kind, but a modus of three half-pence is paid for every foal. The Easter offerings are two-pence for every person who is sixteen years old or above, throughout the whole parish, under the name of communicants, and every house-holder pays a penny for his house, and a half-penny for his reek or smoke, and one penny for his garden. If any person comes to reside in any family, and hath laid nine nights in his house before Easter, the master or mistress of the family is obliged to pay for him or them as communicants. All these small tithes and other dues (except those in the chapelry of Haworth) are to be paid before Easter; the vicar sitting in the Free School (then near the church) to receive, on Thursday before Palm Sunday, and on Thursday, Friday and Saturday before Easter. But in the chapelry of Haworth the vicar receives them there every Easter Monday, after he has preached a sermon at that place."

The old custom of sitting to receive the vicar's tythes has often furnished a theme for poet and painter. While some divines looked forward to the "yearly distress" with feelings of satisfaction and complacency, others regarded it as a terrible ordeal, and dreaded its approach.

In sooth, the sorrow of such days
  Is not to be expressed,
When he that takes, and he that pays,
  Are both alike distressed.

Oliver Heywood has given us a glimpse, in his diary, of the gathering of Easter dues at Haworth in the year 1692. "The vicar of Bradford," he says, "sat all day in an ale-house there gathering his Easter dues in Haworth parish. There was wont always to be a sermon in the church that day, but Mr. Pemberton (the vicar) laid it aside. Many flocked to him to pay their Easter money and then came to hear me (preach.)" There is a tone of bitterness in the remark that follows—"I got nothing for my pains, except four or five put six-pence a-piece into my hands."

Despite this reflection upon vicar Pemberton, who was only claiming what was honestly due to him, he has come down to us as a man "who displayed all the qualities of a scholar and courteous gentleman, and, although High Church in principle, exhibited great tolerance of the religious opinions of others."

Since its erection the Parish Church has undergone many alterations, but the massive, stubborn-looking tower, which has weathered the "bitter storms and biting blasts" of four hundred winters, remains intact as on the day of its completion.

A glance at our sketch shewing the interior of the church, previous to its recent restoration, will suffice to shew the striking contrast presented between *then* and *now*. The side galleries still remain as mementos of past deformity and ugliness. It will also be seen that the east window was completely hidden from view by a gallery which occupied the space now used as the choir. The fine timbered roof was also covered in by a flat plaster ceiling. With the angels (in plaster) gazing pitifully down upon the worshippers below, and the ancient pulpit with its no less ancient sounding-board surmounted by the peaceful dove, we dare not find fault. They were relics sacred to antiquity, and to associations linked with the memory of generations of townspeople who had assembled within those hallowed walls in years long gone by.

Old Pulpit—Parish Church.

But with all our veneration for the past, we yield to none in our admiration of the church as it appears to day. Well may the parishioners of this generation exclaim,—"This is our holy and *beautiful* house." But let not the "faith and works" of bygone generations be forgotten or despised. It is the fashion now-a-days to condemn severely the action of the venerable John Crosse in causing the erection of the galleries which so long disfigured the church. It should however be borne in mind that if he erected the galleries, he also filled them to overflowing with anxious hearers, and so great was the demand for still more accommodation that it became necessary to erect other churches.

The movement for restoring and beautifying the church was projected by the eminent Dr. Scoresby, but was not fairly taken in hand until about the year 1860 when Dr. Burnet was vicar. The efforts put forth by the latter, with the co-operation of the churchwardens, in carrying out this good work, are worthy of all praise. Among the many improvements effected, were the removal of the east and west galleries; the clearing away of the plaster ceiling; the re-seating of the church, and the substitution of a pulpit more in keeping with the improvements. The bells were re-hung; five stained-glass memorial windows inserted; the boundary wall of the church-yard rebuilt, and the work of restoration was brought to a successful conclusion by the erection of a beautiful reredos—the generous gift of Mr. M. W. Thompson.

The interior of the Parish Church now presents a grand and imposing spectacle to the eye. It may not, indeed, boast of marble

PARISH CHURCH AFTER RESTORATION.

effigies and tombs of "Lords and Knights and high-born Dames," but its venerable walls are not without some memorials of old and worthy Bradford families, although we have to confess with profound regret that many of these have, in exceeding bad taste, been stowed away in the dark western tower where their inscriptions can be neither seen nor read. Fortunately the choice piece of sculpture by Flaxman, to the memory of Abraham Balme has escaped the touch of the Vandal and remains undisturbed. It was regarded by the great sculptor himself as one of his finest conceptions, and it has called forth the admiration of that severest of critics—John Ruskin.

The old vicarage in Church Bank, (now occupied by Mr. Thomas Bollans) is an ancient building. It was purchased as the residence of the vicars of Bradford in 1695, at a cost of £153. Among the "principal inhabitants" by whose "help and bounty" the purchase money was raised were the following:—John Rookes, of Royds Hall, £10; Francis Lindley, Bolling Hall, £6; John Weddall, of Bradford, £6; John Field, of Shipley, £5, and many others who contributed

Old Vicarage, Church Bank.

smaller sums. The list, however, was headed by John, Lord Archbishop of York, a native of Bradford, for the handsome contribution (at that day) of £50.

The vicarage previous to that in Church Bank was a house situated in Goodman's End, a little below where the Neptune Inn recently stood. From the fact that in a deed dated 12th February, 1695, it is described as being in a decayed and ruinous condition, it may be inferred that it had served as the house of the vicars of Bradford for many years in the far remote past. Francis Pemberton was the last of the vicars who resided here, but how many of his predecessors had made this their dwelling-place or at what precise date it first became their abode will probably never be known.

Christopher Taylor, who was vicar in 1568, and the owner of considerable property in Bradford and Horton, bequeathed to his daughter Alice, "a cottage, garden, and a little croft adjoining the vicarage of Bradford." In the Parliamentary Survey of church livings made in 1650, (time of the Protectorate), there is this brief reference to the vicarage:—"Wee finde belonging to the p'ish church of Bradforde a viccaridge-house, small tithes, and profitts worth about seaventye pounds p. ann., but by reason of the late warrs not nowe worth above fortye pounds p. ann. or thereabouts. . . . There is no mynister, the viccaridge being vacant."

Mr. James, the historian, very naturally draws the inference that Goodman's End owes its name to the fact of the vicars of Bradford having formerly resided here. He also believes that the thoroughfare known as Vicar Lane was so called because it would probably form the track of the vicars from their residence to the church. This, however, is open to question, as the name "Vicar Lane" is but a modern designation. For some years, even into the present century it was called "Dead Lane," and had been so called long before the siege of Bradford, although it was popularly believed that it came by this ghastly name through the large number of slain that were found in it after the siege.

It is a natural and easy transition from the vicarage to

The Vicars of Bradford.

A catalogue of these and of the patrons of the living, from the earliest to the present times will be found on page 38. Not much is known of the vicars prior to the venerable Crosse, beyond what is to be learned from a perusal of their wills at York. From these documents, as well as from the wills of prominent laymen, some curious information may be gathered.

Prior to the Reformation, it is evident that the priesthood reigned all but supreme over the people, "The dominant control of the local clergy over the popular mind was a necessary result of the isolation of the village and the town. The friar and the parson were the only superior persons that mixed intimately with the burgess and the yeoman, and they only through the same intercourse with the higher ranks, could tell of public affairs beyond the range of their own districts."

As the priests in early times, were the only men of learning, it naturally followed that upon them devolved the making of wills, and they were often the only witnesses to the signing thereof. There is no disguising the fact that their influence was often brought to bear upon the bequests that were made. From certain Bradford wills ranging from 1420 to 1560, we select at random a few items which clearly show that previous to the latter date they were of a pronounced Roman Catholic character:—

Thomas Gell (1430) left VI^d. to be given at his burial to the chaplain "for a trental (thirty masses) of St. Gregory to celebrate for my saull."

William Thornton (1440) gave to the fabric of St. Peter, Bradford, 3/4; his best animal for mortuary, and for two torches for the altar 6/8.

William Leaventhorp (1480) "of sane mind," gave his soul to Almighty God, the Blessed Virgin Mary, and all the Saints; his body to be buried in the church-quire of Bradford, and made gifts for masses to priests at Bradford, York and Knaresborough.

Thomas Balie (1527) gave to "Our Ladie Altar to buy a vestment LIII^s IV^d."

Parish Church and Vicarage in the Year 1810.

Elizabeth Dobson, widow, Allerton (1528) gave to Tristram Horton (priest) "to pray for my husband's saull and myne Vs." Also paid for two torches for Bradford Church.

John Rawson (1530) gave to the high altar "for tythes forgotten IIs."

Miles Warde (1536) gave "towards painting the rode (rood) in Bradford Kirk Vs; towards painting Our Ladie in the Kirk porche IIIs IVd."

In almost every will occurs the item—"I bequeath my best animal for mortuary." We have seen a receipt for mortuary fee dated Feby. 7th, 1833, in which the vicar, Rev. Henry Heap, fixes the amount at 10s.

The list of Bradford vicars begins with the name of Richard de Halton (1293), but the first of whom anything is found recorded, is Henry de Latrynton (1335), who appears to have been a sad transgressor in the matter of illegally appropriating manorial land. He was charged with several other offences, for which he was fined, among which was that of felling wood and carting away three loads, together with an entire oak tree from the "Park of Bradford." He was only vicar, or chaplain, for two years.

The next vicar of whom we have any details is William Rodes, who was presented to the living in 1401. He is described as a rich and liberal man. His will is an interesting document. After giving his soul to Almighty God, the blessed Mary and all the Saints, and his body to be buried in the chancel of the church of St. Peter at Bradford, and after bequeathing certain legacies to his friends he gives "to William, chief parish clerk 12d., and to William Northrop, minor parish clerk 12d. I give to the fabric of the mother church of St. Peter, York, 6s. 8d. To the Friars of the order of the Holy Trinity, Knaresborough, 40d. To the Friars minors of Doncaster 12d. . . . To the Carmelite Friars of York 12d. I give to my sisters Matilda and Eliste each 6s. 8d. I give to the fabric of *the new work* of the blessed Mary in the church of Bradford, 40s. I bequeath to Dom William Scholes, Chaplain, six of my best silver cups, a cloak of wool with fur, and all my books. The rest of my goods I give to my executors to be disposed of by them for the health of my soul."

From the allusion made in this will to the church of Bradford, it is inferred, that the present structure had been commenced in Rodes' time. The inference is also drawn that this vicar was a learned as well as a rich man, for the possession of books at that early period was something uncommon.

Passing over the subsequent vicars, whose wills are to be found in our list of "Early Bradford Wills," we come to the Rev. Caleb Kemp, who obtained the living from the Crown in 1595. Vicar Kemp was a genuine Puritan, and it was said that during his twenty year's vicariate here, he sowed an amount of Puritan seed," the fruit of which was seen for many days." To this period belongs the erection of the chapel of ease at Thornton, which, but for its cupola and bell, might very well have been taken for a Dissenting meeting-house. The phraseology of Mr. Kemp's will affords sufficient evidence of his

Puritan character, and is in striking contrast to those of his predecessors. It begins "Caleb Kemp, a servant of Jesus Christ, in the preaching of the Word of God, and ministry of the Gospel. Into Thy hands, O God! I commend my spirit, for Thou hast redeemed me."

There is some uncertainty concerning the vicars, and the dates of their institution both during, and for some time after the Civil Wars. The times were altogether out of joint, and everything was disturbed and in disorder. Men's fortunes changed with changing events, and even church benefices shared the common fate.

King Charles the First, previous to disposing of the Bradford rectory to the citizens of London, had presented one Francis Corker to the living, but he being a royalist, and probably a Roman Catholic, did not meet with much acceptance by the Bradford Puritans, for he says that he found the town to be "a place verry full and popolous, soe verry factions and seditiory, yet I prevailed with the best part of them (although not the greatest) to hold fast their allegiance."

The Rev. Francis Corker was an adventurer, living in adventurous times, and the story of his eventful career reads very like a romance. Finding himself unable as he admits, to secure the allegiance of his parishioners to the King's side, he and the few whom he had won over, were compelled to seek refuge in the King's garrisons. Afterwards we find him doing duty as chaplain to Sir John Ramsden's division in the garrison at Pontefract during the siege of the castle, and on the garrison being reduced to the last extremity, he was despatched with an escort of sixteen men, through the enemy's lines, to join Prince Rupert, and to make the King acquainted with the condition of the garrison. So well did he succeed in this undertaking that the castle was soon relieved by the King's forces, and Corker boasted with no little pride of his daring and successful feat. "I was sent" he says, "from Pontefract Castle to Oxford through the Parliament's garrisons to procure relief for that place, which was happily effected by Sir Marmaduke Langdale. I was his Majesties chiefest guide in the Northerne Expedition, and he would often call for me by the name of his honest guide; he would employe me into his Enemies' Armye to discover unto him their strength and posture: wherein I soe well pleased him that he would saye to me—"Well, Corker, if it ever please God to restore me, thou shalt be rewarden."

Henceforth the erstwhile vicar of Bradford followed the fortunes of the King, and acted in the dual capacity of spy and guide. If he still considered himself a cleric as well as a soldier he was certainly entitled to rank as a "muscular Christian" of the highest type, for he says, "I received some wounds in his (the King's) service, the effects whereof I must carry to my grave. I have had two horses killed under me in fight . . . my sufferings have not been ordinary, for besides the losse of my benefice (at Bradford), since the beginning of the warr, my house hath been three times plundered and all that I I had taken from me. I was taken prisoner at Gainsborough in Lincolnshire and sent to Lincoln gaole, from whence (General)

Lambert sent for me to execute me upon the same Gybbett with Mr. Beaumont, but I unhappilie made my escape the night before. I say unhappilie, because if it had not soe faln out, I had died in a good cause, and with a better conscience."

At the time of writing the foregoing narrative, Corker was a prisoner in the Tower of London. After the King's defeat, he had ranged himself on the side of the Commonwealth, for which "fearfull apostacye" he was, on the Restoration, regarded as a traitor, and committed to prison. He sent forth a pitiful appeal to be set at liberty, and probably in recognition of his bygone good services in the cause of the unfortunate King, he was set free and allowed to return to his former benefice at Bradford. During the time of Mr. Corker's absence from Bradford, much unhappy wrangling and contention had been going on. Sir John Maynard, the patron of the living had generously tried to meet the wishes of the parishioners in the choice of a minister, but as these could not agree amongst themselves, the vicarage was for a time vacant. A Mr. Blazet was appointed, but he must have soon vacated it, as on the passing of the Uniformity Act, Jonas Waterhouse was vicar.

But here again, a difficulty arose in the fact that Waterhouse would not conform, and he was therefore "ejected," although for a while he clung tenaciously to the living. After much "disputation and litigation," an arrangement was effected, by which Francis Corker was restored to his benefice, and Waterhouse, who was possessed of considerable real estate in Bradford, retired into private life. Calamy speaks of the latter as "a learned man, a lover of peace, and greatly esteemed for his works' sake." He was on friendly terms with the principal nonconformist families in Bradford and the district, and especially with the Sharps of Horton Hall. He kept a Sunday evening service in his own house, in which Oliver Heywood often took part.

The Rev. Francis Corker, now "a sadder and a wiser man" doubtless, was permitted to retain his position as vicar of Bradford until his death in 1667, but with what measure of acceptance to his parishioners we do not know. After the vicissitudes through which he had passed he well deserved a season of rest and repose.

His son, Mr. Edward Hailstone informs us, afterwards turned Roman Catholic, and became chaplain to the wife of James II.

Mr. Corker was followed by a succession of vicars who, if not distinguished for eccentricity of character, or excess of zeal, were at any rate men of learning and piety—holy men who went about their Master's business, "cheering the downcast, encouraging the strong, consoling the sick, and smoothing the hard pillow of the dying. They blessed the mother on the birth of her child, and took it in baptism into the Christian church. They married the young men and maidens, and buried the dead around that venerable pile, the church. They all fulfilled the mission of their day; were lights in their time, and if they were good men, their spirits dwell with the ever adorable Redeemer."

Rev. John Crosse.

It was in the year 1784 that the Rev. John Crosse became vicar of Bradford—a man whose virtues were the theme of successive generations of parishioners. When he came here, he was not the blind and venerable pastor, afterwards so well known, but an active and energetic man in the prime of life. He was born at London in 1739, but previous to obtaining the vicarage of Bradford he had held the joint livings of Todmorden and Crosstones, his predecessor being the famous Wm. Grimshaw (afterwards of Haworth) whose daughter he married. Crosse's life among the bleak and wild hills of this part of the West Riding, bringing him, as it did, in contact with their scattered but rough population, was of great service to him, as it enabled him to become acquainted with the character and habits of Yorkshire people—an acquaintance which he needed, for even in Bradford he found among his parishioners a spirit of sturdy independence much more calculated to repel than attract a man of culture.

For some years prior to the appearance of Crosse upon the scene, the Dissenters in Bradford had not worked in harmony. A love of controversy on the part of both ministers and members on points of doctrine had created a spirit of bitterness and strife. The question was not so much whether a man was a good Christian as whether he was an Arian, Armenian, or Antinomian. Crosse was of the Armenian school, and on more than one occasion placed his pulpit at the disposal of John Wesley when he visited Bradford, but he was tolerant in his religious views and lived on the friendliest terms with the other ministers of the town, content to overlook differences on questions of doctrine in order that he might be the more at liberty to promote the wellbeing of his parishioners.

A marked improvement in attendance at church soon became apparent, and ere long increased accommodation had to be provided, which was met by the erection of the galleries to which allusion has already been made. The vicar was a zealous worker and his figure soon became a familiar object in the streets and lanes.

When visiting such outlying districts as Clayton, Heaton, or Shipley he invariably travelled on foot, and in all kinds of weather. He was a liberal and cheerful dispenser of charity. Indeed he was sometimes found fault with for being *over-generous;* but his failings "leaned to virtue's side," and he would risk a dozen impositions if he might but meet one real case of distress. He lived in the plainest possible style in order that he might have the more to give away. When going out he used to fill his pockets with good things, and always returned with them empty. Rarely had he any money for any length of time. On one occasion, during service, the vicarage was broken into and twenty guineas stolen. This was a large sum for him to lose, but on learning of the theft he merely remarked, "I am rightly served, I ought to have given it away."

During the years 1800 and 1801 there was great scarcity of food, and much distress prevailed among the poor of Bradford. A malignant fever broke out and death was almost in every house. The labours of Mr. Crosse at this trying time ought never to be forgotten. Utterly regardless of his own health and life, he ran from house to house, day and night, to relieve the suffering inmates; providing them with food, blankets, or such other means of comfort as they most needed. In many a lost, filthy dwelling too, where no restoration to health seemed possible, he personally superintended the thorough cleansing and whitewashing thereof.

The last years of Mr. Crosse's life exhibited a painful and afflicting, yet venerable picture. He became blind. It was intended that the operation of couching should be performed upon him, and he went to town for that purpose, but as he could not bear the thought of the necessary confinement which that operation would involve, he returned as he went.

Henceforward he walked in darkness, and as he went about the town on his errands of mercy he was led by the hand by a little boy or girl. He spoke of it as a great mercy that he had lost the use of his eyes and not his ears, and that though he could not see, he could still preach and visit the sick.

The Rev. Legh Richmond, author of the "Dairyman's Daughter" visited this town in the year 1814. The following extract from his diary gives his impression of the visit—"Oct. 2, 1814. Preached in the morning at Bradford Church; a fine congregation. Preached in the afternoon at the same church; a still larger congregation. Preached in the evening; overflowing congregation. I never saw anything like it—not less than 4000 certainly. Three collections, £115. Such a day, such a church, such a vicar, such life, such attention, such liberality, and such general success are rarely seen. I desire to praise God from my heart for the interesting, animating, encouraging scene presented. I received the sacrament from the hands of the venerable, blind vicar."

The Christianity of John Crosse was of a practical sort. His views of religion were of a simple yet elevated cast. He was a faithful and diligent student of the Bible, and took his belief directly from it, and he neither plagued himself nor others with theological wranglings.

His sermons were plain and simple, and though there might be a lack of variety in the mode of treating his subjects, there was an unction and heartiness in his address which rendered him always acceptable to his hearers. Immediately after service on Sundays, both young and old would wait in the church-yard to receive his parting smile or benevolent wishes. We doubt if any survive who can remember these scenes. Many years ago we were privileged to know some old Bradfordians who did, and their testimony was that they were moments never to be forgotten. It was a genuine feeling of respect and not of servility, that then prompted the people to make their obeisance to the vicar, after the good old-fashioned style of paying that compliment.

We have no wish to present a faultless picture of Mr. Crosse. He had his failings and weaknesses, but indeed what man has not? In the vexed controversy between him and Mr. Baldwyn the Grammar School Master, on the question of the appointment of Afternoon Lecturer to the church, he did not come out with quite clean hands, but his temper and language during that unseemly squabble will at any rate bear favourable contrast with that of his opponent. Our estimate of his character is based upon the testimony of those who knew him well. In acts of piety and self-sacrificing benevolence the later years of the good vicar passed away. At all times active and energetic, he did not till within a few days of his death abstain from the customary round of his duties. He was a true friend to the poor, and in many a lowly dwelling his name was as a "household word."

On the 17th of June, 1816, the solemn notes of the passing-bell announced to the inhabitants of Bradford that they had lost the vicar, benefactor and friend, who for thirty-two years had laboured unceasingly in their midst.

Mr. Crosse was succeeded by the Rev. Henry Heap, a native of Todmorden. During the incumbency of Mr. Crosse at Todmorden and Crosstones he became acquainted with Mr. Heap's father, and it was through the persuasion of the former that the son was educated for the church. On Mr. Crosse's death, Mr. Heap was presented to the living at Bradford, and he was vicar here from 1816 to 1839. Although church matters made but slow progress during that period, Mr. Heap's name will be held in remembrance for the energetic and successful measures which he took in alleviating the great distress prevailing in Bradford during the weavers and woolcombers' strike of 1825, and for the prominent share he had in the establishment of the Bradford Dispensary in the same year.

But the most remarkable, and certainly the most distinguished man of learning that ever held the vicarage of Bradford was the Rev. William Scoresby. It lies outside the scope of the present sketch to speak of him other than as the vicar of Bradford. His eminent career as scientist, Arctic discoverer and philosopher, has been recorded in the annals of biography.

Dr. Scoresby was born in the month of October, 1789, at the village of Cropton, near Pickering, and was the only son of William Scoresby of Whitby, a daring and skilful seaman in the Northern Whale Fishery.

In early years he took to the sea-faring life, and accompanied his father in eight expeditions, working his way from the foot of the mast to the maintop gallant. On his twentieth birthday he was promoted to the command of the *Resolution* in place of his father, who had retired for a while from active service. He made no less than twenty voyages to the Arctic regions, the last of which took place in 1823.

A desire he had long cherished to study for holy orders was now realised, and in 1824 he entered the University of Cambridge, where he pursued his studies so successfully that in the following year he received orders from the Archbishop of York, and was ordained to the curacy of Bessingby near Bridlington, where instead of his usual annual income of some £800, he received the very small stipend of £30 per annum.

Rev. W. Scoresby, D.D.

But he had now leisure to pursue his favourite studies in which he made astounding progress, and soon earned a world-wide reputation as a writer on scientific subjects. His famous work "The Arctic Regions" which some regard as his best performance, and for which he received £250 for an edition of a thousand copies, had already appeared and paved the way for future effort. In 1827 he was appointed to the chaplaincy of the Mariner's Church, Liverpool, where he spent five of the happiest years of his life. Subsequently he spent seven years at Exeter whither he had removed on account of his wife's delicate health. These however, were embittered by the loss of both his sons within an interval of twelve months; one at the age of sixteen, the other at twenty-six.

Dr. Scoresby came to Bradford in July 1839; having been presented to the living by the Simeon Trustees; but his stay here of a little over eight years was by no means the brightest spot in his career. Unhappy disputes with some of his parishioners on church rates and other matters, engendered much bitterness, and sadly impeded his usefulness. There may have been faults on both sides, but we never could resist the impression that Bradford was then no congenial clime for such a man as Dr. Scoresby. His tastes and pursuits were altogether out of harmony with his surroundings. He incurred the displeasure of employers by the vigorous part he took in trying to shorten the hours of labour, for he saw fortunes being built up by sordid and unscrupulous men at the cost of over-worked children whose education was wholly neglected. He stirred up the wrath of the Dissenters (then, as now, an important factor in Bradford) by an attempt which he made to levy a church rate, which was not only most strenuously resisted, but even supplemented by a threatening letter in which he was told that "if he but dared to collect the obnoxious rate, he might get a bullet where he expected to receive a shilling."

But indeed the times were sadly out of joint. Trade was bad; work was scarce, and many of the poor were but too ready to take sides with the Chartist movement then flourishing in Bradford. Social and political disorder was widespread, and the unfortunate introduction of the new Poor Law Bill so enraged the people that open riot was the result.

The vicar of Bradford held no enviable position during this trying time, but Dr. Scoresby was a brave and fearless man, and held on his way in the face of all opposition. In the interests of the poor and down-trodden—and these were but too numerous—he laboured unceasingly, and in deeds of benevolence gave every penny which he derived from his living as vicar.

When peace and order were again restored, he devoted his energies to the establishment of parochial schools which were much needed, as, when he came to Bradford, he found to his dismay that there was not a single child under daily education in connection with the Parish Church. When he left the town four large schools had been erected through his efforts, at a cost of not less than £4000. He was the leading light of the Bradford Philosophical Society, of which he was president for a time, his lectures on magnetism and other scientific subjects contributing greatly to its life and activity. He was also the founder of the Church Institute, and frequently gave literary and philosophical lectures to its members and the public.

Partly on account of failing health, but chiefly we fear by reason of his unpopularity with the Dissenters, and the obstructions that were placed in his way, Dr. Scoresby determined to resign his post as vicar, and the useful career of this highly-gifted and good man was brought to a close in Bradford, in June 1847.

For a time he lived in retirement at Torquay, but his ever active mind seemed to find no rest but in employment, for even while here he devoted himself to the study of magnetism and the influence of iron ships upon their compasses. In 1856 he undertook a voyage to Australia for magnetic study, and was received at Melbourne with great enthusiasm. He returned, however, exhausted with his labours, and after a lingering illness died in 1857, at Torquay, aged 67.

On the resignation of Dr. Scoresby in 1847, the Rev. John Burnet, of Trinity College, Dublin, was chosen as his successor. The twenty-three years of his vicarship at Bradford were characterised by great moderation, and a wise perception on his part of the responsible position which he held as vicar of a town like this. It was during his term of office that the extensive improvements in the church, to which reference has already been made, were brought about.

Dr. Burnet was an eloquent preacher, and his clear and forcible style of address both in the pulpit and on the platform, will be long remembered. He took an active part in several movements for the benefit of the town, and held various public offices of importance. For long previous to his death he suffered greatly from ill health. Ash-Wednesday, 1868, was the last occasion on which he preached in his own church at Bradford. He died at his residence at Coniston, near Windermere, on March 8th, 1870.

The late Right Reverend Vincent W. Ryan, D.D., Bishop, was appointed to the Vicarage of Bradford, by the Simeon Trustees in May, 1870. He was born in the year 1816, and was educated at Magdalen Hall, Oxford. Having held a small cure in one of the Channel Islands, he became successively head of the Liverpool Institution, Principal of the Training College at Highbury, and in 1864, Bishop of the newly-founded See of Mauritius, which includes that island and its dependencies.

He resigned his See in 1868 on account of ill-health and returned to England. He was Archdeacon of Suffolk for a time, and held the Rectory of St. Nicholas, Guildford, from February 1869, to May 1870, when he was called to Bradford. He had been vicar here for a little over ten years, when he was invited to accept the vicarage of Bournemouth, which he did, but before taking leave of his parishioners, he was presented with a costly testimonial as an evidence of the esteem in which he was held by them.

The Rev. Canon Bardsley, M.A., is the present vicar of Bradford.

Before passing on to speak of other Bradford churches, it may be well to notice here that in the wills of Bradford people dating from about 1500, the Parish Church was not referred to singly as "St. Peter's," but as "Saints Peter and Paul." In the absence of information to the contrary, it may be safe to assume that "St. Paul's" was merely a side chapel attached to the present church.

The chapel of St. Sitha mentioned in Leland's "Itinerary" was a sacred structure "for the celebration of masses and other divine offices" that is supposed to have stood on the south side of the bridge at the bottom of Ivegate. It was one of the many way-side shrines erected in the early days of the church for the use of travellers, and generally placed in or near to bridges. Mr. Edward Hailstone, of Walton Hall, near Wakefield, is of opinion that Ive-bridge, now called Sun-bridge, was so named from *Ave*-bridge—a deed in his possession mentioning Ave-gate in Bradford, doubtless the same as Ivegate.

It is probable that we should never have known of the existence of this ancient sanctuary but for the discovery of an ancient record in the York Archiepiscopal registers from which it appears that it was erected some time previous to the year 1466.

Catalogue of the Vicars of Bradford.

Time of inst'ion	VICARS.	PATRONS.	How vacated.
1293	Richard de Halton, Presbyter ...	Robert Rector, with the assent of Alice de Lacy ...	Resigned.
	Richard de Irby	Same	
1309	Richard de Eure, Presbyter ...	Same	Resigned.
1327	Robert Moryn, Chaplain ...	Robert, son of Reginald de Baldock, Rector ...	Resigned.
1328	Robert de Byngham, Presbyter ...	Same	Same.
1331	Wm. de Preston, Chaplain ...		Same.
1335	Henry de Latrynton, Chaplain ...	Same Robert	Same.
1348	Adam de Lymbergh, Pbr. ...	Same	Same.
	Richd. de Wilsden, Pbr. ...		Same.
1364	William Frankelayn ...	Wm. de Mirfield	By death.
1369	William de Norton, Pbr. ...	Same	Resigned.
1370	William de Cotes, Pbr. ...	Same	
1374	Stephen de Eccleshill, Pbr. ...	Same	
	William ——— ...		Resigned.
1401	William Rodes, Pbr. ...	Wm. de Wynceby	Resigned.
	Thomas Banke, Pbr. ...	Dean and Canons of College of Leicester	Same.
1432	Dyonis Gellys, Pbr. ...	Same	Resigned.
1464	Henry Gellys, Pbr. ...	Same	By death.
1476	John Webbester, Pbr. ...	Same	Same.
	Richard Strateburell ...	Same	Same.
1503	Mr. Gilbert Beaconshaw, Decr. B. or Beaconhill ...	Same	Same.
1537	Wm. More (Suff. Bp. of Colchester)	John, Bishop of Lincoln	
1541	Wm. Weston, S. T. B. ...	Assigns of the Col. of Leicester	Resigned.
1556	Thomas Okden, Clerk ...	Other Assigns	By death.
1563	Laurence Taylor, Clerk ...		Same.
1568	Christopher Taylor, Clerk ...	Queen Elizabeth	Same.
1595	Caleb Kemp, Cl. S. T. B. ...	Same	Same.
1614	Richard Lister, Cl. A. M. ...	Archbishop of York ...	Resigned.
1615	John Okell, A. M. ...	Francis Morrie and Francis Phillip	By death.
1639	John Kempe, Clerk ...	Charles the First	Same.
1640	Edward Hudson, Clerk ...	Same	Same.
1642-3	Francis Corker, Clerk ...		Same.
	During the Civil Wars ...	Mr. Blazet, ordained minister	
	Then Francis Corker until his death	Jonas Waterhouse, M.A., minister	
1667	Abraham Brooksbank, Clerk, A. M.	Mary Maynard and Jonas Waterhouse	By death.
1677	Francis Pemberton ...	Buller and wife	Resigned.
1698	Benjamin Baron ...	Archbishop of York, by lapse	By death.
1706	Bradgate Ferrand ...	Buller	Same.
1710	Thomas Clapham ...		Same.
1720	Benjamin Kennet, A.M. ...	Francis Buller	Same.
1752	John Sykes, A.M. ...	Joseph and Jane Sykes ...	Same.
1784	John Crosse, A.M. ...	Hammond Crosse, Esq. ...	Same.
1816	Henry Heap, B.D. ...	Daniel Sykes and others ...	Same.
1839	William Scoresby, D.D. ...	Trustees of Mr. Simeon ...	Resigned.
1847	John Burnet, LL.D. ...	Same	By death.
1870	Vincent Wm. Ryan, D.D., Bishop of the Mauritius ...	Same	Resigned.
1880	Joseph Bardsley, M.A. ...	Same	Present Vicar.

CHAPTER III.—Modern Churches.

NEXT to the Parish Church in point of seniority, was the old Christ Church, at the top of Darley Street. To our mind there is something sad in the remembrance of this once sacred edifice, erected little more than seventy years ago, but of which at this moment not a trace remains. We speak, of course, of the building only, for a new Christ Church has within recent years been reared in place of the old one, but upon another site. True, the old structure was no striking object of beauty, nor could it ever, even in its best days, have been regarded as an architectural ornament to the town. But for more than sixty years it was the spot where large congregations of devout Bradfordians were wont to meet for Divine worship, and it witnessed the labours for thirty-six years of that faithful and earnest pastor—the Rev. William Morgan.

Old Christ Church.

As it was pulled down (for street improvements) so recently as the year 1879, the locality and general appearance of the old Christ Church will be fresh to the memory of many of our readers. To pedestrians who daily passed along Darley Street, the edifice, notwithstanding its sacred character, was regarded as a great obstruction.

To many it was a puzzle as to how it ever came to be reared right across what is now one of the busiest thoroughfares in the town. In justice however to those who selected this site it should be borne in mind, that in the earlier years of the present century, the only means of approach to Manningham Lane was either by way of Skinner Lane (Cheapside), or Westgate and Northgate, if we may except a footpath across the fields from the top of Darley Street to near Piper's Grave. When the church was built it stood almost alone amid rural surroundings, one side of the street being appropriated by the Manor Hall and its garden and plantation, and the other side being occupied by one or two private residences surrounded by gardens.

It was also a puzzle to many as to how it came to pass that there was never a church-yard attached to the place. Thereby hangs a tale. The site for the church was given by the then Lord of the Manor, Mr. Benjamin Rawson, but by some oversight or other no seat was set apart for that gentleman when the church was completed. He took offence at this, and refused either to give or sell any land for the purposes of a church-yard.

The foundation stone of the church was laid on the 4th June, 1813, by Mr. Chas. Hardy, on behalf of the venerable vicar Crosse, who by reason of his blindness was unable to perform the ceremony. Towards the cost of erection the former gave £300, and his brother Mr. John Hardy (Lord Cranbrook's father) gave a like sum. Mr. Crosse gave £100.

The first incumbent of Christ Church was the Rev. William Morgan, who had previously been curate under Mr. Crosse at the Parish Church. Shortly before his promotion he married, and the event was noticed as follows in the *Gentleman s Magazine* for the year 1813 :—"Lately, at Guiseley, near Bradford, by the Rev. W. Morgan, (Bradford), Rev. Patrick Brontë, Minister of Hartshead-cum-Clifton, to Maria, third daughter of the late T. Branwell, Esq., of Penzance; and, at the same time by the Rev. P. Bronte, Rev. W. Morgan, to the only daughter of Mr. John Fennell, head master of the Wesleyan Academy near Bradford." From this announcement it would seem that Mr. Morgan was the officiating clergyman at the marriage of his friend Mr. Brontë, and that then immediately the latter acted in the same capacity at Mr. Morgan's.

Mrs. Gaskell in her "Life of Charlotte Brontë" makes no allusion to this odd double wedding, but she does tell us that Mr. Fennell was Miss Branwell's uncle, and that he had a daughter Jane, who was "engaged." A little further explanation however, is needed here. Mr. Fennell, (whose wife was sister to Mrs. Brontë's father) was at this time head master of Woodhouse Grove Academy, and Mr. Crosse, who was an admirer of the Arminian school of theology, took a great interest in his students, and often invited them to the vicarage at Bradford. One of these was a young Mr. Branwell, whose sister sometimes came to see him all the way from Penzance. On these long and toilsome journeys—for travelling was a serious matter eighty years ago—this young lady had for her companion a cousin of hers—also a lady. Through their acquaintance with Mr. Branwell, the two clerical friends, Messrs. Brontë and Morgan, very naturally became acquainted with the young ladies from Penzance, and in course of time, Mr. Brontë fell in love with Miss Branwell, while Mr. Morgan became equally attached to her fair cousin, with the ultimate result that both couples were married in the novel and romantic manner recorded above.

It will be seen that Mr. Fennell was not at this time, as stated by Mrs. Gaskell, a clergyman of the Church of England. He however, afterwards became such, and was for a time Mr. Crosse's curate at the Parish Church, and occasionally assisted his son-in-law, Mr. Morgan, at Christ Church.

Mr. Morgan was a remarkable man, and laboured hard and sacrificed much in the interests of the place which he served for so many years as pastor; but we doubt if his industry and good intentions were appreciated as they deserved to be. He was sadly harassed by a heavy debt that was left upon the church at the time of its erection, and by an insufficient salary for the position he held. He was an author as well as a preacher, but certainly did not excel in that line. His writings were religious, moral and didactic, but were lacking in originality and force. At a time when books, and especially local books, were both costly and scarce, they would doubtless be thought something excellent, but would, we fear, possess little charm for present day readers. His chief works were, "The Parish Priest Pourtrayed," (Life of Rev. John Crosse); "The Pastoral Visitor," (a serial); "Christian Instructions," (also a serial), and a "Selection of Psalms and Hymns." Mr. Brontë was one of his contributors, but in the writings of that reverend gentleman one fails to detect the austere and passionate man that Mrs. Gaskell has painted him, who was wont to discharge pistols into the air in order to let off his tempers.

From an old account-book in the hand-writing of Mr. Thomas Inkersley, who acted as treasurer of the church for several years, we might cull many interesting items, but a few, selected at random, must suffice.

		£	s.	d.
1828, April	—To oil and candles	0	18	7
1832, Oct. 31	—To Joshua Simpson for bell ringing...	1	6	3
,, ,, 31	—To John Simpson for attending letting pews	0	8	0
,, Nov. 6	—To Mary Midgley for cleaning church	3	0	0
,, ,, 6	—To Abraham Scott's salary (clerk)	5	0	0
1833, May 4	—To James Wood for bell rope	0	5	6
,, June 1	—To John Gott's salary (organist) half-year	7	10	0
,, ,, 1	—To John Simpson for poundage in collecting pew rents (no charge)			
,, ,, 10	—To Miss Arthur's half-year's account for Mr. Morgan's little boy	8	12	9
,, July 10	—To Mr. Booth for tuning Organ	2	2	0
,, Sep. 23	—To B. Gissop for a new key for church door	0	2	6
,, Oct. 28	—To Mrs. Clarke for candles	5	4	6
,, ,, 30	—To John Simpson for a pair of listing shoes	0	2	0

The Bradford Gas Company was formed so early as 1822, but it would appear from the last two items, that the authorities of Christ Church did not care to avail themselves of the improved light, as the old "dips" were not superseded till the year 1836. The pair of "listing shoes" (shoes made of cloth list) were for the use of the verger, that he might be able to move noiselessly about in snuffing the candles.

Mr. Morgan had been incumbent of Christ Church for thirty-six years when, in 1851, he exchanged livings with the Rev. W. Ramsden Smith, Rector of Hullcott, Bucks. He had sought this change in order to secure a sphere of usefulness within the compass of his declining activity, but he did not long enjoy his well earned season of repose. He died in 1858, aged nearly seventy years.

In 1878 the site and edifice of the church were required by the Corporation for the improvement of Darley Street, and the £10,000 which were given for these went a long way towards the new Christ Church in Manningham Lane. The last service in the old sanctuary took place on the 27th of October, 1878. The present vicar of Christ Church is the Rev. Vincent John Ryan, M.A.

An interval of twenty-three years elapsed before another church was built in Bradford, after the erection of Christ Church in 1815. This was St. James' in Manchester Road, then known as "Bowling Lane." This beautiful structure—a fine specimen of the Lancet-Gothic style—with its schools and parsonage, was the noble gift of one of Bradford's worthiest townsmen, Mr. John Wood, of the well-known firm of Messrs. Wood and Walker. It was built under the superintendance of Mr. Walker Rawsthorne of this town, who was afterwards architect of the Bradford Infirmary.

The laying of the foundation stone by Mr. Wood, on October 31st, 1836, was a memorable event, and well nigh twenty thousand people were present to witness the ceremony.

The first incumbent of the church was the Rev. G. S. Bull—a zealous co-worker with Richard Oastler in the Ten Hours' Bill movement. Although some people tauntingly styled this worthy man the "Political Parson," his name will be long and deservedly held in remembrance by the class for whom he lived and laboured, and whose rights he so fearlessly advocated through "good report and evil report." He was truly the factory workers' friend.

The Rev. W. Sherwood, B.A., succeeded Mr. Bull to the incumbency, and he in turn was followed by the Rev. Canon Burfield, during whose term of office the living became a vicarage. The Rev. Henry Clark, M.A., was vicar for a few years, and on his retirement was succeeded by the Rev. John E. Loughnan.

The good example set by Mr. Wood was soon followed by Mr. J. Berthon, a gentleman residing in the Isle of Wight, but upon whose generosity Bradford had no claim whatever beyond its great need of church accommodation. At a cost of nearly £4000 he erected St.

Old St. John's, Manchester Road.

John's Church near the bottom of Manchester Road. It was completed in the year 1839, and under license of the Bishop of Ripon service was conducted in it; but for some reason unknown to the public it was closed for a time, and for several years it remained unconsecrated. The place seemed born to misfortunes. The unfortunate loss of a sum of money intended for its endowment caused much embarrassment, and in 1844 the church was offered for sale. The only sources of income for the living were the pew rents and surplice fees, and concerning the latter, unhappy disputes arose between the incumbent, the Rev. C. J. Pearson, and the vicar, Dr. Scoresby, which had to be referred to the Bishop of Ripon for settlement.

The Rev. H. De L. Willis, D.D., was incumbent for several years, and his successor was the Rev. R. W. Loosemore, M.A., during whose time many desirable changes were effected. One of these was the pulling down of the old building, (which, besides being an architectural disfigurement, was inconveniently situated and defective in its arrangements), and the erection in 1871 of the new church in Horton Lane.

St. John's was formed into an ecclesiastical parish in 1854, and its present vicar is the Rev. A. J. G. Nash, M.A.

The Princes' Theatre and the Star Music Hall were subsequently erected upon the site of the old church.

St. John's Church, Bowling, came next in the order of erection. It was consecrated in 1841, and its first incumbent was the Rev. Joseph Loxdale Frost.

St. Jude's Church followed in 1843. The chief promoters of its erection were Messrs. Samuel Laycock, Joshua Mann, J. G. Horsfall and Dr. Macturk. The cost of it (£3000) was raised by subscription. The living was held for several years by the Rev. James Cooper, M.A., and in 1857 the Rev. John Eddowes was appointed his successor. The latter was a clergyman peculiarly fitted to cope with the dense working-class population that rapidly gathered around the church, and the twenty-eight years of faithful and untiring labour which he devoted to the parish bore abundant fruit. For a time however, it was up-hill work. His views on church ritual were too advanced for several of his parishioners, and much opposition and many obstacles were thrown in his way. But these he lived and laboured down, and the early years of conflict were followed by years of peace and great prosperity.

Some three years ago Mr. Eddowes found it necessary to relax his efforts somewhat, and this he did by removing to a sphere of usefulness where the strain upon his energies was less severe. His loss to the parish of St. Jude's was keenly felt.

The church at Manningham, dedicated to St. Paul, is a handsome structure, with a spire of lofty and beautiful proportions. It was erected in 1847 at the cost of Mr. John Hollings. The late Rev. Canon Mitton was for many years the esteemed vicar of this church.

St. Matthew's, Bankfoot, in Bowling, was erected in 1849, and cost about £2000. It is a plain Gothic structure. The living is of the yearly value of about £200, and is in the gift of Sir John Hardy, Bart.

St. Andrew's, Lister Hills, was built by subscription, and opened for public worship September 28th, 1853. The living is in the gift of Simeon's Trustees. The vicarage is now, and for the past thirty-six years, has been held by the Rev. Knight Gale, A.K.C. During that period, a good residence for the vicar, extensive schools and schoolmaster's house have been reared.

Notwithstanding the steady progress that had been going on in the way of church-building, the provision was, as yet, most inadequate to the immense increase of population that had taken place. In the year 1860 Bradford could only boast of four churches in addition to its Parish Church. Manningham had two; Bowling two and Horton one. This was a pitiable state of things; but the good church-people of Bradford roused themselves to a full sense of the situatiou, and by one stupendous effort not only atoned for lost time, but also made a bold step in advance. A movement was started which had for its object the erection and endowment of no less than ten new churches within the borough. The organisation was styled The Bradford Church Building Society, and it was aided in its operations by the Ripon Church Building Society, and the Incorporated Church Building Society. Within the brief span of twelve years the good work was carried to a successful completion. The following is a list of the ten churches and times of their erection—

St. Stephen's	1860.
St. Philip's, (Girlington)	,,
St. Mary's, (Laisterdyke)	1861.
St. Thomas'	,,
St. Luke's	1862.
All Saints'	1863.
Holy Trinity	1864.
St. Barnabas' (Heaton) ...	,,
St. Michael and All Angels'	1867.
St. Bartholomew's ...	1872.

Since the above, the following other churches have been built, viz: St. Mark's, Manningham; St. John the Evangelist, Great Horton (in place of the old Bell Chapel); St. Augustine's, Otley Road; St. Mary Magdalene's, White Abbey; St. Luke's, Manningham, and St. Peter's, Allerton.

Roman Catholics.

Whether or not Roman Catholicism was completely rooted out of Bradford after the Reformation we have not been able to learn, but that there would be families here and there who still clung to the old faith is not at all improbable. It was not however, until the year 1822, that we hear of any attempt being made on the part of this church to regain a footing here—an attempt which caused no little alarm to the Protestants of Bradford. "A room was hired," says

Mr. James, "in Commercial Street, for the performance of public worship, but on account of threats, the owner would not allow it to be occupied. Public mass, probably for the first time in Bradford since the days of Mary, was celebrated in the Roebuck Inn. Some of the persons in authority interfered in a very improper manner, and the landlady being threatened with the loss of her license for allowing her room to be used by the Roman Catholics, they thereupon took a building in Chapel Lane, which had formerly been used by the South-cottians, and worshipped in it till they built their chapel at Stott Hill in 1824."

Old St. Mary's,—Stott Hill.

It was on Wednesday, July 27th, 1825, that the very unpretentious building known as St. Mary's Chapel was consecrated, upon which occasion high mass was celebrated, the officiating priest being the Rev. Benedict Rayment of York, and a sermon was preached by the Right Rev. Dr. Baines, Bishop of Thespia. The event caused no little commotion in Bradford. The service had been announced to commence at ten o'clock, but long before that time, hundreds were gathered at the door hoping to gain admission. Dr. Baines preached an eloquent sermon which occupied an hour and a half in delivery.

Exception was taken by his Protestant hearers to the statement made by him that all countries originally converted from Paganism had been converted by Catholics, and that the number converted by other missionaries hardly equalled the number of converters; and this success of the Catholic missions, he said, was an evidence that the words of Christ "Lo! I am with you alway," were applicable only to the Catholic Church. This assertion afterwards led to a warm controversy between the Rev. J. Taylor, curate of the Parish Church, and the Rev. Francis Murphy, a priest at St. Mary's. A pamphlet by the former entitled—"The Errors, Corruptions and Claims of the Church of Rome, exhibited in a sermon by P. A. Baines, D.D., exposed and refuted," was quickly followed by one of fifty-two pages from the pen of Mr. Murphy. The controversial spirit was quiet for a time, but in 1828 a fresh rupture broke out, through the indiscreet interference on the part of Mr. Maddocks, the priest at St. Mary's, at a Bible Society Meeting. A furious discussion on theological questions, took place at Eastbrook Chapel, between a number of Roman Catholic Priests and Protestant Ministers. The chapel was crowded to excess, and the wrangling continued for two days. Mr. James quaintly observes that "both sides claimed the victory."

The rapid increase of trade and population in Bradford led to the migration here of many families from Ireland, which had the effect of greatly increasing the number of Roman Catholics, and it was found necessary to erect other churches in the town. In 1853 St. Patrick's, in Westgate, was erected; and this was followed in 1871, by St. Peter's, Leeds Road; in 1873 by St. Ann's, Guy Street, and in 1887 by St. Joseph's, Packington Street. The old St. Mary's has recently been superseded by the larger and more imposing structure in East Parade.

Old Unitarian Chapel.

CHAPTER IV.—The Dissenters.

English Presbyterians and Unitarians.

THE history of Dissent in Bradford may be very properly divided into two periods, one beginning with Oliver Heywood, the other with John Wesley. The first of these takes us back to that great struggle for civil and religious liberty known as the Civil War. The passing of the Uniformity Act, shortly after the Restoration, was the beginning of those harsh and despotic measures that were meant to crush out Nonconformity, but which in reality was the greatest blow that ever was dealt at the Established Church. This Act (passed in 1662) was so outrageous in its provisions, that on the day when it came into force, two thousand ministers bade farewell to their weeping flocks, and went out from their homes and livings to face penury and starvation rather than conform to it. The story of the "Ejectment" has become a thrice-told tale. It stands without a parallel in the whole annals of history.

A brave and worthy band of men truly were those who, for conscience' sake went forth to meet the horrors of famine and persecution! It does not come within the province of this work to dwell on this subject, but the names of some of those who shared in this struggle, in Bradford and the district, must be recorded. From the Parish Church of Bradford was ejected Jonas Waterhouse, the vicar. From Thornton went forth Joseph Dawson, a man of venerable aspect and of good report of all men,—a diligent student and affectionate preacher. From Pudsey went Elkanah Wales, of great reputation as a preacher, and withal a man of great holiness and of unspotted life. From Coley (near Halifax) went forth good Oliver Heywood. From Haworth was ejected Robert Town, the elder; from Idle, Thomas Smallwood: from Wakefield, Joshua Kirby, "more abundant in losses and imprisonments than most of his brethren," and from Addle went forth Thomas Sharp, M.A.

The Sharps of Horton Hall, were of the old Puritan stamp, and their name is closely linked with the early struggles of Dissent in Bradford. John Sharp, father of Abraham Sharp, the eminent mathematician, and Thomas Sharp, before named, was a staunch supporter of the Parliamentarians, and fought with Fairfax at the battles of Nantwich and Marston Moor, and for his good services received a gold medal. Thomas Sharp, after his ejectment from the rectory of Addle, returned to his old home at Horton, and during the brief indulgence to Dissenters in 1672, licensed a portion of his library as a preaching room, and formed one of the first societies of Dissenters in Bradford. Here he often preached to great numbers who flocked from all quarters to hear him. Hither also came Oliver Heywood to share in the good work and bask in the momentary gleam of sunshine.

In the year 1688, a chapel or preaching-house was built at Chapel Green, Little Horton, "for the use of the Dissenters of Bradford and the neighbourhood." The land on which it stood belonged to Thomas Sharp, and is referred to in his will. It is to be regretted that some uncertainty exists as to the precise locality of this interesting spot which has been called the "birth-place" of Nonconformity in Bradford. While some incline to the belief that the old building in Chapel Fold, Wibsey, is the place, others maintain that it stood near the Chapel Green in Thornton Lane, Little Horton, and undoubtedly existing evidence is most strongly in favour of this latter view. From this old meeting-house (wherever it may have stood), and its successor in Chapel (or Toad) Lane, sprung the Congregational and English Presbyterian bodies of Bradford. It is disappointing that so little is known either of the pastors or people that were wont to meet here for worship. Mr. James says that "Samuel Hulme, a worthy man and of great repute among the Presbyterians, resided and held the office of minister of Little Horton about the year 1700, and there his son—Dr. Hulme, the eminent physician—was born."

With the year 1717, we come upon more reliable data. In that year, according to Fawcett's "Life of Oliver Heywood," the Chapel in Chapel Lane was erected, and in 1719 the congregation left the old sanctuary at Chapel Green to take up their abode in the new one. From documents now in the possession of Mr. Edward Hailstone, it appears that the cost of the chapel amounted to the moderate sum of £340 3s. 5d. Much of the material, such as the entrance gateway (see page 22), windows, wainscotting, and wood-work came from the ruins of that once magnificent pile, Howley Hall, near Batley. The following items of expenditure are curiously interesting:

1719-20		£	s.	d.
May	21—Paid at Horton Delf	0	0	3
,,	24—Pd. Robert Wilson for six days' work at Hooley	0	9	0
,,	,,—Pd. for Hooley Windows...	3	0	0
,,	26—Pd. for 14 loads of ye same leading to Bradford at 5/- per load	3	10	0
,,	,,—Spent at Hooley Hall in Carters	0	3	4
,,	,,—Spent on them at Bradford	0	3	6
,,	,,—Their dinners at Bradford	0	7	9
,,	,,—Pd. John Aked for leading sand at Eshold	0	0	6
,,	27—Scowring Stone at Delf, 4 days...	0	2	8
June	20—Pd. John Hollings for Wood from Harding	14	17	3
July	10—Six loads of Windows and gobbys from Hooley	1	15	0
,,	18—Pd. Scratcher for 4 loads stones bringing	1	0	0
,,	,,—Spent when the balks were slabbed	0	1	0
,,	31—Pd. Joshua Hartley for 1000 slate pins	0	1	8
Aug.	10—Pd. for 3 small pillars at Hooley	0	5	6

,,	23—Pd. James Virr for 292 loads Wallstones from Horton, being 48 rood, 4 loads at 2/6	6	1	8
,,	25—A load of old doors from Skinner Lane	0	0	6
,,	27—Gave ye mason for a thacking pott	0	2	0
,,	,, —Paid for 24 balls and 2 pinnacles	0	4	0
Sept.	11—A sack of malt for rearing 15d., bruing it 6d., ¾ hopps 1d., 79 lbs. beef 14/6, small meat 9/-, butter 1/6, oatbread 1/6, tobacco 4d., pipes 4d. ... ... in all	2	3	8
,,	19—Pd. Ed. Walsh for 3500 short latts	2	4	4
Oct.	9—Pd. Robt. Swales for 11 loads Otley lime	0	12	10
1719.				
July	2—Pd. John Crocker for Hooley Gates leading	2	5	0
,,	23—Pd. workmen to drink at footing of gates	0	1	0

The conveyance of the land on which the chapel was built bears date December 2nd, 1719, and the parties to it were Robert Stansfield and the several trustees of the chapel. Stansfield, who is therein described as a "gentleman" was a drysalter in Bradford. He had married Elizabeth, daughter of the Rev. Thomas Sharp, of Horton Hall. The land was the gift of the Sharps, and the name of Abraham Sharp stands at the head of the list of trustees. He attended service in Chapel Lane, and though somewhat eccentric in his habits was withal a pious and charitable man. It is related that among other devices of his for relieving the poor, was that of filling his pockets with half-pence, before going to chapel, which he suffered to be taken out of his hand behind him, his object in doing this, being literally to carry out the divine precept, "When thou doest alms let not thy left hand know what thy right hand doeth." This was at any rate a *practical* fulfilment of the scriptural injunction, however much it might be at variance with the sentiment expressed in the same verse, "not to be seen of men when giving alms." But charity may cover a multitude of peculiarities as well as sins. It is said of Abraham Sharp that he had a full purse, and to the poor and needy he was an ever ready and bountiful giver. Peace be to his memory!

From our illustration it will be seen that the old chapel was a plain and unadorned structure. Its builders certainly could not be accused of reckless extravagance in the cost of its erection. In former years it would not be out of harmony with its rural surroundings, standing as it did amid green fields, and with the sun shining through a clear atmosphere on to the quaint old sun dial that might have been seen on the southern wall of the chapel.

On Sunday, October 6th, 1867, the congregation assembled for the last time for public worship within its ancient walls, previous to its being pulled down to make way for the present chapel.

The old place had braved a hundred and fifty years, and was one of the few remaining links between the old time and the new. But it has left other and more enduring associations than any that we have named. Its pulpit was successively occupied by preachers and pastors who were as eminent for their learning as they were esteemed for their piety, benevolence and zeal. At a time when popular education was looked upon with feelings of distrust and suspicion by other religious bodies, these men held high the standard of learning, and laboured beyond their own sphere of duty for its dissemination amongst the people.

The first minister at Chapel Lane was the Rev. Joshua Hardcastle, concerning whom, however, not much is known. In the autobiography of Thomas Wright, of Birkenshaw, an interesting reference is made to him. He states that on leaving the Bradford Grammar School, he went to the school of a Mrs. Betty Ward, in Broadstones, where he fell in love with a young girl named Nancy Dawson. "She boarded," he adds, "with Mr. Hardcastle, of the old Dissenting Chapel, and the people where I lodged attended there, and told Mr. H., who sent me a jocose invitation to his house with an assurance of a cordial welcome."

Mr. Hardcastle was succeeded in 1783 by the Rev. John Smith, a man of learning and an excellent preacher. It is said that he had very advantageous offers to enter the Established Church, but which he refused. During his ministry he drew large congregations, even to the crowding of the aisles of the chapel. Then followed the Rev. John Dean, who is spoken of as a gentleman of literary attainments, and taking great interest in all the philanthropic affairs of the town. His name will ever be associated with the Bradford Subscription Library, in the formation of which, in 1774, he took a prominent part.

Rev. Joseph Dawson.

Contrary to his usual accuracy, Mr. James is nct correct in stating, in his "History of Bradford," that the Rev. Joseph Dawson, of Royd's Hall, was for some time pastor of Chapel Lane, and the immediate predecessor of Mr. Dean. He was never the stated minister, although he was long connected with the place and sometimes preached from its pulpit. His remains were buried in the chapel yard, as were also those of his son Christopher, and his two daughters, Rachel and Mary, both of whom died in their ninetieth year. Mr. Dawson was indeed an extraordinary character—a man of philosophic and sagacious mind. He was the friend of Priestley and of most of the leading philosophers and scientists of the age, and yet one of tho most unassuming of mortals. "It would require," says Mr. J. Horsfall Turner, "a Smiles to do justice to his industry, and a Faraday to give him due credit for his scientific acquirements." He it was who first discovered and directed attention to the vast mineral wealth of Low Moor.

His first settlement in these parts was at Idle, where for a time he was minister at the Independent Chapel. While here he could not resist the bent of his mind, and contrived to work a coal-mine on Idle Moor, in spite of the duties of the ministry and of a private school that devolved upon him. His eccentricities led him into many strange devices in the pursuit of his "worldly" affairs, such as storing away fodder for his cattle in corners of the chapel, and rearing pens for his poultry among the gravestones of the chapel-yard. Nevertheless he was a man of great liberality and kindness, and his knowledge of medicine was of real service to the inhabitants of Idle.

After the ministry at Chapel Lane of the Rev. Henry Turner, which was of but a few years' duration, the Rev. Nicholas T. Heineken was appointed. He was the son of a Bremen merchant, a Lutheran, who had settled in London, and joined the ranks of the "Old Dissent." He began his pastoral labours in Bradford in 1817, and continued in the same with great acceptance till 1841.

Rev. Nicholas T. Heineken.

His acts of benevolence will be long remembered. One day a poor man came to his door just as the family were sitting down to dinner, and he asked for alms. There was a joint of meat on the table, and Mr. Heineken at once cut him a big slice, and taking some bread, carried it to him. When he came back his wife said to him, "You might have cut the slice off the worst end of the meat." "No," said he, "he has had it off the worst end long enough, poor fellow." This was but one of many instances of the reverend gentleman's true kindness of heart. Mr. James has left on record the following tribute to the memory of this good man. "It was my good fortune," he says, "to often converse with Mr. Heineken at his own house; and his knowledge was so extensive and varied, his manner of imparting it so pleasing, that no one listened to him without instruction and gratification. He was kind-hearted, generous, tolerant of all classes of belief, and urbane in manner."

The Rev. George Vance Smith, of York, was minister here from 1841 to 1843, when he removed to Macclesfield. The Rev. J. H. Ryland, his successor, will long be remembered if it were only for his long and useful connection with the Mechanics' Institute, of which he was elected president in 1858. He was deeply and widely respected.

On his retirement in 1860, he was succeeeded by the Rev. T. W. Freckleton, (who removed to Plymouth in 1866) and was followed by the late Rev. Richard Pilcher, B.A. The Rev. Mr. Knapton, Dr. Laird Collier, and the Rev. John Cuckson have subsequently served in the ministry of Chapel Lane, and the present minister is the Rev. J. Ceredig Jones.

The Quakers.

In point of antiquity the Quakers, or Friends, unquestionably claim a foremost place in the history of Puritanism in Bradford. Their register of births takes us back to so early a date as the year 1652. This may appear strange when it is remembered that George Fox, the founder of the sect, had only begun to make a declaration of his views some seven years previously; but the mystery is explained by the fact that the friends were so very careful and precise in their records of membership, that they even entered the *births* of those who joined them in middle life or old age.

That the Society of Friends gained an early footing in Bradford is evident from their register of burials, the first entry in which bears date 1656, two years prior to the death of Oliver Cromwell.

Up to the close of the seventeenth century, the locality of the Friends appears to have been almost strictly confined to the town, but afterwards they began to spread out over a wider area, and the burials of members from "Bradford-Moorside," Bowling, Bierley, Eccleshill, Manningham, "Phrizinghall," and Shipley are frequently recorded. Some are even mentioned as being brought from Allerton, Thornton, Thackley, Rawdon, and Pudsey. Thus widely dispersed and with the most wretched roads on which to travel, no wonder that one of the most useful appendages to the meeting-house which they erected at Bradford, should have been a commodious stable in which the horses of "Friends from a distance" might be comfortably disposed of during service.

The first name that occurs in the register of births (1652) is that of John Marshall, of Bradford. Those immediately following are Abraham Jowett, of Bowling, and Robert Pearson, —— Croysdill, and Abednego Bonas, of Bradford. The first name recorded in the register of Burials is Thomas Judson, of Bradford, followed by those of Richard Thornton, Grace Marshall, Elizabeth Sykes, Esther Birkby, Thomas Kitchen, Dorothy Verity (Wibsey), Zacariah Yewdall, Jeremy Crousdale, and Mabel Sykes, all of Bradford. These were all interred in the burial ground at Horton, near to the present Quaker Lane in that township. Burials continued to be made here for some time after the burial ground in Goodman's End came into use.

The piece of land in Goodman's End, of which the Friends became possessed in 1672, was the gift of a Matthew Wright, described as a clothier of Bradford. He gave the land for the purposes of a burial ground, and, strange to relate, was himself the first that was buried in it. The land was conveyed to the Friends by a deed of feoffment, and is described as "a croft or piece of land containing about one acre, lying and being in Goodman's End, on the south side of the highway, and is conveyed to John Green, John Winn, and Joshua Dawson, upon trust for the Children of Light whom the people of the world commonly call Quakers, to use as a burial ground for them and their succeeding generations." About twenty years ago, while some alterations were going on in the grave-yard, two tombstones were unearthed, which proved to be those of Matthew Wright and his sister. The tombstone of the latter was in a rather dilapidated condition, but every letter on that of Matthew Wright was perfect. The stones are preserved by the Friends as interesting relics, and have since been removed to their new chapel in Fountain Street.

In the career of John Winn (or Wynn), one of the above named trustees, we have a striking instance of the persecuting spirit of the times, and especially of the sufferings to which the Quakers were subjected. Wynn was a native of Bradford—by calling a clothier. In his younger days he enlisted for a soldier, and while quartered in London became a convert to the doctrines of Fox, obstinately refused to fight, and with great difficulty obtained his discharge from the army. He then returned to his native town, took to himself a wife, and both became noted preachers in the Society.

The Friends had no meeting-house here as yet, and were in the habit of meeting in Wynn's house. This fact, coupled with the energy with which the minister and his wife promulgated their doctrines, rendered them peculiar objects of persecution. Their house was repeatedly stripped of all they possessed, and heavy sufferings fell to their lot. Wynn died in 1699, after an arduous ministry of thirty-six years.

For several years after the death of Wynn, the Friends held their meetings in each others' houses. Benjamin Bartlett, the apothecary, specially licensed his house in Westgate for the purpose.

It was not till somewhere between the years 1710 and 1720 that the first chapel or meeting-house was built. This building, with stables adjoining, was erected in front of the land given by Mr. Wright, and with occasional repairs did good service for a hundred years.

The decided preference of the Friends for old scriptural names is strikingly shown by a glance at the registers for this period. Among the females are Deborah, Ruth, Esther, Rebecca, Tabitha, and Judith, interspersed with others such as Grace, Mercy, Faith and Christiana.

The males rejoiced in such old-world names as Abraham, Nehemiah, Amos, Caleb and Lazarus.

At a very early date the Friends appear to have become closely interwoven with the trading pursuits of the town, and from the minuteness with which their various callings are set forth in the registers, we get an interesting glimpse of the trades and professions that were in vogue, in Bradford and the district, about the middle of last century. Cloth-makers, weavers, woolcombers, shoemakers, slay-makers, woolsorters and husbandmen, are pretty plentiful. Some members are also described as yeomen, farmers, linen drapers and thread-makers; and mention is made of one surgeon and apothecary, and one "breeches maker."

Among the old family names that occur during the latter half of the century are those of the Yewdalls of Eccleshill and Idle; the Learoyds of Allerton; the Liveseys of Horton, and such familiar names as the Hoylands, Pearsons, and Bleazards. Before the close of the century we come upon the Hustlers, Peckovers, Mauds, Biltons, Norths, and Wilsons—names deservedly held in remembrance for their long and devoted connection with every good and philanthropic movement for the benefit of the town and its inhabitants. Some of them call for more than a passing notice, and are mentioned in the chapter on "Old Bradford Families."

With the growing importance of the town in the present century, the Friends appear to have kept pace, and instead of the simple callings of weavers, shoemakers, threadmakers, &c., we find them taking rank among the new trades and professions that earlier times did not seem to require, such as bankers, attorneys, physicians, chemists, manufacturers, etc.

The Friends had so far increased in numbers and influence, that it became necessary, early in the present century, to "arise and build." This was done in the year 1811, when a new chapel was erected on the site of the old one in Goodman's End. Though extremely plain in outward appearance, its interior was both commodious and comfortable. It faced to Wakefield Road, and boasted of a colonnade, and circular carriage drive in front. The Hustlers, at Undercliffe, could very distinctly see the front of the chapel from their residence, and discern when the congregation were dispersing at the conclusion of Sunday service. There was then an uninterrupted view from Undercliffe House to Goodman's End, and the gently sloping estate of the Hustlers reached all the way down to the old Leeds Road. There was no lack of lovely scenery on this side of the town, and even the new meeting-house stood amid surroundings both pleasant and grateful to the eye. The chapel was opened under favouring auspices, for the great distress which prevailed when the century was ushered in had happily given place to a season of peace and prosperity to the inhabitants of Bradford. Wages were perhaps not so high as at this day, but rents were low, and working folks were content to live on frugal fare and homely diet. The weaver followed the "peaceful labour of the loom" without disturbing dreams of savage opposition against the inroads of machinery; and the woolcomber was to be seen trudging along with bag of wool on his head, and paper cap and oil can in hand, with no unhappy forebodings of the wretched strikes and struggles that were looming in the distance.

The successive changes that followed the erection of the meeting-house in 1811 may be briefly stated. In 1825 it became necessary to enlarge the chapel building, which involved an outlay of £1611. 9s. 1d. a sum that was raised with no little difficulty in those days. This was the year of the weavers and woolcombers' strike, when large numbers of working people were out of employment, and widespread distress prevailed. But the Quaker Society in Bradford had no lack of substantial and generous patrons within its borders, and three of these staved over the difficulty by lending the amount required till such time as the congregation could see its way to wipe off the debt.

In 1847 the Lancashire and Yorkshire Railway Company required a portion of the burial ground for their intended line of railway, and more recently the same Company intimated to the Friends that they should require the entire plot of land, including the site of the chapel, for the contemplated enlargement of their station premises.

For this final disposal of the Goodman's End property, they received £16,000, a sum which went a long way towards enabling them to build the new chapel in Fountain Street.

The Friends met for the last time as a congregation in their old and venerated sanctuary in the month of October, 1877. Our sketch shews the old chapel and curator's house as seen from Wakefield Road.

Quaker Chapel—Goodman's End.

In that interesting book, the "Private Memoirs of B. & E. Seebohm," a pleasing picture is given of Quaker life in Bradford some sixty years ago, which we feel tempted to reproduce.

"The Hustlers, with some other families of position, were the aristocracy of the place, but such was the freemasonry and republican equality within the community, increased by the natural independence characteristic of the West Riding, that the small farmer or shopkeeper felt himself upon a footing of perfect equality with them. The Hustlers of Bolton House, had an only son, and so also had the honest couple who lived in the cottage at the meeting-house and had the care of the premises. Notwithstanding the difference in their social position, the two mothers were on such friendly terms that one Sunday Mrs. Hustler was accosted by her friend with the observation, in a most patronising tone and in broad Yorkshire dialect, 'I'll tell thee what I've been thinkin'; my Benjamin and thy William are t'finest young men i't' meetin!'"

A frequent and welcome guest at Undercliffe or Bolton House, was Andrew Pearson—a genuine Yorkshireman. He was a native of Wibsey, and had in turns been an Infidel and Chartist, but now he had become a Quaker preacher. A female minister of the Quaker persuasion having held a meeting in a barn at Low Moor, Andrew, through curiosity, had gone to hear her. He had perched himself on one of the long bars of the folding barn doors, intending to scoff and jeer at her; but her preaching, to use his own words, "tracked me through all the lanes of my life, and fair fetched me down." After this he became both a Quaker and a preacher. Though an unlettered man and speaking the broadest of Yorkshire dialects, Andrew was a sterling character, and a powerful preacher too. With a sound judgment and an honest fearlessness in saying just what he thought, he possessed a stubborn spirit of independence. When, after "Sunday meeting" the carriage of the Hustlers drew up in front of the chapel to receive the guests for dinner at Undercliffe, and Andrew was requested to join the party, he politely but firmly declined the invitation. He had conscientious scruples about "Sunday carriages, and preferred to walk the distance."

Of late years the Society of Friends has passed through a striking change in many of the peculiarities which had come to be regarded as almost the very essentials of Quakerism, and a general relaxation of traditional views on points of dress and speech has taken place. Many belonging to the old school of the community looked upon this revolution with feelings of alarm; but the opinion that seems now to prevail is that the main principles of Christian truth and duty are of greater consequence than these. And after all, it would seem that the regulation of dress was no part of the principles of the early Friends, and it is an error to imagine that what is generally regarded as *the* Quaker dress, was the original distinctive costume of the community. George Fox himself, who usually wore a common leather suit, beyond advising simplicity and neatness of attire, regarded the question of dress as one of trifling importance.

The history of the Society of Friends will be remembered by something more enduring than the changing fashions of a day. Their first and greatest principle of peace and good-will towards men; their brotherly love, which they have carried further than any other religious community; their unflinching courage and resignation under the bitterest persecution; their abhorrence of war and all its atrocities; their love of freedom, and hatred of slavery; and lastly, their unbounded philanthropy, must ever inspire the highest admiration, and the remembrance of these will be imperishable when all minor and insignificant matters have long been buried in oblivion.

John Nelson in the Bradford Dungeon.

The Wesleyan Methodists.

Peculiarly interesting were the circumstances under which Methodism was introduced into Bradford. The first Methodist service was a prayer-meeting held at the door of a miserable dungeon, and the first place of worship a room in an old cock-pit.

John Nelson, the preaching stonemason of Birstall, of whom Southey said, that "he had as high a spirit and as brave a heart as ever Englishman was blessed with;" was one of John Wesley's most faithful disciples. His bold advocacy of Wesley's views soon brought him into trouble, and there were those among his enemies who were only too glad of a pretext for getting him out of the neighbourhood where he had been accustomed to preach. Soldiers were wanted in the army at this time (1744), and all "able-bodied men" who led disorderly lives or had no apparent means of earning a livelihood, were pressed into the service with very little scruple. Among those who shared this fate was John Nelson—an able-bodied man certainly, but one who neither led a disorderly life, nor was wanting in a real or an "apparent" means of earning his livelihood. He, however, was apprehended while preaching in a house at Adwalton, and brought before certain commissioners at Halifax, who, in spite of abundant evidence to his good character, condemned him to serve His Majesty as a common soldier.

The Vicar of Birstall has been accredited with the bringing about of this unjust persecution of a good and harmless man, and that he did it as a means of getting John and his preaching removed out of the parish. Nelson was ordered to be taken to York. On his way thither he was lodged for a time in the dungeon at the top of Ivegate, Bradford; a filthy hole, which he said "stunk worse than a hog-stye, by reason of the blood and filth which sink from the butchers who kill over it." At night several good folks came to the dungeon door, brought the prisoner candles, and put him meat and water in through the hole of the door. Comfortless as the place was, John said that his soul was so filled with the love of God that it was a very paradise to him. "When I had eaten and drank," he says, "I gave God thanks, and we (himself and the good people who had come to sympathise with him) sang hymns almost all night, they without and I within."

At five o'clock in the morning of next day, Nelson was removed from this disreputable place and taken on to Leeds. Afterwards, through the kind influence of the Countess of Huntingdon he obtained his discharge, and returned home.

John Wesley's first visit to Bradford was made in the summer of 1744, on which occasion he preached at Little Horton—tradition says at Horton Hall. He was in Bradford again during the following year, and also in the years 1746 and 1747. To the latter year belongs the formation of the first Methodist Society in Bradford. One of the first members of this small organisation was a Thomas Mitchell, who, after serving as a soldier, became one of the earliest Methodist preachers. Alluding to Mr. Wesley's visit in 1747, he says, "He (Mr. Wesley) joined several of us together in a class, which met about a mile from the town. But all of them fell back and left me alone; yet afterwards some of them returned."

If we may take the "home-spun" verses of William Darney as authentic evidence of the fact, it would seem that Methodism, up to the year 1751, had not gained a very firm footing in Bradford.

> On Bradford likewise, look Thou down,
> Where Satan keeps his seat;
> Come, by Thy power; Lord! him dethrone,
> For Thou art very great.

The Methodists took possession of a large room in the old building known as the Bradford Cock-pit, in 1756, which they used as a place of worship. Strange that the spot that was to witness the revival of religion in this town should have been noted as the favourite resort of "the most profligate characters then to be found," and that the place where Wesley, Whitfield, and Grimshaw were wont to address multitudes of anxious hearers, had but recently been the gathering-place of disreputable gamblers and black-legs, who revelled in such brutal sports as cock-fighting and bull-baiting.

It would, perhaps, be difficult to find another spot that has been put to so many "base uses," as this old building. It was much shorn of its former proportions on the opening out of Bond Street into Aldermanbury, but our sketch shews its east end, and the steps from the top of which Wesley addressed the large crowds that came to hear him. Besides being successively the first meeting-room of the Baptist and Methodist bodies, it could also boast of being the gathering place of the followers of Baron Swedenborg and Joanna Southcot. Every Sunday afternoon Prophet Wroe held a sort of service in the upper room of the building, to which he walked from Dudley Hill, in procession with twelve virgins dressed in white, and with long white falls.

Old Cock-pit.

As to the secular uses of the place, they are untold. At one time it was used as an assembly-room for the soldiers quartered in the town during the riot at Horsfall's mill; at another it served the purpose of a court-house. Besides doing service also, at various times, as a vagrants' refuge, school-room, joiners' shop, and soap and oil warehouse, it was once used as a cloth-hall. The circumstance of its being let to the Methodists as a meeting-room led to the following lines being penned by some inspired local poet, which appeared in the *Gentleman's Magazine* for 1798.

O, wondrous pile, who can thy use relate?
At once to God and mammon consecrate!
Here Christ is preach'd, and saving faith is taught,
Here goods are sold, and merchandise is bought.
Strange union! so the Temple once was made
The house of praying, and the house of trade.
Close underneath, an airy ample pit,
For cocks and bloodshed; oaths and wagers fit,
   The Synagogue of Satan!
Below a stable, humble, useful cell,
Where quadrupeds do innocently dwell.
Hail, medley Dome! most comprehensive plan,
That e'er, since Noah, fill'd the brain of man.
Such was his ark, with three-fold storey join'd,
Which in its spacious cavity confin'd
Clean and unclean of every sort and kind.

The Methodists took possession of the large room in the Cock-pit in 1756. Wesley, in a visit which he paid in the following year, thus refers to it:—"Thursday, May 12th. The latter end of the week I spent in Bradford. Sunday, 15, at five, the house contained the congregation, but at eight they covered the plain adjoining to it. The sun was hot till the clouds interposed; it was a solemn and comfortable season." The plain here alluded to was an open space between the Cock-pit and the beck, which was known as the Turls Green. Here assembled the crowds who came to hear Mr. Wesley preach. From the same spot William Grimshaw, of Haworth, and the eloquent Whitfield also addressed large gatherings.

On the discovery being made that the room in the Cock-pit was no longer safe for public worship, on account of the floor having given way, the erection of a new chapel was contemplated, the land purchased, and the enterprise set on foot with all the zeal and energy characteristic of the followers of Wesley. The site chosen for the new sanctuary was in Horton Road, a little above the present Alexandra Hotel. Truly the people "had a mind to work." Several of the members cheerfully assisted in digging the foundation, while two earnest and devoted "brothers" went forth to collect funds in the district, and though the first contribution which they received did not exceed the modest sum of two-pence, they were by no means discouraged. The building involved an outlay of £997. 8s. 9d.; a large sum in those days, when there were no wealthy religious patrons or bazaars to fall back upon for help, as in these.

The style in which the chapel was to be built was one to which Mr. Wesley was himself very partial, namely, the octagon, which, while it possessed the advantage of seating a greater number of worshippers than other buildings, and its acoustic properties were superior, had nevertheless the drawbacks of being less secure in point of safety, and was incapable of enlargement except by entire rebuilding.

The new chapel was opened on Sunday, July 27th, 1776. Wesley in his journal, says:—"There was so large a multitude, and the rain so damped my voice, that many in the skirts of the congregation

Octagon Chapel—Horton Road.

could not hear distinctly. They have just built a preaching-house in a square of 54 feet, the largest Octagon we have in England, and it is the first of the kind where the roof is built with common sense, rising only a third of its breadth, yet it is as firm as any in England."

But notwithstanding this eulogium in its favour, the Octagon Chapel in Horton Road had to be abandoned in little more than forty years after its erection, the walls having so far given way as to render the place unsafe for public worship.

Bradford was one of the spots that Wesley delighted to visit. He lived to see his cause here prosper and flourish beyond his greatest expectations. The cause has never ceased to prosper up to the present time, and promises to do so into the far remote future. Wesley paid his last visit here on the 2nd May, 1788, having then nearly completed his eighty-fifth year. On the Morning of Sunday, May 4th, he preached in the Parish Church, which was so densely filled that it was with extreme difficulty he reached the pulpit. "It was, however," says he, "worth all the labour. I strongly applied those words in the epistle for the day—'The end of all things is at hand, be ye therefore sober and watch unto prayer.' It seemed as if the whole congregation was moved. I believe that hour will not soon be forgotten."

Such was the last appearance in Bradford of this venerable and good man. A touching and impressive picture surely! Wesley was then very near the end of his long and useful pilgrimage on earth,—full of years and well-earned honours. Still more impressive was this occasion rendered by the fact that the venerable and blind vicar of Bradford, beloved of his people, took part in the service.

The earlier years of the present century were marked by great prosperity to the Methodist cause in Bradford. The members in society rapidly increased, and it became necessary to erect both new chapels and schools. From Mr. Stamp's useful little work on "Wesleyan Methodism in Bradford and its Vicinity," we learn that in 1805, Bradford was favoured with "one of those extraordinary visitations which have occasionally marked the progress of our Zion. The doors of the Octagon Chapel were for ten or twelve weeks scarcely ever closed by day or night, one party of worshippers frequently waiting without till those within had fulfilled the appointed hour of service."

The result of this revival was that the demand for greater accommodation became very urgent throughout the whole district. Shortly after the abandonment of the Octagon Chapel, the erection of a large building in the centre of the town was determined upon. Accordingly a piece of land in Kirkgate was bought, and a chapel erected thereon which was opened on May 11th, 1811. The total cost of the work was £12,000.

This was followed by the erection in 1825, of Eastbrook Chapel. The age of fine public edifices in Bradford was not yet, hence the erection of a building capable of holding 1500 persons was an event of no ordinary moment. The chapel even at this day cannot but be regarded as a grand and spacious structure. Sixty years ago it held a prominent position and had few rivals, and was a vast improvement on the style of architecture then in vogue among the Dissenters. The architect was Mr. Joseph Botham, of Sheffield.

The opening of Eastbrook Chapel, which took place on Friday, September 2nd, 1825, was a memorable event in the history of Methodism in Bradford. The fact that the eminent divine and profound scholar, Dr. Adam Clarke, was to take part in it, brought together a large concourse of strangers. The Doctor took the morning service; the Rev. William Atherton the afternoon, and the Rev. Jabez Bunting the evening. On the Sunday following, the interest seemed to have increased rather than diminished, for early in the morning vast crowds of people of all ranks in life thronged the roads and avenues leading to the town. This time the attraction was the chapel in Kirkgate, as Dr. Clarke was appointed to preach there. Many hundreds were unable to gain admittance, and William, better known as "Billy" Dawson, addressed the overflow in the adjoining burial ground. The services in Eastbrook were on this day conducted by the Rev. David Stoner, who had been recently stationed in Bradford, and had already endeared himself to all classes by his eminent usefulness and talents. The collections realised by all the services amounted to £580 2s. 8¾d.

The remark made by Dr. Clarke that he feared the chapel was *too far out of the town* strikes one as somewhat strange when looking at Eastbrook to-day. The locality certainly presented a very different aspect then to what it does now. On each side of the new Leeds

Road were open fields from Bridge Street to the chapel, and the space between Vicar Lane and Hall Ings was unbuilt upon. Behind the chapel stood Peckover House, surrounded by a well-wooded park, and, stretching away in an easterly direction, nothing met the eye but an unbroken succession of cultivated fields. The only populated part in proximity to the chapel was that in front of it, where a colony of dwellings, chiefly inhabited by woolcombers, had just sprung up. But for this, Eastbrook Chapel might indeed have been said to be "out in the country." Besides the two Methodist Chapels, there were then nine places of worship in Bradford belonging to other denominations. The population had reached to about 32,000.

The two Wesleyan chapels, Kirkgate and Eastbrook, have as yet no rivals in the heart of the town, but in the district and outlying villages, many fine and spacious buildings have been reared in order to keep pace with the large and ever-increasing population. We cannot enumerate all these, and our notice of the numerous off-shoots from the "old body" must necessarily be brief.

The Primitive Methodists erected their chapel in Manchester Road in 1824. It was destroyed by fire in 1861 and rebuilt soon after at a cost of £1,400. This community has made great progress, and now owns several large and handsome chapels in the district.

The New Connexion Methodists in Bradford are an influential body. Their first chapel, Ebenezer, at the bottom of Horton Lane, was built in 1839, and as a large and commodious structure, was regarded as being fully "abreast of the times." It had six hundred sittings, and the cost of its erection, including the site, amounted to £2,500. The building had not stood more than twenty-five years however, when, from some defect in its construction, it was considered to be unsafe, and it was pulled down and replaced by another a little more elegant in outward appearance, in which particular there was scope for improvement. This edifice however, has been superseded by the splendid chapel and school buildings at Mannville, Horton Road, which were opened in March, 1879.

The Methodist Free Churches have steadily increased in numbers and influence in and around Bradford. The chapel in Bridge Street was erected in 1838.

The Wesleyan Reformers have also several chapels.

The Baptists.

The Baptist Church at Bradford had a very humble origin. Some piously disposed people quietly met together for worship, at the house of a godly woman named Elizabeth Frankland, who resided at Manningham. This was in 1751. After an existence of about a year, this little society felt emboldened to invite certain Baptist preachers to recognise it, and for a time Mr. Smith of Wainsgate, Mr. Hartley of Haworth, and Mr. Lord of Bacup, preached at Manningham once a quarter. As the result of these services, eight persons "received the gospel and were baptised."

It was while the cause was thus in its infancy that their first minister, William Crabtree, was recommended to them as an acceptable preacher. Indeed, the recommendation went so far as to state that "the Lord had cut him out for a preacher." On the 4th of December, 1753, the Baptist Church at Bradford, consisting of twenty-three members, was formed, and on the following day Mr. Crabtree was ordained. His first sermon was from the significant text, "Therefore came I unto you without gainsaying, as soon as I was sent for; I ask therefore for what intent ye have sent for me?"

As the members now increased, the private house in which the handful of brethren had hitherto met was found to be too small. The large room in the Cock-pit (already described) was engaged in which to hold divine service; the good people exulting greatly that they had "dispossessed Satan of a portion of his dominions, and raised instead the standard of the Cross." This was indeed "the day of small things" for the infant church. It is related that so poor were the members at this time that they could not afford to provide benches for their meeting-room, and the old women wended their way thither with stools under their arms! It must have been a touching as well as a novel sight, to witness these lowly-minded worshippers thus threading their way through the quiet streets of old Bradford to their humble sanctuary on "the beck side." Such zeal and faithfulness to the cause they had at heart, was a certain augury of future success. William Crabtree, the first Baptist minister in Bradford was a remarkable character. He was left an orphan at a very early age, and from being a poor Halifax weaver became successively a member and a deacon of the Baptist Church at Wainsgate, and then he began to preach. When on his "preaching rounds" he made such a favourable impression at Bradford that he received an invitation, as we have seen, to become minister here, which he accepted. The choice was well made, for his ministry was highly successful. The absence of a proper training for his post was a great disadvantage to him, and no one felt it more than himself. But perhaps it may have been that his plain yet forcible style of preaching, produced a more beneficial effect upon his audience than greater learning or loftier eloquence would have done. In his pastoral duties he was ever active and energetic, and there was not a more familiar figure in the streets than that of William Crabtree the Baptist preacher, and his partiality for a white wig and small cocked hat made him none the less conspicious.

But while the congregation was small in numbers and poor in this world's goods, they could ill afford to support a minister. To the honour of Mr. Crabtree be it said that for a while after he came to Bradford he earned the greater part of his livelihood by still following his trade of shalloon weaver, thus staving over the hard times which then prevailed. Brighter prospects soon came. The dark clouds that had long hung over the town at length cleared away, and with better employment and higher wages came a happier state of things.

In the year 1755 a more suitable place of worship was erected, and the Cock-pit abandoned. The site of the new sanctuary was the top of Westgate, and it soon became widely known as the "Top o'taan Chapel," and by this familiar name the place is yet known to many.

One of the most distinguished members of Mr. Crabtree's flock was John Fawcett, afterwards known to the world as the learned Dr. Fawcett—a name, deservedly held in honour and veneration by the Baptist Church. In 1755 Bradford was favoured by a visit from that most popular of preachers George Whitfield, and while addressing an audience of several thousand persons in front of the Bowling Green, a lad of some sixteen years was so captivated by the eloquence of the great poet-preacher that he followed him all the way to Birstall, where on the same day Whitfield addressed a gathering of more than twenty thousand people. This attentive listener was young Fawcett, who was then serving his apprenticeship as a staymaker in Bradford. He was a native of Lidget Green, near this town, and at the age of twelve lost his father, who left behind him a widow and several children.

John was a studious and thoughtful lad, and although his hours of toil reached from six in the morning till eight at night, he still found time to indulge in his favourite occupation of reading, but it was at the expense of the long silent hours when he should have been asleep. As a means of preventing him from sleeping too long in the morning, he would tie a weight to his foot or fasten his hand to the bed post.

He had the good fortune to become acquainted with the Rev. Mr. Butler, the Master of the Bradford Grammar School, who took kindly to him, lent him books, and gave him much valuable assistance in his study of the classics. Fawcett afterwards attained an eminent position as a scholar and divine. In 1765 he was ordained a Baptist Minister, and became pastor of the congregation at Wainsgate near Halifax. Afterwards he established an academy at Ewood Hall, near Hebden Bridge. He was a fine linguist, and during his life wrote many valuable works, the best-known of which were a "Commentary on the Bible," and an "Essay on Anger," for which it is said George III. thanked him in very flattering terms. He died July 25th, 1817, "crowned with honour, and followed to the grave with the blessings of thousands."

As a rigid Calvinist, Crabtree's doctrinal views, of course, differed widely from those of Wesley. Indeed, so stoutly was he opposed to the Arminian view of the Scriptures that he indiscreetly allowed himself to be drawn into a public discussion. One of the members of his congregation had accepted a challenge from two Wesleyan preachers in the town to engage in a public dispute on the question of "The final perseverance of the Saints." Upon reflection, he afterwards wished to avoid the contest and begged his pastor to take it. This Mr. Crabtree consented to do, and the other side were agreeable to the change. A platform was accordingly erected in Burnet Field, Little Horton, and the discussion on the points at issue was carried on in right good earnest in presence of a large crowd of spectators. Mr. Crabtree and his supporters claimed the victory, and one of the Wesleyan preachers, Mr. Titus Knight, was so convinced by Mr. Crabtree's arguments, that he ceased to be a Methodist, and became minister of the Independent Church at Halifax. Bitter feelings and unkind words were, however, the outcome of this contention, and Mr. Crabtree sincerely regretted that he had allowed himself to be led into it.

Mr. Crabtree continued to exercise his ministry till upwards of eighty years of age. He died on February 14th, 1811, having attained the almost patriarchal age of ninety-one.

The congregation found a fitting and able successor in the Rev. William Steadman. The circumstances of the times were such as to call for ministers of religion and philanthropists who could look beyond the borders of their own communities, and make their influence for good felt outside their pulpits and private studies. A dense population was growing up whose religious and moral tone was at a low ebb. Of popular education there was none, while ignorance and superstition were but too abundant. Intemperance was greatly on the increase, and the sports and amusements of the "lower orders" were of a cruel and degraded character. On the formation of the Bradford Mechanics' Institute in 1832, of which Dr. Steadman was appointed the first president, there were certain "influential people" in the town who regarded the project with considerable disfavour and suspicion, and were greatly concerned lest the common people should be educated beyond their station in life. But William Steadman was little affected by such opposition as this, and he and his colleagues carried the enterprise to a successful issue, though in the face of many difficulties.

A heavy trial fell upon Dr. Steadman in the seventh year of his ministry, which for a time impeded his usefulness. This was the loss of his wife and three children within the brief space of eighteen months. The severe blow brought on such a depression of spirits that at times he felt tempted to abandon his post; but he laboured on, and after a while "the gloom was dispelled, mercy smiled, and God revived his work."

The highest degree of prosperity to which Mr. Steadman brought the Baptist cause in Westgate was in the year 1825. The chapel had been enlarged, a large Sunday School established, and the congregation greatly increased by repeated additions of members. It was not until after he came to Bradford that baptisms took place within the walls of the chapel. Previous to this they had been administered in the Mill Goit near the bottom of Silsbridge Lane. But the Goit and its surroundings were then the very contrast of what they were as known to modern Bradfordians. The water was quite clear, and abounded with such live-stock as small sticklebacks and minnows. The banks of the stream were lined with pleasant hedgerows, and there are those still living who have gathered blackberries there, and who remember the "mill-race" as a favourite bathing place for the juveniles of the town.

The first stone of Sion Chapel, in Goodman's-End, was laid on the last day of February, 1823, and it was completed in May the following year. The sermons on the opening were preached by the Rev. Robert Hall, A.M., Mr. J. Saffery, and Dr. Cox. A young student of "great promise" was then stationed at Horton Baptist College, as classical and mathematical tutor, and upon him fell the choice of the people as minister for the new chapel. This was the Rev. Benjamin Godwin. In him Dr. Steadman had an able and intelligent colleague and the names of the two worthies are inseparably associated in all their acts of public benevolence.

The life of William Steadman was brought to a close on the 12th of April, 1837, after a long career of public usefulness and a successful ministry of nearly thirty-two years. He had been a faithful servant

Old Sion Chapel—Bridge Street.

of his Master—generous, large-hearted, and charitable. Sectarian exclusiveness had no part or share with him, and he was intolerant of nothing so much as bigotry and self-righteousness.

Although so much of his time and energy was given for the good of his townspeople it will be seen that the duties of his pastorate were by no means neglected. During the term of his ministry, and the directorship of Horton College, he preached about eleven thousand times; baptised nearly seven hundred candidates for membership; educated for the ministry a hundred and sixty young men; attended more than a hundred ordinations, and officiated at the opening of forty places of worship!

Dr. Godwin, in the year 1834, resigned his tutorship at Horton College in order to devote himself more fully to pastoral work. It was in that year that the advocates of Atheism in Bradford, who were both numerous and bold, threw out certain challenges to discuss the

REV. BENJ^{N}. GODWIN, D.D.

principles of religion. Dr. Godwin was induced to take up the same, and during the months of February and March he delivered his celebrated "Lectures on Atheistic Controversy" in Sion Chapel.

The interest taken in these lectures was far greater than had been anticipated. The chapel was crowded to excess on each occasion, and the most rapt attention was manifested, although each discourse on an average occupied about two hours and a quarter in delivery. At the urgent request of the sceptical party, and of the public generally, the lectures were published, and to this day it may be truly said that no contribution to this controversial theme has been made, within the same compass, at once more fair, complete, eloquent and convincing. The lectures attracted great attention in America, where they were republished and largely circulated. The University of Columbia conferred upon their gifted author the degree of Doctor of Divinity.

In the slavery question Dr. Godwin always took a profound interest, and by a series of able lectures thereon contributed largely towards preparing the community for the great emancipation measure of 1832.

In the stirring events connected with the county election of 1830 and the Reform agitation he also interested himself, not that he was a lover of politics, but because he felt it to be his duty to speak a word on behalf of freedom whenever opportunity offered.

Dr. Godwin in the year 1836 retired from the charge of Sion Chapel and removed for a time to Liverpool. Two years subsequently he accepted the pastorate of the Baptist Church at Oxford, which had for some time been in a declining state. His long and arduous labours now began to tell upon his health, and in 1846 he returned to Bradford in order to recruit his strength for still further usefulness, and for some years after this he was as indefatigable as ever in the cause of philanthropy, and the social, intellectual, and spiritual well-being of the people. Gradually his public appearances became fewer, and at length his familiar voice ceased to be heard among the people whom he loved so well. In 1855, he removed to Rawdon to the residence of his son Mr. J. V. Godwin, where he spent the declining years of his life in retirement and peace among his books and papers, and in the society of a few congenial friends. Here his span of life was lengthened out to its eighty-sixth year, when he quietly passed away, without a struggle or a sigh, to enter upon the more perfect and better life.

In the year 1836, the Rev. Henry Dowson, then pursuing his studies at Horton College, was called to the service of the Baptist congregation at Westgate, in which he laboured with acceptance and success for many years. He resigned the pastorate in 1866, and in that year was invited to become president of the newly-founded College at Bury. He departed this life on the 23rd November, 1884.

Another young collegian, who was summoned from Horton College to enter upon the responsible duties of the pastorate, was the Rev. J. P. Chown. From the diligent pursuit of his studies under Dr. Ackworth and the Rev. F. Clowes, he was called to succeed the Rev.

Thomas Pottenger as minister of Sion Chapel; with what measure of success it is needless to state. The number of members doubled during his first seven years' service, and his popularity became such that he was in demand at nearly all local and provincial religious gatherings.

In 1865 he paid a visit to America, and on his return was presented by the public of Bradford with his residence, which cost £900, and £100 in cash. When the erection of the new Sion Chapel was proposed, Mr. Chown announced that he would be responsible for £1000. The movement was so complete a success that after all expenses had been met, a balance remained of some £250, which was equally divided between the Stockwell Orphanage and the Bradford Fever Hospital. On the occasion of the opening services of the new chapel in October 1873, the Rev. C. H. Spurgeon preached in St. George's Hall.

Mr. Chown accepted the pastorate of Bloomsbury Chapel, London, in April 1875, and previous to taking leave of his townspeople at Bradford he was presented with £1000 as an acknowledgment of his great usefulness, and estimable character. Enfeebled health compelled him to resign in 1885, and in July of the following year he entered upon his eternal rest.

The life of such a man as Mr. Chown needs no eulogy. The gifts and energies that he possessed were dedicated to the service of God, and used unstintedly for the good of his fellowmen. The "good and faithful servant" has been called to his reward, but the indelible impression that he has left behind can never be effaced.

The main features connected with the development and extension of the Baptist Church in Bradford, during the long and successful ministry of Mr. Dowson and that of Mr. Chown, are of too recent a date to call for notice here. We may mention, however, that Trinity Chapel in Horton Lane, a handsome and commodious structure, was erected in 1856, and Hallfield Chapel in Manningham Lane,—an offshoot from Sion, was built in 1863. Other chapels have been reared in the outlying districts.

The General Baptists (that is, those who do not hold Calvinistic views), built their chapel in Tetley Street in 1836, and the one in Infirmary Street in 1852. The late Rev. Benjamin Wood was for many years the esteemed pastor of the former of these.

Zoar Chapel in Westgate, erected in 1846, was a plain and modest-looking building in which the Strict Baptists met for worship. Their present sanctuary is in Darfield Street, Lumb Lane.

The Congregationalists.

The origin of the Independent or Congregational Church in Bradford is to be traced to several sources. To take the most distant it would be necessary to go back to the old Dissenting chapel at Chapel Green,

Little Horton, and its successor in Chapel Lane, which gave birth to the Presbyterian, Congregational, and Unitarian bodies of Bradford. Soon after the Rev. John Dean entered upon the ministry of the latter place, many of the congregation adopted Unitarian views, through the teaching, it is believed, of his predecessor the Rev. John Smith. There were some, however, who clung to the Evangelical doctrine of "the old Dissent," and who rejoiced greatly when the same was revived through the preaching of Wesley, Whitfield, and Grimshaw. They ceased to attend the Presbyterian Chapel, and while some cast in their lot with the newly-formed Methodist congregation, others, who leaned more towards Calvinism, remained for a time without any "local habitation," and were content to attend the ministry of the Rev. James Stillingfleet (a grandson of the celebrated bishop of that name) of Bierley Chapel, who was a powerful preacher and Calvinistic in his views. Mr. Stillingfleet's stay at Bierley, however, was but of short duration, and an attempt was now made to establish an Independent "interest" at Bradford. For a while they met in small companies in each other's houses, and a young man from Wakefield named Edward Hales, "a good speaker and of liberal education," was encouraged to preach to them. An attempt was made to secure his services as their stated minister, and with this end in view he was bought off from his apprenticeship. He proved to be but a "broken reed" however, and to the surprise and disappointment of the small but hopeful flock, he suddenly abandoned the project and returned to his secular calling.

The immediate agency in forming the Congregationalist Church in Bradford was undoubtedly the faithful ministrations of the Rev. Joseph Cockin, minister of Kipping Chapel, Thornton, who, though he declined the urgent invitation of the people here to become their pastor, took an active interest in the cause, and kept them united till they were successful in the appointment of a stated minister. On the occasion of his first visit to Bradford he met with some opposition, and it was with no little difficulty that he succeeded in preaching to an audience gathered around him as he stood on a fine evening on the steps in front of a shop facing the old market at the bottom of Westgate. But he was cordially welcomed by the small and patient band that had rallied around young Hales, and his efforts soon resulted in the gathering of a congregation. Until better provision could be made, the kind offer of Mr. James Garnett to use one of his rooms in the Paper Hall, Barkerend, was gladly accepted. After meeting here for a short time they engaged a room, a malt chamber in the Old Brewery premises at the bottom of Horton Road. It is to be regretted that no record has been preserved of the circumstances under which the small church assembled in this lowly place of worship. The names of a few of its members have, however, been rescued from oblivion. These were Mr. John Smith, a bookseller, of whom the books for the Bradford Subscription Library were for several years purchased; Mr. Hodgson of Scholemoor; Mr. Balme, and Mr. James Garnett and his wife Eleanor.

That the cause now made rapid progress, in the way of development and accession of members, may be inferred from the fact that they were soon in a position to rear a large and convenient chapel in Horton Lane. The first minister was the Rev. James Crosley, whose connection with Bradford was, however, of so short a duration that it may be summed up in the few but significant words that he accepted the call here, preached one Sunday, and—died! Crosley had been the pastor of the Congregational Church at Booth, to which he was deeply attached, and though he was influenced by the hope of more extended usefulness at Bradford, and accepted the call, so much did the prospect of separation prey upon his spirits, that, after keeping service for one Sunday (May 11th, 1782), he died, it is supposed, of a broken heart, on the following Lord's Day.

The beginning of the church in Horton Lane has been variously given as 1781, 1782, and 1783. The first of those years is doubtless the correct date, as the congregation began to worship in the building for some time before it was finished—a practice by no means uncommon in those days.

The pastor appointed to succeed Mr. Crosley was the Rev. Thomas Holdgate, of whom little is known beyond the fact that he was a quiet, earnest man, and discharged the duties of his position with steady zeal and faithfulness. He served the congregation in Horton Lane for twenty-five years.

It was not, however, till the ministry of the Rev. Thomas Taylor, who succeeded Mr. Holdgate in 1808, that the real progress of the church began. To his long and useful career belongs the honour of that growth in position and influence for which the Horton Lane congregation has for so many years been distinguished.

Mr. Taylor was a man of great weight of character and a powerful preacher. He possessed all the solicitude of a pastor for the children belonging to his own church, but his heart yearned with pity for any young people who had no means of receiving a religious training. One of the first movements which he set on foot on coming to Bradford was the formation of a Sunday School, in which he took a deep and practical interest.

This school, which has so long enjoyed a high reputation in the town, was begun in the year 1808, and its first secretary was the late Mr. Robert Milligan, who afterwards became Bradford's first mayor, and one of its representatives in Parliament. Among those who took a prominent part in the conduct of the school may be mentioned such familiar old Bradford names as those of Richard and James Garnett, John Russell, Jonathan Holdsworth, John McCroben, Mr. (afterwards Sir) Titus Salt, Thomas Greenlay, William Milnes, Thomas Wyrill, and William McKay. In more recent times Mr. (afterwards Sir) Henry Ripley, and Ald. James Law were closely connected with it. The work greatly prospered in the hands of men like these, and it was a happy circumstance that the school rarely lacked the countenance and support of the congregation; the pecuniary assistance required for its successful working being invariably met in a liberal and generous spirit.

Horton Lane Chapel, and Minister's House.

The "anniversary" of the Horton Lane Sunday School was for many years a grand and auspicious occasion, and an event always looked forward to with exciting interest by the young. Then the old custom of "sitting up" was in vogue, when the girls dressed in white, and the boys in "bran new suits" were so arranged with an eye to effect as to produce a most dazzling display of well-dressed juvenility; a more prudent and circumspect age has seen fit, and perhaps wisely, to put such demonstrations aside, but it will be long before the memory of these happy days will be forgotten by those who were privileged to share in their enjoyment.

During the whole of Mr. Taylor's public life in Bradford he lived on terms of the most friendly intercourse with the ministers of the town of almost every denomination. Among his co-workers were the honoured names of Dr. Steadman, Rev. W. Morgan, Dr. Godwin, Mr. John Hustler, Mr. Benjamin Seebohm, Mr. John Rand and others, with whom he laboured harmoniously in the formation of societies and charitable institutions for the benefit of the inhabitants.

Mr. Taylor lived to see his own place of worship, after repeated enlargements, made spacious and commodious. What was at his first settlement in Bradford a feeble church and a small congregation, became the parent stalk from which several communities in the town and neighbourhood have sprung. In 1832 he was bereaved of his greatest earthly comfort and wept over the grave of his beloved wife. Three years after this event, his eldest son, the talented Thomas Rawson Taylor who had given promise of the possession of a rare poetic genius, died a premature death. These afflictions, and the increasing infirmities of old age led to his retirement from the ministry in 1835, and from that period, his life, up to its close in 1853 was one of quiet retirement and private devotion.

On Mr. Taylor's retirement, the choice of his successor fell upon the Rev. Jonathan Glyde, a native of Devonshire. Mr. Glyde was descended from eminent divines who had suffered by the Act of Uniformity, and to the last he clung tenaciously to the principles of his forefathers. Describing his first impressions of Bradford, in a letter to Mrs. Glyde, he says—"Look which way you will you see huge tall chimneys pouring forth volleys of smoke, which, when you are near, is not very pleasant, but when seen from a distance is interesting enough. There cannot be fewer than a hundred of these chimneys in Bradford and its vicinity; a cloud therefore is continually hanging over it, and this together with the furnaces of the ironworks in the neighbouring hills, the flames from which, though not visible by day, become so by night; have led me to think that Bradford must be a very favoured spot, having, like the Children of Israel, its cloud by day and fire by night."

To enlarge upon the high position which Mr. Glyde held in Bradford as one of its "townsmen" would be to exceed the limits at our disposal. The various religious and philanthropic institutions of the town could always command his sympathy and patronage. He was an earnest educationist, and the daily sight of streams of young people passing along the streets at certain hours of the day, whose rough and unpolished manners were but too sure an index of the ignorance of their minds, strongly appealed to his pity and aid. Mr. Glyde was no mere sentimentalist. To regret the existence of an evil was with him but the preliminary to a vigorous attempt at its removal. Through his exertions the Borough West Schools were erected, and still exist as a fitting monument to the memory of their worthy founder.

To Mr. Glyde the Bradford Town Mission is indebted for its origin and it was a source of great satisfaction to him to see it commence, and, during his lifetime, carry on its operations with great success. The strenuous efforts put forth by him on behalf of the distressed woolcombers, and in pleading for a public park, as a place of recreation for the toiling population of Bradford, are worthy of lasting remembrance. The latter movement he had the pleasure of seeing realised by the purchase of the beautiful grounds now forming Peel Park. But what must have been the delight of this earnest advocate for "more breathing room" could he have seen the position which the town now holds in relation to its public parks!

Early in the month of December, 1854, the useful and well spent life of Mr. Glyde was brought to a close. It is no easy task to attempt to depict such a character as his. It was indeed many-sided. His Christian manhood; his genuine catholicity; his vivid sense of the beautiful, both in nature and art; the gentleness of his temper, and his genial sympathy are but some of the many points that those who knew him might fondly dwell upon. As a faithful and beloved pastor he is held in loving remembrance by his own people. As one of Bradford's worthiest citizens his honoured name will be handed down as a man whose greatest happiness was in seeking the good of others.

The late Rev. James Robertson Campbell, D.D., entered upon the pastorate of Horton Lane in the year 1855. During his former residence in Edinburgh he was for several years editor of the "Congregational Magazine," and also edited Dr. Wardlaw's "Systematic Theology" and other works. Soon after his arrival in Bradford he received the degree of D.D. from the University of Glasgow. He has since been chairman of the Congregational Union of England and Wales, president of the Bradford Mechanics' Institute from 1868 to 1871, and was a member of the first School Board in this town.

Finding his strength and vigour declining, Dr. Campbell in October 1883 retired from the ministerial life,—a retirement which he enjoyed but for a few years when he was summoned to enter upon his final rest in the better land. During the whole of his successful ministry of twenty-eight years at Horton Lane he enjoyed the respect and affection of his congregation.

The Congregationalists have made great progress in Bradford and the district. The project of building a second chapel in the town was entered upon in Mr. Taylor's time, and resulted in the erection of

The Rev. Jonathan Glyde.

Salem Chapel, which was completed in December 1835. The Rev. James G. Miall was appointed the first minister, and his abilities as a preacher and pastor soon gathered around him a numerous congregation. His literary attainments are of no common order, and to his versatile pen we are indebted for several standard and useful works.

Some fourteen years ago Mr. Miall brought his connection with Salem to a close, after having held the pastorate for an unbroken period of nearly forty years.

On the 6th of April, 1838, the foundation stone of another Congregational church was laid. It was called "College Chapel" from the fact that it was built for the Rev. Walter Scott, then and for many years subsequently the esteemed president of Airedale College.

In 1852, Greenfield Chapel, Manningham (an off-shoot from Salem); was erected. The chapel at Lister Hills, opened in 1854, was in a great measure built by the Horton Lane congregation, and a considerable number of members were "dismissed" from the latter place to form a church. The chapel at Bowling from the time of its erection, in 1865, was nourished and strengthened by the Horton Lane people, who transferred several members to it. The chapel and schools at Little Horton were built by the Horton Lane congregation, and for many years continued to form part of it.

To the period of Dr. Campbell's ministry belongs the crowning achievement of the parent-church in Horton Lane—the erection of the present chapel and schools, the entire cost of which was defrayed before the conclusion of the opening services.

It would perhaps be difficult to point to a more striking illustration of progress and development than that afforded by the Congregational Church of Horton Lane. A century ago, a mere handful of members were worshipping in the malt chamber of a brewery;—to-day, the congregation assembles in one of the largest and most imposing edifices in the town. Like a plant whose tender shoots have been well watered, and whose roots have taken hold of a fruitful soil, it now stands forth in all the majestic proportions of a full grown tree. Though shorn of some of its branches from time to time, this has but served to give enlarged strength and greater beauty to the parent stem.

Other Denominations.

THE MORAVIANS OR UNITED BRETHREN established societies or preaching stations in the districts comprehended between Halifax, Leeds, Wakefield and Bingley, as early as the year 1742. Smith-house, a large mansion at Lightcliffe, was for a time their head quarters, but this was afterwards superseded by the settlement at Fulneck. The diaries of the period contain the following item referring to Bradford—"Here is a little society and promising, since a new breeze of grace has lately blown over it. It is the likeliest to make a little church of any of this group." No further mention is made of it, however.

There was a society at Little Horton in 1742, and the curious fact is recorded that the rent of the house in which lived the minister, or "labourer" and his wife, was £3 per annum, while their weekly stipend was eight shillings! Several of the ministers at this early period were German brethren who had but an imperfect knowledge of the English tongue—a circumstance which placed them at some disadvantage. But an infinitely greater hindrance to their progress than this was the simple fact that they were *foreigners*, and so strong was the prejudice against them by reason of this, that some of the people charged them with being Papists in disguise, others with being Antinomians, and not a few with being leagued with the Pretender.

All this, however, they eventually lived down, and the Moravian Brethren soon became widely known and esteemed as a people remarkable as much for their untiring zeal as for their genuine piety.

In 1745 the preaching room at Great Horton, which was situate in Paternoster Fold, was licensed for worship—a step the Brethren were reluctant to take except that it saved them from much annoyance; but even then the protection of the law did not shield them from persecution. The station at Little Horton was in a house opposite the present chapel, while that at Wibsey was located at Chapel Fold, Brownroyd Hill. In this place Mr. Joseph Hinchcliffe, of Horton House Academy, afterwards opened a Sunday-school which he personally superintended for many years. He too, was the chief promoter of the present Moravian Chapel at Little Horton, erected in 1838, of which the Rev. John Carey was the first minister.

As compared with other religious communities the Moravians made little progress in this country in the way of rearing chapels and forming congregations. By its founders it was regarded as a missionary and not a proselytising church, and so it was that while other, and perhaps more vigorous bodies established themselves, the Brethren gradually withdrew in order that they might enter upon other fields of labour.

The Presbyterian Church of England have a large and handsome chapel in Infirmary Street of which the present minister is the Rev. R. S. Coffey. It was built in 1849, and the Rev. Alexander Wallace was the first minister, who, previous to its erection, addressed large gatherings in the Temperance Hall. During his brief ministry of three years, he formed a numerous congregation, and his removal from Bradford was felt to be nothing short of a public loss. He was truly a useful man, and interested himself in all matters for the well-being of the people. His public lectures were very popular and attracted large audiences. He was the author of the well-known work "The Bible and the Working Classes"; also a volume entitled "Poems and Sketches," and other smaller works. Dr. Wallace has for many years been stationed at Glasgow. Occasionally he visits the scene of his former labours and receives a cordial welcome from his numerous friends and admirers in Bradford. He was succeeded in the ministry here by the Rev. David Sim.

The members of the NEW CHURCH (SWEDENBORGIAN) hold their meetings in Drewton Street, and it may be taken as an evidence of progress that they are now contemplating the erection of a more commodious place of worship.

In December 1849, Mr. William Dyson, a member of the Dalton Society of the New Church, Huddersfield, came to reside in Bradford. There was then no New Church Society in the town, but here and there might have been found some diligent students of Emanuel Swedenborg's writings. One of these, a Mr. George Aspinall, who had heard of Mr. Dyson's residence here, wrote to him suggesting the desirability of forming a weekly meeting for the purpose of reading and conversing upon the Holy Scriptures, and the writings of Swedenborg.

This letter was the origin of the first organised New Church Society in Bradford. The two friends met together once a week and during their study of Swedenborg's "True Christian Religion," were joined by others who wished to share in this means of mutual edification. Presently the week-night gathering gave place to a short devotional service held on Sunday afternoons in each other's houses, and in this way the little band patiently persevered in the good work, believing that where unity and sincerity of purpose prevail a large congregation is not essential to true religious worship.

During the winter of 1856, a course of six lectures was delivered in the Mechanics' Institute by the Revds. R. Stoney, of Dalton, and R. Edleston, of Leeds, on the principal doctrines of the New Church. These attracted large audiences, and at the conclusion of the last lecture those who were favourable to the movement were invited to meet in the ante-room in order to consider the propriety of engaging a place in which to hold weekly Sunday service.

The outcome of this was the engagement of Mr. Child's School-room in Drewton Street at a rental of £8 a year. Subsequently the building was purchased and refurnished, and to the present time it has served as chapel or meeting-room. For several years there was no recognised minister of the church, but in October 1873 Mr. J. Robson Rendell, a student who had taken his degree of B.A. at the London University preached his first sermon at Bradford, and in the following year at the unanimous invitation of the Society became its pastor. He was soon after ordained by the Rev. Dr. Bayley and has continued to be the first, and as yet, the only minister of the New Church in this town.

THE GERMAN EVANGELICAL CHURCH became established here by means of a special mission work carried on by the Church of England in the autumn of 1875. The German population of Bradford was taken notice of, and services were set on foot on their behalf. At the close of the mission several gentlemen made use of this opportunity to continue the meetings in Christ Church School-room, and on this becoming too small, afterwards in the Lecture-hall of the Church Institute, kindly lent to them by the council of that institution. Chiefly through the help of Moravian ministers in the neighbourhood, who could speak the German language fluently, a regular and well-attended Sunday evening service was conducted here until December 1882, when the Rev. E. Just, assistant preacher at the German Church of Liverpool, was induced to undertake the pastorate of the congregation. The building in Horton Road, formerly Manville School, was secured, and is now used as chapel and minister's residence.

The Bradford Synagogue. This place of worship for the Jews of Bradford, is situated in Bowland Street, Manningham Lane. It was erected in 1881, and its present minister is the Rev. Joseph Strauss. Services are held every Saturday morning at 10-30, and on festivals specially fixed. The sermons are delivered in German and English alternately.

The Catholic Apostolic Church have a place of worship in Lansdowne Place, Horton Lane, and

The Bible Christians. have one in Toller Lane.

Wesley preaching from the Steps of the Old Cockpit.

CHAPTER V.

Educational & Literary Institutions.

The Free Grammar School.

BRADFORD has long been famous for its Grammar School. In point of antiquity that institution is entitled to rank next to the Parish Church. The period of its origin is unfortunately involved in obscurity, but there is sufficient evidence to show that several centuries have run their course since it began its existence. Mr. James, the historian, thinks it probable that it dates from the time of Edward III., five hundred years ago; that being a great era for the endowment of schools.

Five hundred years ago! Then the De Lacies were Lords of the Manor, and the feudal system was so firmly rooted in the soil that many of the inhabitants were liable to be sold and dealt with any day, just as so much "goods and chattels" pertaining to the manor. To this far-off period belongs the grand old story of the wild boar of Cliffe Wood, familiar to every Bradford school-boy of to-day and therefore unnecessary to be repeated here. The outside world was then very busy weaving its thread of history. The brave Edward Third had been successful in his wars abroad, and the kings of France and Scotland were prisoners in England at one and the same time. The art of weaving cloth had been but recently introduced from Flanders; and Thomas Blanket of Bristol had established looms for the weaving of those comfortable cloths that still bear his name.

But contemporaneous history fails to throw any light upon the old Bradford Grammar School, assuming that it was in existence at this early date, and we are left in ignorance both as to its position and character, and the standard of education that would then be provided for the children of such Bradfordians whose good fortune it was to be ranked as freeholders.

It is not until the year 1553 that we come upon any local records relating to the Grammar School. In that year there was a law suit in the Duchy Court to decide as to the right of the Crown to certain lands in Bradford, and in a decree pronounced in Easter Term of the same year we find that two messuages, about three acres of land, and two shillings and fivepence rent charges which "*anciently* belonged to the living and sustentation of a schoolmaster teaching grammar within the town of Bradford," were settled to the same use for ever. An inquisition taken at Elland in the reign of Elizabeth confirms the fact that the above property formed part of the Grammar School estates at a very remote period, as it "had been so employed time whereof the memory of man was not to the contrary."

A hundred years had well nigh elapsed since the suit referred to, when certain Commissioners appointed to enquire into charities, took an inquisition at Bradford, which showed that the possessions of the Grammar School at that time were very considerable. This took place during the Commonwealth. Within three years after the Restoration a Charter of Incorporation of the school was granted by Charles II. Only a few of the provisions of this charter need be noticed here.—The school should be called the "Free Grammar School of King Charles the Second at Bradford;" that it should be established "for teaching, instructing and better bringing up children and youth in grammar and other good learning and literature," and should consist of "one master or teacher, and one usher or under-teacher." The charter also provided that there should be "thirteen men of the most discreet, honest, and religious persons in the neighbourhood, whereof the Vicar of Bradford shall always be one, who should be governors," and "the governors, master and usher before they enter upon their offices," were to "take an oath before a Justice of the Peace of the County of York, to be faithful and careful for the good of the school in all things appertaining to his office and charge, and also the oaths of allegiance and supremacy."

As to how far the governors who, since the charter, have successively held office have been thus "faithful and careful" for the interests of the school it does not come within our province to enquire. For many years however, previous to its reconstruction under the Endowed Schools' Act, the school came far short of answering the purposes of a free institution for the benefit of all classes. It certainly failed to keep pace with the requirements of the times, and the number of scholars did not increase in proportion to the growth of the town.

The original Grammar School building, it is believed, stood on the site of the one near to the Parish Church, which was vacated in 1820 in order to take possession of the one in Manningham Lane. This inference is drawn from the circumstance that from the earliest times there seems to have existed a strong link between the church and the school. The vicar, by virtue of his office had most important rights over the school—he used the school-room moreover, as the place where he collected and received his tithes; the boys of the school were recognised as choristers; there belonged to the school by right a number of pews and sittings in the church; the head-master sometimes laid claim by virtue of his office to the post of "lecturer," at the church, and he performed in certain instances, the functions of both vicar and head-master.

On the granting of the charter of 1663 the old school was rebuilt, and it was in this building that the most distinguished pupils of the Bradford Grammar School received their training.

The playground was at the bottom of Well Street, so called from the School-house well, on the opposite side of the street now occupied by Foster's Buildings. The well lay in a little hollow and was reached by descending three or four steps, while the beck—a brcad but shallow stream, with willows growing on its banks—ran close past, soon to mingle its waters with the main current at the bottom of Kirkgate.

But in 1818, it was found that the old School-house was no longer fit for the purposes of a public school, and the governors, under powers given by Act of Parliament, built the school and master's house in Manningham Lane.

The Old Grammar School

The information that has been brought to light concerning the early masters of the Bradford Grammar School is very fragmentary. Mr. James' list goes no further back than 1658, but Mr. Lister of Shibden Hall has recently called attention to the fact that in the will of Thomas Okden (a former vicar of Bradford) dated January 13th, 1563, there is the following bequest—"To Robert Hall, schoolmaister of the school at Bradforde, for such paynes as he hath taken for me, XXs of money." This is the earliest known name in the list of head-masters of the Bradford Grammar School. Nothing is known of Robert Hall beyond the mere mention of his name, but the circumstance that he was "schoolmaister" here at so early a date goes to add one more link to the chain of evidence proving the antiquity of this school.

The first name of head-master that occurs after the charter is that of John Sturdy, M.A., of whom Thoresby speaks as "the quondam famous schoolmaster of Bradford." He severed his connection with the school, however, by turning Roman Catholic and removing to Furness, where he took to scientific studies bearing chiefly upon the ironstone of the district.

The Rev. Thomas Clapham, M.A., a learned and popular man, became master of the school in 1698, and in 1710 he was appointed vicar of Bradford. He did not relinquish the former office on being presented to the latter, but continued to hold them both and to enjoy the emoluments thereof for a period of eight years. His income from the Grammar School was £40 a year. To him is attributed the origin here of the playing of comedies by the boys.

The Rev. Benjamin Butler was appointed master in 1728, and he held the office for upwards of fifty-six years. For fifty years he was afternoon lecturer at the Parish Church. His character appears to have been a happy blending of superior attainments with genuine kindliness of heart. He was not without his eccentricities, and one of these was a very strong aversion to east winds. It is said that he had a weather-cock put up in front of his house in Barkerend Road to indicate the state of affairs outside, and to decide the point as to whether he should turn out or remain indoors. When old and infirm he would have the boys of the elder classes of the school to go up to his house to say their lessons. An easterly wind meant that the boys must of necessity make this visit, and as they regarded this as something of a treat they sometimes adopted the cunning device of tying the weather-cock to point in the direction which best served their purpose.

One of Mr. Butler's pupils was Thomas Wright of Birkenshaw, grandfather of the distinguished author and antiquary of the same name. In his autobiography, he refers to his connection with the Bradford Grammar School, and says "At this school they taught every day in the week; began every morning at seven o'clock, and closed every evening at five except Wednesdays and Saturdays, the afternoons of which were devoted to writing, and we lay by at three o'clock. This was the practice summer and winter, so that living a mile off (Laisterdyke), I had to go and return morning and evening during every winter season, in the dark. Mr. Wright adds, that on leaving the Grammar School he went to a Mrs. Betty Ward, who resided in Broadstones to learn writing and accounts, with whom he states, "I learned to write a plain, legible hand, sufficient for my purposes of common life." Mrs. Ward, by the way, was a useful member of society at a time when schoolmasters were not over-plentiful. She often acted as "letter writer" for those who were unable to discharge that duty for themselves, and for several years she was employed as law stationer to the lawyers of Bradford.

Another useful and interesting character, but more closely connected with the Grammar School was Henry Hopper (often styled "Hoppy") the usher. In addition to his work at the school, he copied out for thirty years the accounts of the Parish Church, and his name frequently occurs in the "Wardens' Accounts." He was a well-known man in his day, and his house, the White House at the foot of the Church Steps, was known as "Hoppy's House," and the bridge over the stream close by as "Hoppy's Bridge." On resigning his post, as usher (in 1707) after thirty-seven years' service, the Governors magnanimously voted him a gratuity of £5 "for his services since the feast of St. Bartholomew last, and a testimony of his having acquitted himself very well in his said place of usher for many years past."

On Mr. Butler's resignation in 1784 the Rev. Edward Baldwyn was appointed his successor. Mr. Baldwyn's name will long be remembered as the author of some clever pamphlets which created no little sensation in their day. Some bitterness it would seem had arisen among some prominent gentlemen of the town with reference to certain charges brought against the Rev. Mr. Crosse, the vicar, for alleged misappropriation of church funds. The quarrel, for such it was, at length became so serious that almost every leading man in the town and neighbourhood became involved in it. Mr. Baldwyn certainly did not espouse the cause of the vicar, nor did he take a very prominent part in the matter until the appointment of the Rev. Mr. Atkinson to the lectureship of the Parish Church, to which post he felt himself entitled as it had been held by previous masters of the school, and to which he had been the only candidate till the day before it was given to Mr. Atkinson.

Stung to the quick by this unexpected blow, then it was that Mr. Baldwyn assumed a decided front, and became the adopted leader of the party opposed to Mr. Crosse. Then it was that his masterly genius as a wit and satirist fully displayed itself, and his pen was wielded with a power that struck dismay in the camp of the enemy. Mr. Atkinson was no mean antagonist, but he was not equal to a foe so formidable as the master of the Bradford Grammar School.

Though powerful in intellect, Mr. Baldwyn was but small in person. He is described as having "a light, fresh complexion, bright blue eyes and sandy hair." He lived in a house near the Wharfe Tavern, Bolton Road, and the gardens, in which he used to walk much, reached down to the canal side.

It is believed that his bitter attacks on those who had opposed him, had led to so much unpleasantness as to render his position at the Grammar School very uncomfortable. Probably his disappointment in not obtaining the lectureship may have had some share in this, and in bringing about his final resignation, after having held the post eighteen years.

The masters who have successively held office since Mr. Baldwyn are the Rev. John Lockman Crane, M.A., the Rev. James Barmby, M.A.; the Rev. Samuel Slack, M.A.; the Rev. John Richards, M.A.; and the present master the Rev. W. H. Keeling, M.A.

Mr. Slack is described as "a most excellent classic scholar and successful teacher," but his pupils appear to have remembered him best for his very severe system of discipline. "Mr. Slack's caning" says an old pupil "was a study in high art. He selected a cane of close grain, not too thick, but as elastic as possible, and laid it on the soft parts of the legs behind, on the breech, and (sometimes) the soft part of the forearm, where it would sting and do no damage. The strokes were delivered in succession with lightning rapidity, and the cane changed hands from right to left marvellously. Every stroke meant business. Few things enraged him more than the attempt to deceive his experience by a subterfuge or a trick. In person he was short, round, and fat, and in school usually wore a long coat, which had been black in the early part of the century, but had grown greenish through the influence of time. Long before my time he was once prosecuted for cruel caning, but the magistrates dismissed the case on the ground that they themselves had suffered equal severity with good results."

From an old document which has recently come to light, and is now in the possession of Mr. Lister, of Shibden Hall, we learn that in the year 1720, the school fees were two guineas per annum, and the pupil's board, outside the school, for the same period, eight pounds. The sports then in vogue were "marbles, football, bowls, tops, kites, shuttlecocks, sliding and skating."

Several men who rose to eminence in their day were educated at the Bradford Grammar School. Among these may be mentioned Joseph Lister, author of the "Genuine Account" of the Siege of Bradford; John Sharp, Archbishop of York; Abraham Sharp, the astronomer; Thomas Sharp and David Clarkson, the divines; Dr. Richardson of Bierley Hall; David Hartley the philosopher; Dr. Arthur Chartlett, an eminent classical scholar, who in a letter to Dr. Richardson said—"It is long since I contracted a debt to the *famous* school of Bradford"; the Rev. S. Disney, LL.B., vicar of Halstead; Joshua Walker, M.D., who became a distinguished physician and scholar; John Fawcett, D.D., who, though not perhaps a regular pupil of the Grammar School, was instructed in the classics by Mr. Butler; Colonel William Sykes, M.P., who "did good service in several battlefields," and Thomas Rawson Taylor, the gifted poet.

By the appointment of the Endowed School Commissioners in 1870 the opportunity was afforded of having the Bradford Grammar School remodelled. A new scheme was drawn up and approved by Her Majesty in Council in 1871. New schools capable of accommodating a large accession of scholars were erected, and were opened by the late Right Honourable W. E. Forster, in July 1873.

There is now a large and efficient staff of masters, and the school has been so re-organised as to secure that the classical instruction, which was its leading characteristic in the past, shall be fully maintained, while the more practical subjects of modern education—so essential to a town like Bradford—receive the prominence and importance due to them.

In 1873 the late Mr. Henry Brown endowed the school with £6,000 to be expended in scholarships; the late Sir Titus Salt gave £5000 for the like purpose, and, on the occasion of his presiding at the annual "speech day" held at St. George's Hall, on July 31st, 1889, Mr. S. Cunliffe Lister, some of whose ancestors had, in bygone years, been governors of the school, gave £5,000—£1,000 towards a cricket and athletic field and £4,000 for scholarships. Other bequests have been made by the late Right Honourable W. E. Forster and Sir Henry Ripley. These magnificent gifts for the creation of scholarships have thrown open the resources of the school to scholars from the elementary schools who are thus enabled to pass through to the universities. The Grammar School has also the privilege of sending candidates for exhibitions under the will of Lady Elizabeth Hastings.

Rich in the traditions of the past, and venerable with years, the Bradford Grammar School has, under what is known as "the new scheme," taken a new lease of life, and at the present moment takes rank as one of the foremost schools in the land. In view of the vast population and importance of the town this is as it should be. The school now boasts its literary organ, *The Bradfordian*, which gives periodical statements of its progress and activity, and to which original papers are contributed by the pupils. Recently a very able and useful history of the school has been written by Mr. W. Claridge, M.A., one of the masters.

The Girls' Grammar School was opened by Lady Frederick Cavendish on September 29th, 1875. It is situated at the bottom of Hallfield Road, and was formerly a private school belonging to the late Mr. M. Watson. It was purchased for the sum of £5,000, and is capable of accommodating 320 pupils. So far the career of this useful institution has been one of "gratifying prosperity."

The Mechanics' Institute.

Although yet in its infancy as compared with the Grammar School, the Mechanics' Institute may point with pride to a wonderful career of usefulness and activity since it began its existence some sixty years ago. It has pre-eminently been an institution of the people regardless of creed and political colour, and this has been the secret of its success. Its patriarchal rival, the Grammar School, came far short of answering the purposes of a *free* institution for the benefit of *all* classes. This state of things was to be accounted for partly by reason of the restrictive nature of the laws affecting endowed schools, but in a greater measure to the fact that the governors were a self-elected body, and pretty nearly men of one creed and of one shade of politics. Since its recent reconstruction under the Endowed Schools' Act, this is happily no longer the case.

The times were fully ripe for the formation of a Mechanics' Institute in Bradford. There was a toiling population of some forty-three thousand persons for whom there was but scant provision in the way of education. Along with many another industrial town, Bradford was rapidly gaining ground after the long and severe drawback of the Napoleonic wars. Its commercial growth had fairly set in, and with extending trade and increasing population great and sudden changes were taking place. The Mechanics' Institute dates its birth from St.

Valentine's Day, 1832, and it is worth remembering that it was not until near the close of that year that Bradford received its enfranchisement, and with it the privilege of sending two members to parliament. The town had then no newspaper of its own. Its streets had not long been lighted with gas, as there was no Corporation to see to such things, and the power-loom had been introduced here only some five years previously. It goes without the saying that there was as yet no penny post or electric telegraph and no railway communication with the outside world. Good Bradfordians therefore who wished and could afford to visit London had to do so by the stage coach, as it was not until 1834 that the rail-road from Leeds to Selby was completed by which means Hull was easily reached, and the remainder of the journey to the great City was accomplished by packet.

It is in the light of facts such as these that we should read the earliest reports put forth by the Committee of the Mechanics' Institute. Old-fashioned notions still prevailed as to the wisdom of spreading enlightenment broadcast, and of educating the poor beyond their station in life. Theatre-going was condemned from the Dissenting pulpits, and the "irreligious tendency of a philosophising spirit" was glibly talked of by the then vicar of Bradford. Living now in the full blaze of Mr. Forster's Education Bill it does strike one as strange that little more than fifty years ago there should have been those who believed the Mechanics' Institute would be "a seminary of disaffection, a school for infidelity, and a nursery for political demagogues and anarchists." The founders of the Institute are, however, by no means deterred from their purpose by such alarmists but simply state that they "look forward with confidence to a period when *all* their fellow-townsmen shall feel that 'wisdom and knowledge are the stability of our times;' that a people will always be virtuous and happy in proportion as they are enlightened and well-informed, and therefore that it is the duty of all who love their country and their kind to unite their efforts in the great work of popular education."

As time wore on it became no longer necessary to make apologies on behalf of "popular education." Good men rallied around this "people's college" and made it what it has been for so many years the most useful seminary of learning the town has ever had, and to which hundreds of young men have been indebted for the means of education which enabled them to occupy prominent and useful positions in society.

The Bradford Mechanics' Institute was the outcome of a meeting of gentlemen held, near the close of the year 1831, in Mr. Lamb's private school behind the Odd-fellows' Arms in Manchester Road, among whom were Dr. Godwin, his son Mr. J. V. Godwin, and Mr. Joseph Farrar. When it was formerly constituted, its board of management comprised the names of the following gentlemen:—President, Dr. Steadman; Vice-Presidents, Messrs. Samuel Hailstone and Benjamin Seebohm; Treasurer, Mr. Alfred Harris; Secretaries, Messrs. J. Reid Wagstaff and Joseph Farrar.

At first the Institute went into lodgings in a room in Piccadilly (now the Bradford Law Institute,) at a rental of £13 per annum; then it removed to rooms at the bottom of Albion Court (afterwards used by the Church Institute,) at an increased rental of £15, and in 1837 we find it in a much more flourishing condition in rooms over the shop of Messrs. Henry Farrar & Co., Kirkgate, where the Committee first indulged in the luxury of gas,—for previous to this the financial statements contained such oldfashioned items as "Coals and candles, £2 16s. 8d.;" "Candlesticks, 14s. 6d.;" and Mr. Wyrill in a generous moment had presented the Committee with "a pair of brass candlesticks."

Old Mechanics' Institute, Leeds Road.

That such an Institution as this was greatly needed in Bradford was clearly proved by the fact that the first year of its existence saw a membership roll of three hundred and fifty-two names. The library contained eight hundred volumes; classes were formed for instruction in writing, arithmetic, grammar, and mathematics, and lectures were delivered on scientific and literary subjects.

The movement for the erection of a suitable building was started in 1838, and in the following year the site at the junction of Leeds Road and Well Street was purchased and the new Institute actually commenced. In 1840 it was completed, occupied, and in full working order.

The first mention of donations to the building fund is made in the report for 1835 when the Committee acknowledge the receipt of "the very liberal donation of £50 from E. C. Lister, Esq., your highly respected and patriotic member for the Borough of Bradford." A subsequent report mentions "the spontaneous offer of £10 from Lord Viscount Morpeth, M.P.," and of £30 from "John Hardy, Esq., the worthy representative of the Borough of Bradford."

Great exertions were made to raise the necessary funds for the new building, and the reports frequently acknowledge the Committee's deep obligations to Mr. Joseph Farrar "for his indefatigable exertions in forwarding the building movement."

The cost of the land and the building was nearly £3,300, towards which the holding of an exhibition of "Natural Curiosities and Works of Art" in the rooms of the new Institute, realised £685, and £1800 had been received in subscriptions.

It was not, however, until 1850 that the Committee were able to report that the Institute was out of debt. This desirable end was accomplished by the generosity of Mr. (afterwards Sir) Titus Salt, who gave a hundred guineas on condition that the whole of the debt (£750) was raised within the month of October of that year. Towards this Mr. Henry Forbes, who succeeded Mr. Salt as mayor, Mr. C. H. Dawson, Mr. Robert Milligan, Mr. W. Murgatroyd, Mr. G. Rogers and Mr. Samuel Smith each gave fifty guineas, while Messrs. Henry Brown, W. Cheeseborough, T. G. Clayton, W. E. Forster, J. Garnett, S. Laycock, W. Rand, H. W. Ripley and T. Smith each contributed twenty-five guineas. Other sums came in which raised the amount to £804 19s. 6d., being £54 19s. 6d. in excess of what was required.

From this point the course of the Bradford Mechanics' Institute was one of uninterrupted success; and for some time before the third decade of its career had been reached it was found that the building, which at the time of its erection was believed to be quite in advance of the times, was now altogether inadequate to the requirements of its largely increased number of members. The state of affairs was therefore laid before the public, and an appeal made for funds necessary for rearing a more suitable and convenient structure. It was significant of the vastly improved commercial position of Bradford, and the enlarged proportions of its "public purse," that while the largest single donation in the early days of the Institute did not exceed one hundred guineas, the subscription list for the proposed new building included such generous gifts as £1,200 by Mr. (afterwards Sir) H. W. Ripley; £1,000 by Sir Titus Salt, and £1,000 by Messrs. Isaac Holden and Son. Indeed, the large sum of £10,000 was raised by the subscriptions of about eighty-five persons or firms.

The foundation stone of the present Institute was laid on January 28th, 1870, by the late Lord Houghton, and his Lordship made a memorable speech on the occasion. Referring to the education movement then agitating the country (and which culminated in the passing that very year, of Mr. Forster's famous Education Act), Lord Houghton said—"I don't know any way in which I could more strongly express my feeling towards Mr. Forster than is illustrated by the fact that I am able in so mixed an assembly as this, of gentlemen of all politics, differing upon many points of religious and social opinion, to express to them my high esteem for that gentleman with perfect confidence in their response. It is now some thirty years since I first knew Mr. Forster, and it is to me a matter not only of gratification, but perhaps of some little individual pride, that I recognised from the first, the elements of greatness in him, and predicted to all about me that that man was a man of the future. . . . . It is therefore, I think, a matter of congratulation to all of us, that it is mainly to such a man that, the proposition of that great question of national education is now entrusted; and I think it is a matter of legitimate pride to Bradford that he is the man they have returned to parliament."

On the 2nd October, 1871, the Institute was completed and formally opened by the right Hon. W. E. Forster, M.P., Minister of Education.

Of the "inner life" of this useful institution a brief notice must suffice. The library has been a most important branch of its operations, and still continues to be so notwithstanding that a public Free Library has been in existence for several years. In the year 1833 it boasted of eight hundred volumes, with an issue for that year of not less than 4,600. In striking contrast with these figures the latest report of the Committee shews that the library now consists of 16,608 vols. with an annual issue of 44,368.

For several years the Committee felt themselves justified in excluding "works of fiction and light reading generally" from the shelves of the library. This was characteristic of the times, and of the worthy men who felt themselves in some measure responsible for "public morals"; but it was found to be a mistake, as by so doing they not only shut out much of the best literature of the period, but also debarred a toiling and industrious population, from the mental recreation and amusement which it so greatly needed. The Committee, in one of the earliest reports, speak somewhat proudly of the fact that the library "includes many of the best works on science, the arts, and general literature." The same may be said with equal truth to day, and it is pleasing to be able to record that this useful auxiliary to the life of the Institute has at no time been allowed to suffer from neglect or lack of patronage.

Another interesting and important branch of usefulness has been the lectures of the Institute, in the benefits of which the public have been allowed to share by paying a small charge for admission. The list of lecturers contains an array of eminent and honoured names of which the Institute may justly feel proud. Among the "Lecturers from a distance, whose presence have reflected a glory on the place" may be mentioned Elihu Burritt, Ralph Waldo Emerson, Sheridan Knowles, W. M. Thackeray, John Ruskin, Dean Stanley, Hepworth Dixon, George Macdonald and H. M. Stanley, the African traveller.

Lectures and entertainments were given by others hardly less distinguished than these, several of whom had engagements to make an annual appearance here. Among those who might always reckon upon a cordial welcome were Charles Cowden Clark, George Dawson, George Grossmith, Mrs. Fanny Kemble and Mrs. Clara L. Balfour.

The Committee of the Institute were fortunate in being able to secure the services, often gratuitous, of able and accomplished lecturers in Bradford and the neighbourhood. To mention the names of some of these will be to revive pleasing memories of the past in the minds of many old Bradfordians:—Dr. Scoresby, Mr. Edward Baines, junr., Dr. Beaumont, Dr. Godwin, Rev. J. G. Miall, Rev. J. Glyde, Dr. Ackworth, Rev. Walter Scott, Rev. J. H. Ryland, Rev. Joshua Fawcett, Dr. Burnett, Mr. James Hanson, Dr. Fraser, Rev. J. P. Chown and others.

Mr. W. E. Forster gave four lectures here in the month of October, 1848, on "Pauperism and its proposed remedies: Communism, Competition, and Organisation of Labour." On the 16th December, 1852, he lectured on "St. Augustine, his Life and Times"; on the 21st February, 1856, on "Passages from the History of the House of Commons"; on the 25th November of the same year on "Slavery in the United States," and in November 1858, on "Passages from the History of the House of Lords."

In 1853, Mr. William Jackson, musical composer, gave a lecture on "Melody and Harmony," with illustrations by Mrs. Sunderland and others.

For some years past the instruction given in the classes of the Institute has ceased to be confined to the mere rudiments of education, but has extended to the classical, linguistic, scientific and artistic branches. Many old pupils who were indebted to the Mechanics' Institute for the "little learning" that gave them their start in life, will yet remember the honoured names of those who took so active a part in the practical working of the classes in the earlier years of their existence. Among these were Mr. Clough, Mr. Charles Lund, Mr. James Hanson, Mr. Thomas Potter, Mr. Wainwright, Mr. Newboult and Mr. Laycock.

The Church Literary Institute.

It is a noteworthy coincidence that the old building in Albion Court, which had done service in 1833, as the Bradford Mechanics' Institute should just twenty-five years subsequently be selected as the birthplace, and for several years, the home of a kindred society—the Church Literary Institute.

There had, however, previously existed in Bradford an organisation which bore the name of "The Church Institution," and which had for its objects "the union of the members of the Church resident in the Parish in one association for the support of the Church; and the promotion of the Glory of God by the religious and intellectual instruction of her members in accordance with her Scriptural principles and sound doctrine." This Society was founded in 1843 by that pioneer of popular enlightenment, Dr. Scoresby, the vicar, and its meetings were held in the large room of a warehouse at the corner of Booth Street and Swain Street. The work of the Institute consisted of lectures on church subjects, sacred history, etc., and on matters relating to science, art and literature. A library was formed and classes established for the benefit of the most advanced pupils in the Parochial Schools, or adult members of the church. Performances of sacred music were also given by the Church Choral Society, for which purpose the room was furnished by a fine organ built by John Nicholson.

From its first annual report we learn that this useful institution had not less than 694 members, besides a branch association at Low Moor of 150 members. Dr. Scoresby was president; Mr. Alfred Harris and the Rev. W. Sherwood, Vice-Presidents; Mr. James Wade, Treasurer; and Mr. John Croft and the Rev. James Cooper, vicar of St. Judes, Secretaries. Among the members of the Committee were the Revs. John Barber, J. Bickerdike, J. C. Boddington, Joshua Fawcett, J. L. Frost, and Messrs. J. A. Busfeild, John Hollings, G. R. Mossman, Richard Ridehalgh, and E. J. Mitchell.

This praiseworthy movement flourished well while Dr. Scoresby was at its head, for he was the life and soul of its activity; but from the time of his unfortunate removal from Bradford in 1847, it began to droop and ere long ceased altogether to exist.

In little more than ten years, however, the need of a Church Institute was strongly felt, and at a meeting held in the Saloon of St. George's Hall on the 22nd April, 1858, the present institution was formed and a council of management elected. The Rev. John Burnet, the vicar, was President, and Messrs. George Wood, William Rand, W. M. Selwyn and W. B. Addison were Vice-Presidents. Mr. Addison, however, declined the office, and Mr. John Taylor, who proved himself to be a true friend to the movement, was elected in his place. Dr. Burnet spared no pains in his efforts to establish the Institute on a sound and permanent footing, and in Mr. George Ackroyd, who is alluded to in one of the reports as "one of the Institute's best friends," he had a faithful ally and zealous co-worker. Mr. Robert Barr has laboured long and earnestly in promoting the success of the Institute, and for upwards of sixteen years served as one of its Honorary Secretaries.

The library, which now numbers about five thousand volumes, was formed from "The Christian Knowledge Society's Depository" and Dr. Bray's library, and has since been augmented from time to time by gifts and purchases.

As the work of the Institute progressed and the number of its members increased, the need of more suitable accommodation became apparent, and at a general meeting held in April, 1865, it was decided that an attempt should be made to select or build a more commodious edifice, but it was not until 1870 that the site of the present building was purchased of Mr. J. L. Margerison for £4,800. The foundation stone was laid on the 10th of June, 1871, by the then President, Mr.

M. W. Thompson, and the members of the Institute entered upon the full enjoyment of the new premises in May, 1873. Increased facilities were soon followed by various new and attractive branches of education and entertainment, among which were a News-room stocked with all the leading newspapers and periodicals of the day; a handsome Gymnasium; Classes in Singing, Languages, Chemistry, etc., and a School of Art. The new enterprise was, however, of so costly a character as to be the means of incurring a heavy debt which considerably impeded the usefulness of the Institute. This was happily cleared off by the holding of a splendid bazaar in June 1882, in St. George's Hall, under the patronage and in presence of their Royal Highnesses the Prince and Princess of Wales, who had come to Bradford on the occasion of the opening of the new Technical College.

The Philosophical Society.

Bradford of the olden time was not without its philosophers—lovers of wisdom and eminent for their scientific knowledge and literary attainments. This is more than can be said for Bradford of more modern times. Somewhere in his "History of Bradford," Mr. James makes the remark that this town has produced "more useful than literary men," by which he does not mean, we take it, that literary men are not useful, but that theirs is not the sort of usefulness which bears directly upon the special industry for which the town has become famous—the manufacture of worsted goods. Bradford has been unquestionably a more congenial soil for the growth of men of business than of philosophers, and this doubtless accounts for the fact that so many attempts have been made and failed, to establish a philosophical society here. When the effort was vigorously put forth some five years ago to revive the Society, some of its older friends prophesied that the revival would only last a couple of years, and that it would then lapse into its former state of lethargy.

The prophesy has not been fulfilled, for the two years have been passed, and the Society is now entering upon its fifth session with the brightest prospects, we believe, for its future.

It should be remembered, however, that the conditions are changed, and that obstructions which formerly impeded the Society's progress no longer exist. Education has, of late years, made rapid strides, and the old spirit of exclusiveness and class distinction which formerly existed, has, in the Society itself, wisely given place to a more liberal and generous feeling of fellowship and co-operation.

The earliest attempt at forming a philosophical society here was made well-nigh a hundred years ago, under the auspices, it is said, of the eminent scientist, Dr. Joseph Priestley. It appears to have had but a brief existence, and nothing more is heard of a similar movement until the year 1823, when, through the exertions of Mr. Samuel Hailstone, a praiseworthy effort was made to establish such a society.

In January of that year a public meeting took place in the Court House (then held in the Piece Hall), at which it was resolved to form a literary and philosophical society, and no less than forty-two persons subscribed £50 each towards raising a fund for erecting a hall, purchasing a library, etc. The then vicar of the parish, the Rev. Henry Heap, discouraged the movement, and by preaching a sermon "in which" says Mr. James "he enlarged on the irreligious tendency of a philosophising spirit, several of the subscribers took fright and withdrew their subscriptions, and thus a society so auspiciously formed was broken up."

Again an attempt is made, after an interval of sixteen years, to establish a society, one of the leading spirits of the enterprise being the vicar of Bradford, but this time in the person of Dr. Scoresby.

To Mr. Wm. Sharp, surgeon, who then resided in a gothic-gabled house at the bottom of Dale Street, belongs very much of the honour of founding this Society, for, during the winter of 1838-9, he had delivered a course of scientific lectures which attracted considerable notice. The lecturer spoke of the desirability of forming such an institution, as he felt persuaded that the time was now fully ripe for it. A number of gentlemen therefore met on the 12th April, 1839, to talk over the matter, and it was ultimately decided to establish a philosophical society on a sounder basis than the previous efforts. Mr. Sharp, then senior surgeon of the Bradford Infirmary was elected President; Mr. J. G. Horsfall, Vice-President; Mr. Alfred Harris, Treasurer; and Mr. John Darlington, Secretary. Among the Members of the Council were such well-known townsmen as Messrs. C. H. Dawson (Royds Hall), John Hustler (Bolton House), Charles Hardy, Rev. Joshua Fawcett, Dr. Macturk, George Pollard, and John Rand. The list of honorary members included such distinguished names as those of Sir John Herschell, Sir David Brewster, Roderick Murchison, and Professors Sedgwick, Faraday, Lyell, Phillips and others. Some of these manifested their interest in the project by sending presents of books, etc., towards the formation of a library and museum.

Of the first twelve monthly meetings of the Society eight were held in a large room of the New Inn, but as the attendance increased, subsequent gatherings took place in the Lecture Hall of the Exchange, Kirkgate.

Dr. Scoresby was elected President of the Society for the third year of its existence. His lectures had become an important feature of its operations. The following are some of the subjects which he treated: "On the Influence and Advantages of Scientific Institutions"; on "Astronomy, or the Arithmetic of the Planetary System"; "Some Account of my Magnetical Investigations." Mr. Sharp gave a paper on "The Formation of Local Museums"; Mr. John Darlington also gave one on "The Mineral, Vegetable, and Animal Kingdoms. These were followed by papers on "Grecian and Roman Architecture" by the Rev. Joshua Fawcett; on "The Construction of Carriages" by Mr. J. G. Horsfall; on "Intermitting Springs," by the Rev. Theodore

Dury, of Keighley; on "A Restoration of St. Mary's Abbey, York," by Mr. Samuel Sharp, of Leeds; on "Phrenology," by Mr. John Crofts; on "The Possession of Reason by the Inferior Animals," by Mr. T. Nunnely; on "The History of the Woollen Manufacture," by Mr. Darlington; on "The Circulation of the Blood," by Mr. Thomas Beaumont: and on "Funeral Rites in all Ages," by the Rev. Joshua Fawcett.

Among the lecturers specially engaged by the Society were the following: Professor Taylor gave a course of lectures on "English Vocal Harmony"; James Montgomery, a course of six lectures on "The Poets of England"; Mr. R. Addams, a course of lectures on "Accoustics, and the Solidification of Carbonic Acid"; and Mr. I. F. Gornoszynski (member of the Polish Historical Society) three lectures on "The History of Poland.

The first report issued by the Society was of a very hopeful character. After regretting that so large and important a town as Bradford should have been so long without a philosophical society it went on to express surprise that the present attempt should have excited such general interest, and advanced with such rapid progress. It is sad to think that in spite of these bright anticipations the Society was doomed to have but a brief life. After the removal from Bradford of its originator, Mr. Sharp, its career appears to have been cut short, for we have been unable to find any trace of its existence after the year 1843.

The subsequent history of the Bradford Philosophical Society may be briefly told.

On December 23rd, 1864, a meeting, consisting of many of the most influential gentlemen of the town, and at which Mr. Charles Semon, the mayor, presided, was held in the Exchange Rooms with the object of re-establishing the Society, and of placing Bradford in this respect, on an equality with such towns as Manchester and Leeds. Among those present were the Revs. Dr. Burnet the vicar, J. R. Campbell, S. G. Green, J. G. Miall and Henry Leach; and Messrs. John Rand, H. W. Ripley, Alfred Harris, junr., John Hollings, Samuel Laycock. John Priestman, Jacob Behrens, James Law, W. Byles, John Taylor, James Hanson, and Drs. Bridges, Bell, and Brady. Reports were submitted to the meeting showing the results of enquiries that had been recently made as to what was being done in other large towns in the way of establishing similar societies. Dr. Burnet remarked that if any of them knew of the flourishing condition of the Leeds Philosophical Society, it would make them blush for Bradford, and wish that a similar one existed here. Alluding to the two previous attempts at establishing a society here, he said the first began at the wrong end in seeking to commence with a formidable building. The second appeared to have been little else than a literary club, and in a town like this a literary *exclusive* club would carry with it the seeds of its own dissolution. Any society instituted in this town, to exist, must be very extensive, very elastic,—of a general and public character, and it must hold out the right hand of sympathy to other literary institutes however humble they might be.

Wise and prophetic words these, and well deserving of remembrance. We venture to believe that it is to the absence of this class exclusiveness that the Mechanics' Institute is largely indebted for its great success and usefulness.

The outcome of the above-mentioned meeting was the constitution of a philosophical society, the object of which, as set forth in its programme, was to be the giving of high-class lectures; the founding of a museum and library, the opening of a reading-room, and the formation of classes under competent professors. The Earl of Rosse held the position of President, and the Rev. Henry Leach (vicar of All Saints), and Mr. Arthur Briggs, were the first Honorary Secretaries. A wise step was taken in the appointment of Mr. L. C. Miall as paid Secretary and Curator.

The first important step taken towards the formation of the museum was the purchase, at a cost of £350, of the geological collection of the late Mr. Richardson, of Southowram. Many other valuable additions were made from time to time to both museum and library. The Society for a while occupied premises in Duke Street, but these proving too small they were vacated in June 1866, for more convenient accommodation in Manor Row. The erection of a suitable building for the Society was mooted, and Mr. Ripley made the offer of a substantial sum towards that object, but the project failed to meet with a hearty response.

In 1884, it became necessary to resuscitate the Society. This was done by first clearing off a debt that had long been a heavy burden and greatly crippled its activity, and by linking itself more closely with the other Societies of the town, thereby extending its advantages over a much wider area than heretofore. Since this fresh start in life the Society has passed through five years of prosperity of which it may justly feel proud, and, as at this moment it holds a position not unworthy of the intelligence and importance of the town which it represents, we trust that its future may be one of long-continued advancement and success.

The Bradford Subscription Library

is an institution that has grown to a respectable old age and is still "hale and hearty." It has passed through none of the vicissitudes which fell to the lot of the Philosophical Society because it has ever been content with a steady onward progress, following the motto of walking gently before attempting to fly. With a very lowly origin its career has been one of slow but safe advancement, and its proprietors may now with great satisfaction look around on the spacious and handsome building in which they assemble, viewing with no little pride the splendid collection of thirty thousand volumes that now form its library, and no less proud of an income more than thirty times its original amount.

The year from whence the Subscription Library dates its birth—1774—was a memorable one in the history of Bradford. The town, then composed of some four thousand inhabitants, was bestirring itself after the stupor of a century, and, with its new worsted industry which it had fairly laid hold of, was assuming quite the proportions of a small commercial community. It was the year of the opening of the Canal, an event of vast importance at that day as it put the town in easy communication with other centres of industry. The great religious revival of last century was then agitating the whole country, and 1774 was the year when John Wesley first visited Bradford, and when his faithful disciple John Nelson was arrested for preaching "the new doctrine."

The formation of the Bradford Library in that eventful year would attract but little notice, as it began its career in a very modest and unassuming manner, and the place that witnessed its birth is not even known. It is known, however, that one of the principal instruments in originating it was the Rev. John Dean, Unitarian Minister in Bradford, a man of considerable literary attainments.

For several years he acted in the capacity of Treasurer; an office involving no great responsibility, as there were only about seventy subscribers who paid each an entrance fee of a guinea and an annual subscription of five shillings.

The first disbursements the Treasurer was called upon to make are worth quoting:

		£	s.	d.
1775—To	John Aked for a book-case and desk ...	3	13	1
,, ,,	Mr. Priestley for books	7	16	3
,, ,,	Mr. Priestley for more books	3	12	0
,, ,,	Dr. Wright for books	1	4	0
,, ,,	Mr. Thomas Wood for books, &c. ...	0	10	0
,, ,,	Mr. John Smith for a book	0	3	0
,, ,,	Mr. Dean for books	0	7	6
,, ,,	J. Bowling, printer, for work done ...	1	2	6
,, ,,	The Librarian for Sundries	0	19	8½
,, ,,	Mr. Smith, bookseller, for books, binding, commission, carriage and stationery ...	34	1	0½

The Mr. Priestley, named above, resided at Stott Hill House, and was a prominent townsman in Bradford, and for upwards of fifty years was the chief business man of the Canal Company.

Bradford could not yet boast of a printer of its own, hence the printing of catalogues, &c. was done by the well-known printer at Leeds,—J. Bowling. It was not, however, without its bookseller and stationer, as a well-to-do tradesman in that way of business, named Dudley Rocket, had a shop in Goodman's End as early as 1744. The John Smith above-named was also a bookseller, and was one of the first members of the small Congregational church that met in the old Malt Chamber.

The first Librarian was a John Whitaker who discharged the duties of his office for the salary of five pounds per annum.

John Aked's account of £3 13s. 1d. was made up of the following items:—

	£	s.	d.
To wood for book-case	1	15	4
,, work at do.	1	7	9
,, glue and nails	0	1	0
,, hinges, locks and screws ...	0	4	0
,, a desk in Library Room	0	5	0

The Treasurer's accounts were audited for the first time in 1776 and showed "Receipts, £24 14s. 11d.; Payments, £31 2s. 0½d.; Balance due to Treasurer, £6 7s. 1½d."

The titles of the first batch of books purchased for the Library with their prices, will be read with interest—

		£	s.	d.
Blackstone's Commentaries—	4 Vols.	1	10	0
Hume's History of England—	8 do.	2	5	0
Pope's Shakespeare—	16 do.	1	4	0
Sterne's Works (complete)—	4 do.	0	15	0
Priestley's Examination of Dr. Reid	... ...	0	4	0
Beccaria on Crimes and Punishments	... ...	0	6	0
Gregory's Comparative View ...	... ...	0	2	6
Dodsley's Poems—	6 do.	0	15	0
Boswell's Corsica	... ...	0	2	0
Robertson's History of Scotland—	2 do.... ...	0	9	0
Hook's Roman History—	6 do.	1	10	0
Swift's Works—	17 do. ...	2	2	0

Whenever the funds permitted, fresh additions of books were made. The entries of some of these in the treasurer's book are sometimes oddly mixed with other items,—thus

	£	s.	d.
To Cicero on Old Age—Calf...	0	5	0
,, The Hermit of Warkworth ...	0	2	6
,, Fire and Candles	0	7	0
,, Three Weeks after Marriage ...	0	5	0
,, An ounce of Wafers	0	0	1½
,, The Silent Woman	0	4	6
,, 30 quils and a pencil	0	0	3
,, Coal and Candles at four Committees	0	4	0

The titles of some of the books purchased at this far off period are very quaint and curious, and such as one never hears of now-a-days. These are some of them—"Alexander's History of Woman;" "A Treatise on Chimneys;" "Hey, on Duelling and Backing;" "Memoirs of the Year 2500;" "Choleric Men;" and "Sermons to Young Women."

One is scarcely surprised to find that the Library during Mr. Dean's connection with it was kept well supplied with the works of Priestley, the scientist and philosopher.

The first mention made of printing being done in Bradford for the Library occurs in 1781. The printer was John Nicholson, and his office was at the top of the present Albion Court in premises now occupied by Mr. Ben Johnson, draper and hosier. This was doubtless the first printing office in Bradford, and although the earliest known book printed by Nicholson bears date 1785, it is clear that he was located here at least four years previously, as an account of his for printing catalogues, &c. amounting to £6 0s. 11½d. was paid in 1781.

John Nicholson had two sons, Samuel and George, the former of whom had a shop in New (afterwards Market) Street. George was a remarkable man, and lived to be the means of bringing about a great revolution in the publishing trade. He removed to Manchester where he remained some years and then went to Ludlow in Shropshire, and established himself at the beautiful hamlet of Poughil, near that town in 1799, where he continued for some years to publish books which were remarkable for their good taste and good printing, and which had a large circulation. He was his own compiler and editor, and his own traveller; the latter task being almost always performed on foot. He died at Stourport in 1825.

While the father and sons were stationed in Bradford, they appear to have done most of the printing and other work for the Library, and after the year 1781 the name of J. Bowling, of Leeds, no longer appears on the books. In 1791 the following items occur—"Paid John Nicholson for books, £31 3s. 0d." "Paid George Nicholson for printing catalogues, £2 17s. 0d." "Paid Samuel Nicholson for binding, 7/-." On the resignation of Mrs. Mercer as librarian in 1814, and the removal of the Library from her house (called White House) at the bottom of Church Bank, to the west corner of Chapel Court, in Kirkgate, Mr. John Nicholson was appointed librarian at a yearly salary of £20. In 1820, Miss Mary Nicholson, probably his daughter, was appointed to the same post, and at the same salary.

Two hundred volumes were added to the Library in 1778—an increase which appears to have necessitated enlarged accommodation, for soon after, a removal was made to the house of Mrs. Bradford, then Librarian.

Where the Library was originally located is unfortunately not known. In 1793 it was removed to Mrs. Mercer's at the bottom of Church Bank, afterwards to Kirkgate as already stated, and in 1829 to the Exchange Buildings at the bottom of Piccadilly, when Miss Eliza Croft was appointed librarian in place of Miss Nicholson. This post has since been held by Miss Mason, appointed in 1848, and Miss Rhodes, who after a service of twenty-seven years as assistant was appointed full librarian in 1881, which office she still holds, with two assistants, Miss Clay and Miss Walker.

The present library building in Darley Street, purchased in 1854, was formerly the Bradford Dispensary. It is most admirably adapted for its present purpose, is well constructed, replete with every comfort and convenience, and its shelves contain a splendid assortment of books in all departments of literature. Several years ago a plain and unassuming man might often have been seen in one of the retired nooks of the Library, quietly poring over some carefully-chosen volume. This was the late Mr. John James, who in gathering the materials for his "History of Bradford" often availed himself of the privilege of consulting this treasure-house of Archæological lore. Another "kindred spirit" who shared in the same privilege, and who gave to the public the benefit of his industrious researches, was the late esteemed author and antiquary, Mr. Abraham Holroyd.

The minute and account books of the Bradford Library contain many particulars interesting to the local antiquary. The lists of subscribers and office bearers unquestionably furnish the most complete record in existence of the names of the leading families of Bradford for the past hundred years. Among the members of the first committee occur the names of Messrs. Nathan Jowett, Francis Duffield, Thomas Outhwaite, Henry Oates, John Rand, senr., Robert Ramsbotham, Joseph Priestley, Edmund Peckover, John Bentley, John Eagle, Thomas Skelton, Matthew Sedgwick, and J. Swaine; and in the list of very early subscribers we come across such familiar names as those of the Revs. John Crosse, Wm. Atkinson and W. Baldwyn (a remarkable trio); also the Revs. Patrick Brontë and N. T. Heinekin; Messrs. John Hustler, Francis Simes, Joshua Field, Richard Lambert, Dr. Mossman, Miss Bower, and many others who may be regarded as fair representatives of a race of Bradford gentry belonging to a bygone generation.

Airedale College.

In attempting to trace the history of this institution we must go back to the religious revival of last century, when England felt the awakening and enlightening power of religion through the preaching of Wesley and Whitfield; and we must look away from the spacious and imposing structure now overlooking Lister Park, to a plain and humble building on the outskirts of the thriving town of Heckmondwike, in which a hundred and thirty years ago, a tutor and a mere handful of pupils were quietly prosecuting their studies.

But the Airedale College of 1756 was only known by the simple title of "Mr. Scott's Academy," although it was soon to acquire a wide reputation and shed its influence for good over an extensive area.

A society called the Northern Education Society had been formed in London for the purpose of "dispelling the cloud of Socinian darkness then spreading over the northern counties of England, and by which many congregations might be blessed with godly preachers, sound in the faith and exemplary in their lives." As an important step towards securing these objects it was determined to establish an academy in the North of England. The tutorship of it was offered to Scott, who accepted it, though not without some hesitation on the score of his fitness for so responsible a post.

James Scott was a native of Berwickshire, and was born in the year 1710. Little is known of his early life beyond the fact that in the session of 1728-9 he entered the University of Edinburgh, and after spending some years as a private tutor he resolved to dedicate himself to the work of the ministry. On hearing that many congregations in England were in need of pastors, he crossed the border, bringing with him the most satisfactory credentials of character and ability.

The original Airedale College.

He travelled on foot with a companion, over districts miserably supplied with roads, till he reached Staunton, where he settled for a time, but afterwards removed to Horton-in-Craven, from which place he was called upon to undertake the tutorship of the proposed academy.

Mr. Scott entered upon his new vocation *with three pupils.* Their names were Thomas Waldegrave, of Bury St. Edmunds; Timothy Priestley, of Kipping, and Richard Plumbe, of Nottingham. Such was the small beginning of the movement that has developed into the Airedale College of to-day.

The plain-looking structure shown in our sketch was the place where the students followed their studies, but Mr. Scott resided in a substantial house adjoining. The situation of the Academy was at any rate open, healthy, and quiet—three essential features—being some distance from the high-road, and far enough away from the surrounding towns.

As the reputation of the Academy spread, its pupils increased, and the list of those who received their training under Mr. Scott from 1756 to 1783, when he died, shows an array of not less than seventy names. Several of these attained honourable and important positions in the Independent Church. It would indeed be difficult to place a limit upon the usefulness of the small and unpretentious seminary at Heckmondwike. Under the agency of its students many new congregations were started, which to-day are flourishing and influential churches.

But those were rough times for preachers of the gospel, and when the young students went forth to "break up the fallow ground," they had verily to "carry their lives in their hands," for they were often treated with great violence by rough and unruly mobs.

Mr. Scott was greatly beloved by his pupils, and little wonder, for his kindness to them was as that of a father for his children. His useful career was brought to a close in 1783, his connection with the Academy having extended over twenty-seven years.

His successor, the Rev. Samuel Walker, of Northowram, had been one of his pupils. To Northowram the Academy was transferred, but it failed to prosper as it had done in the hands of James Scott.

We cannot here enter into all the details of how it became eventually necessay to dissolve the Northowram Academy and begin a fresh one at Rotherham, but we may state that this was an arrangement not satisfactory to all parties. The Rev. W. Vint, the Congregational minister at Idle, near Bradford, was requested as a temporary expedient, to take charge of the four students that remained on the breaking up of the Northowram Academy, and a Mr. Edmund Hanson, of London, (a Yorkshireman), contributed £60 annually for the tuition of two young men, and at his death left £150 per annum for the Academy, thus revived, "for ever." The institution took the name which it still bears of "The Airedale College," and was regarded as the continuation of the one which had existed at Heckmondwike and afterwards at Northowram.

In Mr. Vint the Academy found a tutor of zeal and ability, and under his care it flourished beyond all expectation. It was found in 1817, that the number of Independent Chapels in the West Riding had increased to fifty-six. In keeping many of these supplied with preachers the students at Idle had travelled, during the space of twelve months, over 17,400 miles. During the first ten years of Mr. Vint's term of office he would not accept more than £50 a year as salary, and the terms of board for each student during sixteen years were only £25 per annum. Afterwards Mr. Vint's salary was raised to £100 a-year.

One of the most interesting and accomplished of Mr. Vint's students was Thomas Rawson Taylor, who has been already mentioned as a Grammar School pupil. He was a youth of rare promise, and was for a time classical tutor at Airedale College. He was trained for the ministry, and entered upon his work at Sheffield, but only to be soon snatched away from it by death.

Airedale College, Undercliffe.

The college at Idle has long been demolished, but the tutor's house is yet standing, and was till recently the residence of Mr. J. Horsfall Turner, the distinguished Yorkshire antiquary, who has written an interesting volume on the history of "Nonconformity in Idle."

Of the subsequent career of Airedale College we have little to say, as the object of this sketch has been to treat more particularly of its early history.

In 1834 the College at Idle was superseded by the one at Undercliffe—the massive looking building on the hill top overlooking Bradford—the site of which was given by Mrs. Bacon, a wealthy and benevolent lady then residing in the town. It was opened on the 5th of March of that year, and on the 13th of the same month Mr. Vint,

Baptist College, Horton.

who had held the office of president for thirty-four years, was removed from the scene of his long and faithful labours by death. He was succeeded by the Rev. Walter Scott,—a man of superior mental powers and rare virtues. On Mr. Scott's retirement from the office in 1836, the Rev. D. Fraser, LL.D., was appointed to take his place, and he has been succeeded by the Rev. A. M. Fairbairn, D.D.

The new College now standing on the pleasant hill side beyond Manningham was opened on June the 20th, 1877, the anniversary of the foundation of Airedale College.

Horton Baptist College.

While the present century was yet very young, a building in Little Horton was engaged by the Northern Baptist Education Society for the purposes of a college and tutor's residence, The place was not well adapted to meet those requirements, but this was "the day of small things" with the Society, and its funds did not admit of the taking of more costly premises. This building, which afterwards came to be so well known as "Horton College" had formerly been the residence and warehouse of Mr. John Balme, and was sufficiently near the town, and yet far enough out in the country to combine the advantages of both. The Horton side of Manchester Road was not yet invaded by the capitalist and builder, and beyond the two mansions, Horton Hall and Horton House, and one or two residences in Horton Lane, the College was entirely surrounded by fields that were green and by an atmosphere innocent of impurity.

The origin of this institution is to be traced back to the year 1773, when Mr., afterwards Dr. Fawcett, received into his family at Ewood Hall, near Hebden Bridge, several young men who were piously inclined upon whom "he employed his great intelligence and learning in awakening their mental powers and guiding their intellectual enquiries." The names of men like Sutcliffe, Foster, and Ward must ever be linked with that of the venerated Fawcett, and the large and flourishing Baptist College now located at Rawdon may feel justly proud of a matured age whose infancy produced such eminent and honoured divines as these.

The object of establishing the Horton Baptist College was to form an academy for the assistance of such young men as the churches to which they belonged might recommend, that they might have leisure and opportunity to attend to a course of preparatory studies under the care of a solid and judicious tutor. It began its useful career in 1806, on a very small scale indeed, having but one tutor, Mr. Steadman, and one solitary pupil. Before the year expired, however, two more pupils were placed under the tutor's charge, and the number steadily increased as the years rolled on.

The College was not without its friends and patrons. The first of these was Mr. James Bury of Pendle Hill, Lancashire, who generously offered £5000 in annual instalments of £100 as part of the capital to sustain its future operations. The Rev. John Sutcliffe, of Olney, bequeathed his library worth £500 to the Academy upon certain conditions that were readily complied with. Up to the year 1817, the business of the College had been carried on in hired premises, but by the gift of £1271 by Mr. Thomas Key, of York, the entire College buildings were purchased. In 1834, Miss Ward, of Bradford, left a legacy of £500, and in the following year, Mr. Samuel Broadley, an old and worthy Bradfordian gave by will the munificent bequest of £5000, upon trust that the interest thereof should be applied to the purposes of the College for ever.

Other benefactors came forward from time to time by whose aid the premises were greatly enlarged, and a new president's house was erected. This house may yet be seen immediately behind the comfortable hostelry known as "Armstrong's Hotel," but the old College building was pulled down several years ago in order to make way for the thoroughfare called Park Road.

After an existence reaching over more than half a century, the old Horton College was found to be no longer fitted for the requirements of such an institution. Its accommodation was insufficient for the number of its students, and, moreover, its situation was no longer in harmony with a seminary needing seclusion and quiet. Its once rural surroundings had given place to long streets of houses and to a dense population that had sprung into being with marvellous rapidity.

A new College was therefore erected at Rawdon, and taken possession of in 1859. With increased resources and a healthier locality the Academy entered upon a new phase of its history. Of the old Horton College little remains to show that it ever existed, but it has left associations that time itself can never destroy. For upwards of fifty years it was the home and nursery of men who were destined to exert a powerful influence for good in nearly all parts of the globe, and its record of presidents and tutors contains a list of worthy men of whom any religious community might well feel proud. It is enough to mention the names of Drs. Steadman, Godwin and Ackworth, and the Revs. Isaac Mann, J. P. Chown, F. Clowes, H. Dowson and S. G. Green.

Sunday Schools.

For fully eighty years these institutions have carried on their beneficent operations in Bradford, and during that period have not only acted upon its population as a powerful moral and religious agency, but have been also instrumental in imparting elementary instruction to thousands of children, who, but for them would have remained in profound and hopeless ignorance.

Those well-meaning but prejudiced people who looked upon the education and enlightenment of the "humbler classes" with fear and suspicion, do not appear to have regarded with much favour the giving of secular instruction in Sunday Schools; for when the Kirkgate Wesleyan Sunday School issued its report on the occasion of its anniversary held in February 1817, it seemed necessary to offer a sort of apology to those who believed that "education would make the lower orders of society less disposed to submit to the constituted authorities and to act in a subordinate capacity." After recording, on the authority of one who had been an active and successful teacher for eight years, that during that time, fifty-four children belonging to one class only, who could not read at all when they entered the school, had to his knowledge been enabled to read the Bible well previous to their leaving it, the report is bold enough to assert that "those who are best acquainted with the Holy Scriptures, and with what they owe to God, their parents and *superiors*, will ever prove the most humble Christians, and the most faithful servants."

But if an apology like this were necessary in 1817, one cannot help wondering as to what would be thought of the action of that pioneer in Sunday School work—the Rev. John Crosse, the vicar, who as early as 1786 had no less than three such schools in active operation in Bradford; one in Tyrrel Street, another in White Abbey, a third in High Street, and—a few years later,—a fourth in an old house at Little Horton Green. These he not only established, but, with the aid of his co-worker the Rev. W. Atkinson, the lecturer at the church, also attended to catechise the children, and in other ways encouraged the good work.

It is impossible to fix the precise date when Sunday School teaching first began in Bradford, as individual efforts in that direction would doubtless be made long before any organised system was contemplated. Such an effort, it is said, was made by one John Brown, a Wesleyan residing in Mill Bank, who in 1773 began a school in his own house and had about twenty scholars. A similar attempt was made in 1777 at a cottage-house in Lower Globe Fold, Manningham, but by whom we have not been able to learn. These early enterprises it should be borne in mind were made several years before the idea of Sunday Schools was broached by that apostle of the movement, Robert Raikes of Gloucester.

For some years prior to the death of Mr. Crosse, the Parish Church Sunday School was held in what was known as the "Assembly Room" of the old Market in Market Street. Each year brought its anniversary, or "Charity Sermons," when special efforts were made towards improving the financial position of the School. The hymns sung by the Sunday School children were printed, as at the present day, and on the fly leaf was set out an "Abstract of the Treasurer's Account." The account for the year ending April 1822, shews the receipts to have consisted of a collection at the Parish Church of £56 15s. 0d. with sundry gifts varying from one to five guineas from the following gentlemen, viz: William Smithson, John Hustler, Joseph Peckover, Charles Harris, Henry Harris, John Hustler, junior, and John Farrer. The payments were made up of balance due to treasurer

£7 14s. 10d.; books for children, joiner's work in school and sundry bills, £47 11s. 4d.; Benjamin Rawson for one and a half year's school rent, £22 10s. 0d.; James Speight's (schoolmaster) salary, &c. £6 9s. 5½d. Total number of scholars, 419, being an increase of more than a hundred during the year.

Accounts for subsequent years contain such items as "By one Instructor for the children and Coals during winter, £6 6s. 0d.;" "By one year's salary for one teacher, including attendance upon the children, £4 4s. 0d.;" "By half a year's salary for one female teacher, including attendance, £1 1s. 0d." These entries clearly point to the fact that some, at least, of the Sunday School teachers were then paid for their services. These payments along with the substantial item for rent paid to the lord of the manor, who owned the old Market Hall, were serious items of expenditure and helped to swell out the balance due to the treasurer at the end of each year.

But not all the Sunday Schools of those early times could afford the luxury of paid teachers. In some the curriculum of instruction was of the most primitive kind, the letters of the alphabet being taught by the simple method of drawing the finger across a tray full of sand, or of sliding wooden letters along a couple of bars with a stick, and forming them into words. Truly the pursuit of knowledge by our forefathers was one beset with difficulties.

The Rev. Henry Heap who succeeded Mr. Crosse as vicar in 1816, took an active interest in the Sunday School movement. In 1827 the new schools near the bottom of Bolton Road were erected, and the old Assembly Room vacated. From this point, great and rapid progress was made, the number of scholars in 1830 having increased to upwards of a thousand, while the scholars then in attendance at Christ Church School (established in 1815) were not less than six hundred.

The Wesleyan Methodists were hardly less vigorous in Sunday School work than the Church people. With them the movement in Bradford dates from February, 1808, when a gathering of school children was begun in the Octagon Chapel in Horton Road. This was afterwards superseded by the upper room of a warehouse in Union Street belonging to Mr. Richard Fawcett who took a great interest in the Sunday School movement, and whose father had for many years been a Methodist leader and local preacher.

In 1824, the school in School Street was erected, which was soon followed by others in the outskirts of the town.

The Congregational Church in Horton Lane were early in the field with their Sunday School. For a while the scholars were taught in the body of the chapel, but the large school-room adjoining was erected in 1819 and soon had an attendance of some three hundred scholars. This has for many years been one of the most flourishing institutions of its kind in the town, and its roll books contain the names of many of Bradford's most prominent and useful citizens.

The Baptists date the origin of their first Sunday School here to the year 1814. It has proved a most important and useful auxiliary to the church in swelling the ranks of church membership from time to time from the senior classes.

The Sunday School movement has kept pretty even pace with the rapid increase of churches and chapels in Bradford during the past half century. In 1845 it had taken firm root in the soil, and its powerful influence for good could no longer be questioned, for there were then in the borough no less than thirty-four Sunday Schools and eleven thousand, five hundred and seventy scholars in attendance upon them. Up to the present time the movement has gone on increasing and prospering, but in recent years it has passed through a peculiar crisis. As a means of imparting elementary instruction to children Sunday Schools have served their day and generation, for in the light of the present educational facilities they are far behind the race. This is no longer their vocation, but it is a mistake to suppose that their existence has ceased to be necessary because "the schoolmaster is abroad," and the face of the land is covered by Board Schools. The object of Sunday Schools is to teach religious truth and form religious character, and according to the measure in which this object is attained will they answer the great end of their existence, and accomplish the same good in the future that they have done in the past.

Modern Institutions.

Of late years education has grown apace. This is doubtless as it should be, in view of the present magnitude and importance of the town, and of the fact that the English Minister of Education, the Right Honourable W. E. Forster, was for several years its senior representative in Parliament. Looking around us to-day, in the full blaze of the gigantic operations of the Board School movement, and of the various other educational institutions of which Bradford may justly feel proud, it may not be uninstructive to look back "across the years" for a while, to see how our forefathers fared in the matter of education, and to note the striking contrast between the Past and Present. We have before us a document dated "Lady Day, 1825," purporting to be a covenant, on the part of the tenants of certain cottages in Bradford with their landlord, that in case of default in payment of their rent when the same was duly demanded, it should be lawful for such landlord to distrain upon their goods. The document contains the names of thirty-one tenants, but out of that number only six were able to write their own names, the remainder being marksmen. This illiteracy was not by any means confined to the humbler classes, for we have it on the authority of one well acquainted with the fact, and he was one of the unfortunates himself, that seventy years ago the majority of those who attended the Bradford market were wholly uneducated, or nearly so. They knew how to make pieces well enough, and still better how to sell them; they could calculate the cost of yarns, and rates of wages, and had a desperately good idea of profit and loss, and many of them were even so far learned as to be able to read the Bible with the aid of a little spelling of the long words; but their notions of book-keeping were of the most primitive description, and the author of the system of "Double entry" would have stood aghast if he had seen their account *books*, which were not unfrequently exhibited in chalk on the backs of their shop doors. The writer hereof, remembers, when a boy, being hailed by a well-to-do farmer from Horton, and asked to read (a feat he was unable to perform himself,) a sale-bill just posted on the wall.

Some praiseworthy attempts were, however, occasionally made to place the means of education within easy reach of the poorer classes, and to the honour of the Society of Friends be it recorded, one of the most practical and successful of these is to be ascribed to their benevolence and zeal. "The Quakers' School," as it was called, began its existence in 1816, and made such steady progress that in 1831 it became necessary to erect a larger building. The commodious school in Chapel Street, Leeds Road, was opened in that year with an attendance of 200 boys, 140 girls, and 130 infants. The site of it was the generous gift of Mr. Charles Harris, and the cost of erection, £2,300, was raised by subscriptions among the Friends, Mr. John Hustler himself contributing £300. In 1831, the commemoration of the emancipation of British slaves took place in Bradford, when the scholars of the Quaker-school were treated to a "feast" at Undercliffe House, the residence of Mr. Hustler; the procession passing on its way through the beautiful grounds of Peckover Park. Each scholar wore a medal in honour of the event.

The Parochial-schools, originated and carried on by Dr. Scoresby at the cost of much labour and anxiety, was one of the most comprehensive and successful schemes of popular education ever attempted in Bradford. Not only did he collect the contributions necessary for their maintenance, but he also gave lavishly from his own purse. From Dr. Scoresby's printed report of the working of the schools, we learn that the "Parochial School Fund" was begun in 1839, and that Mr. Alfred Harris was Treasurer, and soon after that date the Model School in Manchester Road, the New Leeds School, the Daisy Hill School, and the School at Eccleshill, in addition to the large and flourishing School at Stott Hill, were established and in successful operation. These were followed by the Schools at Heaton, Manningham, Bowling, Sticker Lane, and Croft Street, making in all nine schools, through which passed during the six years covered by the report (1839 to 1846,) not less than twenty thousand children.

In the year 1839, a meeting of Dissenting ministers and influential laymen was held in Bradford to consider what steps should be taken towards better promoting the education of the people. A scheme was drawn up in which it was proposed to erect a number of schools in different parts of the borough, but it fell through because it aimed at accomplishing too much at once. The Rev. Mr. Glyde, minister of

Horton Lane Chapel, interested himself greatly in this project, and was disappointed at its failure. He was not the man, however, to be disheartened by defeat, and he at once called his own people together and proposed the erection of a public day school in their own behalf. Subscriptions amounting to £940 were promised; a grant of £240 was obtained from the Privy Council, and the fine buildings known as the Borough West Schools were erected, and opened in September 1843.

The Female Educational Institute established in 1857, chiefly through the instrumentality of the late Mr. S. C. Kell, had for its object the instruction of young women and mothers whose education had been neglected in their early days. For a time it carried on its operations at a house in Horton Lane, where on four evenings in the week lessons were given in the elementary branches of education, and in sewing and domestic economy. The capital fund of the Institute was augumented by a bazaar held in St. George's Hall, which raised about £1000, and for some years the movement enjoyed a season of prosperity. When the Board School system came into operation, and ratepayers were called upon to provide the means of education, many of the subscribers ceased to pay their contributions, and the falling off of the funds was soon followed by the closing of the Institute, which had had an active and useful existence of some twenty years.

The Bradford long-pledged Teetotal Association carried on for some time an educational movement in the shape of a night-school held in the Southgate Hall, Westgate. At the twelfth annual meeting of the association held April 7th, 1855, the Committee acknowledged their indebtedness to the late Mr. Tom Potter for the zeal he had displayed from the commencement of the school, and for his masterly and admirable management of it. Only two-pence per week was charged to the pupils, and for this small fee all school materials, except copy books were provided. The Committee were therefore compelled occasionally to make appeals for collateral aid in order to meet expenses. In December 1854, they requested Charles Dickens to give a reading of his "Christmas Carol." The request was complied with, and on the evening of the 28th of that month the famous author of "Pickwick" made his first appearance before a Bradford audience. The performance (which was one of Mr. Dickens' earliest attempts as a public reader) was given in St. George's Hall, and after all expenses had been defrayed a balance of £54 remained for the benefit of the Association. Mr. Dickens generously declined to receive any payment, and even bore his own expenses.

It is impossible, without carrying this chapter beyond reasonable limits, to dwell upon the various literary and educational institutions that have sprung into life during the past few years, such as the Board School movement, the Free Library, and the Technical College; moreover they do not come within the scope of "word-pictures" pertaining only to *Old* Bradford.

The tendency of the "modern institutions" which have been briefly noticed has been to develop and strengthen the commercial prosperity and material success of the town, much more than to open up sources of intelligent refinement and true elevation. The higher walks of science and philosophy have not been trod in Bradford as they ought in view of its vast wealth and its dense population. In this particular it has long been behind the race with many other centres of industry; but we would fain believe that in the recent formation and development of such institutions as the Philosophical Society (as reorganized); the Historical and Antiquarian Society; the Scientific Association; the Microscopical and Naturalists' Societies; the Literary Club, and the various Art and Musical Societies, we may read aright the "signs of the times," and thereby redeem very much of the past by a nobler and more glorious future.

Back of the Old Paper Hall.

Toll Booth and Old Shops,—Ivegate.

CHAPTER VI.

Old Public Buildings.

The Old Law Courts, Prisons, &c.

THE History of Bradford may almost be said to be written in its public buildings, for according to the growth and development of the town have these been called into requisition. If we were to begin at the very beginning, however, with a view to tracing out the order in which the public buildings of Bradford have succeeded each other down to the present day, we should require a much longer chapter than the one now at our disposal. The preservation of "law and order" has in all periods of history been one of the first requirements of society—hence the first building of a public character in this town of which we have any authentic record was the Toll-Booth and Hall of Pleas at the top of Ivegate, which was not only Bradford's most ancient place of confinement, but also the scene of its "Courts Baron" and "Courts Leet," at which the Abbot of Kirkstall and his colleague Sir William Calverley used to sit and dole out the sort of justice that our forefathers were wont to receive in the "good old times." In a bill that was filed by the inhabitants of Bradford against a certain John Rawson, sometime during the reign of Henry VII., occurs the curious item—"The old Court Rolls of Bradford were wont to be kept in a chest within the Toll-booth of Bradford, which chest had three locks and three keys, and one was kept by the Steward, the second by the King's freeholders and the third by the Bailiff of the town." It is not of much moment as to what has become of this ancient chest and its locks and keys, but the important question of the present whereabouts of those ancient records of Bradford's early history, the "old Court Rolls" is one deserving the attention of our local Antiquarian Society.

The passing of certain Acts of Parliament, and the incorporation of the town in modern times have stripped the old memorial courts of their ancient glory and privileges. The duties of the Court Leet lapsed into the hands of magistrates, and punishments for paltry cases were dealt with at the quarter sessions. But the old Court Rolls, wherever they may be, would tell us of the far-off times when the Manorial Steward and the Parish Constable were the most important of public functionaries; and when the ducking-stool for scolding house-wives; whipping at the cart tail, and incarceration in the pillory or the stocks were modes of punishment of every day occurrence.

The duties of the Pindar who had charge of the pinfold for strayed cattle; the Ale-taster who tested the quality of the liquors sold at the hostelries; the Beadle who looked after absentees from church have ages ago fallen into disuse, and instead thereof we have to day the unromantic and matter-of-fact Policeman.

The Court House which came next in order after the Hall of Pleas and Toll Booth was the one at the top of Westgate, nearly opposite the end of John Street. It has recently been altered beyond all former recognition, but a stone over the doorway still bears the date of its erection—1678—and the initials "H.M. I.M.;" indicating that it was then the property of the Marsdens, lords of the manor. By various purchases, Henry Marsden, of Gisburn, had become sole owner of the Bradford manor, from whom it descended to Henry Marsden of Wennington Hall, Lancashire, who in 1780 was succeeded

Old Justice Court.

by his brother and heir-at-law John Marsden, of Hornby Castle, who in 1795 conveyed the manorial property to Benjamin Rawson, in whose family the manor yet remains.

Several years ago the old Court House was occupied by Mr. John Hill, the maltster, who took a pride in showing the royal arms on the wall (in plaster) marking the position of the spot where the judge of he court used to sit.

Prior to the erection of the Court House in Hall Ings in 1834, our law-administering magnates were put to sad and undignified shifts for suitable accommodation in which to "hold court." At one time they sat in the old Court House in Westgate; at another in a room of the old Piece Hall, and for a time they occupied a shabby-looking building behind the New Inn (see sketch) which eventually came to be known as the "Old Justice Room." From the columns of the

Bradford Courier (Bradford's first newspaper) for 1825 and the two following years, we are enabled to catch a glimpse at the sort of "cases" that were dealt with by the magistrates at this place. Thus, at a petty sessions held here on May 24th, 1827, before the Rev. Lamplugh Hird, and E. C. Lister, Esq., W—— E—— of Tong, was convicted in the penalty of £5 and costs for poaching pheasants on the grounds of Col. Tempest, of Tong Hall. Three lads from Wibsey were convicted for stealing rooks from the rookeries at Bierley and Bowling. Three men, the two principals and a "bottle holder" in a fight at Fairweather Green, were adjudged to pay 50s. damages and costs, for a trespass by them during the fight in question; and John Thornton *alias* "Black Toppin," who had been apprehended at Black Abbey, was convicted on the charge of sheep stealing.

The Court, we may add, was held in the room at the top of the steps, and the culprits were confined in the hole underneath pending their being marched off to "durance vile."

Mr. E. C. Lister of Manningham Hall, who for nearly half a century was an influential Magistrate and Deputy-Lieutenant, for several years held regular petty sessions at the Spotted House, Manningham Lane, where a large share of Bradford's magisterial business was transacted. It was often observed that no man's opinions and decisions gave more general satisfaction than did "Justice Lister's."

The first prison in Bradford of which we have any authentic record, was the one beneath the old Toll Booth, at the top of Westgate. It was best known as "Nelson's Dungeon" from the circumstance of John Nelson's incarceration there in May 1744. From John's description of it, it must have been a miserable hole, but its successor, the old "lock-up" near Sun-bridge, appears to have been little better, as from its close proximity to the beck, it was so damp that prisoners who had been lodged in it but for a night presented a most wretched appearance when brought before the magistrates in the morning. For a time, one of the rooms in the old Cock-pit building was improvised as a prison, and was under the charge of John Ingham the constable. The public had every opportunity of "taking stock" of the prisoners in those days, for the wretched criminals had to walk all the way to Wakefield, under escort.

It was proposed to build a new Court House as early as the year 1825, and £2,000 were subscribed by the inhabitants, and a grant of £3,000 was made by the West Riding Magistrates at the Pontefract Quarter Sessions, but as the wish of the subscribers to have a voice in the selection of the site was strenuously opposed, the project fell through and nothing further was done until 1834.

For several years the Court House was considered to be the finest building in the town, though it has long since ceased to be regarded as such. As a public building it will of course be best remembered as a legal tribunal for many years. It will also be associated with the parliamentary elections of Bradford, for, from the election of 1835 almost down to the passing of the Ballot Act, the hustings for the nomination of members were erected here. Striking indeed is the contrast between the hard-fought struggles of those early political contests, and the sedate and orderly manner in which these things are now done; and yet there are those whose memories fondly turn to the "good old times" and who do not by any means regard the Ballot Act as an unalloyed blessing.

That relic of antiquity, the Manor Court, whose history goes far back into the "forgotten years" now exists in little more than its name. The altered conditions of property and the development of municipal legislation have done much to deprive this institution of its time-honoured duties and privileges. Once upon a time it had to decide all disputes as to encroachments, etc., and was responsible for the proper regulation of weights and measures. It was also the tribunal for the recovery of small debts; its debtors' prison being the notorious "Will Lee Hoil," (so called from the name of its custodian William Lee) in North Wing, which was closed in 1844 by virtue of the act for abolishing imprisonment for debts under £20.

Some of the old manorial customs did not die without a struggle. The "riding of the boundary" was kept up until 1823, and several small duties devolving upon the constable or bellman have only been given up within very recent times. This latter office was discharged for many years by members of the Bentley family.

Down to the year 1866, when the Corporation purchased the manorial rights of Bradford, the custom of "crying the fair" was faithfully observed, when the town-crier, in his dress of green and gold, appeared in the streets on the morning of the fair, and, after ringing his bell, made the announcement that the fair was to be holden for three days, "under our Sovereign lady the Queen, and Mary and Elizabeth Rawson, the ladies of this manor;" that all dues and tolls must be paid without any molestation, and "for every bloody fray, you'll have ten groats to pay. God save the Queen and the ladies of the manor!" The threatening portion of this announcement was hardly in keeping with these refined times. It smacked more of the middle ages, but did not sound amiss as coming from the lips of a functionary whose lineage was to be traced back to feudal times.

The duties of the Court Baron for the recovery of small debts passed into the Court of Requests, which had its offices on the site of the present Friends' Provident Institution, Darley Street. The Act establishing the latter Court, to represent Bradford and certain neighbouring towns, was passed in the year 1793. Its work is now discharged by the County Court.

The Old Workhouse

Was built for the poor of Bradford in the year 1738, and the structure, which only incurred an outlay of about £360, may yet be seen at Barkerend. No provision, however, was made in it for the relief of vagrants, and it was not until 1827 that any steps were taken

Old Workhouse, Barkerend.

to provide for this department, when it had become an institution in nearly all the neighbouring towns.

At a meeting held in the vestry of the Parish Church on the 29th June, 1827, Mr. Aked, senior Constable, in the chair, a committee consisting of the following gentlemen was appointed for the purpose of establishing the new vagrant office:— Messrs. William Maud, Thomas Inkersley, Richard Thornton, John Ward, John Bonnell, John Stead, Benjamin Wilkinson, Thomas Milthorp, James Bilton, Robert Ward, James Ellis, John Lee, J. A. Illingworth, and John Aked. Mr. John Ingham was appointed Vagrant Master. By reason chiefly of its central position, the old Cock-pit building was fixed upon for the vagrant office, which was at once put into thorough repair.

Some idea may be formed of its original proportions when it is stated that as a vagrant office it consisted of a watch-house; a lock-up room; three sleeping-rooms with beds for male and female vagrants, and a room for the vagrant master and for committee meetings.

"On the whole," says the *Bradford Courier*, of that date, "a more commodious spot could not have been chosen. Not being a thoroughfare it is comparatively retired, yet it is centrical and near the place where the magistrates hold their weekly meetings."

The first monthly report showed that twelve persons had been relieved and 115 lodged and relieved at a cost of £1 3s. 5d. In addition twenty-six persons had been induced to leave the town, not having any visible means of obtaining a livelihood while in it. Afterwards weekly reports were issued which showed that the average number of persons relieved per week was about fifteen, and considering the small outlay incurred (about four shillings) the ratepayers could hardly complain of reckless or unnecessary extravagance.

The Bradford Union was instituted in February, 1837, and included the whole of the townships in the parish (except Haworth) and several important out-townships. It was placed under the direction of a board of thirty-two guardians, the magistrates residing within such townships being guardians *ex-officio*. Six members of the board were appointed by Bradford, three were returned for Horton, and two each were appointed for Bowling, North Bierley, Pudsey and Thornton. Mr. J. Reid Wagstaff, solicitor, was appointed Clerk to the Board, and Superintendent Registrar-general, which offices he held until his death in 1851, when he was succeeded by Mr. John Darlington. On the 29th September, 1848, the Bradford Union was divided into two, one to embrace only the borough, and the other to include the out-townships. This division took place in consequence of the Union having become too complicated and cumbersome for convenient management.

One of the most extraordinary disturbances of the public peace that ever happened in Bradford was that known as the Poor Law Riot of 1837. So very well satisfied were the inhabitants, especially the lower classes, with the old pauperising system of administering relief, that the introduction of the new poor law was regarded with detestation, and resisted by violent opposition. The story of the riot will be found recorded in another chapter.

In course of time it was found that the new system was, with all its faults, a vast improvement upon the old. The "Bradford Union" became a thoroughly organised institution, and when the first half of the century had been reached it was found necessary to replace the old Workhouse at Barkerend by a larger and more commodious building. Mr. Charles Rhodes, then one of the guardians, took an active interest in this movement, and helped to carry it to a successful completion. He laid the foundation stone of the present Workhouse at Little Horton in 1851. The cost of the building and site amounted to £11,000, but enlargements have since been made involving an outlay of not less than £16,000.

The Old Piece Hall.

Old Piece Hall.

The erection of this building in the year 1773, takes us back far beyond the age of factories and steam engines. The population of the town was not much more than four thousand, but Bradford dale and the surrounding villages were fairly populated with hand-loom weavers and spinners who brought their pieces—calamancoes, shalloons and tammies—to the Bradford market for sale.

Previous to the erection of the Piece Hall, those manufacturers who came from a distance had been in the habit of exhibiting their pieces in a large room in the White Lion Inn, Kirkgate, which was divided into closets; but those who resided in the town had piece rooms in or near their houses, while some displayed their goods on the side walk in Kirkgate in pretty much the same fashion as the vendors of pack-thread have done in more recent times in front of the Nag's Head and Shoulder of Mutton.

But, as Bradford became noted for its stuff trade, and the number of merchants who came to purchase goods rapidly increased, it was found that this sort of market accommodation would not do. The proposed building of a suitable Piece Hall was therefore hailed with joy, and from the moment of its opening it was a pronounced success. One may well imagine that an erection costing above £1,500, as the Piece Hall did, would in those simple times create no little sensation.

Plain and homely folks were the people who first gathered within its walls to buy and sell and get gain. The well-to-do half farmers and half tradesmen would be dressed in hodden-grey, and knee breeches, set off with the wig and cocked hat that were worn a hundred years ago. Rough in speech they would be, for they used the guttural dialect then spoken in Bradford-dale and beyond. Hard-handed and hard-headed were they also, for they were themselves hard workers, being both woolstapler and spinner, and perhaps weaver too. But we have it on good authority that they treated their work-people—weavers, combers, and farm servants—with kindness, and were themselves so honest that when one of them "benked," as they termed it, it was the talk of the whole country side for many a day.

Unlike some of the manufacturers of our own day, they did not make haste to be rich, but were satisfied if their money came in slowly and surely. This sturdy and honest old race have, however, long been laid in the church or chapel yard, and the building in which they met, and where our infant worsted trade was nurtured and brought to nearly its present growth, is now a thing of the past.

At the time of the erection of the Piece Hall, Bradford was fortunate in having its chronicler to make due record of the event. This was James Hartley, the schoolmaster, whose useful little book was printed in 1776. After describing the dimensions of the building, its plan of operation, and the kind of goods that were bought and sold in it, he winds up with this sublime peroration—"'Tis wonderful to behold to what perfection this most useful branch of business is arrived at within the compass of a very few years, comparatively speaking, in this part of *Yorkshire*, but especially at Bradford. How amazingly great is the goodness of God towards us, who from one period to another is raising up a set of men, endowing them with power and faculties suitable to the employment they are set apart for; stirring them up ever with emulation; blessing their endeavours, not only with a sufficient competency, but many with great abundance, to the mutual welfare and happiness of thousands of their fellow creatures, who are constantly employed by them: for trade and commerce is the bank of plenty, not only to us, but to every part of the globe!"

Notwithstanding its "large and commodious" proportions, not many years had passed away ere it was found necessary to add a large wing to the Piece Hall. But when the old hand-loom weaving gave place to steam and factory labour, even this enlargement was found to be insufficient and unequal to accommodating all the Bradford manufacturers, and thus it came to pass that the old market building on the other side of Hustler Gate began to be used for piece rooms. Mr. John Foster, of Queensbury, migrated here, and others soon followed him.

One of the greatest drawbacks to the usefulness and success of the Piece Hall was its system of stalls or closets, which did not afford sufficient privacy to their several occupiers for transacting business, and it was a cause for complaint that when a merchant was in treaty with a manufacturer for the purchase of goods, unscrupulous manufacturers in neighbouring stalls would crowd around to hear what was said, and to learn the prices at which pieces were being sold.

The stringent bye-laws, framed as far back as the year 1790, were allowed to remain in force too long. They had long ceased to be applicable to the changed condition of things. Read in the light of the present day they will at least amuse the reader, especially when he is told that at the time when they were drawn up it was considered nothing short of a privilege to be permitted to purchase Bradford goods. We give them unabridged.

RULES and ORDERS to be observed by the Merchants,
Buyers of Goods and Occupiers of Stands, in the Manufacturers' Hall,
in BRADFORD.

I.

That the Gates of the Hall shall be opened from the First of April to the Twenty-ninth Day of September, every Thursday morning, at Eight o'clock, and from September the Twenty-ninth to the First of April, at half past Eight, for the Reception of Woollen Goods, and at Ten, on the Ringing of the Bell, the Merchants and Buyers shall be admitted and not before.

II.

That if any Horse shall be found standing in the Hall Yard above the space of Five Minutes after the Bell rings on, the Owner of such Horse shall forfeit One Shilling to the Keeper of the Hall, who shall seize and keep the same till the Penalty be paid.

III.

That at half-past Eleven o'clock, the Bell shall ring off, and the Market shall be closed; the Merchants and Buyers shall quit the Hall, and the Gates be shut at half-past Twelve.

IV.

That every person who sells Goods either before the Bell rings on, or after the Bell rings off, shall forfeit Five Shillings for every such offence, Two Shillings and Sixpence to the Informer, and Two Shillings and Sixpence to the Fund belonging to the Hall; and if the said penalty be not immediately paid after full proof thereof, the Hall-keeper shall seize a Piece, the property of the Offender, and keep the same one week, and if the Offender do not discharge the said penalty, the said Piece shall be publicly sold, and after the Forfeiture and Expenses be taken thereout, the remainder shall be returned to the Owner.

V.

The Market for the sale of Yarn to be opened at Two o'clock in the Afternoon, and continue till half-past Three.

VI.

Every person who sells Yarn in the Hall either before the bell rings for the market to begin, or after ringing off, shall forfeit One Shilling for every Gross so sold, and for smaller Quantities in proportion, the Penalty and Forfeiture to be recovered as in the Fourth Rule.

VII.

That if any Person or Persons be found exposing Goods to Sale, which are not his own Property, or the Property of a Subscriber, or Occupier of a Stand, shall forfeit Five Shillings, the same to be recovered as in the Fourth Rule.

VIII.

That no person shall be suffered to take a Partner into his Stand on Penalty of Five Shillings per Day, One Shilling to the Informer, and Four Shillings to the Hall Fund, the same to be recovered as in the Fourth Rule.

IX.

That if any Manufacturer's Property be invaded by the encroachment of his neighbour, or any Manufacturer behave himself in a rude or disorderly manner, so as to give public offence, complaint being made to the Trustees, with full proof thereof, it shall, and may be lawful for the said Trustees to expel and turn out of the Hall, such rude and disorderly Person or Persons, except he or they make suitable satisfaction, returning him or them, (if a Subscriber,) half of his or their Purchase Money.

X.

That all Goods be delivered a Quarter of a Yard longer than they are commonly called, to wit, those called Thirty yards, to be Thirty yards and One Quarter; Forty yards, to be Forty yards and One Quarter; Forty-two yards and a half, to be Forty-two yards and three-quarters. If they measure the length called, and not One quarter over, to abate Sixpence. If they do not measure the length called, to be optional with the Buyer, whether he take them or not; but if the Buyer insist of having the Piece or Pieces, he shall abate no more than Sixpence each Piece, excepting with the consent of the Seller.

XI.

As Broad Calamancos and Russels are of greater value than common Goods, if they do not measure Forty-five yards and a Quarter, to abate One Shilling; if short of Forty-five yards, to be optional with the Buyer, as in the foregoing Rule If any Piece be cut, if it does not measure half a yard more than it is called, to abate Sixpence.

XII.

That a Standard Yard be kept in the Hall, and when any dispute ariseth betwixt the Buyer and Seller about the Length of any Piece or Pieces, the goods in dispute shall be brought to the Hall, and measured by the Keeper thereof, and both Parties shall abide by his admeasurement, and the person found in the wrong, shall pay to the said Keeper One Penny for each Piece he measureth.

N.B. That the Dispute about the Length of Pieces be settled the Day the goods are bought.

When it was discovered that the manufacturers were deserting the place in order to take possession of piece-rooms of their own, attempts were made to adapt the old stalls to suit modern requirements, but with little success, as on the 28th July 1853, it ceased to be the "Piece Hall" any longer, and the building passed into private hands. The manufacturers, meanwhile had located themselves in various parts of the town, but chiefly in the neighbourhood of Charles Street, while the merchants erected the large and palatial warehouses which are now the pride and ornament of the town.

As the scene of local political events the old Piece Hall could justly claim to be the parent of the Court House in Hall Ings. From the steps in front (see illustration), Lord Morpeth, and Mr. (afterwards Lord) Brougham, in the contest of 1830, addressed the (county) electors of Bradford, when the audience had the privilege of listening to two of the most eloquent speakers of the day. On the 13th December 1832, a large and enthusiastic audience assembled at the same place, for by the passing of the famous Reform Bill, Bradford had received its enfranchisement and the right of sending two members to parliament, and this was the occasion for nominating its first candidates for election.

Old Market House.

This interesting old place, which in former times was known as the "Market House," was one of the most quaint-looking erections that ever adorned the streets of Bradford; indeed it looked much older than it had any right to do for it was only built at the close of the last, and brought into use during the first year of the present century.

It was erected by Mr. Rawson, Lord of the Manor, in order to provide better accommodation than was to be found at the bottom of Westgate, where from time immemorial the market had been held; and it is worthy of note that that gentleman had been at the pains (so he said) of going all the way to Italy in order to meet with a suitable design for the new market building.

It was regarded as a wonderful architectural embellishment to the town in its better days, but we doubt if its merits were sufficiently appreciated by a more recent generation. It would certainly be a striking object when Bradford was not very prodigal of public buildings. At the period of its erection it was looked upon as a great stride in advance of the times, inasmuch as it covered a considerable area, had two bazaars and an assembly room, in which were held the concerts and oratorios of the Philharmonic Society, and the gay and festive assemblies of the Bradford aristocracy. The lower part was let as butchers' shambles and green market, and there were besides two butter crosses and "divers other conveniences." The part opposite the Hope and Anchor Inn was first erected, and at that corner was the staircase leading to the upper room in which the Rev. Mr. Crosse held his Sunday School.

Such, however, were the rapid strides that Bradford now made in commercial prosperity and population, that even this place became altogether inadequate to its marketable requirements, and in 1824 the larger and more commodious market near the Manor Hall was built. Henceforward its fate became linked with the Piece Hall in close proximity, and it was better known as a market-place for the sale of worsted pieces.

But if the career of the old Market House was a short one, it was not without some honour in its day. It had been the means of gathering around it and centralising—if not actually calling into

Old Market Building.

being—certain other useful and important institutions. Moreover it gave the name to the best and most central of Bradford thoroughfares —Market Street, which had formerly been known as New Street. Just across the way (in Bank Street) was the Post Office, which like a faithful companion, had kept the Market good company for many a day before its departure from Westgate. In 1803, Mr. Edmund Peckover of Eastbrook House, established the bank, afterwards so well known as "Harris's Old Bank," which gave the name of Bank Street to the thoroughfare connecting Market Street with Hustler-gate. In this same street that useful citizen and staunch conservative, Thomas Inkersley, began his career as a printer and publisher, and in one of the bazaars of the market opposite, was printed by him the very first newspaper of which the town could boast—the *Bradford Courier*.

We cannot notice all the surroundings of the old Market, but must not omit the old building that occupied the site of the present tower of the Exchange. This corner, which for many years prior to its demolition was known as "Bartle's Corner" formed part of the market building, and was used as the butter cross. A large room above supported on massive stone pillars, was devoted to the drama at such times and seasons as Mr. L. S. Thompson (senr.) the proprietor, deemed to be most advantageous to the public in general, and his own personal interests in particular. Here was the favourite resort of such patrons of the "sock and buskin" as dared to brave the evil repute then attaching to "playhouse visiting," and here they were treated to such high-class performances as *Tom and Jerry*, *The Spoilt Child*, &c., in all of which Mr. Thompson, and his sister Mrs. Lamb took the leading characters, while Mr. Lamb attended to the door and took the money.

Those of our readers who "dote upon the military" may be interested to know that in the year 1826 the old Market House was used as a barracks for the 32nd Regiment of foot. It was not large enough however to accommodate the entire regiment, and so the remainder were lodged in a large warehouse in Tyrrel Street.

There is yet another landmark that calls for notice before taking leave of the old Market House. We allude to the old Market Cross—or at least all that remained of it—that formerly stood at the junction of Bank Street with Hustler-gate. If Mr. James' conjecture be correct that the old cross may date its origin to the days of the De Lacies, this is indeed the most ancient of all our time-honoured relics. What a link between Past and Present, and what a span of centuries of history is taken in by the sight of this rude emblem of bygone ages! We are at least taken back to that far off period when the Charter (dated 1251) to hold a market at Bradford was granted to Edmund de Lacy, which set forth that he and his heirs should have *(inter alia)* "one market every week, on Thursday, at his Manor of Bradforde." It may perhaps, be always a matter of uncertainty whether the Market Cross reared its head at so early a period as this, but we do know that more than two centuries ago it stood erect near the bottom of Westgate, where the market was then held, for in the Court Rolls of the time it is ordered "that the street be repaired round the Market Cross." Those were the days when Bradford like all other towns in good old England had its Puritan bigots "who, (says our chronicler) in their zeal against the emblem of the Cross, broke off the top, so that only a portion of the shaft and the pediment remained." It is not generally known that all that is left of this time-worn relic, as shewn in our illustration, has for some years past had a peaceful resting place in a secluded corner of Peel Park.

Old Market Cross.

The old Exchange.

This building which yet stands at the bottom of Piccadilly, and has recently been purchased by Mr. George Brown and transformed into a huge shop, was built for the purposes of "a public news room, a ball-room, a billiard-room and their necessary adjuncts." It was the first attempt at providing the town with a building that should meet its social as well as its commercial requirements.

Previous to its erection in 1828, the inhabitants had often been put to sad and inconvenient shifts for accommodation in which to hold meetings of an instructive and entertaining character. Musical oratorios were frequently performed in Christ Church. Lectures were sometimes given in Thompson's Theatre, or in the school-room in the Market House. In 1831 William Cobbett was invited to give a lecture in Bradford on a subject then agitating the country, viz: "The return to cash payments, as adopted by the Government," and it was with some difficulty that a lecture room was secured for him. It may have been that his peculiar views on that subject stood in the way of the Exchange-room being placed at his disposal, A news-room over the Roebuck passage in Market Street was offered, but declined by Mr. Cobbett, and eventually a large room in the Talbot Hotel was selected. All the leading magnates of the town were present to hear the popular orator, and Mr. John Rand, then an enthusiastic politician of the Tory school, put several questions to the lecturer.

Bradford was greatly indebted to Dr. Outhwaite for the erection of the Exchange, who not only in this, but in many another instance showed how much he had the interests of the town at heart. It was in February 1825, that a committee was first formed for carrying out the project. The gentlemen who composed it were Drs. Outhwaite and Sharp, and Messrs. John Wood, junr., Geo. Stansfeld, Henry Leah, John Pearson, Joshua Mann, Richard Thornton, Henry Harris and Thomas Rishworth. The money was proposed to be raised in shares of £25 each; each shareholder to have a vote or votes according to the number of the shares he held. The ladies who had honoured the subscription list with their names were to have a power of voting by proxy.

The site opposite the Piece Hall was fixed upon, and the cost of this and the building was estimated at £6,000. The *Bradford Courier* availed itself of the opportunity to offer a few hints as to the architecture of the proposed building. "This," it goes on to say, "is a matter about which we feel particularly anxious, because there are so many public erections throughout the kingdom which stand the monuments either of bad taste or of niggardly economy. It by no means follows that the most *expensive* is therefore the most *beautiful* architectural design. There is often more loveliness in the most perfect simplicity than in the greatest departure from it. We particularly recommend to the committee to hold fast to the models which have been handed down to us from the days of Greek excellence. Gothic is of course out of the question for an erection of this nature, and no mongrel or nondescript style which we have ever seen is at all comparable with the unadorned chastity of the Doric or the Ionic."

However widely opinions might have differed as to the architectural merits of the building, its situation was unquestionably a good one, and the fact that the venture was a successful one was but another evidence of the growing prosperity of the town. At first it was only known by the modest title of "The Public Rooms," but when it became known to be open (for an annual subscription) to the merchants, manufacturers, and tradesmen who attended the Bradford market, it soon got the name of the "Exchange," and the street in which it stood was called "Exchange Street." When this street afterwards changed its name to Piccadilly (a most unnecessary change we venture to think), the good people of Skinner Lane also went in for an alteration, and styled their thoroughfare Cheapside—a piece of snobbery which did not escape the notice of Professor Blackie on the occasion of his recent visit to Bradford.

Many and brilliant have been the scenes witnessed within the walls of the old Exchange. At the balls and assemblies held here were to be seen "all the quality and fashion of the town and neighbourhood—a numerous and stately group." On the occasion of the return of Bradford's first members to Parliament in 1832, (Messrs. Lister and Hardy) all the rooms were thrown open for a ball in Mr. Hardy's honour, and were crammed by that gentleman's political supporters. Again, in 1839, a grand fancy dress ball was given to commemorate the septennial return of the Bishop Blaize festival, the proceeds of which were to be handed over to the Poor Relief Fund. This was a magnificent affair. The tickets were a guinea each, and in order to raise as large a surplus as possible for the relief of the poor, the splendid supper which was served up was furnished by the families of the committee of management, the wine being gratuitously and liberally supplied from the cellars of Mr. J. G. Horsfall. The large room was brilliantly decorated. At the upper end was a transparency of Her Majesty the Queen, on the right of which was a representation of Bishop Blaize, and on the left a figure of Jason surmounted by the fleece. The windows were richly decorated by blue damask curtains.

But as there is no gold without some alloy, it so happened that even these grand and joyous events did not give satisfaction to everyone. They were regarded as too much restricted to the "upper ten,"—a fact which gave rise to a spirit of rivalry between what were then styled the "aristocracy" and the "shopocracy" of Bradford. The latter, not to be outdone, commenced a series of assemblies hardly less fashionable or gay than those at the Exchange, which were held at the Sun Hotel, when that fine old hostelry was in its rosiest days.

The foundation stone of the New Exchange in Market Street was laid by Lord Palmerston on the 9th of August, 1864, "with such a display of pomp and circumstance," says Mr. James, "as has rarely been witnessed in Bradford." In 1867, the Old Exchange was purchased for £9000 for the Bradford Post Office, and it was used as such up to the time of entering into possession of the new Post Office in Forster Square, on September 1st, 1887.

The Dispensary and Infirmary.

The Bradford Dispensary, which it is almost needless to say was the germ of that most useful of all our public institutions, the Infirmary, was born and cradled in troublous times. The year 1825 was one of the most disastrous that has ever befallen this town, and it was in that year that the Dispensary was established. The twenty-three weeks' struggle between the weavers and woolcombers of Bradford and their employers, for a higher rate of wages, had produced an amount of distress and misery the like of which had never been known before; and in November, the painful fact was revealed that not less than three thousand persons were out of employment, and in actual want of the bare necessaries of life. Noble and praiseworthy efforts were made to alleviate the distress as much as possible, and an organisation, of which the vicar, Mr. Heap, was at the head, was formed for the dispensation of charity. Large funds were required, and happily were forthcoming, in order to stave off the threatened famine, and some idea may be gained of the magnitude of the work of charity that was carried on when it is stated that within one week nearly seventy loads of flour and oatmeal alone were distributed among two thousand families. Famine and privation were soon followed by their grim companions, sickness and disease, and it became necessary to turn the stream of charity in the direction of supplying healing medicines to the sick and dying.

A meeting of gentlemen was held in the vestry of the Parish Church for the purpose of considering what had best be done, and it was ultimately resolved that a dispensary should be established in Bradford "for the use of the indigent poor of the town and its vicinity." A committee was formed; the town was canvassed for subscriptions, and a house, the property of Mr. Charles Harris, at the junction of Peckover Street with High Street, was engaged at a rental of £23 per annum.

This was the origin of the Bradford Infirmary, and in this unpretentious building, the kindly offices of this noble charity were faithfully discharged until the erection in 1827 of the larger and more convenient edifice in Darley Street, now used as the Bradford Subscription Library.

Old Dispensary, High Street.

In contrast with the systematic means now adopted of raising the necessary funds for so gigantic an institution as the Infirmary has become, it will be interesting to notice how such funds were raised previous to the adoption of any organised method. In August 1825, Messrs. James Ellis & Co., the occupiers of the Soke Mills, resolved to appropriate the whole amount of fines that should from time to time accumulate, for the support of the Dispensary, and which up to that date amounted to £5. The talented editor of the *Bradford Courier*, Mr. Henry D. Inglis, who under the pseudonym of "Derwent Conway" had gained a high reputation as an author, gave a lecture on "Phrenology"—price of admission 2s. 6d.—the proceeds of which were devoted to the funds of the Dispensary. Sermons were preached as follows in aid of the same funds; in Sion Chapel by Dr. Steadman, when £10 were collected; at Tong Church by the Rev. Mr. Heald (the "Cyril Hall" of *Shirley*), collection £7; at Bierley Chapel a special service was given which realised £6 6s. 0d. and by a service in the Bradford Roman Catholic Chapel the sum of £10 was raised. On October 1827, a grand oratorio of sacred music was performed in Christ Church, the band "comprising the whole of the musical talent of Bradford and the neighbourhood," consisting of a hundred performers, all of whom gave their services gratuitously. The charges for admission were—body of the church 3s.; gallery 2s.; side aisles 1s.; and the amount realised for the Dispensary amounted to £80 4s. 0d.

Among the earliest bequests of private individuals may be mentioned £50 each from Mrs. Bacon and Miss Balme; £200 from Mrs. Simes; a legacy of £150 left by Mr. Samuel Broadley, and the gift of £100 by Richard Fountayne Wilson, M.P., who wisely suggested the erection of fever wards as important accessories.

The ceremony of laying the foundation stone of the new Dispensary, which took place on May 29th 1826, was to have been performed by Mr. Benjamin Rawson, the Lord of the Manor, but for some unexplained reason that duty was discharged by Mr. Heap the vicar. The institution had then been in existence a year, and during that time upwards of 2,000 patients had been admitted on its books of whom 1,559 had been discharged cured, 115 relieved, and 520 still remained under treatment. Between five and six hundred patients had been the objects cf medical or surgical treatment at their own homes.

In view of these important facts and figures it was felt that the Dispensary had fully justified its existence. A dinner was prepared at the Talbot Hotel for its officers and subscribers, at which several of the officers of the regiment then quartered in the town were invited to be present.

It was believed that the new structure in Darley Street would be fully "abreast of the times" for many years to come, but so rapid an increase of population with a corresponding increase of patients, had not been reckoned upon, and in little short of fourteen years it was discovered that it was too small for the further development of the objects and purposes of an infirmary. Accordingly the new erection at the top of Westgate was reared and completed in 1843 at a cost, including site, of £9,500. From this fresh starting point this most beneficent charity has gone on developing and extending its resources until it has assumed the gigantic proportions that we behold to-day.

Increased responsibilities have however necessitated a larger increase of its funds, but we believe that no appeal for public sympathy and support on behalf of this institution has ever yet been made in vain. The Bradford Infirmary has had many friends and patrons who during life have contributed liberally to its financial necessities, or at death have left substantial sums to swell out its capital fund. Others again, as in the case of Mr. Charles Rhodes, and the late Rev. J. P. Chown, by kindly words and noble deeds have kept alive the public interest in its welfare. Nor must we omit to refer to those who in their character as physicians and surgeons to the institute—promoted its best interests and raised it to its present high and honourable position by the most faithful and disinterested services. The names of men like Drs. Sharp, Outhwaite, Mossman and McTurk are yet fragrant to memory.

The old Theatres.

THE early days of the drama in Bradford may not furnish a very illustrious chapter of local history, but the subject is one by no means void of interest, and we think that no apology can be necessary for attempting to show how our forefathers found amusement and recreation.

It was not till the close of last century that Bradford could boast in anything approaching to a permanent platform for theatrical performances. Previous to this the pleasure-loving portion of the community had to be satisfied with such stage representations as were produced periodically by such strolling companies as found their way hither on each returning Bradford fair. However questionable these may have been as exponents of the drama in country towns and villages, they could at least lay claim to considerable antiquity, for the stereotyped "penny gaffs" were a time-honoured institution, and could date back their origin for three centuries.

And who shall say that even these attempts to pourtray the "sublime imaginings of the immortal Shakespeare" did not exercise a refining and elevating influence in times when the common people were in the most deplorable ignorance, and delighted only in sports of a low and degrading character?

But even when the population had increased in numbers and intelligence, Bradford was far from being a congenial soil for the cultivation of the drama. The more respectable and well-to-do of the working people, many of whom inherited the puritanical prejudices of their fathers, regarded the "play-house" as no fit place for honest folks to be seen at, and had about as much sympathy for it as they had for the brawling tavern or the roystering cock-pit. Actors and actresses were men and women to be pitied and avoided.

Coming down to more recent times when the town had lost much of its rural aspect, and the former quietness of its streets had given place to the bustle and commotion of factory life, we still find Bradford far behind some lesser towns, both in the matter of its appreciation of the drama and the general character of its amusements. When its population had reached to 35,000 and its wealth had increased in a still greater degree, no provision whatever had been made to meet the social and intellectual demands of the people. There was no Mechanics' Institute, no lecture or concert hall worthy of the name, and need we add, no theatre that deserved to be called such; while such towns as Doncaster, Wakefield and Halifax had long been honoured by the visits of the Keans and Kembles and other eminent actors of the day. "Fifty years ago," writes the author of "Natterin' Nan," "even the legitimate drama had small chance of success in Bradford. For so large a population, playgoers were not numerous. There was no regular theatre. The few gentry living amongst us—always too few in a manufacturing town—for the most part discountenanced the stage. Working people were too illiterate to enjoy and too ill-paid to support it; and tradesmen, shop-keepers and others were altogether too sordid or too sanctimonious. The long hour system which had then too long prevailed everywhere had ground down both master and workman to the lowest point of mental degradation. Robbed of leisure, and all but without the means of improvement, the working orders were given up in the main to hard drinking, the natural result, and apparently the natural solace of unhealthy, of exhausting, and of ill requited, and consequently hopeless toil. The recreations of the period were in harmony with this brutal state—man-battles, cock-battles, dog-battles, etc. . . . . Turning from these to the upper portion of the working classes—the employers—and we find that for the children of the sock and buskin the prospects were not much brighter. It may well be believed that those who were grinding the very children of the poor for twelve, nay fourteen hours a day, were not distinguished for refinement of thought or tenderness of feeling. What did men like these, whether rich or poor, want with a theatre—a theatre, the home of Art, of Eloquence, of Music, of Poesy, the fairy-land of Imagination, of Fancy, of Genius? Why, to such beings as these—mere Gileadites—hewers of wood and drawers of water—the very Temple of the Muses seemed but a synagogue of Satan, a flimsy and painted palace of the enemy of souls."

The stage on which Thespis the Greek first trod was nothing more than a cart covered with planks. That upon which his disciples at

Bradford first appeared was quite as lowly and unpretentious, for it consisted only of a few boards shaped into a platform in an old barn. The parallel goes no further, however, for while Bradford numbers its two hundred and twenty thousand inhabitants, and yet can barely support two theatres, the rapid development of the drama with the Greeks was such that within fifty years from the first dramatic effort of Thespis, the finest of the tragedies of Æschylus and Sophocles had been performed, and at no great distance of time after this, the large stone theatre of Athens had been built, a structure capable of holding thirty thousand spectators!

The old barn we have referred to was located in Southgate (now Sackville Street), Westgate; and here it was that in the year 1810 the first permanent stage was fitted up in Bradford for dramatic performances. Its proprietor and manager was Mr. L. S. Thompson, father of the once famous Lysander Thompson, hence it came to be known as "Thompson's Theatre." But, unassuming as the place was, it served as a starting point from which to aim at higher things. In course of time Mr. Thompson vacated the barn, and engaged a fair-sized room, reached by a flight of steps, in the back yard of the King's Arms Inn, Westgate. In its better days it had been used as an Assembly room, but that was when the King's Arms was a place of some consequence—a real *bona-fide* hostelry of the grand old type, when dram shops were unknown.

Here Mr. Thompson had a stage fitted up, and continued his theatrical business for a few years. An old account book belonging to the late Mr. Booth Illingworth, builder and contractor, contains this interesting item:—

"To fitting up Stage and Seats for Mr. Thompson, £7 19s. 3d."

On the opposite side of the yard was a building known as "Longbottom's School," afterwards occupied by Mr. Anthony Nesbit as a Commercial and Mathematical Academy, where the junior members of several old Bradford families were first initiated into the mysteries of the three "R's."

In the year 1820, Mr. Thompson left the King's Arms Yard, and started a theatre of some pretensions over the butter-cross, in Market Street. The place formed part of the building afterwards known as "Bartle's Corner." This theatre was capable of holding seven or eight hundred persons, and was well fitted up and furnished with stage, scenery, and other accessories.

Mr. Thompson, the proprietor, was himself an actor of no mean order. By his skilfulness in impersonating Yorkshire characters he obtained the sobriquet of "Yorkshire Thompson." But clever as he was, his son, Lysander, afterwards far excelled him in this particular line.

It was at this time that Mr. Thompson persuaded the poet John Nicholson to write for him a drama in three acts, entitled the "Robber of the Alps," which was so well received that he was induced to try his dramatic powers again, and produced the "Siege of Bradford."

This was successfully acted for the benefit of Mr. Macaulay, one of the company, and yielded a profit of £47; but Nicholson derived no benefit from the performance, although he had been led to believe that he would receive a share of the profits.

During his connection with the theatre in Market Street, Mr. Thompson brought some good talent to Bradford. The Abbott family, consisting of Mr. and Mrs. Abbott, and two sons and a daughter, were much thought of in their time. Altogether the place was ably managed, and possessed many attractions, but failing to meet with sufficient patronage and encouragement, the worthy proprietor became disheartened, and finally abandoned it, after a varying career reaching over two or three years.

On the vacation of the theatre over the butter-cross by Mr. Thompson, which happened soon after the winter fair, "Jemmy" Wild, whose travelling booth was more familiarly known as "Old Wild's," took it for about two months, and here, with the addition of a clown to his usual stock-in-trade, and with the advantage of the scenery and stage left behind by Mr. Thompson, he entertained admiring audiences by his customary round of conjuring tricks, juvenile acrobatic exploits, and the wonderful feats of the pony "Billy;" with small extras in the shape of ballet dances and short farces, "never before attempted" previous to his removal here.

But as yet, Wild had not started upon his dramatic career, and we must leave him for the present, in order to continue our notice of what were then termed "patent theatres," as distinguished from the travelling booths that received their permission to play during fair time, by privilege of the lord of the manor.

Next to that of Thompson's the "patent" theatre known as "Smedley's" follows in order, although they were separated by an interval of fourteen years. Mr. Smedley came to Bradford in the summer of 1836, and from his play-bills we learn that he was here during the latter half of that and the two following years, 1837 and 1838. His theatre, a large wooden structure capable of holding about twelve hundred persons, and of a superior sort to the ordinary wooden buildings of that time, stood upon the site of Messrs. McKean, Tetley & Co.'s warehouse, in Peel Square.

The surroundings of it were, it need hardly be said, in striking contrast to what they present to-day. The warehouse-building period had but just begun, and Smedley's "Temple of the Muses" stood almost alone. The space between it and Well Street was frequently used as the fair ground, and here the travelling showmen periodically pitched their tents, before the green market in front of Rawson Place and the ground adjoining the old Christ Church were brought into use for that purpose.

Mr. Smedley came from Sleaford in Lincolnshire. He was a tragedian *on* the stage, but *off* it, a dandified gentleman, full of self-confidence and importance. He was proud of his establishment, and very enterprising, and certainly *deserved* success, if he might not always command it. His theatre was "highly respectable," comfortable, well arranged throughout, and possessed good scenery, some of which was from the brush of J. Wilson Anderson, a local artist of considerable ability. The company, though not large, was select and good. In his play-bills, Mr. Smedley states that "It is quite certain the town of Bradford is entitled to amusements on the scale of talent and respectability equal to any in the country, *but if so, they must be paid for at the same rate.* Accordingly he fixed his "bill of fare" at "*Boxes*, 3s.; Pit, 2s.; Gallery, 1s." This scale he sustained throughout his stay in Bradford, and had good houses too, his best patrons, however, being the "gods" of the gallery.

Although he had a good company, Mr. Smedley nevertheless went in for the "Star" system. One of the most distinguished of these was the great tragedian, G. V. Brooke, whose tragic fate on board the *London* will long be remembered. He fulfilled a six nights' engagement here, beginning on Monday, June 19th, 1837. Brooke was at this time creating a great sensation in Dublin, and Bradford was the third place at which he appeared after leaving that city. His performances here were chiefly confined to Shakspearian characters.

One of the members of Mr. Smedley's stock company was Mr. Rogers, afterwards so well known as one of the Haymarket staff. He was an Oddfellow, and such was the estimation in which he was held by his brethren of that Order, that no fewer than thirty-nine Lodges of the town and district assembled to do him honour on the occasion of his benefit. The foundation stone of the Oddfellows' Hall, Thornton Road, had just been laid, and from this place the procession started on its way to the theatre.

Mr. Mosley, afterwards for so many years lessee of the Theatre Royal, Duke Street, was another member of Smedley's company. In the performance of *Hamlet*, Mr. Smedley took the leading character, Mr. Mosley, "Horatio," and Mr. Rogers, the "Ghost." The following appear to have been among the favourite pieces of this company:—*Jane Shore; George Barnwell; The Jewess, or the Council of Constance; Speed the Plough; The Rake's Progress;* and *A New Way to Pay Old Debts.* These were often interspersed by Shakespeare's dramas, the production of which did not then, at any rate, mean bankruptcy to the proprietor. There was, of course, the inevitable (or what seems to have been *then* inevitable) interlude between the first piece and the farce. This was invariably made up of a song or dance, (notably the "Highland Fling") or both. The very best actors, whether they could sing or not, were sometimes required to take part in this portion of the evening's programme. Thus, in one of such interludes, Mr. Rogers is put down for the song "Has your Mother sold her Mangle?"—Mr. Mosley takes part in a trio entitled "O, tell her I love her!"—And even the great Lysander Thompson could not escape taking part in this humiliating business, as he is announced to sing a piece bearing the following curious title—"The Improvements of Bradford, or a peep at the Wool Trade, with sketches of Jason and the Golden

Fleece, Queen Medea, the two Brazen Bulls, and the Wide-Awake Dragon, with Dobbys, Plainbacks, Piece makers, Combers, Comb pots, Charcoal, Landlords, the Beer-Bill, Freemasons, Oddfellows, Druids, Foresters, Gardeners, Slivers, Wool Wigs, and—Old Bishop Blaize."

Mr Skerret's theatre, which was located in the large upper room of the Oddfellows' Hall, was one of the best attempts ever made at supplying Bradford with superior dramatic performances.—The Oddfellows' Hall, then recently erected (1840) at a cost of about £3,000, and regarded at that time as a structure of some importance, was unfortunately not favourably situated for a theatre. A greater drawback than its mere locality, however, was its very limited accommodation for a *paying* audience, the gallery especially being very small, and the admission to it—a shilling—too high a figure for the "gods," who, when the price is in accordance with their pockets, are undoubtedly the best patrons of the drama.

Mr. Skerret aimed high, and spared no expense in making his little theatre as comfortable and attractive as possible, but his efforts were not appreciated as they deserved to be. Special attention was devoted to the musical department. There was a good band, and good singing was a prominent feature. The stage, scenery, proscenium and decorations were all the workmanship of Mr. J. Wilson Anderson, and reflected great credit on his artistic taste and ability. The acting was always good, for Mr. Skerret kept a good stock company. Among these was Miss Walton, who took the leading female characters, and was a favourite with the audience. Mr. Macaulay was also an actor and elocutionist far above the common run. He made his debût at the Halifax Theatre when quite a young man, and early developed a liking for the "legitimate" school of English dramatists. It is but a few seasons since he took his farewell of the stage, at the Bradford Theatre Royal, being then more than eighty years of age. He took the character of "Iago," in *Othello*, and delighted a crowded house by his marvellous impersonation of that part. Those who associate actors with pothouse society, may be interested to know that Mr. Macaulay was almost as distinguished for his scientific knowledge as for his dramatic powers. When in Bradford, he was often the guest of Mr. Richardson, of Southowram, with whom he was on the most friendly terms. On these occasions, he was wont to exhibit to an admiring circle, his wonderful powers of memory. Shakespeare, Massinger, Ben Jonson, Beaumont, Fletcher, Rowe, and Otway, among the elder writers, and Sheridan Knowles, among the modern, were his favourites. It is said that one evening he recited from memory the whole play of the *Honeymoon*, without committing a single mistake. He died at the age of eighty-six.

Mr. Skerret was himself a good comic actor; happy in mannerism and inimitable as a laughter-provoking fellow. As an actress, Mrs. Skerret was excellent in "all-round" characters. Like her husband, she was a good singer, and sang the parodies made by him with delightful effect. She has been described as "a very fascinating, lively woman—good looking and lady-like, and far too good for a Bradford theatre of that day."

But in spite of superior acting, good music, fine scenery, and able management, it seemed impossible to draw good houses. Strange as it may seem at this day, it was no uncommon occurrence for the audience to be dismissed without performance by reason of its smallness in number. It was, of course, impossible that things could go on long under these adverse circumstances, hence, after a few brief, struggling seasons the Oddfellows' Hall Theatre was brought to a close. On taking his farewell, Mr. Skerret delivered an address (for once to a "numerous and respectable audience") both unique in style and characteristic of the man. We can only give the latter portion of it—

"The circumstances under which I entered on the management of this theatre were of a peculiar nature, and far from inviting. As of all other undertakings, so of this, I found different opinions entertained; yet I could not suppose that in a town like Bradford, the legitimate drama could for any length of time be altogether overlooked. To a certain extent I was right, but unfortunately the patronage received has not been sufficient to enable me to obtain an adequate return for the immense outlay which undertakings of this kind involve. It is true, in the first and second seasons, I had many excellent houses; but, ladies and gentlemen, a manager of a theatre is not like a lecturer on magnetism, mesmerism or humbugism. The lecturer's expenses are comparatively nothing; but the unfortunate manager has some five-and-twenty individuals looking up to his treasury chest for the means of subsistence. Frequently, during the best of my business, when the Saturday came round

Not a guinea remained, not a one-pound note,
As my actors from the treasury hurried,
Nor left me, in pity, one farewell shot
In the chest where my hopes lay buried.

Few and short were the words they said,
And those not the words of sorrow,
And cheerfully off with the money they fled,
And I, not a rap for the morrow.

Slowly and sadly I sat me down,
With my hand on my upper storey, (*striking his forehead*)
And felt as I pressed my only crown,
That cash was better than glory."

Mr. and Mrs. Skerret, who took with them the sympathies and good wishes of many real lovers of the drama, removed to Carlisle, and, we believe, never again visited Bradford.

Fast dying out is the generation that remembers the periodical visits of such strolling companies as Holloway's, Thornes, Parrish's, Chatterton's and others, who for many years pitched their tents in such open spaces in the town as might be available. What a strange and adventurous career the old strolling-player appears to have led, as contrasted with the refined and easy-going life of the Thespian of to-day! The vicissitudes of life do not seem to have affected the former as they do ordinary frail mortals. The stroller's existence was made up of such a continuous round of eventful changes; of pleasures and hardships; of hopes and disappointments, that the freaks of fortune, and the ups and downs of life came to be regarded by him very much as a matter of course.

The history of that chief of strolling players, "Old Wild," and of his remarkable family, furnishes a striking example of the wandering showman's life of fifty years ago, and it is pleasing to know that so interesting and eventful a life has not been allowed to pass unrecorded. In a handy volume recently published, entitled "Old Wild's," by "Trim," the narrative has been faithfully told, and will well repay perusal.

Not only was Jemmy Wild himself the pioneer of wandering theatres, but his "establishment" became the home and nursery of the most noted strolling players that afterwards figured before the public. Among the more noteworthy of these, were Mr. and Mrs. Thorne; Wallett, the "Queen's Jester;" Professor Anderson, the "Wizard of the North" whom Wild taught the art of conjuring; David Prince Miller, author of the "Life of a Showman," and Arthur Nelson, who, afterwards became famous as a clown, and for his wonderful geese-driving feats upon the water and performances upon the "Rock Harmonicon."

Wallett appears to have been an all but indispensable acquisition to several of the strolling companies. As a clown, he had few equals, and as a scene painter his services were often in demand. Indeed, it usually fell to his lot to get up the scenery for the different companies with which he became connected. He kept a portfolio always at hand, and was ready at a moment's notice to suggest an idea for any new scene that might be required. He, however, delighted in being a "free lance," and went from one company to another, as a butterfly flits from flower to flower. One week he would be with Old Wild's; another with Thorne's, and a third with Holloway's; but this was long before he became celebrated as the Queen's Jester. It falls to the lot of few men to pass through such a career. In the character of jester or clown, he has frequently been to Bradford, and latterly has paid several *farewell* visits, and has been honoured by large audiences. He has given to the world the story of his life, in the form of a shilling pamphlet. It is a remarkable book, and abounds in humourous and extraordinary adventures. Two of these relate to his early connection with Bradford, and, from their local interest, are worth repeating.

It was during Wallett's engagement with Old Wild's, that the farce for one evening's programme was entitled *Raising the Wind*—rather an ominous title, for a storm came on after the conclusion of the performance. "At four in the morning, I and others were called up to disentangle the wrecked theatre of its sails and tackle. The canvas roof, and the new scenery I had painted were torn to rags. While sitting upon the ridge-pole of the demolished roof, clearing the *debris*, the factory bells rang out the hour for work. Then, hundreds of the workpeople passed by, and many stopped to look at the ruin. I believe I gave vent to my feelings in very emphatic language, for a small urchin called out, "Nay, Mr. Wallett, doant grumble, ye were raising t'wind yersen yester neet."

We have before us a play-bill dated March 10th, 1835, setting forth the performance of a popular melodrama, entitled "*Jack Robinson and his Monkey*," at Thornes Theatre, in which Wallett appears as "Musapug," the "man-monkey." This piece, however, is unhappily associated with a sad disaster which befel one of the company—Jem Farrar. The accident had taken place on the 2nd of February, and the play was again put on the boards in order to raise a benefit for the poor fellow, who, it is stated, "has now so far recovered as to render practicable his removal from the Dispensary in a few days." The story of the sad occurrence is thus told by Wallett:—

"My second appearance as Monkey had an unfortunate conclusion. Just at the close of the drama, the property man, Jem Farrar, was charging a horse pistol when it exploded in his mouth, shattering his jaws frightfully. I saw him fall, and instantly rushed to his assistance. Seeing his state, I took him on my back, and, though a heavy man, I carried him to the Dispensary in Darley Street. It was then past eleven o'clock, and the place was closed. I rang at the door, which was opened by a woman with a candle in her hand. Her fright may be imagined when she saw the apparition of a man-monkey with his tail trailing on the ground, and a half dead man on his back with the blood streaming down. One glance sufficed, she fell senseless to the ground, and the candle was extinguished. I strode over her in the dark with my heavy load. Knowing the building well, I ascended the grand staircase, and perceiving a light issuing from beneath a door, with one knock I brought out the house surgeon. As he opened the door, and the blaze of gaslight from within revealed the horrible figures, he too, nearly fainted away. A few words convinced him that I was of earthly mould, and he promptly summoned several surgeons. Surrounding the bed of poor Farrar, they had but one opinion, that his case was hopeless. One of them remarked—"We can do nothing for him." Farrar, on hearing this, shook his fist at him, being unable to speak. A fine old surgeon, Dr. McTurk, seeing this action said, "Come, boys, the man has pluck enough to live through anything. Off coats, boys, and let us do the best we can to save him." They did so; his life was preserved, and I believe he survives to this day."

One of the best of the wandering theatres that came to Bradford for the winter fair, and sometimes stayed, according to the patronage received, till over Christmas, was that of Mrs. Chatterton, who always announced her advent by a liberal display of "posters, and a still more liberal distribution of hand-bills. In these she announced that her establishment was brilliantly illuminated with gas; that her wardrobe was of the most costly description, embracing the costumes of every nation, and that the scenery of her theatre was entirely new and beautifully executed by the best artists of the day. She then goes on to say that she feels assured "the play-going inhabitants of Bradford are still numerous enough to render it once again as in *the olden time (?)* the rendezvous of the intelligence and wealth of this enlightened neighbourhood."

The decline of the drama in Bradford, she ascribes to "the scandalous disregard to propriety, and the low and ribald nature of the entertainments given by other companies, which have vitiated the public taste, and estranged from theatres the moral and intellectual part of the population."

After such a high-flown style as this, one would certainly have expected something exceptionable on Mrs. Chatterton's own boards in the way of purity and excellence. Her fine promises, however, were "more honoured in the breach than the observance," for instead of the "plays of the best established authors," her performances were chiefly of the "Sweeney Todd," and "George Barnwell" type, occasionally varied by such high-class tragedies as *The Wife of Seven Husbands, or the Fatal Secret;* and *The Walking Ghost, or the Spectre Bridegroom.*

To do the lady justice, however, she sometimes treated her "moral and intellectual" patrons to such goody-goody pieces as *The Factory Girl of Bradford, or Virtue Rewarded; The Bottle, or the First Step to Crime*, and *The Children in the Wood.*

Plays of a local character were invariably well received in Bradford, and Mrs. Chatterton was not ignorant of this. One of her play-bills announces a performance of such local interest as to call for special notice. This was the "first and only appearance" upon the boards, of "five gentlemen of Great Horton." The play was *Eugene Aram, or the Murder at St. Robert's Cave, Knaresbro'*, and the characters were allotted as follows:—

Eugene Aram	Mr. Smith.
Richard Houseman	Mr. Sowden.
Squire Courtland	Mr. Jennings.
Corporal Bunting	Mr. Priestley.
Peter Dealtry	Mr. Forrest.

Unfortunately history is silent as to how these Horton gentlemen acquitted themselves as exponents of the legitimate drama, but we may be sure they would give every satisfaction to their patrons, and bring into renown the village which they represented.

Although the audiences that gathered at the old strolling theatres were fond of strong sensation, and vulgar display, there is this to be said for them that the production of Shakespeare's tragedies rarely failed to attract large houses, and such high-class plays as the *Love Chase*, *The Stranger*, and *Green Bushes* were always favourites.

One of the most successful pieces performed at Mrs. Chatterton's theatre was entitled *The Stanfield Hall Murders, or, The Last Crime.* The crimes of the notorious murderer, Rush, were just then (1849) the topic of the day, and the opportunity was seized for dragging the horrible details of the tragedy on to the stage, while the public fever-heat was at its height. The writer of the play states that his object is "to bring as forcibly as possible before the public the almost imperceptible steps by which a person once induced to commit a crime approaches nearer and nearer to the awful climax, which plunges him in earthly ruin, and hurries him prematurely before his eternal Judge." Following closely upon this little speech is the announcement that "The Awful Denouement, The Scaffold, The Execution and The Grand Tableau will be effected in a most singular manner, never yet attempted upon the stage."

The production of this piece was a most successful hit. As a means of replenishing the coffers of the proprietors it was a triumphant success. But in a large and mixed population like that of Bradford forty years ago, such performances as these could not fail to draw large houses. But, indeed, does not this remark apply with equal force to our own day, in spite of our boasted refinement and advance in taste? For a reply, it is surely enough to point to the glaring and sensational pictures that may any day be seen on the hoardings of our principal streets and thoroughfares.

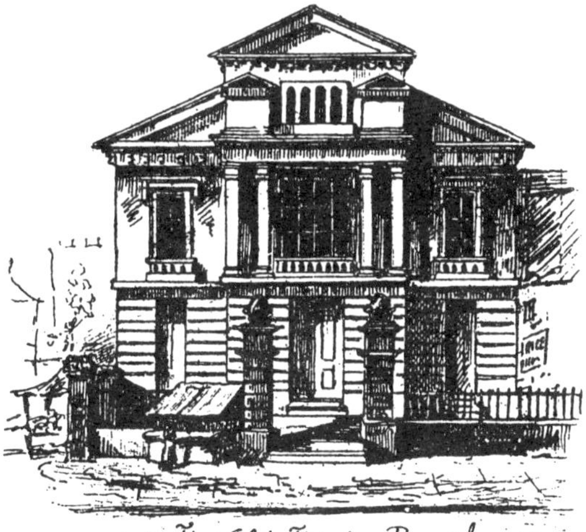
The Old Theatre Royal.

The old Theatre Royal in Duke Street will yet be remembered by many an old Bradford playgoer. As the home for so many years of the "legitimate drama," it was but a shabby concern. It had been built in 1841 as a theatre for Mrs. Wild, and went by the name of the "Liver" theatre. Then it did service for a time as a circus, and in 1844 was engaged by Messrs. Mosley and Rice for the purposes of a theatre. Before being opened by them, however, it was altered and improved very much. A grand new front, designed by Mr. Charles Rice, was put on, and the old stone gate posts that had stood for many a long year in front of the

Manor Hall, Kirkgate, were carted away and reared in front of the theatre, where they remained as dignified relics of bygone days for another long space of time, until finally removed a few years ago to make way for Mr. Willey's new warehouse.

But notwithstanding its alterations and improvements, what a strange place the Old Royal was to be sure, with its small and stuffy "dress boxes" on each side, looking very private and select, no doubt, but very much like so many shut-up beds. And what a place was the pit when fairly taken stock of, with its rude planks for seats, but with nothing, (rude or otherwise) as supports for the back. The old stage with its proscenium ornamented by panels of looking-glass and gilt borders, and the drop-curtain with its Oriental view are yet familiar to memory. How strange at this day would seem the old system of putting the scenes together by halves! The process was a clumsy one, but the "scene-shifters" were expert at their work, although they did at times make droll mistakes in the way of putting wrong scenes together, such as placing a gentleman's library somewhere in the middle of a sea view.

There were other associations, however, clinging to the quaint looking building in Duke Street of infinitely greater interest than these. It was the cradle of histrionic talent of no common order. Here was the birth-place of such reputations as those of Amy Sedgwick, Julia St. George, Maria Jones, Lysander Thompson, Rogers, Belford, J. E. Shore, Stoyle, and others,—names which reflected a glory back upon the place whence they sprang. The boards of that old "wooden box" (as it was often called), had been honoured by the tread of actors no less distinguished than Macready, Vandenhoff and his talented daughter, Mr. and Mrs. Charles Kean, Phelps, the Misses Cushman, Helen Fawcett and others.

The audiences at the old Royal were chiefly made up of the sons of toil—horny-handed men, who liked good acting and plenty of it. It was the play they went to see—not blue fire and saltpetre,—and if it was not to their liking, they had a way of showing their disapproval which could not possibly be misunderstood. To most of them, a good play was a wonder as well as a joy, and they were not tardy in giving expression to their appreciation. It was on Saturday nights that the rough-and-tumble element most prevailed, when there was a general gathering of the clans from Low Moor, White Abbey, and other select quarters. A rough lot they were, and some lively interludes between the acts were often performed in the pit. It was thought lightly of to propel some offending person from the back of the gallery down into the pit, where his limbs were kept in active exercise until he found himself landed at the bottom, somewhere in the neighbourhood of the orchestra. Messrs. Mosley and Rice were, however, determined to put an end to this state of things, but it was some time before they succeeded in doing so, and before the following notice ceased to appear on the play-bills :—

"Notice!!! is hereby given, that persons entering the Theatre in a state of intoxication, smoking, throwing orange peel, nutshells, etc., etc., or personally addressing the musicians or other individuals in the Theatre, or in any way annoying the audience, will be instantly removed by the Constables in attendance. No admission behind the scenes on any pretence."

Messrs. Mosley and Rice first made each other's acquaintance at the market town of Oundle, in Northamptonshire, where the former was then carrying on theatrical performances in a barn. The acquisition of Mr. Rice, who entered into an engagement with Mr. Mosley, gave a new impetus to the concern, and enabled it to reach a higher point in the dramatic scale. For a time the small company were content to display their abilities before such audiences as could be attracted to barns or other places of an equally lowly character, but they were hopeful of better times; nor did they hope in vain, for a few seasons previous to their settlement in this town, we find them performing to good houses at Wakefield, from whence they removed to Huddersfield, and in the autumn of 1844 they came to Bradford.

It was on the evening of August the 12th of that year that the first performance under the lesseeship of Messrs. Mosley and Rice took place at the Theatre in Duke Street. The first play put on the boards was that of *The Hunchback;* followed by the laughable farce of *The Illustrious Stranger, or, Married and Buried.* The "cast" was a very superior one for a provincial theatre, and as the company became augmented during this and the following season by such high-class actors as Lysander Thompson, Mr. and Miss Woolgar, and Miss Julia St. George, it certainly would have contrasted favourably with any other then in existence off the London boards.

Few, if any, of those who saw the beginning of the old "Royal" now survive. Among those who had the longest connection with the old place, some of whom even saw the beginning and end of Mr. Mosley's engagement, were Mr. Robinson, actor and scene-painter, Mr. Roughton, Mr. Mackay, and Mrs. Nunn.

Mrs. Nunn was an undoubted favourite with old Bradford play-goers. Although claimed as a Bradford lady from her long connection with the Theatre Royal she had won her laurels before coming to this town. She was born at Southampton. Her father, Captain Boyle, commanded His Majesty's ship "The Arab," which was wrecked off the coast of Rio De Janeiro, when all on board perished. She showed an aptitude for the stage very early in life, and at the age of fourteen actually appeared on the boards of the Old Royalty, East End, her character being that of young Norval in the play of *Douglas.* After this she made rapid strides in her profession, and gathered fresh laurels at every stage of her progress. It was while visiting Sheffield that she entered into an agreement with Messrs. Mosley & Rice to come to the Theatre Royal, Bradford, where she at once assumed the position to which her abilities fully entitled her, as the leading actress in tragedy, comedy, and drama. She possessed an extraordinary study, and a wonderfully retentive memory, added to which she had a commanding appearance and a physique admirably fitting her for the *role* of male Shakspearian characters, in which she excelled. The press criticisms of this period of her career speak in glowing terms of praise of her delineation of Romeo and Hamlet. During an engagement at Hull with the elder Vandenhoff she appeared as Claude Melnotte to the Pauline of Miss Vandenhoff, and so delighted was the great tragedian with Mrs. Nunn's performance, that he presented her with a valuable jewel as a mark of his appreciation.

In the old stock-company days the capabilities of actors were severely taxed by laborious study and long rehearsals. Some conception of this will be formed when it is stated that Mrs. Nunn has appeared in as many as fourteen characters in one week, each part or character reaching an average of twelve lengths (a length being forty-two lines). What would artists of to day think if they were called upon to embody such a variety of characters in so short a time, making each individually a success, and going through the Herculean labour of studying until midnight and rehearsing until noon, to be ready for the evening's performance; and to continue in such an arduous career throughout a long course of years, as was the case with Mrs. Nunn?

Mrs. Nunn took her farewell of the stage in 1863, her next appearance in public life being in the character of landlady of the Bermondsey Hotel, of which her husband had become the proprietor.

Mr. Nunn, familiarly styled "Jack" by his friends and associates, was a nephew of Nunn the celebrated lace maker, and patentee of the "Nunn's lace" sported so lavishly by the court of George IV. As an actor he was most successful in what are known as character parts, such as Robert Macaire, Jeremy Diddler, Blueskin, and Caliban. His Mercutio was a finished and well-studied delineation.

As the landlord of the Bermondsey Hotel, Mr. Nunn will be remembered by many as a genial-hearted, amiable fellow. Possessed of an unlimited fund of anecdote and being a good musician to boot, it is little wonder that he was the centre of a large circle of friends who sought and relished his company.

The daughter, Miss Annette Nunn, was early discovered to have inherited much of her mother's talent for the stage. She has since given abundant proof of the possession of dramatic genius of no mean order.

Mr. Nunn as Jeremy Diddler.

One of the most prominent and familiar names associated with the earlier days of the Bradford stage was that of Lysander Thompson the younger, a man whose gentlemanly manners gained him many friends, as his superior acting won him many patrons and admirers. Mr. Thompson was a local celebrity, and his society was sought for and enjoyed by those who loved

"The feast of reason and the flow of soul."

To form one of any convivial gathering of which he was the "centre of attraction," especially after his *debut* on the London boards, was indeed a privilege not to be thought lightly of. Mr. Thompson's favourite resort was the Nag's Head, Kirkgate, not then degraded into a dram-shop, as it afterwards was, but a real old-fashioned hostelry, with a bar seated round with "long-settles," and where people used to take ale by the tankard."

As an actor, Mr. Thompson's greatest *forte* was unquestionably that of a delineator of rustic character, and in this particular walk of the drama he stood without an equal, as unrivalled as Macready was in the highest rank of tragedy. Nothing could surpass the excellence of his Robin Roughhead; his Tyke, and his Zekiel Homespun. Throughout the whole of his performance there was not the least appearance of art; no straining after effect; no mannerism or stage trickery, but all was natural and kept within the bounds of moderation. His dialect (genuine Yorkshire), action, and good humoured grin were in strict keeping with the character of the unsophisticated artless countryman. In scenes of pathos and tenderness he was equally successful, and never offended by approaching to anything like buffoonery.

Mr. Thompson was induced to go to London, where he met with a most flattering reception, the press being loud in its praise of his performances. His reputation was now thoroughly established, and he returned to Bradford full of honours. His laurels had been well won, and his old patrons were not slow in showing that they shared his triumphs and were proud of his achievements. Henceforth he was a local magnate of no ordinary type.

But great as he was as a delineator of rustic character, he was scarcely less so in other walks of the drama. His Caliban, for instance, was a marvellous personation of that wonderful character, and it is doubtful if he has ever been surpassed in it.

It must have been no ordinary treat to have witnessed the *Tempest* as performed by Mosley & Rice's company in the year 1845 with Hamilton as Prospero, Miss Julia St. George as Ariel in which she was without a rival, and Lysander Thompson as Caliban.

This was a most interesting period in the history of the Bradford stage. The finest of the grand old tragedies and comedies were put upon the boards and were performed in splendid style by one of the best companies then in the provinces. Of the character and variety of these a good conception may be formed by a glance at the play bills of the time. Selecting one week's performances at random we find *The Stranger* given on the Monday, and the other evenings respectively occupied by *Speed the Plough; Eugene Aram; Romeo and Juliet; The School for Scandal;* and *Richard III.* Each of these plays was followed by one or more after-pieces, interspersed by songs and dances.

Occasionally the programme was varied by plays of what may be termed an eccentric character, made up generally of local incidents and surroundings. Mr. Rice's aptitude for dramatising local events was brought to bear on more than one of these performances. *The Gibbet Law of Halifax, or, a Legend of Kirklees Abbey*, was specially written and put on the boards by that gentleman for the benefit of his co-lessee, Mr. Mosley. Another play of local interest, also written by Mr. Rice, was entitled *The Fire Raiser, or the Prophet of Low Moor;* a third of these domestic dramas was called *The Merchant of Bradford, or, the Fatal Duel, and the Bride of Kirkgate.* On one of the benefit nights of Mr. H. Loraine, a play specially written for the occasion and bearing the title of *The Manufacturer, or a Tale of Yorkshire* was performed. The manufacturer, a Mr. Joshua Ramsley—is, of course, the vagabond of the piece, and he begins a long course of evil-doing by seducing the daughter of one of his work people, a woolcomber who is held up as a model of virtue and uprightness. It goes without the saying that ultimately villany is defeated and innocence is triumphant. Lest the moral of the play, however, should be regarded as reflecting too strongly upon the class of tradesmen to which Mr. Ramsley belonged, the following epilogue is thrown in by way of apology.

> But think not that our scenes shall here disclose
> *All* manufacturers as virtue's foes;
> Though Ramsley's drawn with pencil free and true,
> His faults are only common to the Few;
> A Host of Honourable Men remain,
> Stern Foes to Fraud, and Friends to virtue's Reign.

Prior to the engagement of Mr. Lysander Thompson, the then new and popular play of *Richelieu* had not been produced here, and being desirous of putting it on the Bradford boards he obtained the sanction of the lessees to this being done. The necessary preliminaries had been made and the appearance of the piece duly announced, when on the day previous to its performance, Mr. Thompson discovered that he had lost the play. Unfortunately another copy could not then be had nearer than York. He was not, however, a man to let the grass grow under his feet, so he at once mounted a horse and rode to York and back reaching home at two o'clock in the morning. The book was cut up and distributed to the actors; the piece was ready for rehearsal by eleven o'clock, and was performed at the time announced. Mr. Thompson took the part of Richelieu, and Mr. Rice that of De Mauprat.

One of the well known members of the company at the period now under notice, was "Old Mackay" who, played the irritable old fathers, although he himself was not married till late on in life. He would however threaten to cut off his children (on the stage), with a shilling; made the course of love anything but smooth; then would relent, and, with a salary probably of fifteen shillings a week, gave daughters away with large fortunes with this laconic benediction, "Take him, you puss, and be happy." Poor Mackay! we fear the uses of adversity were not sweet to him. The termination of his long career at the old "Royal" was but to find him old, poor, and friendless—a sad requital for one who had spent a lifetime in trying to amuse his fellows. Those, unfortunately, were not the days of benevolent organisations for the aid of worn-out actors, and to many—alas! how many—there was no brighter prospect in view than an old age of utter neglect and poverty. The life of an actor was then no enviable lot, and nothing surely but a strong and deep-rooted love for the drama could have enabled him to brave a career beset with so many trials and hardships.

Mr. Phillips, father of the leader of the orchestra, was connected with the company from its commencement up to the time of his death. When young Phillips first led the orchestra, he was only in his fifteenth year, and wore a tunic. His two sweet-looking sisters were children of the stage when children were needed. The elder one developed into a beautiful woman, married, and left the stage of fiction for one of sober reality. Mr. Robinson, the clever scene-painter, played quiet subordinate parts respectably. He married a Bradford lady, and was always a credit to his profession. Mr. Roughton roughly combined in himself robber, "bobby," and carpenter; was the Jove of the stage, and produced thunder and all other magical effects. Mrs. Kirk was a widow lady, sister to Mr. Mosley, and played well the parts of aged spinsters and mothers. Her daughter, Miss Lizzie Kirk, was a great favourite on the Bradford stage. Besides being a good actress she sang well, and between the two accomplishments was kept pretty well employed.

The management of Mr. John Mosley (who became sole lessee on Mr. Rice's retirement in 1847) was successful in rearing some actors who were to become "pillars and ornaments" of the stage, although he was severe and imperious towards those whom he employed. In his later years he became possessed with the all-engrossing idea of money making; hence he lost much of that enterprise and interest in the drama by which he had formerly been characterised. He continued to tread the boards as an actor for several years after he became lessee of the theatre, generally as light, genteel comedian, his favourite parts being Romeo, and Evelyn (in *Money*.) But he was never a good actor. He was a ponderous and artificial lover, and a very unheroic hero; still, he had the reputation of having "that within him which passeth show," and this served him, as it has done many another, in very good stead. A gentleman of more than local literary fame, has kindly furnished us with particulars of an incident coming within his own experience, which will serve to give a good insight into Mr. Mosley's character. "I remember well, when a young man, sending

Mr. Mosley a farce upon which I had tried my 'prentice hand. I was persuaded that it was one of the finest farces ever written—young authors always *do* think such things—and I verily believed that it would pave my way to fame and fortune. Well, Mr. Mosley wrote and asked me to call upon him, and I did so. He then lodged in a house in Manningham Lane. With a fluttering heart, I waited upon him at the time he had named. He received me with an air of courtly condescension that at once gave me to understand that he did not undervalue his own importance. He told me that he had read my farce, and was disposed to think there was something in it. He would produce it at an early date, and I must attend the rehearsals. I was overjoyed. He then invited me to drink wine with him, and as we sat together he discoursed to me in a very stilted fashion upon the decay of the stage, and told me the many sacrifices he had made for his art and for an unrequiting public. He showed me that he had suffered little short of martyrdom on behalf of the play-goers of the West York Circuit, and when he had fully impressed me with this idea, and not before, he allowed me to depart. How far he was sincere in his sentiments I could not judge, but I shall never forget his pompous manner and his grand condescension. This was my first and last interview with John Mosley. I may add that my farce *was* produced; that it was announced to be "by a gentleman of Bradford," and that I believe now, it was one of the very worst farces ever represented before a discerning public."

One of Mr. Mosley's most talented and precocious pupils was Miss Maria B. Jones, who received her theatrical education here, chiefly under the tuition of Mrs. Nunn. Her first appearance on the stage was as one of the immortals, in the first pantomime produced at the Theatre Royal (1846), entitled *Harlequin and the Magic Pancake;* Miss Jones being then but a mere child. Her father then acted as prompter, and her mother, so well known for many years on the Bradford boards, held a prominent position in the company. One of Miss Jones' earliest impersonations was as Eva, in *Uncle Tom's Cabin*, in which she displayed a remarkable aptitude for the stage, and her infantile efforts met with such approval that she at once became a general favourite. In after years she became the leading actress here, and her fine performances will yet be fresh in the recollection of many patrons of the old "Royal." One of her chief triumphs was in the part of Eily O'Connor, in the *Colleen Bawn*. Miss Jones afterwards became leading lady at Drury Lane, where she fully sustained the expectations of her admirers at Bradford as an actress of great promise, but, alas! her career was suddenly cut short by an attack of acute rheumatism, from which she never rallied. She had married an officer in the army, named Fairlie, and at the time of her death was but in her thirtieth year. She will be long remembered as one of the brightest ornaments of the local stage.

The first Bradford pantomime above alluded to, was a very different kind of performance to those we are accustomed to see now-a-days—especially since they were brought to such a stage of perfection by the late Mr. Rice. The brilliant and costly transformation scenes of to-day were not so much as dreamt of, and the only extra outlay then involved was in respect of one or two new scenes, some new dresses, and a fresh musical programme. To the delight of the juveniles, the clown's tricks formed a prominent part of the entertainment. These, of course, consisted chiefly of the old stereotyped red-hot poker and butter-slide trick, the squeaking live pig and Christmas goose, and the murdered baby brought to life again by a liberal dose of "pap," roughly supplied by the clown out of the largest of basins and with the biggest of spoons. The pantomimes rarely ran beyond the month of January; but even this short interval of rest was very acceptable to overworked actors, although the idea of making a whole night's performance of the pantomime had not yet been conceived, and it was invariably preceded by a heavy drama.

The pantomime season was brought to a close by the usual round of benefits. To Mrs. Nunn belonged the honour of having reached the highest sum ever realised in the old "Royal" on the occasion of a single benefit. The largest amount that it was possible to raise, with a crowded house, and at the ordinary prices of admission, was £50. While in former years a respectable stock company might have been got together at the rate of from £25 to £30 per week, it is now impossible to do this for less than £70 or £80. This may possibly account for the fact that formerly the benefit season was such an anxious time for actors, the issues of which were often fraught with disastrous consequences. Occasionally there were seasons alike distressing to the proprietors and the members of the company. The year 1845 was regarded as a successful one, the lessees having the sum of £450 to divide betwixt them as nett profits.

Mr. Mosley found it desirable to introduce new actors occasionally. In 1850, Mr. Montague Smythson succeeded Mr. Henry Loraine in the leading *roles*, and a very painstaking and competent actor he proved himself to be. In that year, too, Mr. J. D. Stoyle made his first appearance at Bradford. Young as he then was, he soon became known as "Owd Stoyle." The owner of the name, at first, did not like this, but he soon discovered that it was only the real favourites who were honoured with the appellation "old," and that it was used as a term of endearment.

Mr. Stoyle soon satisfied his Bradford patrons that he had the true gift of comedy in him, and the genuine ring of an actor. His connection with Mr. Mosley's company reached over five seasons. He then joined Mr. Copeland at Liverpool, and subsequently had engagements at all the best theatres in London and the provinces.

Mr. J. D. Stoyle as "Prince Paul."

Whatever character he took in hand he made his own, hence the difficulty in pointing to those in which he may be said to have excelled. His Mr. Dodge in *The Artful Dodger* and Prince Paul in *The Grand Duchess* were impersonations by which he will, perhaps, be best remembered. By his long connection with the Duke Street Theatre, and his marriage with a Bradford lady (sister of Mr. Ald. Duggan), it is almost needless to say that Mr. Stoyle had many friends and admirers in this town. He, too, delighted to return to the scene of his former exploits whenever opportunity presented itself for him to do so. Recalling his remembrance of the past, Mr. Stoyle, in a letter to the writer hereof, said:—" I was very young when I first became a member of 'the Bradford Circuit' as it was then called, and was proud of my position as first low comedian in a company among which were such artists as Lysander Thompson, Montague Smythson, William Belford, Amy Sedgwick, Mrs. Nunn, Josephine Shalders, and other inimitable performers who made up one of the best companies then in the provinces. . . . . When I remember how the fine old comedies and the best of tragedies were acted in those days, and how they were mounted and put upon the boards, I blush as I reflect on what I have since seen and acted in, even in London, where lavish expenditure and royal patronage and most attractive audiences are seldom, if ever, wanting. For much of my own success as an actor, I honestly believe that I am greatly indebted to the tuition which I received at Bradford, and while I live I shall ever look back with feelings of unalloyed pleasure to the good old times associated with that happy period of my history."

Mr. Stoyle's versatility was very great. Not only was he an accomplished actor, but he was a really good vocalist also, his singing in the part of Hecate in *Macbeth* being always a great treat. During the latter part of the year 1880 he was with the Imperial Theatre, London, but was seized with a sudden illness which cut short his engagement. He died on the first day of the new year, 1881.

Miss Amy Sedgwick was the most distinguished member of Mr. Mosley's company, and one of the most accomplished and popular artistes that ever trod the boards of the old Theatre Royal. Very early in life she was inspired with a longing for the profession of which she was destined to become so bright an ornament, and she made her first appearance on the stage when not more than sixteen years of age. She soon became a popular favourite, and her rising fame reached the ears of Mr. Mosley who was quick at discerning true dramatic talent. Young as she was he offered to engage her as his leading actress. The offer was accepted, and Amy Sedgwick's first appearance before a Bradford audience took place in the autumn of 1854. Her reminiscences of this period of her career will be best told in her own words.

"I made my first appearance at Bradford," she says, "in the character of Constance, in *The Love Chase*, with the most flattering success, when under seventeen years of age. I also acted as Pauline in *The Lady of Lyons*, with the late G. V. Brooke, who complimented me highly, and said he hoped to see me holding the position my talents would merit, with study, on his return from Australia, whither he was then going, poor fellow. I remember how happy and proud his words made me feel. I *did* study, and his encouraging words greatly cheered and strengthened me in my early struggles to attain the position which he had led me to hope I might one day reach. I also remember with something akin to pride how, on the occasion of my farewell benefit in Bradford, a number of poor factory girls awaited my exit at the stage door, and joining their hands took hold of me and carried me home, cheering and crying out 'Bless tha, lass, we do love tha; tha mun come agean,' etc. Well do I recollect an amusing incident in connection with poor Mr. Mackay's benefit. Anxious to 'draw a house,' as he said, he got some local gentleman to write a farce on *The Sayings and Doings of Sebastopol, or the Recruits of the Crimea*. I will not be certain, but I really do not think the gentleman had finished writing the farce until the day before it was acted. Consequently, with a number of other pieces to study, we knew little or nothing about it. I know *I* did not, and all I could say through the roaring and firing off of guns was 'On, comrades, on! Victory or death!' Oh! I shall never forget it, the recollection of it even now affords great amusement both to myself and my friends. Well, the 'gods' bore it for a short time, when they commenced hissing. Poor Mackay, half frantic, rushed to me saying, 'Miss Sedgwick, do for pity's sake go forward and say something to quiet them, or I shall never dare to show my face in the town again.' I replied that I dared not; but he pushed me on the stage, saying, 'You are such a favourite with them they will listen to you.' There I was trembling, frightened, and unable to speak. At last, after the applause had subsided, I said, 'Ladies and gentlemen,' . . . . (pause) 'Ladies and gentlemen,' . . . (another pause) . . . when a boy cried out, 'Speyk up, lass, doan't be freeten'd.' 'Well, I replied, 'I am very sorry to say that we have not had time to study our parts. We had hoped to have taken Sebastopol to-night, but, unfortunately, our numbers are not sufficiently strong and we have failed. I hope you will kindly assure us of your pardon by giving us a helping hand in the shape of applause, when I promise you that if Sebastopol be not taken within a month, Amy Sedgwick will take it herself.' I drew my sword, flourished it above my head, and amid rounds of applause the curtain fell. For months after, whenever the boys met me in the streets they would say, 'Hey, lass, hes ta ta'en Sebastopol yet?'

Miss Sedgwick's engagement with Mr. Mosley did not extend beyond the year 1855, but brief as it was, it served as a useful season of probation. Her progress in the dramatic art was both thorough and rapid. Happily, she was not one of those who believe that culture is unnecessary where natural gifts abound. By careful and unremitting study she acquired a chaste and delicate appreciation of the lights and shades of the characters she impersonated that was remarkable in an artiste so young in years. The great charm of her acting was its perfect truthfulness and freedom from all artificiality and restraint. While full of warmth and spirit, she was easy, graceful, and natural in her whole deportment, and exaggeration and affectation were conspicuous by their absence.

We need not follow Miss Sedgwick through her marvellous career on the London boards, where she became the leading actress of the Haymarket in the best days of that company, and justified beyond all expectation the high hopes that had been raised of her future. One feature in her character must, however, be noticed, and that was her great benevolence. She was ever ready to devote her talents to objects of philanthropy and mercy. By her splendid dramatic recitals, given gratuitously, she was the means of raising large sums of money in aid of the Lancashire Cotton Famine; also in 1871 on behalf of the suffering French, when she gave a dramatic recital in Exeter Hall before a splendid audience, that was electrified, as well by her high-toned oratory, as by the sweet chord of charity which pervaded her whole bearing. The Dublin Hospital and many other institutions were the recipients of substantial aid through her untiring generosity.

It was a fitting tribute that the devotion of such a genius as that of Amy Sedgwick's to the ends of charity should be recognised by the Queen. Miss Sedgwick had the honour of reading before Her Majesty at Osborne House, who complimented her and said, "The late Prince Consort and myself always admired you, and I shall like to hear you again."

Mr. Mosley was professedly a great admirer of the legitimate drama, but there were times when he stooped considerably from his high position, and the same boards that might on one evening be honoured by the tread of a Vandenhoff or a Macready, would, on another, give place to some dog and monkey performance as utterly unworthy of a respectable theatre as could well be imagined But he atoned for this in some measure by the occasional engagement of "stars" of the brighest lustre, and this was not done, as at some theatres, at the sacrifice of a good stock company.

Vandenhoff made his first appearance at Bradford on the 9th of November, 1846, when he began a week of Shakesperean performances. He came again in January, 1848, when his talented daughter, Miss Vandenhoff, appeared as Portia, in *The Merchant of Venice*.

Mrs. Fitzwilliam, of the Haymarket, began a four nights' engagement on November 30th, 1846. She was then at the height of her fame, and her appearance at Bradford was regarded as an event of no small moment. She was a fine vocalist, and had a catching style which rarely failed to "fetch down" the house.

The great tenor, Sims Reeves, was another musical "star" who put in an early appearance here. His first visit to Bradford was on the 30th of March, 1848, when he came with Mons. Jullien. Mr. Reeves, who was described as the greatest tenor that had appeared in England since the days of Rubini, took the house by surprise, by his rendering of the fine old song, "In this Old Chair my Father sat."

Miss Cushman, the elder, first appeared on the Bradford boards on January 14th, 1848. She was engaged for two nights only, and took the characters of Katherine in *Henry the Eighth;* Meg Merilies in *Guy Mannering*, and Juliana in the *Honeymoon*. The sisters Cushman afterwards performed here for a week. On the occasion of this visit they were accompanied by Miss Eliza Cook, the gifted author, as their companion.

In January, 1850, came the great Macready. The announcement of his appearance created no little commotion in the local dramatic world. He should have given a week of Shaksperean characters, but through a family bereavement was only able to appear on one night. He took the character of Richelieu.

Miss Helen Faucit was a "star" of considerable magnitude. She began a four nights' engagement on May 16th, 1851, during which she impersonated the characters of Pauline, Julia (in the *Hunchback*), Rosalind, and Juliet.

It was surely no slight compliment to the old Theatre Royal that its boards should have been dignified by the presence of actors so eminent as these. To the names already mentioned we may add those of Mr. Phelps, Mr. and Mrs. Charles Kean, Mr. G. V. Brooke, Charles Dillon, Charles Pitt, and Swinbourne.

On the removal of Mr. Mosley from Bradford, and the final breaking up of his company in 1864, the old theatre was put up for sale by auction, and Mr. Morton Price, a man well known to the theatrical world, became the purchaser. He shortly afterwards brought with him a company of actors, and for a time carried on dramatic performances in the old place.

In 1867 the Corporation required the site of the theatre for street improvements, and it was in that year that the curtain fell for the last time, the lights were put out, and the long and interesting career of the "Old Royal" was brought to a close.

That it was quite time the shabby looking building in Duke Street should give place to a more elegant and commodious structure was beyond all question. The population of Bradford and its district had vastly outgrown the provision made for it in this, its highest, and most attractive form of amusement. The old town had become proud of its progress, its trading enterprise, its public buildings and palatial warehouses, and surely the time had come when its Theatre should no longer follow so far in the rear.

The last of "The Old Royal."

It was in the autumn of 1862 that certain public-spirited gentlemen met together to consider the desirability of erecting a new theatre. To two of these gentlemen may be ascribed the honour of originating the scheme, namely, Mr. James Cater, Solicitor, Bradford, and Mr. William Morgan, so well known as an enterprising caterer for public amusements. Mr. William Douglas, of Ilkley, threw himself heartily into the project, and spared no pains in helping it on. One of the difficulties that impeded its progress was the selection of a suitable site; Cheapside, James Street (Westgate), and Aldermanbury were respectively suggested, but finally Manningham Lane was chosen, and here it was erected.

On Monday evening, December 26th, 1864, the new "Royal Alexandra Theatre," as it was called, (the Theatre Royal being still in existence) was opened in all its freshness and splendour, and the first play put on its boards bore the significant title *All that Glitters is not Gold*, the principal characters of which were taken by Mr. Arthur Wood, Miss Wiber, and Miss Beatrice Shirley. This was followed by the Christmas pantomime *Rasselas, Prince of Abyssinia, or Harlequin and the Happy Valley*, in which Miss Madge Robertson (now Mrs. Kendal) made herself very popular as the Prince. Mr. Wilde, co-lessee with Mr. Buckstone of the theatre, had offered her this prominent position in the pantomime at a salary of £10 a week. To one so young as Miss Robertson then was this seemed a large amount, especially as it was more than all her family were gaining at Bristol. She built high hopes upon it, and resolved that very soon her parents should act no more—a resolution she was soon in a position to carry out.

The late Mr. Charles Rice became lessee of the theatre (now called the Theatre Royal) in 1869. Previous to coming to Bradford he had been connected with a number of the London theatres, and had written pantomimes both for the Britannia and the Grecian theatres. Later on he took up comic *roles* and made a decided impression, falling in for many good engagements both in London and the country. He, however, frequently essayed serious parts and with considerable success. His Rip Van Winkle, played by him three hundred nights was his greatest achievement. Some of the critics yielded the palm to him in preference to Mr. Jefferson in the impersonation of Rip, but it must be remembered that the conception of the character was different, although each was perfectly consistent and original.

Chas. Rice as "Rip Van Winkle."

The best part of Mr. Rice's life was given up to the writing and managing of pantomimes, in many of which he was his own author, scene-painter, and stage-manager, while Mrs. Rice designed the dresses in which art she was especially successful, her knowledge of the harmony of colour, and of elegance of form and design, being something remarkable.

Mr. Rice died on the 12th of April 1880, aged sixty-five; Mrs. Rice, his widow, carried on the theatre very succesfully until her death on the 23rd August, 1887.

The Prince's Theatre in Horton Lane was erected some years ago under the belief that there was ample scope for the existence of two good theatres in Bradford. It was opened on April 17th, 1876, and for the two first seasons some of the best actors of the day appeared upon its boards, among whom may be mentioned Henry Irving, J. L. Toole, H. J. Byron, J. B. Buckstone, Joseph Jefferson, Charles Dillon, Herr Bandmann, and Barry Sullivan. The theatre was then under the management of Mr. William Morgan. Its brief but eventful career was brought to a sudden close on the 16th of July, 1878, by a disastrous fire which caused its complete destruction. It was afterwards rebuilt and re-opened as a theatre, and is now occupied by Messrs. Pullan.

The Odd-Fellows' Hall.

Odd-Fellows' Hall.

The Odd-Fellows' Hall, in Thornton Road, has long been thrown into the shade by erections of a more ornate and imposing character, but it can nevertheless claim a history such as few other public buildings, even of greater age, are able to boast.

It was early in the year 1836 that the Independent Order of Odd-Fellows' contemplated the erection of a building which should serve to centralise its various Lodges, which then held their meetings at different public-houses in the town and neighbourhood. The Order had then about 1,500 members, and the Lodges were the Globe, the Anacreontic, the Industry, the Good Intent, the Golden Fleece, the Faith Hope and Charity, the Friendly Mechanic, the Faith, and the Civil Engineer. At first it was intended to erect the hall at the bottom of Leeds Road, near the present site of Peel's Statue, but the cheapness of the site in Thornton Road—five shillings per yard—led to the selection of this spot. There was some difference of opinion as to the character of the building to be erected. Some were desirous that it should be an hotel; others preferred a more private building, while others again advocated the erection of a Temperance Hall. Ultimately it was decided that a hall should be built in connection with a licensed public-house. The first stone was laid by Mr. Charles Hill, P.G., of the Golden Fleece Lodge, on the 27th June, 1836, in the presence of a large gathering of the members of the Order, who had marched in procession from the Market Tavern, headed by three bands of music. No pains were spared to celebrate the event with becoming honours.

The building was completed and opened in October 1837, and again there was a large procession of the members of the Order, and a dinner at which not less than five hundred sat down. The hall was tastefully decorated, and presented a gay and festive appearance. One of the first applicants for the inn was Jack Flintoff, the noted cricketer, but as he afterwards decided to take the Hope and Anchor, in Market Street, it was let to a Mr. Thomas Bakes, on a three years' lease.

Many and curious were the applications made for the use of the large hall. This was to be attributed partly to the fact of its being let on easy terms, but chiefly because there was then no other room in Bradford so suitable for public gatherings.

The Wesleyan Methodists were the first to request the use of the hall, their object being to have a missionary breakfast in it on Christmas-Day morning. It was let to them for that purpose at the small charge of a guinea, including fires, gas, &c. An application by the Socalists of Bradford for the room was rejected, as the prejudice against that party in certain quarters, was then strong enough to endanger the landlord's license.

Afterwards, however, the room was frequently let to both Socialists and Atheists, and many were the violent controversies and heated discussions that took place on its platform. Here, too, such "leading lights" as Holyoake, Cooper, Robert Owen, and Lloyd Jones have given utterance to flights of oratory such as are rarely heard now-a-days. Ministers of religion in the town were then foolish enough to accept challenges for public discussion of religious subjects—pitiable exhibitions that only served to raise bitter and unkind feelings, and make the disputants the more confirmed in the views which they respectively held.

A license was taken out on the 11th of April, 1844, to use the hall as a preaching room, and among those who applied for the use of it for that purpose were the Latter Day Saints, who were then making vigorous efforts to gain a footing in Bradford. These were followed in 1852 by the Wesleyan Reformers, who were no less vigorous than their predecessors in the cause which they had at heart.

Time and space would fail us to tell of the many political gatherings that have assembled within those walls, when politics were appreciated with a keener zest than now, and "Tory," "Whig" and "Radical" were badges of distinction more clearly defined than are the political parties of to day; or of the varied entertainments that served to amuse "large and admiring audiences" in bygone times—Springthorpe's wax-work, magic lantern and sundry other exhibitions, of an equally innocent and diverting character.

As a place of public entertainment the star of the Oddfellows' Hall has long since gone down. We have briefly endeavoured to chronicle the history of its happier days, before such formidable rivals as St. George's Hall and the new Mechanics' Institute appeared upon the scene.

The Post Office.

The Bradford Post Office is an old public institution, but not until very recent times could it claim to rank as one of the public buildings of the town. As an evidence of the march of progress that has characterised the past eighty years, we could not point to a more striking contrast than is shewn between the old Post Office in Miller-gate, and the graceful structure now standing in Forster Square.

The first Post Office in Bradford of which we have any record belongs to the reign of Queen Anne. William Rawson who built the Manor Hall in 1705, and who is described as "an attorney, and a man of considerable note," was successful in contracting with the Post-master General for the delivery of all letters between London and Tadcaster, and also to some other northern towns. The grant was only for three years, but it produced the nice little perquisite of £1,470 per annum—a goodly sum in those days. It was at this time that the first Post Office in Bradford was started. It was kept at the back of the Manor Hall, but afterwards removed to an ancient house that stood on the site of the late Post Office at the bottom of Piccadilly.

Old Post Office, Miller-Gate.

Towards the close of last century the Post Office was kept by an elderly spinster, named Gwynne, at a house near the top of Miller-Gate, where until recently might have been seen the slit in the door into which the letters of the Bradford correspondents were wont to be *posted*. The Post Office was then in close proximity to the Market which was held, as it had been for many a bygone generation, at the bottom of Westgate.

Afterwards it was removed to Kirkgate again, this time its site being immediately opposite Mr. George Brown's present shop. While here it was kept by Mr. Thomas Trout who died in 1815, and was succeeded by his nephew also called Thomas, or more familiarly "Tommy" Trout. Soon after this date the Post Office was removed to Bank Street, where again it kept company with the Market. Its next removal was to the corner of Toad Lane near the Bowling Green Hotel. As yet however it was but a shabby concern for a public office. The Post Office itself was a rickety wooden pigeon-box-contrivance reared in front of Mr. Trout's residence, and of so frail a construction that once when old John Stanfield, father of the late Mr. Charles Stanfield of Westgate, applied at the window to see the worthy post-master, and received no response, he knocked so vigorously as to upset the whole fabric into the street—an undignified position truly in which to find the Bradford Post Office.

At the period now under notice there was but one delivery of letters per day, and for this one postman amply sufficed. This was Ben Carrington—a well known character in his day.

The mercantile inhabitants of Bradford, who were now beginning to feel of some consequence, were greatly annoyed at the fact that although the London mail arrived at Leeds at six o'clock in the evening, the bags containing the Bradford letters were not delivered here until next morning. The Postmaster General was memorialised upon the subject, but two years of "Time's tardy pace" were allowed to elapse before any alteration was made. The memorial was despatched in January 1826, and in January 1828 the following paragraph appeared in the *Bradford Courier* :—"The new mail from Leeds to Halifax passed through Bradford on Sunday evening for the first time. A great number of persons assembled near the Sun Inn to witness this novel sight. To those inhabitants who recollect the comparatively modern time when Bradford had only the *Royal Mail* and the *Heavy Coach* passsing through, the increase in the number of conveyances, and the despatch with which letters now arrive must create great surprise. The new mail has four horses, and is attended by a guard. It leaves the Golden Lion, Leeds, at half-past five in the evening; arrives at the Sun Inn, Bradford, at a quarter to seven, and the White Swan Inn, Halifax, at eight o'clock, which place it leaves on its return at a quarter before six in the morning, Bradford at seven, and arrives at Leeds in time for the Glasgow mail to London. Letters are delivered at the Bradford Post Office to those who may call for them after seven o'clock."

Some years after the above events, the two solitary clerks of which the Bradford Post Office could then boast, shared alternately between them the unpleasant duty of sleeping (!) at the office, and getting up twice during the night to take in the mail bags.

Mr. Thomas Inkersley became post-master in 1831. He had long been established in Bradford as a printer and publisher, having first started in a little shop in Bank Street, from which he removed to one next door to the Bowling Green Hotel. This was the publishing office of the *Bradford Courier*, printed by him; and here he printed and published so many of the works with which his name will ever be associated. Mr. Inkersley afterwards removed to Kirkgate, and it was while there that he obtained the appointment of post-master.

The *Bradford Observer* of July 30th, 1835, makes mention of a memorial, which was then lying for signature at the warehouse of Messrs. Milligan and Forbes, praying the Postmaster General to grant greater postal facilities to the inhabitants of Bradford. The paragraph is worth quoting for the curious facts it contains :—"It will hardly be credited that the postmaster of this town only receives the paltry remuneration of £100 a year, yet such is the fact. And although the population of the place has been trebled within the last dozen years, and the trade has increased in a still greater proportion, yet the salary of the post-master has been raised only £20—it having formerly been £80 per annum. But even this is liberality itself when compared with the remuneration of the letter carrier. This poor fellow executes both deliveries, each of which takes up four hours! four times a week he has the additional task of walking to Apperley Bridge, thus averaging throughout the week a distance of twenty miles a day, which he performs winter and summer, in wet and dry weather, for the insignificant sum of *fourteen shillings a week*. He has done this duty for upwards of fifteen years, and we believe not a single complaint has ever been brought against him."

An answer to the memorial was received from the Postmaster General authorising certain improvements such as that of having a horse-post for the purpose of bringing the London bag to Bradford immediately on the arrival of the first mail in Leeds; the granting an allowance for an evening letter carrier, and for better facilitating the other deliveries.

John Hudson.

The man who had discharged his duties so long and for so small a remuneration was John Hudson, who with his heavily-laden bags—one in front and one behind—was for many years the most familiar object in the streets of Bradford. Although sorely tried by his excessive duties he was invariably courteous and obliging. He stuck faithfully to his post for upwards of thirty years, when, from increasing age he was obliged to give it up, but without receiving anything in the shape of a retiring pension. A sum of money was however subscribed by the inhabitants of Bradford, which was presented to him, along with a silver snuff box.

Union Passage.

As the postal business increased, enlarged accommodation had to follow, and Mr. Inkersley's shop in Kirkgate eventually gave place to the Post Office in Union Passage, or Post Office Yard, as it was more frequently called. The accompanying sketch from Mr. McArthur's original drawing will serve to remind our readers of this well-known thoroughfare, the site of which was purchased by the Corporation so recently as 1874 for the purpose of forming new Bank Street. The Post Office here was abandoned in 1867, in order that possession might be taken of the premises at the bottom of Piccadilly. It was in 1836 that the system of private boxes came into use. The annual fee for a box was then a guinea, but there were some side-boxes at half a guinea. As the first list of box-holders contains the names of the leading commercial firms of Bradford fifty years ago we give it intact. It will be seen that there were then six foreign firms settled in the town. The late Sir Jacob Behrens, to whom Bradford was indebted for the honour of becoming a postal centre, did not come here until 1838.

First List of Box-holders (1836.)

Bradford Banking Co.
Commercial Bank (Mr. Hill)
Yorkshire District Bank
Bradford Old Bank
Horton College
Hird, Dawson & Hardy
Crosley, Thomas
Holmes, Thomas
Brumfit, Abraham
Wagstaff, J. Reid
Patterson, R.
Salt, Titus
Bateman & Sons
Fawcett, Rev. Joshua
Murgatroyd & Clayton
Russell, John
Haigh & Light
Broadbent & Son, James
Fison & Sons
Turner & Mitchell
Wright, Isaac
Thompson, James
George, W.
Whitaker & Co., William
Milligan & Son, J.
Wharton, Josh.
Schlesinger, Mr.
Outhwaite, Dr.
Kiel, W. C.
Rennie & Tetley
Hammond, Thomas
Lister, E. C.
Hailstone, Samuel
Wells, William
Ackroyd, William
Pearson & Son, William
Rand & Sons, John
Ecroyd, Benjamin
Tolson, R.
Moulden, William
Mann & Co., J. T.
Eckhard, J. & C.
Gaussez & Boissermas
Rawson & Co.
Emmanuel & Son
Haigh, George
Ross, A. G.
Cheesebrough, William
Rawson, Clayton & Co.
Wade & Sons, James
Waud & Co., C.
Wood & Walker
Smith, Wilson & Co.
Anderton, Swithin
Milligan, Forbes & Co.
Nicholson, R.
Heron, J. N. & Co.
Greenwood, F.
Ellis, William
Ramsden, Henry & Co.
Firth, James
Simes, F.
Byles, Mr. (*Observer* Office)
Martin, Mr.
Ackroyd, Messrs.
Willett & Co., Thomas
Willett, Oxley & Co.
Gamble, John
Milthorpe & Co., Thomas
Rouse & Sons
Clayton, T. & J.
Hudson, William
Ellis & Co., James
Selby, Samuel
Pollard & Co., Joshua
Fawcett, Richard
Tolson & Tetley
Hustler & Seebohm
Hustler & Blackburn
Garnett, R. J. & W.
Smith & Sons (Dyers)
Michaelis & Samson
Thornton, John
Pullan, J.
Lee, J. L.
Hollings & Sons, T.
Peckover & Ferrand
Addison & Roper
Clayton, Josh.
Turner, C. F.
Smith, W. & E.
Illingworth, Miles
Fearnley, Josh.
Hardcastle & Sons

FIRST LIST OF BOX-HOLDERS (1836)—*continued.*

Aked, J. & T.	Thistlethwaite & Co.
Horsfall & Bros., W.	Haigh & Atkinson
Milnes & Wilcock	Heap, Rev. Henry
Clayton, James	Cousens, of Bradford
Leach, Clayton & Co.	Milthorp, John
Osborne & Co., G.	Hinchcliffe Josh.
Rogers, G. (Leeds & West Riding Bank)	Bull, Rev. G. S.
Salt, Daniel	Murgatroyd, William
Clayton, William	Schuster, Leo
Smith, John	Hird, Henry
Butterfield, Mr.	Sturges & Co.
Ripley & Son, Edward	Bentley, Mr.
Lupton & Son, R.	Britton, Mr.
Cheesebrough, John	Mossmann, G. R.
Lister, G. T.	Mitchell, Mr.

The more striking events connected with the history of the Bradford Post Office may be briefly summarised as follows:—

In the year 1840 Sir Rowland Hill's important measure known as "the penny post" came into use.

Mr. Thomas Inkersley, the post-master, died in 1844, and was succeeded by Mr. Joseph Watson, second master of the Grammar School, who however, died in May of the following year, when the late Mr. Wm. Coates obtained the appointment. On his death in 1879, Mr. Sayers, who now holds the office, became post-master.

The building at the bottom of Piccadilly (formerly the Exchange) was purchased for £9000, and taken possession of as the Post Office in 1867, but although regarded as a great stride in advance of the old offices in Union Passage, it was soon found that even this place, with the ever increasing demands upon its resources, was not large enough. A movement was therefore set on foot for the provision of more commodious officcs, which resulted in the erection of the present handsome building in Forster Square, which was opened, without any public ceremonial, on the first of September, 1887.

The Old Banks.

None, of the many institutions of which Bradford can boast, are more closely linked with its trading interests than are its banks. As the former prosper or decline according to the vicissitudes of fortune, in pretty much the same ratio do the latter. The present number and position of the banks of Bradford—ranking as they do among the finest of our public buildings—may therefore be regarded as an unmistakable evidence of the prominent place which the town now holds as a "centre of industry."

Very little is known of what is believed to have been the first Bradford bank. Mr. James' investigations of some fifty years ago only brought to light the fact of the existence of some bank notes which he had seen dated 1760, and bearing the names, "Leach, Pollard & Hardcastle." In few but significant words Mr. James adds—*This bank failed.* No data is given, however, to show either when it began its career or when it collapsed. A little more light was thrown upon this subject by the discovery of a bundle of old bankers' drafts on the pulling down in 1877, of the old hall at Stott Hill. One of them ran as follows:—"Bradford Bank, 17th July, 1780. Fifty days after date pay to Messrs, Abm. Bower & Co. or Order, thirty pounds value received. To Messrs. Mildred, Masterman & Walker, bankers, London. For Leach, Pollard & Hardcastle, signed, William Hardcastle, Junr." Here at least was evidence that the bank had a London Agency, and that it was in existence at least twenty years subsequent to the date given by Mr. James.

By the kind permission of Mr. W. F. Atkinson, Solicitor of this town, we have seen an old memorandum book kept by the Rev. W. Atkinson, formerly Afternoon Lecturer at the Parish Church, which contains many interesting notes, interspersed with several rough sketches of local scenes from the pencil of that reverend gentleman. One of these is a plain-looking building which bears the name "The Bradford Bank," (see accompanying sketch). No date is given, however, but as Mr. Atkinson came to reside in Bradford in 1784 and there was no other bank here until the one established by Mr. Edmund Peckover in 1803, which bore no manner of resemblance to the one sketched by Mr. Atkinson, we have no hesitation in claiming this as the veritable first Bradford bank.

Old Bradford Bank.

It is related that when Mr. Edmund Peckover first contemplated the establishment of the bank which afterwards became so well known as the "Old Bank," he wrote to Mr. Birkbeck of the Craven Bank, Settle, and asked his advice as to the prospect of success. Mr. Birkbeck's reply was, that seeing there was already a bank at Leeds, one at Halifax, and another at Settle, he did not think there was scope for one at Bradford.

Nevertheless, Mr. Peckover persevered in his enterprise, and in conjunction with his nephew, Mr. Charles Harris, began the establishment in Bank Street, from which circumstance that thoroughfare got its name. No existing bank in Bradford has had to weather such severe storms as this. The most trying period in the commercial history of this town was the year 1825, but the Old Bank came out of it unscathed, and has since steered its course through a long stretch of years until it has become to-day one of the most influential banks in the West Riding.

Mr. Peckover built, and resided at, Eastbrook House. It was then noted for its beautifully shaded grounds and serpentine lakes, and even yet bears the name of Peckover Park, although it has long ceased to show any traces of its former aspect. It afterwards became the property and residence of Mr. Charles Harris.

On the death of Mr. Edmund Peckover, his eldest brother, Mr. Joseph Peckover, of Fakenham, Norfolk, succeeded him as head of the firm, and about the same time Mr. Henry Harris joined the bank. On the retirement of Mr. Joseph Peckover in 1823 the firm was joined by Mr. Alfred Harris, when it took the name of C. H. & A. Harris & Co. In 1840, when Mr. Charles Harris retired, Mr. William Masterman Harris became a partner, and the name of the firm again underwent a change, this time to H. A. and W. M. Harris. Another change took place in 1850, when Mr. Alfred Harris, Junior, now of Lunefield, Kirkby Lonsdale, was admitted a partner, and the firm became Harris & Co. which title it retained till it became a joint stock company in 1864.

The Old Bank, Kirkgate.

The building in Kirkgate known for so many years as the "Old Bank" was erected about the year 1813, and was not vacated until 1867, when the new bank at the junction of Cheapside with Market Street was completed. The old building was soon afterwards secured by the well-known firm of Beckett & Co. who established their branch here in 1874 with Mr. J. H. Lincey as manager. It has recently given place to a beautiful structure, which to say the least, affords a striking contrast to its old and unassuming predecessor.

The three brothers, Charles, Henry and Alfred Harris, and their sister, Miss Harris, were members of an old Quaker family in the south of England. With the exception of Mr. Alfred who became attached to the Church of England, they all died as they had lived, in close membership with the Society of Friends. It will not, however, be as bankers merely or even as Quakers that these brothers will be best remembered. They were true philanthropists in their day and generation, and as such their names will be ever fragrant. It were needless to mention the many charitable institutions that tasted the sweetness of their benevolence. Their deeds of kindness were done quietly and without ostentation, and it would ill become us to parade them now. It is enough to know that their liberality was generous and unstinted, and that it was extended to every good and deserving cause.

Little more than half a century since, Bradford had only two banks, viz. the Old Bank already noticed, and a branch of the notorious Wakefield Bank—Wentworth, Rishworth, & Chaloner's.

It was the failure of this bank in December, 1825, that put the finishing touch to one of the most eventful and disastrous years that Bradford has ever known. The news of the collapse, coming as it did immediately after the long and bitter struggle known as the Wool-combers and Weavers' Strike, which had utterly crippled the trade, fell as a very thunderclap, and spread the wildest alarm in all directions, for the bank had several branches scattered throughout the West Riding.

After the panic had subsided, some of the leading tradesmen of Bradford conceived the idea that a favourable moment had arrived for starting a public bank. After considerable deliberation, for the step was a bold one, the Bradford Banking Company was fairly floated with a capital of £20,000.

The *Bradford Courier* took great interest in the formation of this bank, and issued weekly bulletins of its progress. It almost went into ectasies at the rapidity with which the shares were taken up. In its issue for May 15th, 1827, it states—"The Committee is empowered to receive subscriptions for shares till the 15th June, when the book will be finally closed. The present number of shares taken is upwards of 2000. It is expected the bank will be ready to commence business by the 1st July." On July 11th, it announces that "The Company commenced discounting on Monday, the 2nd instant;" and on July 25th, it says "Since our last, the Banking Co. have began to issue their £5 notes. The tens have not yet appeared in public." This statement is followed by a minute description of the notes, and of the precautions taken to prevent any possible imitation of them.

It was on the 7th of July, 1827, that the Bradford Banking Company first opened its doors to the public. Until larger premises were available, the building in Market Street, lately occupied by Wentworth & Co., was engaged until January of the following year, when a house in Kirkgate was purchased, which, with additions made to it, was made to answer the purpose of bank and manager's residence.

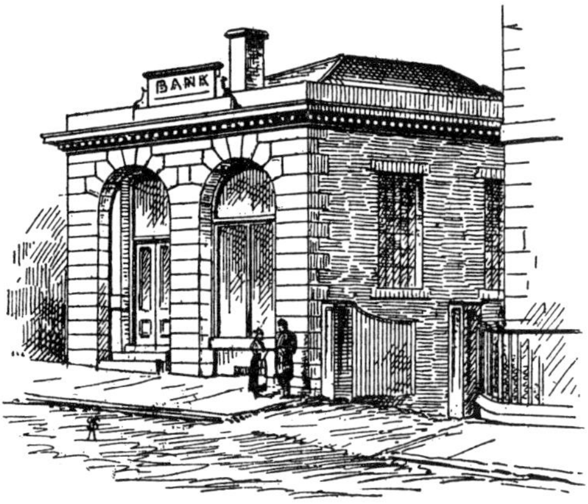

Wentworth & Co.'s Branch Bank, Market Street.

The little bank building in Market Street (now occupied by the Exchange and Discount Bank), and an adjacent house (the present George Hotel), were offered for public sale by Wentworth & Co.'s Assignees, but valuable as this property is to-day, the highest bid that was then made for it was not more than £2000.

The first board of directors for the Bradford Banking Co. was composed of gentlemen who were prominently identified with the commercial interests of the town. Their names will be yet remembered:—Mr. J. G. Paley, of the Bowling Iron Works, Mr. Henry Leach, Mr. Benjamin Thompson, and Messrs. John and William Wood.

Mr. Samuel Laycock was the first manager. He had been first a clerk in Wentworth & Co.'s Bank, and then manager of the Bradford branch previous to his appointment by the Bradford Banking Co. He was a thorough man of business, and yet possessed a refined intelligence and strong political convictions. In his earlier years he wrote imaginative literature, and held very advanced views on social and political questions. He was sobered down, however, by the stern realities of business life. On the incorporation of the town he was appointed Treasurer to the Corporation, and when the Town Council proceeded to select men to fill the office of Justice of the Peace, his was one of the first names selected. It was said of him, that if he had had a spark of ambition, he might have attained to the higher offices in the gift of his fellow-townsmen.

On Mr. Laycock's death, in September, 1867, Mr. George Ackroyd was appointed to succeed him as manager. That gentleman began his connection with the bank when in his thirteenth year. From the position of junior clerk he rose to be cashier, and afterwards manager, which office he held until the 1st of July, 1881, when he retired from active duty, after a faithful service reaching over fifty years.

Mr. Ackroyd is Treasurer of the Bradford Library, the Bradford Church Institute; a member of many of the committees of the charitable institutions of Bradford, and an active worker in connection with the Children's Hospital. It is no empty compliment to say of him, that he is never weary in "well-doing." Like his predecessor, he has a strong attachment to literature. Among his literary associates and friends may be mentioned the late Charles Cowden Clarke; Thomas Wright, F.S.A.; John James, F.S.A.; Edwin Waugh; Ben Preston; the late Abraham Holroyd, and others.

A worthy successor to Mr. Ackroyd in the management of the bank was found in Mr. Joseph Croft whose connection with the place dates from 1840. Mr. John Thompson is the present sub-manager. Mr. Richard Ridehalgh was solicitor to the Company for many years, and on his retirement in 1872, was succeeded by Mr. Walter Gardiner of the present firm of Messrs. Gardiner, Jeffery & Hardcastle. Mr. William Harker, of Pateley Bridge, is chairman, and Mr. Joseph Hardcastle, of Bingley, vice-chairman of the Board of Directors.

The example set by the Bradford Banking Co. in erecting so fine a building for its bank has been recently followed by the other banking companies, and the beautiful structures which they have reared have added greatly to the effect of the splendid street architecture which has so changed the appearance of central Bradford, and made it almost unrecognisable to anyone returning to it after a few years absence.

The Bradford branch of the Yorkshire Banking Co. first commenced business in 1843, in rooms upon the site of Mr. Rogerson's shop in Darley Street, where it continued to thrive until the premises in Market Street, now occupied by the *Bradford Daily Telegraph*, were built for it in 1851. Here it went on prospering until in 1874 it became necessary to build the bank which now stands at the junction of Bank Street and Tyrrel Street. It was designed by Messrs. Lockwood & Mawson, the architects, and is unquestionably one of the ornamental buildings of the town. The present manager is Mr. J. L. Harrison who began his connection with this bank more than twenty years since as a junior clerk. Messrs. Mumford & Johnson are the solicitors.

The Bradford Commercial Bank was founded in 1833 under the title of "The Bradford Commercial Joint Stock Banking Co." Its birthplace was the square little building in Market Street, already referred to as Wentworth & Co.'s branch bank. Here it was carried on until 1868 when a removal was made to the present bank at the junction of Bank Street with Hustler Gate. The first manager was Mr. Joseph Hill, father of its present manager, Mr. Hill, J.P. Messrs. Killick, Hutton & Vint are the solicitors to the bank, and occupy a portion of the premises.

The Bradford District Bank is as yet only in its infancy. It began in 1862 in the building formerly known as the "Rawson's Arms." Ten years later it was replaced by the present structure, of which Messrs. Milnes & France were the architects. The solicitors are Messrs. Rawson, George & Wade.

The two Halifax Banks—the Joint Stock, and the Commercial—have now each a branch in Bradford. The Craven Bank, Limited, has also a branch here. The East Morley and Bradford Savings' Bank has had a long and useful career, and its advantages as a provident institution have been largely made use of by the industrial classes of Bradford. It was established in 1818, and first began in a small room near the Fleece Inn, in Bank Street, but was removed to a new building in Kirkgate, next door to the White Lion Inn. Much of the success of this bank was due to the exertions of its secretary, the late Mr. Thomas Haigh, a truly worthy man and deservedly held in esteem for his many virtues.

The Post Office Savings' Bank and the Yorkshire Penny Bank are now represented in Bradford.

—::—

During the past twenty years, institutions of all kinds have been constantly increasing, and causing the erection of public buildings that were neither required, nor even dreamt of, in more primitive times. The more central portions of the town have been entirely remodelled by the opening out of new thoroughfares, and the rearing of new structures of a most costly and splendid character.

The transformation has indeed been marvellous. And yet, Mr. James, in the "Continuation" to his "History of Bradford," issued twenty-three years since, says, "What an amazing town in wealth, population, and size it has grown! Standing on one of the hills by which it is surrounded, a sight is presented to the eye which baffles description. Where, within the memory of most of even the middle-aged native inhabitants, the noisy rooks made their nests, and where, in the clear brook, numerous trout disported,—buildings, warehouses, rivalling in size and splendour the far-famed palaces of Venice, rear their proud fronts." After this glowing description, he adds,—"No prophetic eye is required to depict the glowing future of the good old town. With an ever increasing trade, and an ever increasing improvement, it is destined to become one of the greatest and most prosperous towns in the kingdom."

We would fain hope that Mr. James' sanguine view of the future of Bradford may be realised. Since the above lines were penned, the "trade" has passed through many fluctuations, but the "ever increasing improvement" in the condition and aspect of the town has never ceased. A new Town Hall has been reared. The New Exchange, Mechanics' Institute, Technical College, Post Office, Market Hall, and other important public structures have sprung up as if in a night, and still the work of transformation is going on, obliterating every trace of the past, and wiping out from sight and memory all the familiar land-marks that served as connecting links between Bradford as a small rural town, and Bradford as a vast commercial metropolis.

The buildings just enumerated have chiefly been the outcome of the commercial and material success of the town. It is gratifying to be able to record that institutions necessary for ministering to the misfortunes of the less fortunate of the inhabitants have not been overlooked. Wealth is now given cheerfully and abundantly to mitigate the sufferings of our fellow creatures. The Infirmary, already noticed, no longer stands alone in dispensing its charity, but is greatly aided by such important auxiliaries as the Fever Hospital, the Eye and Ear Hospital, the Institution for the Blind, the Children's Hospital, and the two Convalescent Homes. There are also numerous other public charities, less known than these, perhaps, but all fulfilling the special objects for which they were called into existence.

The erection of St. George's Hall, in 1853, was a public-spirited enterprise that created no little sensation in its time. It was regarded as a bold venture to raise a building capable of holding four thousand people, chiefly as a place of entertainment. But the projectors of the movement were sanguine of success. A company of shareholders was formed, mainly through the untiring exertions of Mr. Samuel Smith (then the Mayor), whose name will be ever associated with the movement, and a capital was subscribed amounting to £16,000, in £10 shares. The foundation stone was laid in 1851, by the Earl of Zetland, and in August, 1853, the hall was completed, and opened by one of the grandest musical festivals that has ever taken place in Yorkshire.

This event certainly marked a new era in the history of Bradford. Hitherto, the only accommodation available for public gatherings had been the upper room of the old Exchange; the old Mechanics' Institute; and the Temperance and Oddfellows' Halls. Now, there was almost unlimited scope for the holding of oratorios and concerts on the most magnificent scale; mass meetings—political or other—lectures, dramatic performances, banquets, assemblies, or indeed, anything where a fair field and public patronage were requisite in order to ensure success.

As a financial venture, St. George's Hall may not, perhaps, have proved a success, but as a real public boon, its value cannot be over estimated. The musical taste for which Bradford has long been famous, was nourished and developed within its walls, and under the leadership of a Jackson, whose musical reputation was something more than local, was brought to a marvellous degree of perfection.

Great hopes were raised for the future of this public hall, and already great things have been accomplished. Its platform has been honoured by the most distinguished characters in literature, science and art, and memorable and stirring events affecting the political world have taken place within its walls. Here have been heard the voices of Livingstone the missionary and traveller; Kossuth and Burnaby the patriots; Cardinal Manning, George Cruikshank, Charles Dickens, Lord Brougham, John Bright, Lord Palmerston, Lord Cranbrook, Lord Hartington, Sir Frederick Cavendish, and the Right Hon. W. E. Forster; dramatists like Macready, Kean, Fechter, and Henry Irving; such distinguished musicians as Jenny Lind, Thalberg, Rubenstein, and many others hardly less famous.

CHAPTER VII.

The Old Inns, & the Coaching Days.

THE prominence given in these "Pictures of Old Bradford" to the inns and hotels of bygone times, is not by reason of any interest attaching to them as mere beer-drinking places.

Their associations are of a totally different and higher character. The old style of hostelry is, however, now a thing of the past. The conditions are altogether changed; the erection of large and fashionable hotels in connection with railway stations, and the formation of political clubs having rendered their existence unnecessary, except in country towns and villages. In bygone years, a genuine old hostelry was both a serviceable and a necessary institution, not only supplying ease, comfort and refreshment to "man and beast" as no other place could, but even giving birth to movements and projects that have developed in our day into organisations of a most useful and indispensable character.

The Court Rolls of the fourteenth century reveal some curious facts concerning the drinking customs of that far off period. It would seem that drunkenness was not then regarded as a misdemeanour, nor were any restrictions placed upon landlords as to the hours when they should open or close their houses. Anyone could start a public house, with the sanction of the Manor Court, on payment of a shilling for license. Indeed, the only restriction made was as to the quality of the liquor brewed, which had to be tasted, before being offered for sale, by a person specially appointed for the post, and who was called the "ale-taster." It is not a little singular that the man who discharged the duties of this office was named William Nutbrowne, and that there were also innkeepers or "hostilers" of the same name, and perhaps, of the same family, some of whom were fined for selling ale not up to quality.*

In the Parish Church Registers for the latter part of the seventeenth century mention is made of a Jeremy Bower who kept "Ye Swanne," and who was also a tanner and barber, ("hair-beard"); but where "Ye Swanne" was located, or what was its rank among the other inns of the town is left for conjecture.

*** See Paper by Mr. Empsall, in *Bradford Antiquary* (Vol. I.)**

The Wool Packs Inn.

The Pack-Horse, Westgate, was an inn that would be flourishing in those days. It stood at the junction of the pack-horse roads that communicated with the outside world, and was then a very *Tabard* of the "Canterbury Tales" type. Then the old Back Lane, running parallel with Westgate, was a very hive of industry; thrifty housewives bringing their spinning wheels to their doors on summer days, and turning over, as only women can, the newest gossip of the town.

At the close of last century there were not less than fifty public-houses in the town—certainly more than were requisite for the population. Some of them it would seem were not so well conducted as they ought to have been, for good Vicar Crosse found it necessary to present a memorial to the Licensing Justices sitting at Halifax against licenses being granted to ten of them.

The following list of hotels, inns, and taverns in Bradford in 1822, with the names of their several occupiers, will be of interest to some of our readers. Several of them were flourishing until very recently; some have changed from the hostelry to the dramshop, but it will be seen that nearly all of them have been completely swept out of existence.

HOTELS, INNS, AND TAVERNS IN BRADFORD IN THE YEAR 1822, AND BY WHOM KEPT.

Angel, The	Westgate	William Lister.
Beehive	Do.	Benjamin Kaye.
Bishop Blaize	Kirkgate	Hannah Clough.
Boar's Head ...	Market Street ...	Josh. Pollard.
Bowling Green	Bridge Street	Joseph Ward.
Boy and Barrel ...	Westgate	Benjamin Wardman.
Britannia	Market Street	James Field.
Brown Cow... ...	Kirkgate	William Wagstaff.
Bull's Head	Westgate	Jere Illingworth.
Cock and Bottle ...	Barker-end	John Thornton.
Dog and Shovel ...	Kirkgate	John Wright.
Duke of Wellington	High Street ...	Joshua Taylor.
Fleece, The	Bank Street	Samuel Lupton.
Fox and Hounds ...	North Wing ...	Maggie Bell.
Hare and Hounds ...	Westgate	James Forrest.
Hope and Anchor ...	Bank Street ...	Sylvester Forrest.
Horse Shoes	Tyrrel Street	Eunice Clayton.
King's Head ...	Westgate	George Storey.
Lord Nelson	Northgate	John Bell.
New Inn	Tyrrel Street ...	James Wade.
Old Bishop Blaize ...	Westgate	Joshua Lumb.
Old Crown	Ivegate	George Lumb.
King's Arms	Westgate	John Raper.
Nag's Head	Kirkgate	Nicholas Mason.
Royal Oak	Kirkgate	William Baxter.
Pack Horse	Westgate	Samuel Pawson.
Rawson's Arms	Market Street	Francis Snow.
Roebuck, The ...	Sunbridge	Martha Midgley.
Salutation, The ...	Market Street	Robert Smith.
Saracen's Head ...	Westgate	Timy Green.
Ship, The	Well Street	Timothy Rhodes.
Shoulder of Mutton	Kirkgate	Elizabeth Wilson.
Sun, The	Sunbridge	Benjamin Robertshaw.

HOTELS, INNS AND TAVERNS—(continued).

Talbot, The	Kirkgate	Rebecca Wood.
Unicorn, The	Ivegate	Robert Clough.
White Horse ...	Kirkgate	John Gibson.
White Lion	Kirkgate	Joshua Bowron.
White Swan... ...	Market Street ...	John Bradford.

Interesting reminiscences are doubtless associated with many of the old "publics" above named. The "Church Steps Inn" was said to

Back of the Church Steps Inn.

be the oldest licensed house in Bradford. The most attractive part of the building, to the antiquary, was that to be seen in the "ginnel" at the back leading from the old Church Steps to Church Bank. This was all that remained of the ancient portion of the inn, the part fronting to Bolton Road being comparatively modern. In a corner of one of the old rooms was to be seen that relic of bygone times, the old chair in which the eccentric verger, Jonas Tasker, and many of his predecessors used to sit, and preside over select coteries of old Bradfordians who met nightly to discuss the fates of nations, or retail the small talk of the town. Hither, too, gathered the ringers of the church bells to tell of their exploits when commemorating some national or important local event, for which they were wont to receive extra "'lowance"—a well merited boon, poor fellows, for they were but wretchedly remunerated for their ordinary toil. In one of the old churchwarden's account books occurs the item—"Paid the ringers for all the year, 2s. 6d." A more liberal payment, however, was made when the number of bells was increased in Dr. Scoresby's time.

Sixty years ago the "Steps Inn" had the reputation of being a well-accustomed house. For a long period it was frequented by the members of a club called the "Church Steps Society." To this society the town was indebted for the upholding of the once famous Bishop Blaize festivals. Long after the last great celebration in honour of this saint, in 1825, the members of this society commemorated the event by dining together on the memorable 3rd of February.

The Church Steps, the old Inn, and its neighbour the Old Grammar School building were all swept away—all except their traditions—to make room for the new Post Office.

The Bowling Green Hotel, in Bridge Street, was a fine sample of an old English hostelry, with its large open frontage, balcony, bay windows, and its unlimited accommodation for "man and beast." For many years it ranked as the best inn of the town, and no relic of the "olden time" was missed so much as this when its demolition became a stern necessity. It is uncertain when the Bowling Green began its existence, but sufficient evidence exists to date it back to the seventeenth century. Thomas Wright, of Birkenshaw, who was born in 1736, says in his autobiography—"Thomas Wright, my paternal grandfather (after whom I suppose I was named), sometime kept the Bowling Green Inn, in Bradford, where, after he married my grandmother, he lived and died with credit and esteem amongst his neighbours. John Wright, my father, was born at the Bowling Green Inn."

In 1750, the place was entirely re-built, and by an agreement between John Woolmer, the owner, and John Crosley, the occupier, it was arranged that when completed, a lease for twenty-one years should be executed, the rent to be £39 per annum, payable at Whitsuntide and Martinmas, and that the said John Woolmer should pay all taxes and impositions except window money, and that the said John Crosley should be "bound to the usual and customary conditions for the good management of the said inn, and the good husbandry of the land."

At the beginning of the present century, Mrs. Fryer was the landlady of the Bowling Green, but about 1815, Mr. Joseph Ward took the house, and after his death, his widow kept it on for some time. The next landlord was Mr. Joseph Baxter, who fully sustained its good reputation. A worthy successor to him was found in the person of Mr. John Lupton, the last of the race, for it was during his term of office that the old Bowling Green was marked for destruction.

Many and curious were the uses to which the open space in front of the Bowling Green was put in times gone by. On this spot, our forefathers listened to the fervent exhortations of Whitfield and Wesley, and the rugged eloquence of Grimshaw, who were then "turning the world upside down," by what many were pleased to call "the new doctrine."

The year 1832 brought with it the enfranchisement of Bradford. It also brought much strife and discord. The Bowling Green front, and the space facing the Sun Hotel formed a grand arena for the Liberals, who had command of both hotels for election purposes, and here the leading lights of "Yellows" displayed their eloquence, in "broad Yorkshire," from "early morn till dewy eve."

Those were "stirring times" too, when, during the memorable Corn Law agitation the effigy of Sir Robert Peel—life-size and in top boots—was paraded in front of the Bowling Green, and, after being carried through the streets at the head of a long procession, was, amid great excitement, burnt on the very spot (strange coincidence!) where the statue of that eminent statesman now stands. Sir Robert was then as unpopular for the part he had taken in opposing the repeal of the obnoxious Corn Laws, as he was afterwards idolised as the great advocate of that measure, and no community was more ready to do honour to his noble deeds than were the inhabitants of this town. The first public park in Bradford was dedicated to his illustrious name, and the first monument raised in its streets was that of—Sir Robert Peel!

What a cluster of interesting facts are associated with the old Bull's Head, at the bottom of Westgate!

In the days when Bradford consisted of little else than Westgate, Kirkgate, and Ivegate; when the beck abounded with fish; when the space at the bottom of Westgate was filled with butchers' stalls, and farmers' wives, with their butter baskets, gathered around the old butter-cross on market days, then was the Bull's Head a house of some consequence. Fronting the inn might then be seen the bull ring, where bull-baiting, which then formed one of the sports of the people, was carried on. Close by stood the pillory, where lookers-on were allowed to throw eggs or potatoes, *but not stones*, at the poor wretches who had the misfortune to be "pilloried."

But even in later years the old inn stood high in public favour, for here the merchants, woolstaplers, and manufacturers used to resort to talk on politics and trade, forming themselves into a veritable Chamber of Commerce. Here, too, used to assemble the members of the first Bradford Club, when good Mrs. Duckit was hostess, who stood unrivalled in the art of making "genuine rum punch."

The Bull's Head had a musical notoriety extending over a greater period than any other inn in Bradford. Sixty years ago, it was the rendezvous for both town and country musicians, and under its roof the old Choral Society took up its quarters upon its removal from the assembly room in the Old Market. The meeting nights were arranged for the Tuesday *on* or *before* the full moon, in order to accommodate the country musicians on their homeward journey.

Bull's Head Inn.

Mrs. Illingworth was the landlady at that time, and a kind hostess she was to "t' singers," never omitting to lay before them some "tit-bit" after their evening's practice. Nothing but oratorio was then attempted, public performances being left to the newly-formed Philharmonic Society.

The New Inn, like the Bull's Head, would furnish material for a very copious notice if space permitted. *New* it doubtless has been once upon a time, and even yet is not old as compared with such houses as the Bull's Head and the Old Crown. We cannot give the date of its erection, but Mr. Stamp in his "History of Methodism in Bradford" says that where the New Inn now stands was then (1756) a low, old-fashioned house in the occupation of the Aked family.

The New Inn was the scene of the first flower show held in Bradford. It took place on Wednesday afternoon, 15th August, 1827. The Bradford Florist Society had then been newly-formed, and the event was one of more than ordinary interest. A pair of silver sugar-tongs were given for the best scarlet bizarre, and a copper kettle for every first prize of the other classes. The secondary prizes consisted of sums of money varying in amount according to merit. Ladies and gentlemen paid one shilling for admittance from two to five, and after that, persons admitted paid "what they chose."

When James Wade was landlord, some sixty years ago, the New Inn was the head-quarters of a club called the Querical Society, the like of which has not existed since in this town. In more modern times this old hostelry has been noted for its spacious yard, extensive stabling, and its pig-market, and to-day it is the favourite resort of small contractors, waste dealers, and divers other tradespeople.

The Old Sun Hotel.

The Sun Hotel building at the bottom of Ivegate is yet standing though it has been so shorn of its ancient glory by its transformation into shops and offices as to be scarcely recognisable. This fine old inn has "played many parts" in its time. Once it was noted for its great dancing assemblies. Its entire arrangements from the time of Mr. Belcher, in 1807, down through the several occupancies of Messrs. Gascoigne, Wade, Hirst, Whitworth, and Harrison, have all been in keeping with its character as a leading hotel. It was an awing sight to youngsters of the present generation to look upon the head waiter of the Sun—all starch and black cloth—as he ushered the latest postchaise arrivals into the hotel. It was worth something being a head-waiter in Bradford in those days! The last landlord of the Sun, Mr. Wilman, seems to have been the last of his race. He was a genuine specimen of the old style of landlord.

The Talbot Hotel still exists, but under altered conditions, although it still sustains its high character as a commercial house. In recent years it has been entirely rebuilt, two "bran-new" dogs having taken the place of the old wooden one which passed into the hands of Mr.

Edward Hailstone of Walton Hall, near Wakefield. The old hotel never seemed to find favor with the middle and working class people of Bradford. There was always a select and "snobby" air about it that repelled them. It was a famous house in early election times, as will be hereafter noticed, and on these occasions it was invariably the head-quarters of the "Blues," and it is said that there was one room in the hotel that was kept sacred for the leading Tories, into which none other were ever allowed to enter. But be that as it may, the Talbot was a fine and well conducted hotel, and it had a long succession of worthy hosts, of which any house might have felt proud.

Old Talbot Hotel.

The George Hotel in Market Street is but an erection of modern times compared with those already noticed. When good Miss Reany was its hostess, it was indeed a welcome and hospitable retreat, as many could bear witness. Hither were attracted some of the choicest specimens of local genius that it was then possible to find—some indeed whose position in the world of letters knew no limits of mere locality, such for example as Hartley Coleridge, the talented author of "Northern Worthies" and other works; Branwell Brontë from Haworth, and Leyland the sculptor from Halifax. Robert Storey, the Craven-dale poet, was a frequent visitor here, and shared the "feast of reason and flow of soul" with such "kindred spirits" as William Dearden, author of "The Star-seer," John James the historian, Skerrit the actor, Wilson Anderson the artist, and others.

It was at the "George" that Charles Dickens "put up" on the occasion of his first visit to Bradford (1854) when he read his "Christmas Carol" at St. George's Hall.

A good and "well-accustomed" house was the Hope and Anchor that stood at the junction of Bank Street with Market Street. There were few of the genuine old "pubs" of the town that were not in some way or other linked with such useful organisations as friendly societies, clubs, and social gatherings for the development of various good objects. Such an one was the Hope and Anchor. This house will ever be associated with the early days of the Bradford Cricket Club which began its career in 1836. Chief among its originators were Joseph Clayton; C. D. and Joseph Wade, and Jack Flintoff. The practising-ground was opposite Ashfield Terrace, Horton Road, but the matches were played either at Fairweather Green or Apperley

Hope and Anchor Inn.

Bridge. The members of the club met at the Hope and Anchor of which Jack Flintoff was then the landlord. Jack was a "character" in his time, and on the occasion of a match with the Wakefield Club, was dressed in the height of the fashion prevailing in the old coaching days—light buff kerseymere trousers, very tight about the knees; a waistcoat of prodigious proportions, descending below the hips, with a coat of a kind between a surtout and a topcoat—square lapped, and containing innumerable pockets; while his head was decorated with a semi-clergyman's hat, the brims turned up; his neck was adorned with a white silk or spotted tie that would not have disgraced the greatest hero in the pugilistic arena. A coach-and-four was decided upon, the horses being as gaily decorated as their drivers, so that the whole was a source of great attraction, Flintoff taking every opportunity on the road to show his importance. The result of this match was that Bartlett, one of the Bradford men, scored more runs than were got by the Wakefield eleven in both innings.

The White Swan was a comfortable and busy house, though by no means a typical inn of the "olden time." It stood at the corner forming the junction of Charles Street with Market Street now occupied by the fine block of buildings erected by Mr. Angus Holden, and known as the Swan Arcade. It would be difficult to conceive a more striking contrast between the scene now presented to view, and the modest-looking building shewn in our illustration. In the coaching days the White Swan was the house of call for the "Highflyer" when that and sundry other coaches passed through the town. Mr. Bradford was the worthy host of the house, and he afterwads commemorated his connection with the place by building a row of houses at Bradford Moor to which he gave the name of "Highflyer Row."

Mr. Fox was, we believe, Mr. Bradford's successor as landlord. In his time the figure of a white swan was shown on the swing sign, and underneath was the name "Fox." This, however, had once the effect of greatly perplexing a good old lady from Wibsey, who, after gazing a-while at the picture exclaimed, "Wha, that's nivver a fox i' this world; its nowt bud *a gooise!*"

ANGUS HOLDEN.

MAYOR OF BRADFORD:

Nov., 1878, to Nov., 1881.

Nov., 1886, to Nov., 1887.

From a Photograph by ALBERT SACHS, *Bradford.*

White Swan Inn.

The Three Horse Shoes in Tyrrel Street, was a quaint-looking place that retained its humble appearance to the last, although it was a house that prospered with the prosperity of the town. Soon after the begining of the present century it was kept by Jesse Clayton, who followed the trade of a shoesmith. Probably from this circumstance

Three Horse Shoes Inn.

his wife Eunice was looked upon as the "landlord," and well she discharged the duties, although her customers, chiefly country folks, horse dealers, &c., were none of the best to manage. After her husband's death Eunice became enterprising, and added a "bow window" to the house, but the room it lighted was specially reserved for a class then known as "dobby weyvers." Woe be to any taproom customer who aspired to a seat in the "dobby" room! Eunice also firmly resisted the entrance into her house of any drunken man. She used to say she'd "bother eniff with her own drink without other fowks!"

John Sugden, who married one of Clayton's daughters, succeeded to the house.

Many of our readers will remember the old Bee Hive Inn, (formerly the Horse and Groom), in Westgate. It was the head-quarters of a recruiting sergeant, who was often to be seen about the door of the inn ready to enlist any able-bodied men who were ambitious to join the ranks of their country's defenders. The old house, however, had many other associations connected with it, both anterior to and during the occupation of William Oldfield, Benjamin Kaye, and Joe Foster, brother to the late Mr. John Foster of Hornby Castle.

The Bermondsey Hotel, in Bermondsey, was erected in 1838, and its first landlord, Mr. Isaac Walmsley, was a well-known Bradfordian whose father had discharged the duties of clerk at the old Bell Chapel, Horton, for many years. Isaac first started life as one of the "jolly shoemakers" of Bradford, and had his shop in Ivegate, a little below the Albion Hotel. After leaving the Bermondsey, he became landlord of the Albion. At the former house he was succeeded by Mrs. Dunn, who started the first Bradford concert hall in it, at which the voice of Mr. "Joe" Coates, the well-known vocalist, was often to be heard. Mr. John Nunn, of the Theatre Royal, was afterwards "mine host" of the Bermondsey, and more recently, Mrs. Scott had it, and changed its name to the "London."

Although a thoroughfare of but modern construction, Market Street appears to have been well supplied with "publics" in good time. The Britannia, and the Rawson's Arms will be remembered. The latter was kept by Francis Snow, and afterwards by James Ingle and his son William. The Boar's Head was twice re-built. Three well-known landlords of this house were James Risden, Joseph Pollard, and Joe Blamires. On the opposite side of the street stood the Salutation Inn, but better known as the Soldier and Sailor, from the circumstance that in front of the house there was, formerly, a picture representing the figures of a soldier and sailor shaking hands. The name of the house was afterwards changed to the Griffin, and upon the late Mr. B. B. Popplewell commencing business as a spirit merchant, he opened the dramshop now known as the "Iron Gates."

In Well Street, and at the corner of Canal Road, stood the old Wool Packs, which then pretty nearly covered the site of Oastler's monument of to-day. On the opposite side of the street was the Ship Inn. Both this and the Wool Packs were within a short distance of the canal "basin," where might be seen, at any time, a motley gathering of "fresh-water-sailors," waiting, if not for "the turn of the tide," at least for an odd job that might turn up at "the port."

The Bee Hive Inn, Westgate.

The White Horse and Malt shovel, two low-storied houses, stood "cheek by jowl," in Kirkgate, on the site of Lower Cheapside. The White Lion, a little higher up, is still represented by the dramshop of that name. A portion of it was, until recently, used as Morgan's News Room. On the opposite side was, and still is, the Shoulder of Mutton. The Nag's Head was a little above the White Lion, and was kept successively by Nicholas Mawson, Francis Snow, and Jonas Hill.

The Manor House, the Roebuck, the old Market Tavern, the Fleece, and others of the old inns that have disappeared, might be dwelt upon, but perhaps our readers have had sufficient gossip on this subject. In contrasting the old hostelries of Bradford of fifty years ago, with the dramshops of to-day, it is impossible to resist a feeling of regret at the change which has been brought about. We have no wish to moralise on the subject, but it must be plain to all that it is not in the glaring gin palace that "old friends and true" care to meet together for the pure love of "good-fellowship;" neither is the weary and belated traveller tempted thither in hopes of finding rest and refreshment for mind and body. Truly, the "march of civilisation" has not in this respect, brought with it an improvement on the past.

The history of the coaching days in Bradford is inseparably linked with the old inns. The arrival or departure of a coach was always an interesting event, for indeed, there was little else to vary the monotony of the quiet old streets. Pleasant and familiar sounds were the blowing of the horn, and the clatter of the horses' hoofs to the knots of idlers that gathered at the street corners; and equally pleasant were they to those on the look out for expected friends. Those who came to see the arrival of the coach from a pure love of sight-seeing, did not return disappointed, for it *was* a sight to behold the splendid style in which "Rockingham Bob," with his four-in-hand, drove up to the very windows of the Bowling Green. A sight it was, too, to look upon guard and coachman, the former clad in brilliant scarlet, and the latter in a huge drab jarvey-coat, which, with its three or four laps, or capes, could not, when new, have cost a penny less than five sovereigns! And the polish on the coachman's face, too; the combined work of storm and breeze, of heat and cold, of summer and winter for goodness knows how many seasons, aided by daily supplies of the best Yorkshire ale. When shall we behold his like again?

The running of stage coaches was well established about the middle of last century. Previous to that time the pack-horse mode of travelling was in vogue. As early as 1678, however, there was a coach running between York and Hull, and in 1683 there was a London coach running from York, through Tadcaster, Ferry-bridge and Doncaster, and passengers from Leeds, Bradford and neighbouring towns were obliged to ride on horseback to either York or Ferry-bridge to join the coach.

A great obstacle in the way of travelling with safety by coach in early times, was the miserable condition of the roads. The so-called high-roads in the north of England were in a most deplorable state. Arthur Young, in his "Tours," describes one high-road as so narrow that a mouse could not pass by a carriage, and so deep in mud that waggons were continually sticking fast in them, till so many were in that predicament that the waggoners put twenty or thirty of their horses to pull them out. This state of things led to the passing of the Turnpike Act, and the making of turnpike roads—a movement regarded with great disfavour, as it was believed to be a deliberate plan to make the poor pay for the privileges of the rich. John Wesley joined in the popular cry against the system, for, having to travel much during his itinerating career, he felt the impost of the tolls very heavily.

The process of stirring up public agitation was peculiar. Bands of men in female attire, with blackened faces and veils over their heads, went about by night, creating great commotion, and tearing down the obnoxious turnpikes wherever they could. This led to the rioters being styled "Rebecca," and whenever they went abroad on their errands of mischief, it was said that "Rebecca had gone out to sweep." On the 18th of June 1753, the rioters made an attempt to destroy the Bradford turnpike, but without success. The same day, however, saw

Spink-well Toll Bar.

the destruction of the one at Apperley Bridge. On the 22nd, they assembled again, and this time they were joined by many hnndreds of people from most parts of Bradford parish, when they tore down a turnpike at Tyersal Moor-end, and burnt it and the house together. The same day they burnt one at Newall Hall and Wibsey Bank Foot, and (this time) the Bradford turnpike shared the same fate.

Emboldened by success, their depredations began to spread over a wider area, until the military received orders to fire upon a large mob that had gathered at Leeds and was doing serious damage to property.

Some were killed and many wounded, but this, with the arrest and imprisonment of several of the ring-leaders, had the result of putting an end to these remarkable riots.

But the mysterious and terrible movements of the rioters, when all honest folks were a-bed—the sudden lighting up with lurid flames of quiet country lanes, and the noise and tumult of infuriated mobs, were events highly calculated to play upon the imagination of an ignorant and superstitious people. No wonder that many a "traditionary tale" should have been handed down from father to son, and many a ghostly story "told i' the inglenook," should have been shaped out of the strange going forth of "Rebecca" to sweep.

The establishment of the turnpike system, and the improvement of the high-roads were followed by a rapid increase of stage coach traffic. In 1825 there were no less than fourteen coaches running daily to and from Leeds, usually carrying 196 passengers, while forty years previously only one coach ran between the two towns, which left the King's Arms, Bradford, in the morning, and returned from Leeds in the evening, and carried *four passengers only*.

The Bowling Green Hotel was the posting-house of the "Defiance," which ran from Hull to Liverpool, and arrived here at eight o'clock a.m., and returned at eight p.m. every day except Sunday. From here, also, the "Duke of Leeds" ran to Manchester every morning, and the "Royal Mail," which left Leeds before two in the morning, called at the Bowling Green, and then passed on by way of Halifax and Rochdale, arriving at Manchester at 8-40 a.m., and at Liverpool, its destination, by 3-30 in the afternoon. From the White Swan, the "Courier" left Bradford for London every day.

The names of some of the best known of the old coachmen will yet be familiar doubtless to some of our readers. A well-known character was "Cockle Jack," who drove the "Union" from Leeds to Kendal, and who, in passing through Bradford, put up at the Talbot. Jack got his sobriquet from the fact of his bringing into the town some fine samples of cockles, which he sold at a good figure to those who could afford such luxuries. John Bradford drove the "Highflyer" as already mentioned, and Dick Fletcher was a well-known driver of one of the many coaches running between Leeds and Bradford. A very familiar figure also was Tom Forrest.

Bradford had no railway of any kind until 1846, when the Midland was opened. From this period began the decadence of the coaching days. When it was first mooted that the steam-locomotive was likely to supersede the old "coach-and-six" mode of travelling, great was the alarm in the breasts of those who had "vested interests" at stake, while to many the news came as a terrible wrench upon their old-world notions of custom and usage. It certainly was not difficult to foresee that whatever blessings might follow in the wake of the famous Railway Bill, a change would be brought about that must inevitably cause ruin and disaster to many. Old established way-side inns and posting-houses would become tenantless and deserted, and many a town and city hostelry that had stood for centuries would be shorn of its former glory. At Bradford rival coaches continued to run to and from Leeds for two or three years after the Midland line had been opened, at fares very much lower than what had formerly been charged. But it was an unequal and a hopeless struggle, and one that had to be abandoned for ever in despair by the weaker side.

Old Bowling Green Hotel.

JOHN HARDY, Esq., M.P.
(*From the Painting by* H. W. Pickersgill, R.A.)

CHAPTER VIII.

Early Parliamentary Elections.

IN the civil wars, Bradford showed its political colour pretty distinctly by siding with the "Roundheads," and proved beyond dispute that the radical spirit for which it has long been distinguished, is not of modern growth. A more recent indication of the existence of this spirit was shown during the political agitation raised by John Wilkes, for not only did the people embrace his cause with great fervour, but on his liberation from prison, the town was the scene of great rejoicings, and even the church bells were set a-ringing to celebrate the event.

It was the memorable Reform Bill of Lord John Russell, however, that fairly roused the politicians of Bradford to an attitude of life and energy, as it was by the passing of that bill that Bradford received its enfranchisement, and the right of sending two members to Parliament.

Thursday, the 13th of December, 1832, was a great day in the political annals of Bradford. It was the time set apart for the nomination of its first candidates for Parliamentary honours. The morning was ushered in by the ringing of the church bells, and the crowded streets had all the appearance of some gay and festive occasion being a-foot. The Reform or Liberal party were strong, and conscious of their importance, had mustered in large numbers. Three gentlemen had been selected as candidates, two Whigs and one Tory, and the front of the old Piece Hall, Kirkgate, was the place appointed where the nomination was to be made. At twelve o'clock, Mr. J. G. Horsfall, the Returning Officer, made his appearance upon the steps in front of the hall, and was immediately followed by Mr. Hardy and Mr. Banks and their friends, and also the friends of Mr. Lister,—the last-named gentleman being unable, through indisposition, to be present.

Mr. John Hardy, one of the Whig candidates, was a native of Bradford, and up to this period had spent most of his life here. He was brought up to the bar, and became a leading barrister at the Riding Sessions. Afterwards he was appointed Recorder of Leeds, at which place he resided till he gave up that post, when he removed to Heath Hall, near Wakefield. Mr. Hardy was also a partner in the Low Moor Ironworks, from which source he acquired great wealth. Various philanthropic institutions found in him a liberal supporter. He was among the earliest and most generous friends of the Mechanics' Institute, and four churches were reared by his individual munificence. About seven years prior to his death, he purchased an estate in Staffordshire, where he resided during the later years of his life, and where he died at the age of eighty-two. He had a large family—twelve children, we believe—of whom three were sons, viz. Sir John Hardy, the late Mr. Charles Hardy, and Lord Cranbrook.

Mr. Hardy was a fine speaker, and, as a politician, was a firm believer in Mr. Pitt. At the general election of 1830 he had tried to enter Parliament, and became a candidate for Pontefract, but was not elected. The agitation for the Reform Bill soon followed, and Mr. Hardy for a time forgot his ancient predilections and became a Reformer. The Bill having passed, he aspired to the honour of representing his native town.

Mr. Ellis Cunliffe Lister was the eldest son of Mr. John Cunliffe, of Addingham, at which place he was born, and resided during the early period of his life. Afterwards he carried on an extensive business in the worsted trade at the same village, being the first to produce a hank of yarn in the Bradford market not spun by hand. On retiring from business, Mr. Lister removed to Calverley Hall, and after residing there several years, came to Manningham, near Bradford, where he spent the remainder of his life. For nearly half a century he was an influential Magistrate and Deputy-Lieutenant.

In politics, Mr. Lister was a thorough Whig, and was, moreover, a great favourite with his party for consistent attachment to his political colour. He was not a good speaker, but when in Parliament was distinguished by a cheerful and ready devotion to his duties, whether in the House or on Committee. Mr. Lister had several children, one of whom is Mr. S. C. Lister, of Swinton Park.

Mr. George Banks, of Leeds, a semi-Whig in politics, was brought out by the Tories as a set-off against the two Reform candidates. The most prominent feature in his political programme was his advocacy of the Ten Hours' Bill.

The political questions of the day were those of household suffrage (the voting qualification being then the ten pounds rental); triennial Parliaments; vote by ballot; the abolition of slavery; Catholic emancipation; free trade, and the abolition of the corn laws. Some were bold enough to add to these the separation of Church and State. The candidates gave expression to their views on some of these questions, and were put through a severe course of cross-questioning by persons in the audience.

After the several nominations had been made and seconded, a show of hands was called, which, on being put, showed a majority in favour of Mr. Lister.

Between Mr. Hardy and Mr. Banks the numbers were so nearly equal that a second show was called for, when the returning officer declared that it was in favour of Mr. Lister and Mr. Hardy. A poll was therefore demanded on behalf of Mr. Banks, which was granted, and was to commence on the next day.

In the contest that took place during the two following days there was nothing needed to make the turmoil and excitement that prevailed more complete, and it would have been difficult to say which party

E. CUNLIFFE LISTER, ESQ., M.P.

exceeded the other in keeping up the Babel of noise and commotion. The Talbot formed the head-quarters of the Blues, while both the Sun and the Bowling Green were appropriated by the Yellows. The old, narrow streets were packed with on-lookers, and the bustle and scurrying to and fro from morn to night were such as had never been seen in Bradford before. Occasionally the eccentric Jacob Dawson came upon the scene, and gave in lusty style his threadbare song on the "Talbot Dog and the Blue lights," one verse of which will serve as a fair sample of the rest.

Our fathers have told us that equal laws
  Are the rich and the poor man's true right;
But God defend the poor man's friend
  From the Bread Tax and the Blue light.
    Oh, the grinding Blue light!
    The farmer's curse the Blue light!
    The Talbot Dog, tho' cut from a log,
    Would be starved to death with a Blue light.

But in spite of all this commotion there was nothing that could in the least be regarded as of a riotous nature, and the fact could be truthfully chronicled that Bradford's first election contest passed off without any breach of the law.

Nine hundred and sixty-seven persons voted at this election, and at the close of the contest the poll stood as follows :—

First Day.	Second Day.	Plumpers.
Mr. Lister, 483	Mr. Lister, 650	224.
Mr. Hardy, 321	Mr. Hardy, 471	49.
Mr. Banks, 281	Mr. Banks, 402	114.

The two "Reformers" were therefore elected. In acknowledgement of the compliment they sent their sons to be "chaired," in place of themselves, but the roughs tossed the lads out of the cars, and smashed the "chariots of triumph" to pieces.

The Reformed Parliament of 1832 was not destined to enjoy a long life. Towards the close of 1834 a sudden and unexpected turn of events led to the dismissal of the Whig ministry by the King, and this was soon followed by a dissolution of Parliament.

A greater blow could not well have been dealt to the cause of the Reform party, than the happening of these events at so critical a moment. The Reform mania at this point had lost much of its novelty, and many were losing faith in it because it did not seem to realise all that had been expected of it. The wonderful Bill which some had been sanguine enough to believe would "put a pot on every fire, and a fowl in every pot," had wrought no such miracles, although it had done great things, and would have done still greater but for the faintheartedness of those who should have clung to it through all its vicissitudes.

A reaction now set in, and the weakness of one party became the strength of the other. The Toryism which in 1832 seemed utterly enfeebled and cast down suddenly sprang to newness of life, and stood prepared for battle on equal terms with its foe. Again the country is thrown into agitation by vast preparations for a general election, at which no ordinary struggle is expected to take place. At Bradford there is every appearance that the contest will be a severe one. The "Rads" were now an important element in Bradford, and the present was regarded as a fitting opportunity for carrying a man of their own along with Mr. Lister, whom they regarded as more of a Whig than Mr. Hardy. The object of their choice was Mr. George Hadfield, of Manchester, a gentleman who was said to possess "undaunted courage, resolute principles, and high political intelligence." As a Congregationalist his candidature met with general acceptance on the part of the Dissenters of Bradford. An enthusiastic meeting of his supporters was held at the Sun at which he was present. On the following evening his committee dined at the same house, and a grand affair it was to be sure. The leading characters of the Liberal and Radical sections were present, and all was sweetness and harmony—enough to make one long for a return of the old electioneering days. When the cloth was drawn the following toasts were drunk: "The King, the Queen, and Royal Family;" "The People, the only source of legitimate power;" "George Hadfield, Esq., and Civil and Religious Liberty" (three times three, and drunk standing); "E. Cunliffe Lister, Esq., and union amongst Reformers," (three times three, and one cheer more). Great was the enthusiasm that prevailed, and the unanimous voice of the audience was loud in favour of Lister and Hadfield.

And now began the tug of war, although the day of election was a month distant. Night after night the candidates addressed the electors in public, and day after day made visits to them in private. An announcement having been made that Mr. Hardy would address the electors from the steps of the new Court House, a similar notice was issued by Mr. Hadfield stating that he also would address them from the same spot. At twelve o'clock on the day appointed, the two gentlemen, escorted by their respective friends, repaired to the Court House, where they found a gathering assembled of not less than five thousand persons. Great was the excitement that prevailed, and numerous were the questions put to the candidates by persons of all political shades.

Peter Bussey, whose pertinacity in putting questions, was only equalled by his violent and extreme political views, was a conspicuous figure, and put his many queries in a style that gave little scope for prevarication by way of reply. He was very hard upon the new candidate, and besieged him unmercifully with questions on various points. If Mr. Hadfield were sent to Parliament would he vote for the abolition of tythes, the entire abolition of church rates, and the abolition of punishment by death in all cases; for triennial Parliaments, the abolition of flogging in the army, the reduction of the army estimates, and the emancipation of the Jews so as to place them on the same footing as himself; for the ballot; for the throwing open of the

Universities to all classes of His Majesty's subjects of whatever sect; for corporate reform; for household suffrage; for the abolition of the stamp duty on newspapers; for the repeal of the corn laws; for a careful revision of the pension list; for the abolition of taxes on industry, and for the repeal of the game laws? Each of these questions was put separately to Mr. Hadfield, and with the exception of that on household suffrage, each was answered in the affirmative. His remark that he was not prepared to go the length of household suffrage was received with disapprobation, but all the other answers were followed by loud cheers.

Although the measures submitted by Bussey were regarded at that day as very advanced indeed, yet how few remain that have not since been placed on the British Statute Book!

The show of hands at the nomination, which took place on the 8th January 1835, was declared to be in favour of Mr. Lister and Mr. Hadfield. A poll was therefore demanded on behalf of Mr. Hardy.

No efforts were spared by either party during the two following days in the general squabble after votes and voters, and many were the shifts and stratagems freely practised upon electors either to win them over or to prevent them from voting for the opposition. Many stories are still current of mysterious kidnappings and sudden disappearances, for a time, of men who should have come forward to vote.

At the close of the poll the numbers stood as follow:—

Hardy	611
Lister	589
Hadfield	392

In all, 1013 electors had voted. Mr. Hadfield had only two plumpers. He had twelve "splits" with Mr. Hardy, and 378 with Mr. Lister.

Though rejected at Bradford, Mr. Hadfield was afterwards returned for Sheffield. He was an attached friend of Richard Cobden, and vigorously supported that gentleman in the Anti-Corn Law League. He died at Manchester, on the 21st April, 1879, at the advanced age of ninety-two.

Little more than two years had elapsed since the election of 1835 when the country was startled by the announcement of the death of King William IV. The event took place on the 20th of June, 1837, and was soon after followed by the accession to the throne of our present Queen.

By the dissolution of Parliament, which immediately succeeded these events, the country was again thrown into all the excitement of another election—the third that Bradford had witnessed within the brief space of five years. To those political enthusiasts who love nothing so much as the turmoil and agitation of an election squabble, these must indeed have been the happiest of times.

As the time set apart for the election approached, it became evident that an unusual degree of interest was being excited in the contest of

1837. It was mooted that two new candidates were to be brought into the field. Mr. Hardy was not quite so popular with his party as formerly. An impression was gaining ground that he was trying to accommodate his views to suit two factions, and the Tories of Bradford did not approve of the tone expressed in a couplet which it was said Mr. Hardy was fond of applying to himself,—

> In moderation placing all my glory,
> The Tories call me Whig, and Whigs a Tory.

In response to a requisition signed by six hundred voters, Mr. William Busfeild, of Upwood, near Keighley, consented to become a a candidate. His nephew, Mr. William Busfeild (the late Mr. W. Busfeild Ferrand, of Harden) also signified his intention of entering into the contest. Four candidates were thus brought into the field—two Tories, and the same number of Whigs.

On the day of nomination, the streets of Bradford were thronged with interested spectators, the neighbourhood of the White Lion, Kirkgate, being especially crowded by on-lookers anxiously awaiting the appearance of the two Tory candidates, Messrs. John Hardy and W. Busfeild, junr., who were to proceed from here to the hustings. At length the two gentlemen arrived, and were greeted by "loud and prolonged" cheers. A procession, four abreast, was formed, headed by a brass band, and, amid a lavish display of blue bunting, and sundry other party emblems, the demonstration set forth to the hustings at the Court House. Meanwhile an equal, if not a greater interest was being taken in the Liberal candidates, Messrs. E. C. Lister and W. Busfeild, senr. A large procession, accompanied by four brass bands started from Manningham Hall and made a triumphant entry into the town.

Arrived at the hustings, in front of which, it is said, a crowd numbering not less than twenty thousand persons was gathered, the usual formalities of nomination were gone through. The candidates made fine speeches and sweet promises, and were in turn badgered by loud-mouthed demagogues, who would persist in putting questions or exacting pledges of what they would have to do if elected. On the show of hands being taken, the majority were clearly in favour of Lister and the elder Busfeild. A poll was therefore demanded on behalf of the other two candidates, which was fixed to take place on the following day.

The contest began in right good earnest at eight o'clock in the morning, and it would have been difficult to say which party exceeded the other in zeal and activity. The Liberals came up in good style, and it was regarded as a fine stroke of business that they should have polled as many as 250 for both their candidates within the first half-hour. The hopes raised so early were sustained throughout the day, and, although the Tories fought with the utmost spirit and determination, it was evident they could not overtake their opponents unless by some unexpected stroke of good fortune.

The close of the poll showed the defeat of the two Tory candidates. Mr. Busfeild, junr. did not again enter into the contest for the representation of Bradford, but he afterwards sat for Knaresborough and Devonport.

It was in the summer of 1841 that the Whig ministry, after sustaining sundry humiliating defeats, were compelled to resign, and the country was called upon to face another election. In the eyes of the Radical section, the Whigs were now in disgrace. The four years during which they had held office had absolutely been wasted as contrasted with the great things that had been expected, and the fond hopes that had been raised. Besides all this, a succession of bad harvests, and other causes, had created a widespread distress; and nothing renders an administration more unpopular than hard times, however slight a share it may have had in bringing the same about.

The advanced Reformers felt that their confidence had been betrayed, and that they were simply the victims of Whig deception. The time for temporising was gone by, and sterner measures must now be tried. There were not a few who openly advocated the "physical force" policy of Peter Bussey, and the "signs of the times" were now to be plainly read in the Poor Law Riots of 1837, and the outbreak of Chartism that followed two years later.

We allude to these events, however, only to show their bearing upon the election of 1841. The unpopularity of the Whigs was regarded by the Tories as affording a favourable chance of returning a representative of their own colour. As early as 1838 an "Operative Conservative Association" was formed, its rooms being at "Bob" Waterhouse's, in Bank Street. The late postmaster, Mr. Wm. Coates, who was then a thorough-going politician, was one of its most able and active members, and through his efforts, a requisition signed by upwards of six hundred electors, was presented to Mr. Hardy, desiring him again to contest Bradford, which he eventually consented to do.

Mr. E. C. Lister, who had represented the town since 1832, was now desirous of quitting the "the stormy sea of politics," and of seeking the retirement which his advanced age required. He accordingly retired in favour of his son, Mr. Wm. Cunliffe Lister, a young barrister of great promise, and a gentleman of amiability and intelligence, and holding, it need scarcely be said, the same political opinions as his father.

Mr. Busfeild, senr., the former member, again came forward, and a fourth candidate was added to the list by the appearance of a person representing the Chartists of Bradford, Martin by name, and an Irishman by nationality. Tuesday, the 29th June was the nomination day, and a splendid ovation was made by the Tories in behalf of Mr. Hardy. A procession of people in carriages, on horseback, and on foot, with bands of music and a liberal display of banners, met that gentleman at Low Moor, and escorted him all the way to the hustings.

A large and imposing procession also accompanied the Whig candidates. The Chartist candidate was nominated by Mr. James Clarkson, a Bradford solicitor, who said he had great pleasure in introducing as a fit and proper person to represent them in Parliament, Mr. William Martin—a native of persecuted Ireland. He was born within the precincts of Dublin University, and had received the finishing touches of his education at three of the Whig Universities in England. The first was at York Castle, the second was at Northallerton House of Correction, and the third was at Lancaster Castle. True to his loyalty, he had, while in Northallerton gaol complained of a chaplain not praying for the Queen, and had taken it upon himself to do so.

He challenged any man in the borough to bring the least accusation against Mr. Martin's private character. His principles were comprised in the people's Charter, and he would prove himself a staunch advocate of the peoples' rights.

To the astonishment of the Whigs the show of hands was declared to be in favour of Mr. Hardy and Mr. Martin the Chartist. The latter, however, for some unaccountable reason, at once retired from the contest. The Whigs demanded a poll on behalf of their candidates. The election which took place on the following day resulted as follows:

Hardy	612
Lister	540
Busfeild	536

Within the brief space of four months the inhabitants of Bradford were again called upon to exercise their electoral franchise. The young and newly elected member, Mr. W. C. Lister, had suddenly died while on a visit to Farfield Hall, Addingham, where he had caught a severe cold. His funeral took place on the very day of the meeting of Parliament, and when he should have taken his seat in the House for the first time. In September a new election took place to supply the vacancy. The Whigs again brought forward Mr. Busfeild, senr., who had been defeated at the last election, while the Tories were determined if possible to secure anothei representative of their party. They were very sanguine of success, and the sequel showed that their hopes had not been built upon a false foundation. Never in the whole of the electoral history of Bradford has the town been brought so near to an absolute Tory representation as on this occasion.

The candidate selected by the Tories was no other than William Wilberforce, son of the great philanthropist of that name; and if a gentlemanly demeanour, and most persuasive style of eloquence could have secured his election, his success would have been certain. The full force of the Liberals, however, was brought to bear against the return of another Tory, and the tug of war between the two parties was unprecedented. "Never in the annals of Bradford electioneering," says Mr. James, "had so severe and acrimonious a contest been witnessed. Electors were hocussed and smuggled away; conflicts of a fearful character took place between the respective parties; disgraceful squibs and pasquinades covered the walls, and violent animosities were formed between neighbours and friends which a lifetime did not eradicate."

The election took place on the 15th September 1841, when the numbers were—Mr. Busfeild, 526; Mr. Wilberforce, 522;—a narrow majority which showed that though defeated there had been no lack of spirit and determination in the battle which the Tories of Bradford had so bravely fought.

We now pass on to notice the election of 1847 which was chiefly memorable for the appearance upon the scene of three new claimants for electoral honours, two of whom were afterwards to occupy prominent places in the political history of Bradford, and the third, though at no time a representative of this his native town, was destined to be raised to one of the proudest positions in England's legislature, and to be crowned with honours the like of which had never before fallen to the lot of any Bradfordian.

It is hardly necessary to say that in the last of these three candidates we allude to Lord Cranbrook—then Mr. Gathorne Hardy. This was his first venture in political life on his own account, but for some years previously he had taken an active interest in local politics and had brought considerable influence to bear on securing his father's return for this town. On the occasion of the opening of the Bradford Conservative Club a few years ago he could not refrain from making allusion to this interesting period of his career. "I can look back," he said, "upon Bradford and its neighbourhood for a long stretch of years . . . . It was here that I began my political education, and I am afraid to say how long ago, but certainly over forty years ago, I began to go through Bradford on behalf of my father when he was a candidate for your representation, and from that time I have never ceased to take an interest in the welfare of the town, and in the neighbouring West Riding. I remember those days how different it was even to pass through the neighbourhood of Bradford with a piece of blue flower or blue ribbon about you. I remember up to the year 1841, that so strong was the opposite party in this region that it was almost a dangerous thing to ride with a piece of blue ribbon in the frontlet of your horse for fear you should be taken for one of those abominable Tories."

It was in response to a requisition from the Conservatives of Bradford to himself and Mr. H. W. Wickham, that Mr. Gathorne Hardy consented to stand as a candidate in the interests of this party, and in place of his father who was now retiring from political life.

Mr. H. W. Wickham, who also responded to the request to offer himself as a candidate, now came forward.

The Liberal candidates were Mr. William Busfeild, the last of the old line of representatives, and Colonel Thomas Peronnet Thompson, a man eminent alike as a politician and a man of letters. He was born at Hull in 1783, and was educated at the Grammar School there. In 1806 he entered the army, and by the influence of Mr. Wilberforce was sent out two years afterwards to be Governor of Sierra Leone. Here he exerted himself more vigorously than was pleasing to the Home Government in putting down the project for continuing the purchase of slaves under the plea of apprenticeship, and for this he was recalled. After an arduous military service in India, where he learned Arabic he returned to England in 1821, a hale young man of thirty-eight, and of an experience far beyond his years. In 1825 he was promoted to the rank of Major, and afterwards to that of Lieut.-Colonel. Having cultivated the acquaintance of Jeremy Bentham, he contributed to the *Westminster Review*, of which he afterwards became editor and proprietor, and he wrote from time to time a number of pamphlets and works on various subjects, especially political economy. Among these were his famous "Corn Law Catechism," which did much to undermine the Protectionist system of commercial policy. He was an advocate of the principles of Free-trade, and as one of the authors of the famous Charter, he was popular with the working classes.

Such was the man who along with Mr. Busfeild was brought forward by the Liberals to contest the election of 1847. It was an interesting circumstance that on his nomination, a seconder was found in the person of one who was afterwards to play a most important part in England's political history—Mr. W. E. Forster.

The nomination took place on July the 29th, in a field now the site of the Exchange Station, and the election followed next day. The Talbot and the Sun Hotels were secured by the Tories, at which places the braying of trumpets and the distribution of blue favours, *ad lib.*, were only equalled by the tumult from the Bowling Green, the head-quarters of the Liberals.

The result of the election was, that Mr. Busfeild and Colonel Thompson were declared to be duly elected.

A vacancy was created in the representation of Bradford in the year 1851, by the death of Mr. Busfeild, who, with the exception of a brief interval, had served the constituency for a period of fourteen years. A contested election in order to supply the same, was however avoided by the Liberals bringing forward a candidate who was held in such general respect, and whose political opinions were of so moderate a character, that his election was universally approved, and was allowed to pass without opposition.

Mr. Robert Milligan, the gentleman in whom this confidence was reposed, was a native of Dunnance, in Kircudbright. His parents were farmers—honest and sturdy Scotch peasantry. No lavish expenditure had been bestowed upon his education, but he had received a thorough training in habits of industry and economy, which were of great service to him in after life. It was about the year 1802, that he found his way into these parts, not exactly with the traditionary "clog and shoe" start in life so often ascribed to men who have risen from the ranks, but at any rate with a beginning as lowly as that of a "travelling Scotchman." In 1810 he gave up his wanderings and finally settled down at Bradford as a draper. He took a house in Westgate near the King's Head Inn, which however was so small as to necessitate his removal to a larger one lower down the street, afterwards occupied by Messrs. Ward, drapers. After some years he again removed to a shop next to the Talbot Hotel, to which he was succeeded by Mr. McCroben. Whilst here he was buyer to Messrs. Leo Schuster & Co., of Manchester, and it was while executing their orders that Mr. Forbes, a London traveller, remarked that "if he had patterns he could sell a lot of those goods." The patterns were supplied, and the sales from them were so great, that it quickly led to the constitution of the firm of Milligan, Forbes & Co.

It would be difficult to point to one who better represented the commercial growth of Bradford, from its youth up to its maturity, than did Mr. Milligan. For fully half a century he was closely identified with its advancement in trade, and was no less interested during that period in its benevolent institutions. In politics he was a staunch Liberal though no man was more tolerant towards those who held views differing from his own either in politics or religion. He was one of Bradford's most useful and honoured citizens, and his townsmen were proud to show their appreciation of his services by bestowing upon him the highest honours at their disposal, and this they did by electing him, on the incorporation of the borough, as their first mayor, and afterwards as we have seen, as one of their representatives in Parliament.

At the general election which took place in July, 1852, the great question of Free-trade was agitating the country, and was made the party-cry of the Liberals. It was a question in which politicians of all sections were keenly interested, and the election proved to be one of the severest contests on record. It was the last struggle of the Protectionists, and was the battle by which it was finally decided that the principles of Free-trade should henceforth govern the commercial legislation of England.

The Conservatives, who had doubtless seen the folly of attempting to carry two of their party, now confined their choice to one, and were wise in their choice, for a gentleman more highly esteemed or more popular with a large proportion of the inhabitants than Mr. H. W. Wickham was, it would not have been easy to find.

Mr. Wickham's antecedents, if Mr. James, the historian, be correct, were most illustrious, for he traces them back to the great William of Wykeham, Bishop of Winchester, who founded New College, Oxford, in the fourteenth century. There is no doubt, however, that for the last two centuries the family had been of high respectability, and connected with eminent dignitaries both in Church and State. Mr. Wickham's father was the Rev. Lamplugh Hird, Prebendary of York, and Vicar of Paull, in the East Riding, the youngest son of Colonel Wickham, of Cottingley. Henry took the name of Hird, which was that of his mother, the daughter of Richard Hird, Esq., of Rawdon, but resumed his paternal name of Wickham on his father's death, in 1843.

Mr. H. W. Wickham was first sent to the Bradford Grammar School to receive his education, and afterwards to the University of Oxford. Through his father's connection with the Low Moor Company, he became early linked with the interests of that large concern, and by his business talents and knowledge of metallurgy, contributed in no small degree towards its prosperity. In 1833 he was appointed a West Riding Magistrate, and it is recorded of him that no more just, impartial, and patient an administrator of the law ever sat on the bench. He was also appointed Chairman of Quarter Sessions, and for many years was also Chairman of the Lancashire and Yorkshire Railway Company.

The candidates chosen to contest the election of 1852 were the two former members, Col. Thompson and Mr. Milligan, both Liberals, and Mr. Wickham, Conservative.

The Liberals had been sanguine that they would carry both their men, but the very favourable reception accorded to Mr. Wickham began to create some alarm, especially among the supporters of Col. Thompson. Many were the presentiments and prophesyings as to the result of this contest, and the issues of it were watched with the keenest interest. The nomination was fixed for the 6th of July, and on that day, a large and lively audience gathered in front of the Court House. Mr. Hudson, the Town Clerk, read the precept, and then the Mayor, Mr. Samuel Smith, called upon anyone to come forward that had candidates to propose. Thereupon Mr. W. E. Forster stepped to the front, and, after addressing the electors, proposed Col. Thompson; seconded by Mr. Edward Kenion. Mr. S. Cunliffe Lister, who now took a lively interest in politics, and was a Liberal, proposed Mr. Milligan; seconded by Mr. (afterwards Sir) Titus Salt. Mr. John Rand proposed Mr. Wickham; seconded by Mr. David Ramsden. A fourth candidate was brought forward in the person of Mr. George Julian Harney, a popular Chartist lecturer, who found a proposer in Councillor Hudson, and a seconder in Mr. William Cooke, afterwards proprietor of the *Bradford Times*. As in the case of Martin, the former Chartist candidate, no further effort was made to secure the return of this party. Harney, by the way, was a man of considerable ability. On one occasion he even opposed Lord Palmerston, at Tiverton, though ineffectually. He subsequently went to America, where he became State Librarian for the Government of Massachusetts.

On the show of hands being taken, the hopes of the Liberals were again revived by the fact that a large majority declared in favour of Colonel Thompson, Mr. Milligan having the next largest number. A poll was therefore demanded on behalf of Mr. Wickham, to take place next day.

A poll *did* take place on the following day, and it was an event that will not soon be forgotten by those who took part in it. Never, perhaps, was the hourly announcement of progress watched with a more devouring interest. Mr. Milligan took the lead, but at ten o'clock was outnumbered by Mr. Wickham. Again Mr. Milligan was a-head at twelve, but the Colonel stood lowest on the list. At two o'clock, Milligan was first, Col. Thompson second, and Mr. Wickham —last. The close of the poll was now awaited with breathless anxiety, and great was the joy of some, but equally great the disappointment of others, when it was announced that Mr. Milligan was at the head of the poll, and that Mr. Wickham had a majority over Colonel Thompson of just two votes! The numbers stood thus—

Milligan	1264
Wickham	1151
Thompson	1149

A dissolution of Parliament was brought about in the spring of 1857, by the defeat of Lord Palmerston, on Mr. Cobden's motion condemning the Chinese War. Mr. Milligan, who had not yet sat five years, "finding himself, from his advanced age, unequal to the late hours and onerous duties of the House of Commons," embraced this opportunity of retiring from his post. The question of returning two Liberal members at the election had been already mooted, and the merits of the proposed candidates freely discussed. These gentlemen were Col. Thompson (the former member) and Mr. Titus Salt. In view of the fact, however, that Mr. Wickham, since his return, had voted for so many Liberal measures, and had now almost come to be regarded as a Liberal himself, many, if not most of that party were in favour of his re-election, along with a candidate of a more Radical colour. To avoid a contest, a compromise was therefore effected between the parties by the return of Col. Thompson and Mr. Wickham. No one was more agreeable to this arrangement than Mr. Salt himself, who had the highest regard for Mr. Wickham, although he held different views on some of the political questions of the day.

Mr. Alfred Illingworth, one of the present members for Bradford, had now begun to interest himself publicly in matters political, and at the meeting referred to spoke on such questions as the ballot; extension of the suffrage, and separation of Church and State.

Two years had barely elapsed since the election of 1857, when another dissolution took place, this time through the defeat of Lord Derby's Government on the Reform Bill brought in by Mr. Disraeli, a measure which came far short of satisfying the demands of the Liberal and Radical sections, who wished to see the franchise extended to the industrial classes of the community. A considerable impetus was given to the Reform movement by the appearance at Bradford, in January, 1859, of Mr. John Bright, who, in addressing a crowded and enthusiastic gathering in St. George's Hall, gave the outline of a new Reform Bill, which he thought would settle the question for some time to come.

Three candidates came forward to contest the election of 1859, viz., Mr. Wickham, Mr. Titus Salt, and Mr. Alfred Harris. On Mr. Salt being proposed at a meeting in St. George's Hall, to represent the town, a "working man" in the audience accused him of having been instrumental in causing the incorporation of Bradford, and then of removing his works to Saltaire, in order to avoid the heavy taxation entailed as the result of such incorporation. This called forth an eloquent and forcible reply from Mr. H. F. Lockwood, the architect of Saltaire. He said he would answer the remark that had been made

Sir Titus Salt, Bart.

because Mr. Salt was too modest to do so. There was no one, of whose acts he could speak more worthily than he could of his. It was his own (Mr. Lockwood's) good fortune to be entrusted with the direction of the works at Saltaire, and in that capacity he might tell them that Mr. Salt gave him instructions upon all occasions to study the health, comfort, and happiness of his people, expense being in no case a consideration. He desired him to give them plenty of fresh air, and plenty of pure water. Wonld any man say that Mr. Salt deserted Bradford? He could only tell them that in the enormous contracts for his works, Mr. Salt always gave the preference to Bradford men, and the amount of these contracts executed in the town was £250,000! Did they call that deserting Bradford? At one time there were not less than three thousand men employed belonging to Bradford. Mr. Salt was always doing great good in other ways, and his motto might be written, "Deeds, not words." He had known him go to a clergyman of the Church of England in feeble health, with a handful of notes, and say, "Here, take that; every shilling of it is to be spent at the sea-side!"

This brief but convincing speech had a telling effect upon the audience, and the resolution in support of Mr. Salt was carried with great enthusiasm.

Mr. Salt was a man of few words, but he made a characteristic speech, in which he briefly touched upon his political views. "I have been called upon," he said, "to come forward as a candidate for this town. * * * * It is forty years since I came to this borough. I came as a boy. I have been educated here in commercial affairs, and you all know my political principles. For the last thirty years I have never flinched from them, and they are the principles I now profess. I advocated the Reform Bill of 1832, and I also supported the successful effort to repeal the Corn Laws, and for the extension of education among the working classes. * * * * I shall support the vote by ballot. I think it quite essential to give independence to voters, and whether they are shopkeepers or the working classes, I would have them all independent by giving them the ballot. As a commercial man, you may be sure I shall advocate all possible economy in the expenditure of the public money."

Mr. Alfred Harris, the Conservative candidate, had not hitherto brought himself into prominence by taking a public interest in politics. His was a retiring and unobtrusive nature, and the surprise to many was not so much that such a candidate should have been selected, as that so modest and unassuming a gentleman should have consented to bear the brunt of an election contest. Mr. Harris was held in great esteem by his townsmen both for his private worth and his great benevolence, but it was not difficult to perceive that Mr. Salt was the more popular candidate of the two. The friends of Mr. Wickham felt safe in being able to secure that gentleman's return.

On the show of hands being taken at the nomination, the majority were in favour of Mr. Wickham and Mr. Salt. A poll was therefore demanded for Mr. Harris, which was to take place on the following day.

Next day the polling began in right good earnest, and its progress was watched with the keenest interest. Great was the rejoicing in the Liberal camp when the victory was declared in favour of Mr. Wickham and Mr. Salt. Throughout the day the streets presented a gay and festive appearance, and during the afternoon (being Saturday) the inhabitants of the surrounding districts poured into the town in their thousands—some to hear the result of the contest, others to share in the rejoicings at Mr. Salt's victory. A dense crowd gathered in front of the George Hotel, Market Street, the headquarters of Mr. Salt's committee, and here various lively interludes were performed, such as throwing money into the crowd, which caused an amount of struggling, scrambling, and tearing of clothes, the like of which was never seen in Bradford either before or since.

We are now brought to the year 1861—a period which enables us to pass from the early to the more recent of the Bradford elections. Treating of events that will be within the recollection of most our readers, little more than a brief outline will now be necessary.

For some time prior to the eve of the session of 1861, Mr. Salt had felt his health giving way, and that it would be necessary for him to retire from his Parliamentary duties. In January of that year the inhabitants of Bradford were taken by surprise at the announcement that Mr. Salt had resigned his seat. From the time of his election he had faithfully attended to his duties, his place in the House being always occupied, and his name found on every division list. But the country was to be no loser by the step he had taken, for now began those vast schemes of charity and benevolence for which his name will ever be held in universal gratitude. He was spared to enjoy a season of comparative rest and retirement reaching over sixteen years. In September, 1869, Her Majesty conferred upon him the dignity of Baronet.

The following statement of the expenses incurred by the three candidates, in the election of 1859, will be interesting to many of our readers :—

Election Expenses, 1859.

	Wickham.			Salt.			Harris.		
Hire of Rooms	20	15	3	153	5	2	122	6	7
Printing, Advertising, etc.	88	7	5	186	3	8	208	8	5
Cab Hire	118	10	9	164	8	9	144	9	0
Conveyance of Voters by Rail	4	6	0	21	2	7	7	17	6
Election Agents, Clerks, etc.	167	10	0	149	7	0	69	1	0
Canvassers and Messengers	60	16	0	200	1	0	153	17	9
Miscellaneous Expenses ...	205	17	10	363	13	11	253	19	10
	£666	3	3	£1238	2	1	£960	0	1

With a view to the appointment of a successor to Mr Salt, the Liberal electors held a meeting, at which the names of four candidates were submitted, viz., Mr. Edward Miall, General Thompson, Mr. W. E. Forster, and Mr. John Priestman. Political feeling was just then at a pretty high pitch in Bradford, and opinions touching the views of these gentlemen were, in some instances, expressed with much greater freedom than courtesy. Eventually, two of the gentlemen proposed declined to enter the contest, and Mr. Miall wrote refusing to divide the party. Mr. Forster was therefore elected without opposition, the event taking place on the 11th February, 1861.

THE RIGHT HON. W. E. FORSTER, M.P.

(*From a Photograph by* APPLETON, *Manningham Lane, Bradford.*)

William Edward Forster, who, from an outspoken manner of speech, and certain other characteristics peculiar to the "North Countree," has often been mistaken for a typical Yorkshireman, was born at Bradpole, in Dorsetshire, on the 11th July, 1818. His father, Mr. William Forster, was a well-known philanthropist and minister of the Gospel in connection with the Society of Friends, and had married Anna Buxton, sister of Sir Thomas Fowell Buxton of Anti-Slavery fame. William Edward was educated at the school of the Society of Friends, at Tottenham, and very early in life evinced an interest in public affairs. When only in his twenty-ninth year he visited Ireland during a dreadful famine in that country, and afterwards wrote a clever account of what he had seen, and made a forcible appeal on behalf of the distressed people.

Mr. Forster came to take up his abode at Bradford and start his business career while a very young man. It is related that while staying with his friend, Mr. John Hustler, junr., at Bolton House, he one day fixed upon Rose Cottage, at Low Fold, Bolton, as the spot just suited to his tastes, and for several years during his connection with Mr. Fison he resided there, and laid the foundation of those vast stores of knowledge which were afterwards so valuable to him. Subsequently he removed to Rawdon, and among the distinguished guests who visited him there were Mr. and Mrs. Thomas Carlyle, and Thomas Cooper, the Chartist poet-orator. In 1850 he married Jane Martha, eldest daughter of the late Dr. Arnold, of Rugby, the "dear old doctor" of "Tom Brown's School Days."

Up to 1847 Mr. Forster was more concerned with the social than the political life of Bradford, but in that year he came boldly forward as a strong supporter and ardent worker in the cause of Liberalism. At one particular election, (before the passing of the Corrupt Practices Act,) in which he took a deep interest, intelligence was brought to the committee on which he sat, that the enemy had captured some waverers, and actually had them under lock and key in a certain public house in Westgate, where they were being well-primed with beer. In a moment Mr. Forster disappeared from the committee rooms, cleared Ivegate at three strides, and, not being able to enter by the door, leapt through the window into the room where the roystering backsliders were drinking, and by very force of eloquence so spurred them on to duty that he was able to lead them triumphantly to the poll.

It was not until 1859 that Mr. Forster attempted to secure a seat in Parliament, when he contested Leeds as the Liberal colleague of Mr. Edward Baines against Mr. Beecroft, the Tory candidate. He was, however, defeated on that occasion, but two years later was successful, as we have seen, in becoming one of the representatives for Bradford. At the general election of 1865, Mr. Forster had again the good fortune to be returned for this borough without the anxiety of a contest.

By the death of Mr. Wickham, on the 23rd September, 1867, who had faithfully served his constituents for well nigh fifteen years, another election became necessary. This was regarded by the Radicals as a favourable opportunity for bringing forward their favourite candidate Mr. Edward Miall, a politician undoubtedly of the highest character and repute, but whose views on the Disestablishment question were about as unpalatable to the Church party as they were acceptable to some of the Dissenting bodies. Mr. Matthew William Thompson, the opposing candidate, was a Liberal, but his antipathy to the Disestablishment movement and its advocates was well known, and it was believed the Tories would regard the mere fact of his being opposed to Mr. Miall as a sufficient title to their votes in the absence of a candidate of their own colour. It was evident from the character of the meetings held by both parties that the struggle was to be one of no ordinary severity. We have no intention of raking up the hard and unkind things that were said by both sides. Suffice it to say that on the one hand, Mr. Miall was regarded as the very "apple of discord," brought from a distance by a narrow and bigoted sect for no other purpose than to create strife and bitterness among a peaceful and contented people, while on the other, Mr. Thompson was accused of gaining his influence over the electors by no better means than the power of the beer barrel, and the countenance and support of the Licensed Victuallers. It would have been well if matters had gone no further than this, but, unfortunately, words were exchanged for blows, and the election of 1867 was marred by some disagreeable features that should not have appeared. On the day of election (Tuesday, October 15th) the streets of Bradford presented a miserable aspect. The very elements were unsympathetic. Rain had fallen for several days previously, and made the busy thoroughfares almost impassable with mud and dirt. The large influx of visitors from surrounding districts only served to increase the universal turmoil and confusion. A large and excited crowd took early possession of the street in front of the committee rooms, to watch with eagerness the progress of the poll, which was published every half-hour. The earlier returns of the morning were highly satisfactory to the Miallite party, but, alas, it was soon found that "hope told a flattering tale," and by eleven o'clock the contest was virtually decided. Up to this time the dense multitude in Bridge Street had behaved itself with tolerable decency, but as time wore on, the general good humour gave place to positive viciousness, and instead of the harmless divertisement of pelting each other with paper pellets, pieces of cork, etc., missiles of a more dangerous character, such as wisps of straw twisted into hard knots, and dipped into mud, were freely used. Many of the electors were literally covered with mire before they were able to record their votes. During the afternoon, matters assumed a more serious aspect. The crowd was now largely composed of roughs, who desired nothing better than a thorough breach of the peace. The throwing of a large stone through the window of Mr. Miall's committee room was but the

Ripley's Dyeworks, 1807.

prelude for further depredations of the same sort, and window smashing became the order of the day, with the result that several persons received severe cuts and bruises, while others were seriously injured. Eventually something like order was restored, but not before a large body of police had been summoned with weapons of defence no less formidable than truncheons and drawn cutlasses.

Although the result of the poll was not officially declared until the following day, it was known that Mr. Thompson had won the battle. Mr. Miall, in response to a request from his supporters that he should address them, said—"Gentlemen, in such a contest as this has been, to be defeated is to be honoured. I am by no means downhearted by the result. I thank you all most heartily for what you have done. I mean to come to Bradford again (loud cheers). I hope at that time to find a very different result. My time is not yet come. I have nothing to do in this Parliament, but in the Reformed Parliament I do hope to take a part, and then I hope Bradford and I shall be more closely united."

Mr. Thompson was on the Continent during the election proceedings, on account of his own and the ill health of his son. A telegram was received from him, and read at the nomination, in which he expressed his confidence that he would be placed at the head of the poll.

The statement given at the declaration of the poll was—

Thompson	2210
Miall	1807

It is hardly necessary to state that Mr. Miall redeemed his promise of again contesting Bradford—with what result is well known. Little more than a year had elapsed when a general election took place, his opponent this time being Mr. (afterwards Sir) H. W. Ripley. Again, however, he was defeated; but the outcome of this unhappy contest was the memorable petition against Mr. Ripley, heard before Baron Martin, in January 1869, by which that gentleman was unseated. A counter-petition was at the same time brought against Mr. Forster by Mr. Ripley's supporters, but it hopelessly failed to accomplish the end which it was intended to gain.

These events were soon followed by the election of Mr. Miall to the vacant seat, although he had again to face Mr. M. W. Thompson as his opponent.

At the general election in February, 1874, the borough was contested by four candidates, the two successful ones being Mr. Forster and Mr. Ripley. The two other candidates were Mr. J. V. Godwin and the late Mr. James Hardaker, who were supported by the Liberal Registration Association. In the election of April, 1880, Mr. Alfred Illingworth first appeared as a candidate, and, was returned, along with Mr. Forster, with a large majority over Mr. Ripley, the Conservative candidate. The last named gentleman was soon afterwards created a Baronet.

On May 7th, Mr. Forster was re-elected without opposition, on his being appointed Chief Secretary for Ireland.

The elections that have taken place since the Re-distribution of Seats' Act will be found recorded in the list given below. At the first of these, the Right Honourable W. E. Forster was elected for the Central Division, and held the proud position of being at the head of the poll for the re-constructed constituency of Bradford. That position he had held from the day he was first returned, and it is gratifying to reflect that now that his course was nearly run, and his useful labours all but finished, he had the consolation of feeling that he was still member for Bradford. It was an honour he highly prized, and surely none had ever deserved it better. He died on April 5th, 1886.

In this brief notice of Mr. Forster's political career, we have not attempted to go beyond that portion of it which relates to the constituency which he represented, or to touch upon the great measures with which his name must be ever associated. These are matters of national history, and will be found recorded in its annals. In the recent "Life of the Right Honourable W. E. Forster," from the able pen of Mr. T. Wemyss Reid, a graceful and worthy tribute has been paid to the memory of one of the most distinguished and illustrious statesmen that England has ever produced.

Bradford Parliamentary Elections.

THE NAMES OF THE UNSUCCESSFUL CANDIDATES ARE IN ITALICS.

September, 15th, 1832—Ellis Cunliffe Lister, 650 votes; John Hardy, 471 votes; *Geo. Banks*, 402 votes.

January 10th, 1835—John Hardy, 611; E. C. Lister, 589; *George Hadfield*, 392.

July 12th, 1837—Ellis Cunliffe Lister, 635; William Busfeild, 621; *John Hardy*, 443; *William Busfeild, jun.*, 383.

June 30th, 1841—John Hardy, 612; W. C. Lister, 440; *William Busfeild*, 436.

September 15th, 1841—(In place of W. C. Lister, deceased.)—W. Busfeild, 526; *W. Wilberforce*, 522.

July 30th, 1847—Wm. Busfeild, 940; Col. Thompson, 928; *H. W. Wickham*, 858; *Gathorne Hardy*, 808.

1851.—No Contest.—In place of W. Busfeild, deceased, Robert Milligan.

July 7th, 1852—Robert Milligan, 1366; Henry W. Wickham, 1159; *Colonel P. Thompson*, 1153.

1857.—No Contest.—H. W. Wickham, General Perronet Thompson.

April 30th, 1859—H. W. Wickham, 2076; Titus Salt, 1727; *Alfred Harris*, 1222.

1861.—No Contest.—In place of Titus Salt, resigned, William Edward Forster.

1865—No Contest.—Henry W. Wickham; William E. Forster.

October 15th, 1867—In place of H. W. Wickham, deceased—Matthew William Thompson, 2210; *Edward Miall*, 1807.

November 16th, 1868—W. E. Forster, 9648; H. W. Ripley, 9347; *Edward Miall*, 8768.

March 12th, 1869—In place of H. W. Ripley, unseated on petition—Edward Miall, 9243; *M. W. Thompson*, 7806.

February 4th, 1874—W. E. Forster, 11,945; H. W. Ripley, 10,223; *J. V. Godwin*, 8393; *Jas. Hardaker*, 8115.

April 1st, 1880—W. E. Forster, 14,245; Alfred Illingworth, 12,922; *H. W. Ripley*, 9018. The number of votes polled was 22,108.

May 7th, 1880—W. E. Forster—re-elected without opposition after his appointment as Chief Secretary for Ireland.

ELECTIONS SINCE RE-DISTRIBUTION OF SEATS' ACT.

November 28th, 1885—*Western Division:* A. Illingworth, 4688; *H. B. Reed*, 3408. *Central Division:* W. E. Forster, 5275; *G. Motley Waud*, 3732. *Eastern Division:* Angus Holden, 4713; *John Taylor*, 4367.

April 21st, 1886—*Central Division:* (In place of W. E. Forster, deceased)—G. J. Shaw-Lefevre, 4407; *E. B. Hoare*, 3627.

July 6th, 1886—*Western Division:* A. Illingworth, 3975; *A. W. Stirling*, 2623. *Central Division:* G. J. Shaw-Lefevre, 4410; *C. M. Norwood*, 3951. *Eastern Division:* H. B. Reed, 4519; *Angus Holden*, 4223.

Col. T. Peronnet Thompson, M.P.

CHAPTER IX.

Old Bradford Families, and their Homes.

LOOKING upon Bradford in its present-day aspect, one can hardly realise the fact that "once upon a time" it was so small and insignificant as to consist of little more than its church, its castle, its lord's mill for "grinding ye people's corn," and its burgage-houses, mingled with the huts and cottages of the bondmen,—'villains,' or common people—stretching at irregular distances the whole length of its three lanes, Kirkgate, Westgate and Ivegate. And yet this is no fancy picture, reader, but one truthfully based upon the facts set out in the "Inquisition" made on the death of Henry de Lacy, Earl of Lincoln, and bearing date March 3rd, 1311.

Coming down with a very long stride to the days of Elizabeth and James, when the town had considerably advanced in size and wealth, we arrive at a very important period in house-building in Bradford and the district, the best of the old mansions here dating from that time. With peaceful times, and a sense of security prevailing throughout the land, a more luxurious and domesticated order of things set in. The throwing off of the old feudal bondage gave birth to a wealthy and influential middle-class, who built themselves mansions, which for solidity and durability have not since been equalled. It might then be truly said that an Englishman's home was his *castle.* Quaint-looking buildings they were, those dear old homesteads, with their many gables, chimney stacks, and mullioned windows; furnished within by massive chests, delf-cases, long-settles, and wainscottings, all of sturdy oak. Many of these old mansions yet exist, but, alas, how sadly shorn of their former grandeur! They are impressive still, however, even in their degradation. No longer are they tenanted by the yeomanry of bygone days, but, after being hacked and hewn out of all former semblance have each been made to serve the purpose of some half-dozen tenements for the "humbler classes," in the accomplishment of which feat old wainscottings and rare carvings have been ruthlessly torn down, and mullioned and diamond-paned windows knocked out to give place to patent sashes and "squares"—more convenient perhaps, but not nearly so picturesque, nor yet so substantial.

Happily, however, not all our time-honoured houses have shared this fate. Bolling Hall, Horton Hall, Horton House, Royds Hall, Miryshaw, and a few others are pleasing exceptions. May they long remain so. Of the old mansions erected in the Elizabethan and Stuart periods that formerly adorned the old streets of Bradford—and there were several such in Westgate, Kirkgate, and in the neighbourhood of the Parish Church—barely a trace now remains. The old building at the bottom of Westgate, once a mansion of some consequence, but for many years used as shops by Mr. Gaskarth and his predecessors, and recently pulled down for the extension of Kirkgate, was the last of its race, for not a vestige remains to tell of the time when the best of the Bradford families resided in the very heart of the town. They, too, have disappeared as completely as the old houses which they once inhabited.

Whitaker in his "Loidis and Elmete" states that the eminent families of this parish (Bradford) have never been numerous, and gives as a reason the fact that the greater part of such parish ascended to the confines of the moors, and afforded not many very flattering situations to those who were in a condition to choose for themselves, and, for the rest, the genius of trade had expelled the aristocracy. He adds, however, that in their places had arisen many modern houses in every direction about the town, fruits of prosperous industry, and rising in the scale from simple convenience almost to the confines of splendour.

At the time of Dugdale's "visitation" to Yorkshire in 1665, he made the following entries of gentlemen bearing arms hereabouts:

Manningham	Mr. John Wilkinson.
North Bierley	Mr. Wm. Richardson.
Allerton-cum-Wilsden	Mr. Peter Sunderland.
Bowling	Henry Savile, Esq.
Eccleshill	John Stanhope, Esq.
Haworth	Mr John Ramsden.
Manningham	Mr. John Lister.
Shipley	Mr. Wm. Rawson.

This list it will be seen does not include the name of a single *Bradford* family. Coming down to the year 1798 we find the following names included in a list of persons claiming the use of armorial bearings, and describing themselves as residing in the parish of Bradford:

Duffield, Esq., Francis	Town Hill.
Field, Esq., Joshua	Heaton.
Hird, Rev. Lamplugh	Bradford.
Hodsden, Mrs. Dorothy	Horton.
Jarratt, Esq., John	Bradford.
Lister, Mrs Mary	Manningham.
Preston, Miss Mary	Kirkgate.
Rawson, Mrs. Frances	Bradford.
Sharpe, Esq., C. S. B.	Old Hall, Horton
Stott, Mrs. Susannah	Eccleshill Hall.

The mansions that once clustered around the Parish Church have all disappeared, unless we may except the old Paper Hall, which, however, has been so mutilated and defaced that it is almost impossible to form any conception of its original appearance. But enough remains to show that it has been one of Bradford's finest houses. The long streets of cottages and small shops that now surround it were not so much as dreamt of when the hall was built in the days of the Commonwealth. Green fields bordered both sides of the road, then the only highway to Leeds, while in front of it lay the glebe lands of the church, which, after changing hands a great many times came into the possession of Mr. Edmund Peckover, on a portion of which he built the mansion known as Eastbrook House.

The Old Paper Hall.

We cannot satisfy the curiosity of our readers as to how the old house came to be called the Paper Hall, nor do we know the precise year of its erection, but we do know that it was built by William Rookes, of Royds Hall, near Low Moor, who died on the 25th of October, 1651. From the Rookes it came into the possession of the Bowers, an old and respectable Bradford family.

Towards the close of last century it was occupied by Mr. James Garnett, and it was during his residence here that the first spinning machine in Bradford was set up. Even then the old hall could boast of much of its splendour. The good man took a pride in making its fine old oak glitter with the bees' wax and oil with which it was constantly rubbed. Such is the solidity of the building that some portions of it seem to defy the ravages of Time itself. All the floors, both upper and lower, are of solid black English oak, and every beam and rafter is of the same material. The doors of the hall are studded all over with nails, and provided with huge draw-bars at the back so

Stott Hill House.

as to resist any attempt on the part of the enemy (if there should have been one) to intrude upon the privacy of the owner.

The old hall is not without its bit of tradition in the shape of a ghost story. We have not seen the ghost ourselves, but have it on the authority of the blacksmith whose workshop is just behind the hall, that it may be both seen and heard. It is supposed to be that of a certain old admiral who was murdered here at some time or other, whose spirit refuses to be "laid" as all good spirits should.

Another fine old mansion in the neighbourhood of the church was that known as Stott Hill House. To the present generation it will only be remembered as a filthy and dilapidated old lodging house in which "well-aired beds at tuppence a night" were to be had. It was recently pulled down in order to widen the thoroughfare leading from Stott Hill to Bolton Road.

The old hall bore the date "1660," and the initials "J. A. W.," the latter representing the names of Jonas and Anna Waterhouse. The Rev. Jonas Waterhouse was the ejected Vicar of Bradford to whom reference has already been made. This was his residence, and would then doubtless be regarded as the vicarage.

In more recent times Stott Hill House was the residence of the Priestley family. Joseph Priestley was for several years chief manager of the Leeds and Liverpool Canal Company. His son John, better known as Captain Priestley (in whose memory we have now Captain Street and Priestley Street), was an influential townsman in his day. One of his daughters became the wife of the late Mr. Ferrand of St. Ives, and another was married to the late Mr. J. A. Busfeild of Upwood.

Of all the fine old mansions that ever graced the streets of Bradford there was not one that looked prouder or more dignified than did the Manor Hall in Kirkgate, with its noble frontage, its fine avenue walks, and its extensive and beautiful gardens in the rear.

The building known to the present generation of Bradfordians (see illustration) was only erected in 1705, but it stood on the site of a hall of great antiquity. This was the home of a long succession of Lords of the Manor, and here resided the Rawsons, who were big folks in Bradford as far back as the reign of Henry VII. The earliest mention made of the Bradford branch of this family is that of William Rawson who built the hall, then described as a "fair place," in that reign. There was a long succession of "Williams," who do not appear to have been noted for anything in particular, except that some of them are described as "Attorneys."

It is unnecessary to trace the fortunes of the Rawson family further than to state that very early in the present century the Manor Hall ceased to be their residence. Benjamin Rawson having "considerably increased his fortune by trade," purchased Nidd Hall, near Knaresborough, and went to reside there, and his daughter Miss Elizabeth Rawson, the present Lady of the Manor, now resides at the same place.

The Manor Hall was next occupied by Mr. John Hardy, one of the first members who represented Bradford in Parliament. It was while residing here that several of his children were born, one of whom was Gathorne Hardy, the present Lord Cranbrook, who was born on the 1st of October, 1814. He was educated at Shrewsbury School, and at Oriel College, Oxford, where he was second-class in classics, and graduated B.A. in 1836, being made Hon. D.C.L. at Oxford in 1866. In 1838 he married Jane, daughter of Mr. James Orr, of Holywood House, county Down. He was called to the bar at the Inner Temple, where he practised for some time. Prior to his first election to Parliament, he was appointed a county magistrate, and became a deputy-lieutenant of the West Riding in May, 1856. He unsuccessfully contested Bradford in July, 1847, but there were some who then declared that "young Hardy," as he was familiarly called by his admirers, would one day make himself a name in the country. In 1856, he was returned for Leominster, which place he represented till 1865, when he contested Oxford, and defeated no less an antagonist than Mr. Gladstone. His first appointment, we believe, was that of President of the Poor Law Board, and he has since been Under-Secretary for the Home Department; Secretary of State for War; Home Secretary, and Secretary for India, and at the present time of writing he is Lord President of the Council. He was created Lord Cranbrook in 1878.

Old Doorway, Manor Hall.

His eldest brother, J. Hardy, Esq., M.P., resided at Dunstan Hall, Burton-on-Trent, and was elected for Dartmouth in November, 1860. Charles Hardy, Esq., of Low Moor, the other brother, will long be remembered for his munificence in the erection and endowment of churches in Bradford and the district.

It was in 1824 that the precincts of the Manor Hall began to be used for the purposes of a market, and from this period began the

THE MANOR HALL, KIRKGATE.

"decline and fall" of the greatness of this fine old mansion. Hemmed in on all sides by a beggarly array of stalls and shambles which the inhabitants of fifty years ago were pleased to call *the* market, its resources were required for a great variety of "business purposes." More recently, its once stately rooms, rich in quaint and costly carvings, echoed and re-echoed the discordant voices of eating-house proprietors, hat and cap dealers, and others of the like ilk. To-day, it exists but as a memory, as both the hall and its surroundings have in recent years given place to the present fine market hall. No longer may we listen to the Babel of tongues, pitched in all keys, raised by the Saturday-night characters that gathered around the old hall—vendors of "long, strong, leather laces"; salves for "corns, warts, and bunions"; penny ducks "all hot", and "the best Durham mustard." All, all are gone, the old familiar sounds, with the still more familiar faces of the odd characters to whom they belonged; and gone too are the dear old scenes with all their varied and pleasing memories.

Miryshaw, a fine 17th century mansion at Barker-end is yet in a good state of preservation, and is interesting for having retained so much of its original character. It was for several generations the home of the Smyth family, who at one time were owners of the Bradford Soke Mills, and who afterwards resided at Heath Hall, near Wakefield.

Boldshay, (from *Bolt*, a residence, and *Scarr*, a woody slope,) lies a little below Miryshaw, and is a substantial house of a not very ancient date. It is doubtless built upon the site of one of some antiquity, for "Boldshay" is mentioned in 1345 with "its thirty acres of land." Mr. James found mention made of it in certain pleadings in the Duchy Court, in a suit (13th Elizabeth,) between George Waterhouse and Hugh Charnley, claiming it by grant from the Queen, when Sir John Tempest was steward of the manor. Afterwards Boldshay was the property of Sir John Maynard, who has been previously mentioned as the owner of the Bradford Rectory. Subsequently it belonged to Henry Hemingway, an attorney of some notoriety in his day, through whose line it descended to the Fitzgeralds. It is now the property of Major Fitzgerald, of Richmond, Surrey.

There was quite a colony of good houses of the "better sort" in the locality where Horton Road, Little Horton Lane, and Manchester Road form a junction, and the district was known as "Town End." One of these houses was that which yet stands next to the Unitarian Chapel in Chapel Lane, and is now used as offices, and as part of Mr. Cheetham's coach-building premises. It was formerly the home of the Bower family, who could trace back their connection with Bradford to the time of the famous "Barnard's Survey" of 1577. The residence of good Mrs. Bacon at the bottom of Horton Lane will yet be remembered by many. But if the house were forgotten, the good deeds of its occupant will not, for she spent her life in acts of kindness.

Just across the way was the residence of the Rands, a family that represented the different phases of the Bradford worsted trade perhaps better than any other. Mr. John Rand, the father, who to the last clung to the powdered wig, and knee-breeches peculiar to the last century, was in himself a connecting link between the days of hand-loom and machine labour, and between Bradford as a village and as a prosperous commercial town. In his sons, John and William, the link was continued unbroken down to very recent times. The firm of which Mr. Rand was the head originally came from Norfolk, from whence Bradford received its worsted trade more than a hundred years ago; but the credit of introducing that trade into Yorkshire belonged to Mr. Ramsbottom, a grandson of whom was for some time a partner with Messrs. Rand.

The late Mr. John Rand, the elder son, was connected with the worsted manufacture all his life, and to attempt to sketch his business career would be to trace the changing fortunes of that trade from the introduction of the spinning frame and power loom, some seventy years ago, to the present time. But Mr. Rand was not wholly engrossed with business pursuits. No one could take a much greater interest than he did in the social and philanthropic movements of Bradford. He was a sound churchman, but that circumstance by no means prevented his participating with men of other creeds in the promotion of any good object. He was also a staunch Conservative, and a thorough-going politician, and being moreover a fluent speaker, was for a time regarded as the leader of his party, and many a time did he boldly and eloquently advocate the interests of that party at the hustings and on other public occasions.

Mr. John Rand.

Mr. Rand married a sister of the late Dr. Macturk. He died on the 27th June, 1873.

Mr. William Rand, the younger of the brothers, did not devote his time to public business, although he earned for himself a fair measure of public esteem. He was a Conservative both by birth and education, but nevertheless a genuine advocate of free trade principles. He was also an active member of the Anti-Corn-Law League, and was selected to second the nomination of Mr. Cobden for the West Riding. On the incorporation of the borough, Mr. Rand was

Rev. William Atkinson, M.A.

chosen as one of the first batch of Aldermen, and subsequently was elected Mayor. He died at his residence at Baildon on the 8th December, 1868, aged seventy-two.

Opposite to Mr. Rand's residence at the bottom of Horton Road, there stood side by side two substantial dwellings that were for many years familiar objects to passers by. One of these was formerly the residence of Mr. Hardy (grandfather of Lord Cranbrook), an attorney of good repute, and with whom Mr. Samuel Hailstone served his articles. It was afterwards occupied by Colonel Skelton, a fine specimen of the ancient military *regime*, and an object of reverential admiration to Bradford youths, whom he honoured by an occasional shake of the hand, or a cheerful "How d'ye do?" His sister married Mr. John Thompson, a solicitor and partner with Mr. S. Hailstone. She and her husband were passengers in the ill-fated "Rothsay Castle" which was wrecked in the Menai Straits in 1831, and both perished.

The other house referred to is yet standing, and now forms part of the Old Brewery premises. It was once the residence of the Rev. Lamplugh Hird, and here were born his sons H. W. and L. W. Wickham. The next occupant of the house was Mrs. Anderton, sister to Mr. John Wood (of the firm of Messrs. Wood & Walker), a lady of rare virtues and rich in good works. Subsequently it became the residence of Mr. (afterwards Sir) Titus Salt.

One of the most interesting of the old Bradford homesteads was that which was formerly the residence of the Rev. William Atkinson, Afternoon Lecturer at the Parish Church. Its site (for it has long since disappeared) may be best defined as being near to where Sir Titus Salt's statue now stands. In its halcyon days the surroundings of the house were very pleasant, nearly the whole of the space afterwards occupied by the Old Foundry being then (1790) cultivated as a garden. We were acquainted with an old Bradfordian, who, in his boyhood was wont to scale the reverend gentleman's garden wall with a view to relieving him of some of his surplus stock of fruit.

The Rev. William Atkinson was born at Thorparch, on the 14th April, 1758, and was the fourth son of the Rev. Christopher Atkinson, who was then the Vicar of that place. Having distinguished himself at Cambridge by the rapid progress made in his studies, he became Rector of All Saints', Warham, Norfolk, and in 1784 Afternoon Lecturer at the Parish Church here. His appointment to this post led to the violent controversy which has been already referred to in a previous chapter.

Although not without some eccentricities of character, Mr. Atkinson was a man of rare scholarly attainments and intellectual power. In person he was of herculean build, and far beyond the average height of human stature. He did not preach in his master's gown, nor wear the academic hood of his degree, but in the round, flowing gown of the university scholar of modern times—the Geneva gown. Occasionally he would address his hearers in a plainness of speech not unlike the style peculiar to Grimshaw, of Haworth. In one of his discourses, he divided the inhabitants of Bradford into three classes, one of which he affirmed never attended the service of the Church; another class, he said, did attend, but it was purely from fashion or habit; and the third, he observed, might do it from principles of piety and devotion. But, he asked with much emphasis, whether among these there were *ten righteous*, who worshipped God in spirit and in truth.

Mr. Atkinson had but scant sympathy with Dissent and Dissenters, and in this particular he differed greatly from his patron, Mr. Crosse, the Vicar, who lived on the friendliest terms with the Dissenting ministers of the town. One of his crotchets was the possession of a printing press, which he kept in his house, and from which he often issued pamphlets on ecclesiastical or political topics, under the name of "The Old Enquirer." At one time he issued a small serial called *The Looking Glass*, in which he expressed his views of Dissent and its advocates.

Mr. Atkinson married Mary, daughter of John Cottam, Esq., by whom he had five sons and three daughters. The mother of Mr. M. W. Thompson was his eldest child, and the father of Mr. W. F. Atkinson, solicitor, was his youngest that survived infancy. During the later years of his life the reverend gentleman resided at Thorp-arch, and here he ended his life, on the 30th September, 1846, in the eighty-ninth year of his age. By his long residence in Bradford he endeared himself to many of its inhabitants, a few of whom yet survive and hold his memory in reverence and esteem.

Westgate, though now, and for many years past, a street of shops, was once composed chiefly of the private residences of well-to-do tradesmen, when Bradford was more noted for its woollen than its worsted industry. These same tradesmen manufactured their goods on their own premises. Within the recollection of old inhabitants yet living, the space reaching from Brunswick Place to the end of Lumb Lane was one stretch of green fields, in which were fixed posts or "tenters," for the purpose of drying and stretching cloth. In the "Cropper Lane" of to-day, we have a reminder of Bradford's bygone woollen cloth trade.

A distinguished resident in "Fayre Gappe" (now called Northgate) off Westgate, was Robert Clarkson—a Puritan and yeoman of the seventeenth century. It is believed that he was a mauufacturer of woollen cloths. He was the owner of large estates at Bradford, Manningham, Idle and Pudsey. In 1615 he was made a warden of the Parish Church, and afterwards acted with the Vicar and others as trustees for the sale of the manor. On his death in 1632, he was buried at the Parish Church.

Of his seven children—four sons and three daughters—William was the eldest who grew up to manhood. When a little over thirty, he became Chaplain to Ferdinando, Lord Fairfax, and in 1645 was installed Vicar of Adel, to which he was succeeded by his nephew, Thomas Sharp.

Rev. David Clarkson, B.D.

Mary Clarkson, the elder of the two surviving daughters, became the wife of John Sharp, of Horton Hall, the sturdy Parliamentarian who acted as private secretary to Lord Fairfax.

It is, however, the youngest son, David, in whom we are most interested, and whose portrait we are enabled to give, through the kindness of Mr. Matthew Clarkson, of New York—a worthy representative of this eminent family. From the Bradford Grammar School, young David went to Cambridge University, where he distinguished himself as "a scholar and a Christian," and secured the friendship and confidence of his associates in college. On hearing that his native town was in a state of siege he returned home, for we find from Joseph Lister's interesting narrative, that he was shut up here, when the Earl of Newcastle invested the town in June, 1642. Lister was then serving his apprenticeship with John Sharp, David Clarkson's brother-in-law, who was a clothier and merchant, and in relating the story of the "desperate adventure" of Sir Thomas Fairfax and his men in trying to break through the enemy's army, sword in hand, says,—"My master (John Sharp) being gone, I sought for my mother, and, having found her, she and I, and my sister, walked in the street, not knowing what to do, or which way to take. And as we walked up the street, we met a young gentleman called David Clarkson, leading a horse. My mother asked him where he had been with that horse. Says he, 'I made an essay to go with my brother Sharp, and the army, who broke through the enemy's leaguer; but the charge was so hot I came back again, and now I know not what to do.' Then I answered and said, 'pray, mother, give me leave to go with David, for I think I can lead him a safe way,' for being born in that town, I knew all the bye-ways about it."

It is believed that Clarkson was captured and taken to Leeds and exchanged for some Royalist prisoner, as he returned to Cambridge, and was there soon exalted to competency and honour. In 1645 he left Trinity for Clare, where he received his degree of B.D. During his residence in the University, he had placed under his care, as pupils, his sister Mary's son, Thomas Sharp, and John Tillotson, of Sowerby Bridge, who afterwards became Archbishop of Canterbury, and with whom he retained the closest friendship to the end of his life. He was appointed to the cure of Mortlake, in Surrey, in 1655, which he held until the passing of the Uniformity Act in 1662, which drove him and two thousand of his brethren from the national pulpits. From this time he retired into private life, and gave himself up to reading and meditation, but his pen was ever active in the religious controversies of the day. To this period of seclusion we are doubtless indebted for the writings which made him famous, and with which his name will ever be most closely linked.

Twenty years had elapsed since the time of his ejectment, when he was called upon to engage in active service in the church. He became co-pastor of the church where Dr. John Owen officiated, and on the death of that eminent divine was appointed his successor. This was in 1683. Three years more and the labours of David Clarkson were also brought to a close. As a theological writer he undoubtedly held a foremost place among the divines of the Puritan period, and Baxter, Howe, and Mead, all bear testimony to his worth and ability. In 1696 an edition of his sermons and discourses was published in a large folio volume, and in 1846 the Wycliffe Society issued a fine edition of his collected works, and since then a beautiful edition, in three volumes, has been published in Edinburgh by Mr. James Nichol.

Mr. Clarkson had for his wife a lady of eminent intelligence and piety. She was a daughter of Sir Henry Holcroft, Knight, Essex. They had several children, one of whom—Matthew—went to America, and many of his descendants held high and responsible positions in that country.

The Bartletts were a worthy and honoured family who also had their abode in Westgate. Their name occurs in the Quaker register of this town as early as the middle of the seventeenth century. Joshua Bartlett, described as a yeoman, was the owner of property in Westgate, and, by virtue thereof, of a sitting in a certain pew in the Parish Church. In July, 1676, he married Sarah Hird, or Hurd, daughter of a Sarah Hird, a good Quakeress, who seems to have exercised more zeal than discretion in her "ministry." In the West Riding Sessions Rolls, at Wakefield, it is recorded that "Sarah Hurd, a Quaker, on Sunday, 7th March, 1694, in a very disorderly and seditious manner, com'd into the church of Bradford in time of Divine service, and did then and there by some clamorous speeches disturb the minister in his prayer, and the congregation in their devotions."

The issue of the marriage of Joshua Bartlett with Sarah Hird (the daughter of the over-zealous Sarah,) was Elizabeth (who married Mr. Henry Gurney, of Norwich, and whose descendants afterwards inherited the property of the Bartletts of Bradford), and Benjamin, who was born on the 9th February, 1678. This their only son was brought up to be an apothecary, a calling which appears to have been congenial to his tastes, and one in which he gained some distinction.

The house in which Benjamin Bartlett resided, and practised as an apothecary stood on the site of the shop next door above the Central Coffee Tavern, and in old deeds is described as being "opposite the Market Cross." This property, by the way, had become historic before it became the residence of Bartlett. It had formerly been the abode of the Jeremiah Bower and his wife Rosamond, who acted as such dastardly spies and informers in the unfortunate Farnley Wood Plot of 1663, and who had been the means of bringing more than one honest townsman o grief.

In July, 1713, Benjamin Bartlett married Elizabeth, the only child of Thomas and Mary Green, of Liversedge, and brought his bride to his home in Westgate, which was now becoming reputed as the abode of a skilled and learned man. In July of the year subsequent to their marriage, their only child was born, and they called him Benjamin.

As if to commemorate the joyous event, the house was soon afterwards consecrated (if we may use the word,) for purposes of religious worship, for Benjamin Bartlett, besides being an apothecary, was a devout minister of the Society of Friends. The child was born on the first of July, 1714, and on the 13th the house in Westgate was registered at the General Quarter Sessions for the West Riding as "a place of meeting for religious worship of Protestants dissenting from the Church of England."

It was probably through Mr. Bartlett's position as a Quaker minister that he became intimate with John Fothergill, of Carr End, Wensleydale, and that his son (afterwards the famous Dr. Fothergill,) was apprenticed to Mr. Bartlett for seven years to learn the apothecary business. To that end the youth left school at Sedbergh and came to Bradford in 1728, being then in his sixteenth year. Gilbert Thompson, Fothergill's biographer, has given in few words a pleasing picture of the home that awaited the lad in Bradford. "His (Bartlett's) house," he says, "might be called the seminary of ingenious physicians. How happy to obtain such a master, when to imitate him was to be the gentleman in sentiment and manner; to be generous, good, and virtuous. He had here the completest opportunity of knowing drugs and preparations in their best and genuine state, of compounding them with neatness, visiting patients, and of laying the best foundation in an art to which his mind had an early and strong impulse."

It is unnecessary to allude to Fothergill's career further than to say that he was a worthy pupil of a worthy master. On leaving Bradford he continued his studies at Edinburgh, became a licentiate of the College of Physicians of London in 1744, and F.R.S. in 1768. As a physician and a man of science he was unrivalled in his day. As a benefactor it is only necessary to say that he was the founder of the famous Quaker school at Ackworth, an institution in which he took the deepest interest, and handsomely endowed.

That Mr. Bartlett was successful in his business may be inferred from the fact that he made extensive purchases of property in Bradford, and indulged himself in the luxury of a country residence. There is a plain but well-built house, which is familiar to persons passing along Bolton Lane, and which stands at the bottom of the hill leading up to Low Fold, Bolton. It has been known in the past as "Bolton Banks Farm," and "Walnut House" from the existence of an ancient Walnut tree planted against the house; but it was formerly known best as "Bartlett House," for this was the place chosen by the eminent apothecary for his country residence. The district lying in front, known as Busy Brig Fields, was not then given up to factories and huge gas tanks, nor was its quietude disturbed by the shriek of locomotives. It was a pleasant rural spot, where lovers delighted to ramble, and where Nature asserted its sway in undisturbed repose. At the east end of the house may still be seen the initials "B. E. B.," and the date "1736." These, of course, represent the names of the worthy Quaker and his partner in life, Benjamin and Elizabeth Bartlett.

The son, Benjamin Bartlett the younger, was also brought up an apothecary, and became even more distinguished than the father. He was, however, early induced to go to London, where he was introduced by his father's old pupil, Dr. Fothergill, who had now become famous, to the most eminent scientists and physicians of the day. He also became a distinguished antiquary, and in this capacity acted as the correspondent of Dr. Richardson, of Bierley Hall.

The Society of Friends, in Bradford, is unquestionably rich in its annals of worthy and useful men, good citizens who have delighted in works of benevolence and philanthropy rather than in amassing wealth, or striving after public distinction. The Hustlers were for many years an influential family in this town, and were held in great esteem for their spirited interest in public matters, but still more for their private deeds of benevolence. In 1745, a William and John Hustler are described in the Quaker registers as of Bolton. They were brothers, and in the wool business. John was the father of the John Hustler who built Undercliffe House. The eldest son of the latter was also named John, but it was the father who figures so prominently in the history of Bradford, in connection with the public movements of his day. He was one of the principal promoters of the Bradford Canal, and it was he who in 1781, at the head of a company of gentlemen, began the erection of the Market-building which formerly stood on the site of the present Exchange. He, too, was the first to suggest the construction of what is now the most important thoroughfare in the town, Market Street, although his name is immortalised by another well-known thoroughfare, viz. Hustler-gate.

The second John Hustler, of Undercliffe, had perhaps as much energy and spirit in the affairs of the town as his father. In the attempt made in 1823 to establish a philosophical society we find him taking a leading part; and when the Quakers' school in Chapel Street was in contemplation, he gave £300 towards its erection. He was also one of the founders of the Friends' Provident Institution.

William Wilson, familiarly called "Quaker Wilson," was a philanthropist of no common type. Quietly, yet perseveringly following his business of a woollen draper, he succeeded in accumulating a fortune of some £20,000. He was thrifty, industrious, and—well, a bachelor, and had few wants beyond what a pound or two a week could supply. Having spent half his life in earning his wealth, he nobly resolved to spend the rest in giving it away. It is related of him that "he went out of business, filled his room with clothing and blankets, sent his agents out into the surrounding villages to take note of the wants of whatsoever poor families they found, and a while after a waggon laden with goods would wend its way along the same route. There would be a blanket for one cottage, and warm clothing for another; and so systematically and persistently was the good man's resolution carried out, that when he died he scarcely left as many hundreds as he once had thousands." All honour to thy uame, thou worthiest of Friends! We will not pause to question whether thy charity was sufficiently discriminating according to the standard of worldly prudence, but would rather join in the wish that thy noble example were oftener imitated by others.

James Ellis was a man conspicuous for sterling honesty of purpose. While an apprentice lad he had gone cheerfully to prison rather than serve against his conscience in the militia. In 1855, he and John Priestman were in partnership at the Old Soke Mill as maltsters and millers, and had a monopoly of the right of "milling and malting" for Bradford. Their tolls in connection with malting were profitable, while the milling trade was of but secondary importance. Having adopted total abstinence principles, and having also conscientious scruples against living by a trade which they believed to be productive of much human misery they nobly determined to give up the more lucrative part of their business. They afterwards turned their attention to the worsted trade, and were very successful in it.

John Priestman, whose frank honest face and manly bearing will be yet remembered by many, was not a native of, but came to Bradford when about nineteen years old. He was indeed "successful in business," and at one time employed not less than eleven hundred workpeople. But whatever tended to the moral and social improvement of his employes, and the town at large, always met with his approbation and support. He was an able and sincere advocate of the temperance cause, and in 1879, a beautiful stained-glass window was placed to his memory in the Temperance Hall, Leeds Road.

Two honoured and well-known names in Bradford for many years were those of James and John Bilton, both Quakers, and given to charitable deeds.

William Maud, of the firm of Maud and Wilson, chemists, Sunbridge, was a man of few words but good actions. He was born in Bradford in 1765, and when a young man commenced practice with his father in Westgate, where he soon established a good reputation. He was a member of the Society of Friends, and took an active part in the Slave Trade Question, the Bible Society, Female Friendly Society, Savings' Bank, Dispensary, Sunday Schools, and indeed anything that had for its object the well-being and benefit of his fellows. An upper room of the old druggist shop at Sunbridge was set apart as a meeting place for those who laboured with him in his various philanthropic projects. Among these were the Rev. Henry Heap, Vicar, the Rev. W. Morgan, Drs. Steadman and Godwin, the Rev. Thomas Taylor, Mr. John Hustler, Mr. Benjamin Seebohm, Mr. John Rand and Mr. William Tetley.

Mr. Maud resided in a house that formerly stood on the site of the Lancashire and Yorkshire Railway Station, but he afterwards removed to an old farmhouse in Legrams Lane, to which he added a library and dining-room, and which thenceforth was known as "Horton Grange."

The successor to Mr. Maud at Horton Grange was Mr. Benjamin Seebohm, but before we introduce that estimable and worthy man to our readers, the story of how he found his way to Bradford must be briefly told.

Ludwig Seebohm was descended from a Swedish officer who settled in Germany after the Thirty Years' War. He married in 1790, Julia von Borries, and when Benjamin their son was born they were living at Friedensthal. They had nine children, and they were trained up in Quaker principles. Stephen Grellet, one of the chief preachers among the Friends of modern times, visited Waldeck when Benjamin Seebohm was sixteen, and though the latter was so young, his proficiency in languages fitted him to act as interpreter to Grellet, and soon afterwards to Sarah Hustler of Bradford, who visited Pyrmont, Switzerland, Frankfort and France as a preacher. She and her brother, John Hustler, pressed upon Benjamin to accompany them to their home at Bradford. He consented, and they reached Dover from Calais on the 2nd November, 1814, after a stormy sail of eleven hours, and arrived at Bradford by the Leeds coach on the 14th. Very pleasant to young Seebohm was the Quaker home at Undercliffe, for John Hustler possessed a good library—theological, scientific, &c.; a fair botanical collection, and philosophical apparatus. Sarah Hustler was a lady of the highest mental calibre, and was devoutly religious.

Benjamin Seebohm and John Hustler, junr., were taught the woollen cloth trade, and they then started business together in Bradford, but the former feeling a call to the ministry, got leave from Brighouse monthly meeting, and in 1824 joined Barbara Hoyland in a religious visit to Friends in Cornwall. In 1831 Seebohm married Esther, daughter of Joshua Wheeler of Hitchen, great-grandson of Joshua Wheeler, a Quaker prisoner in Bedford Gaol with John Bunyan. Esther, besides an elder sister, Fidelity, who died young, had two younger sisters, Sarah, who married Isaac Robson, of Huddersfield, and Mary, the wife of James Ellis above mentioned.

This brief sketch we have drawn from "The Private Memoirs of B. and E. Seebohm," edited by their sons,—a beautiful memorial, but not more worthy than these devout Christians deserved. The book is a delightful addition to the annals of Quaker biography.

Seebohm's missionary travels in America, which extended over five years, led to a renewal of his acquaintance with Stephen Grellet, and qualified him to edit the memoirs of that excellent man. The "Memoirs of William Forster" (father of the late Right Honourable W. E. Forster) was also the work of Mr. Seebohm's richly-furnished intellect.

While residing at Horton Grange, Mr. Seebohm took a profound interest in several projects for the moral elevation of the people; but the good that he did was done quietly and without ostentation, though none the less effectively.

Engraved by C G Lewis.

In 1861 the Seebohms left Bradford for Luton, where Mrs. Seebohm died in October, 1864, followed by Mr. Seebohm, her husband, on June 2nd, 1871. Their three surviving sons, Frederick, Henry, and Benjamin have won for themselves conspicuous positions in the literary world.

Manningham Lane was, fifty years ago, a quiet country highway, and its surroundings being pleasant to look upon and easy of approach, it is no matter for surprise that it should soon become a favourite locality for "residential purposes." Several good houses were built parallel with the lane, and styled "North Parade," and among the earliest tenants of one of these was Mr. Daniel Salt, the father of one of Bradford's most honoured and distinguished citizens—Sir Titus Salt, Bart. Sir Titus was not a native of Bradford, but was born at the old Manor House, Morley, on the 20th September, 1803. He came to this town with his father when in his sixteenth year, and on attaining manhood was taken into partnership with him in the

Sir Titus Salt's Birthplace.

wool business, under the firm of Daniel Salt and Son. He married in 1829, Miss Caroline Whitlam, daughter of George Whitlam, Esq., Great Grimsby, and for a time resided near to his father in North Parade. His successful speculations in wool, especially alpaca, became the talk of commercial circles, but when he went out in patriarchal fashion and built himself a city, calling it after his own name, then the world looked on and wondered. Sir Titus Salt however, won for himself another and a nobler character than that of a successful man of business. Years of prosperity were succeeded by a long period of open-handed liberality, and noble gifts were made to all worthy and deserving objects with a more than princely benevolence.

The year 1836 is memorable as being that in which the wool of the alpaca first came under the notice of Mr. Salt. That year is also a memorable one in the life of another eminent Bradfordian who was destined to rank as one of the greatest of England's merchant princes. Mr. Samuel Cunliffe Lister attained his majority in 1836, and at that time was residing at Manningham Hall with his father Mr. E. C. Lister. It was never intended that young Samuel should become a tradesman, and he was therefore educated with a view to his entering the Church. But fate willed it otherwise. When the time arrived for him to go to the University, he decided to follow the bent of his inclination, and give himself up to the pursuits of industry and commerce. Who shall say that his choice was not a wise one?

Unlike many who have embarked in the risks and anxieties of a business life, Mr. Lister could look back on a long line of honoured ancestors who had known nothing of the "taint of trade;" but with him an ever active industrial career appears to have had a peculiar charm. By a wonderful aptitude for business, indomitable perseverance, and sheer strength of will, he has earned for himself a distinguished and proud position—honourable alike to himself and to the townspeople who have so greatly benefited by his marvellous enterprise and energy.

Although Manningham Lane has long been the favourite locality for the homes of well-to-do Bradfordians, there were other select and pleasant spots on the outskirts of the town which were not overlooked. In Horton Road, opposite the present Technical College, stood the large hall known as Mannville, the residence of Mr. Thomas Mann, who had made considerable wealth in business. On the site of the Alexandra Hotel formerly stood the residence of Mr. Richard Fawcett. It was then a delightful spot, and the house overlooked the Thornton valley in one direction, and the Little Horton side of Bradford on the other. Close by was the once famous Randal Well, the water of which was so celebrated for its superior tea-making properties.

We must not, however, venture too far into the suburbs in our peregrinations, else this chapter will assume proportions out of keeping with the others. We feel tempted, however, to stretch out as far as Little Horton Green, a village that still retains much of its ancient rural character. Its old, quaint, and irregularly-built dwellings are pretty much as they were within the memory of its "oldest inhabitant," and, thanks to Mr. Powell, who is now, we believe, sole owner of the village, are likely to remain so for some time into the future. We are also grateful to that gentleman for having recently secured the Horton Hall estate, by which one of Bradford's most venerated relics was saved from falling into the hands of some house-building Philistine, who, we fear would have made short work of all that was ancient or sacred about it in his haste to "run up" some ghastly pile of back-to-back houses.

S. CUNLIFFE LISTER, ESQ., J.P., D.L.

From a Photograph by ALBERT SACHS, Bradford.

The Sharps, of Little Horton, were divided into two main branches, and the elder resided at the Horton Hall shewn in our illustration. The names that stand out most prominently from this branch are those of John Sharp, who fought on the side of the Parliamentarians during the siege, and his sons Thomas, the divine, and Abraham, the mathematician. The younger branch were Royalists, and their family seat was that which now forms the residence of Francis Sharp Powell, Esq., known as Horton Old Hall. Here dwelt John Sharp, the Royalist, (second cousin to the John above-named), who fought in several engagements on the side of the King. His son Isaac re-built the mansion. Mr. Powell is descended from this branch of the Sharps and is its present representative.

Horton Hall.

John Sharp, who became Archbishop of York, came of a collateral branch of the Horton Sharps, and was born at a house in Ivegate which stood a little to the west of the present Unicorn Inn.

For an authentic history of Horton Hall and the family that made it famous, we have pleasure in referring the reader to Mr. Cudworth's recent work—"The Life and Correspondence of Abraham Sharp." Concerning the modern history of this interesting place, there is little to be said. The modern portion of it was for several years the residence of the late Mr. Samuel Hailstone, and of his son, Mr. Edward Hailstone, now of Walton Hall. Previous to its being the residence of the Hailstone family, Horton Hall was the home of Mr. John Wood, for many years the senior partner of the well-known firm of

Messrs. Wood and Walker. As an employer, Mr. Wood was especially kind and thoughtful, and had a way of regarding his work-people as something more than a mere mechanical branch of his business concern. The long and weary hours which the factory people had to work was a subject on which he felt deeply. As early as the year 1825, he had maintained that ten hours a day was as long a time as a mill-master ought to employ his workpeople. But it was not till 1830 that he called the attention of Richard Oastler to the state of the factory system, and the scope which it gave for cruel oppression on the part of employers.

Mr. Oastler, who was at this time on a visit to Horton Hall, was deeply affected when told that little children were worked from fourteen to eighteen hours a day with scarcely a moment in which to snatch their meals. After a long and impressive interview, Mr. Wood concluded by saying "I cannot allow you to leave me without a pledge that you will use all your influence in endeavouring to remove from our factory system the cruelties which are now regularly practised."

The pledge was given, and how faithfully it was kept is best shown by the monument reared in Bradford, by thousands of operatives, to the memory of their benefactor, Richard Oastler. Horton Hall was the birthplace of the Ten Hours' Bill.

We can make little more than a passing notice of the old Bradford families whose names are so closely linked with the great iron industries of Low Moor and Bowling, namely, the Hirds, Dawsons, Hardys, Leahs, Paleys, Woods, Sturges', Pollards and Duffields. Some of the old mansions in which these families lived yet remain as monuments of the wealth and substance of their former owners. They are to be found scattered in places within easy reach of the ironworks above-named. Bolling Hall, Bierley Hall, Royds Hall (now the residence of Laurence Hardy, Esq.), and Odsal House are among those best known at the present day.

Duffield Hall, or "Town Hill House," as it was usually called, was in Wakefield Road, nearly opposite the Wheat Sheaf Inn. The house has long since disappeared, and the family, the Duffields, ceased to be connected with Bradford many years ago. The Pollards were till recently worthily represented by the patriarch of Scarr Hill, the late Joshua Pollard, Esq.

Bolling Hall is beyond question one of the finest of the old baronial mansions of which the West Riding can boast,—a place "familiar with forgotten years" as George Eliot would say, and with the history of "olden times" written on its very stones. For fully five hundred years its storm-beaten walls have withstood the ravages of time. Built in a style that may best be described as half castle and half mansion, it has come down to our own day in a condition such as few of the monuments of feudal times, in Yorkshire, can boast. To form a fair conception of its age we must glance across the page of history beyond the wars of the Red and White Roses, before we approach that far-off period (the fourteenth century), when William

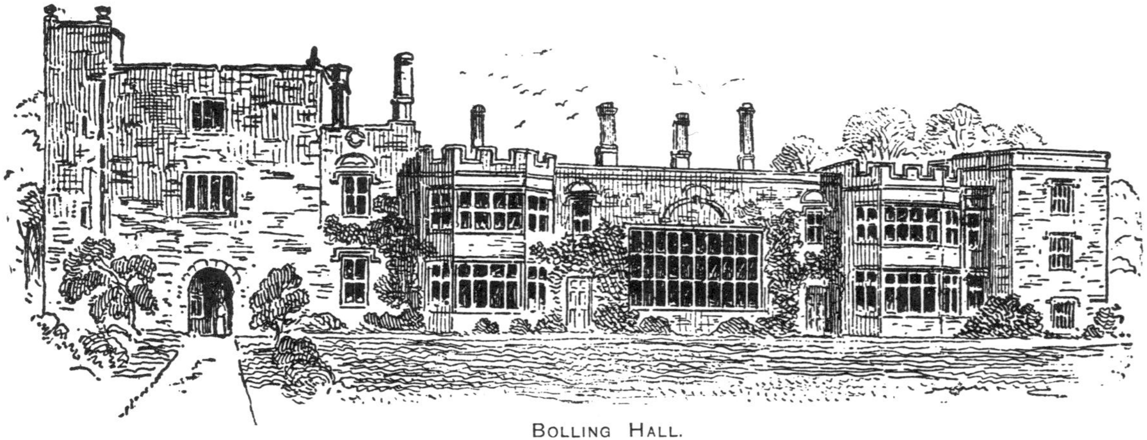

Bolling Hall.

de Bolling, lord of the manor of Bolling, gave certain "common of pasture" to Kirkstall Abbey, and twelve acres of land in Bolling, called "Walters Essart," to the Hospital of St. Peter's, York, in "pure alms." Going further back still, we are told of a certain Sindi who was the owner of Bolling, for, is it not recorded in the Domesday Book that "In Bolline Sindi had four carucates of land," and that "Ilbert (de Lacy) has it, and it is waste."

But was there a Bolling Hall in existence at this time? Probably not, nor would there be until the manor came into the possession of the Bollings, whose connection with it reached from about the year 1250 down to 1500. Then would be built the two massive towers facing the south, which with their small loop-hole windows piercing the thick walls, and the battlemented turret surmounting the western tower, at once tell of the feudal age, harmonising as they so well do with the requirements of that stern period. The central portion, with its deeply embayed windows, and large central window of three tiers, unmistakeably tells of the Tudor period—when the Tempests came in —which brought with it a more luxurious and domesticated order of things.

A long run of good fortune seems to have followed the Bollings down to the adventurous reign of Edward IV., when the unfortunate struggles for supremacy between the houses of York and Lancaster threw the whole country into war. Lord Clifford, of Skipton Castle, espoused the cause of the Lancastrians, and carried things with a high hand among the Yorkshire gentry, who dared do no other than enrol themselves under his banner. The famous battle of Towton was fought on Palm Sunday, March 29th, 1461, and resulted in the defeat of the Lancastrians, and amongst the defeated none suffered more in estate than did Robert de Bolling (the third of that name). He was attainted for high treason against the King and deprived of his possessions. He made a pitiful appeal to have his estate restored to him, and after a time succeeded in regaining it. He made his will at Bolling Hall, in which he directed that his body should be buried before the altar in Bradford Church.

Of the Bollings who succeeded the unfortunate Robert, there are none who call for special notice until we come to Tristram, at whose death, without male issue, the line of the Bollings of Bolling (reaching over nearly four hundred years) became extinct. There was however, a collateral branch of the family who were for a long time after settled at Chellow, near Bradford, but they do not appear to have added much lustre to the family name.

The fortunes of Bowling became first linked with the family of Tempest, when on the death of Tristram Bolling, May 30th, 1502, the heir to his estates was declared to be his daughter Rosamond, who was at this date the wife of Richard Tempest. Richard was the representative of a family (the Tempests, of Bracewell, near Skipton), some of whose members had figured conspicuously in English history. In the Record Office, London, there are many entries among the papers proving that he was a man of much importance. He fought, as his ancestors had done, on the Borders, and is amongst those named by Wolsey, in June, 1513, as "now mustered" with his retinue ready for the coming fray. In the battle fought on Branxton Moor, called the Flodden Field, in September following, the old writer of the "Ballad of Flodden Field" relates:—

Then Richard Tempest with his rout,
In rereward thus th' array did hold. *

Knighted by the King's own hand at Tournay, on Christmas Day, 1513, Richard Tempest from being a "Squire" became a "Knight of the Body," and was elected as one of the personal attendants on King Henry VIII, at Calais, in 1520, at the Field of the Cloth of Gold. He was also one of the three Yorkshire Knights the King and Queen took with them when they interviewed the German Emperor at Gravelines. Sir Richard served as High Sheriff of Yorkshire in 1516, and held various posts under the Crown.

In 1535, we find Sir Richard residing at Bowling, probably finding it a more convenient centre than either Bracewell or Waddington; and if, as we may conjecture, his wife was left much alone, she must have preferred her old home overlooking what, in those days, would have been a lovely fertile valley, instead of Bracewell set on its bleak Craven hill side. Some riots having taken place about Bradford in 1535, we find Sir Richard writing from "Bollyng" on the 27th August to Cromwell, that the rioters were in prison, and adds "Assuredly they have had strait punishment, are poor men, and if they remain in prison their harvest will be ungotten, and they unable to pay their farm." Again he writes the 28th September from the same place, to Cromwell, as to certain difficulties he was experiencing with Dr. Holdsworth, the vicar of Halifax.

The year 1536 was destined to bring much trouble to the Tempest family, as to many another ancient Northern one, over the rising known as the "Pilgrimage of Grace." The 13th of October, 1536, Sir Richard wrote from Bowling to his relation, Lord Darcy, consulting him as to what action he himself and the Earl of Cumberland had better take in the matter; for, writes Tempest, if Darcy and Cumberland will proceed against the rebels, he will also. While he doubted, the King was the same day despatching to him a letter under the privy seal, directing him to assist in repressing "certain traitors lately assembled." Having received his "marching orders," Sir Richard was not wanting in action. We find him writing from "Bollyng, Sunday morning afore daybreak," (15th October) to the Earl of Cumberland. —"This day I repair myself to Wakefield to see to the defence of the King's subjects there, whom I have in rule;" and, as good as his word—"This instant, Sunday," (the 15th), writes Grice, "Sir Richard Tempest came to Wakefield with a number of men well horsed.....

* Ballad of Flodden Field, edited by C. Federer, 1884, page 50.

when at one o'clock he received word by one of his espials out of Lincolnshire, that the host there had dispersed." We have not space to recite Tempest's various movements in this campaign; it is sufficient to relate that though as late as the 23rd October, the Duke of Norfolk writes to the King mentioning Sir Richard's loyalty and energetic action, yet in the end he succumbed to the popular voice, and we find him with his brother, Nicholas Tempest (whose share in the rising cost him his life at Tyburn the following June), and many another "whose name is famous in Border history," amongst the rebels, in the conference at York on the 24th November, and he was one of the thirty-four peers and knights who sat in the hall of Pontefract Castle discussing the affairs of the Commons. The pardon extended by the King to Sir Richard for all offences committed during the rebellion up to the 10th of December, 1536, was proclaimed by the Herald, Thomas Hawley, at Bradford on Thursday the 14th December.

Sir Richard must have felt how near his neck had been to the halter, for soon after this he wrote to his old friend and connection the Earl of Cumberland—"I have bene sor a crasyd, so as I dar not as yet styr abrod," and bemoans that he and the Earl should have been in the same condition.

Perhaps it was this trouble which led Sir Richard to think of making his will, as it is dated the 6th January (1536-7). In it he gives his soul to God Almighty, and his body to be buried in "Our Lady's Queere, in the Church of Bradford." He died on the 20th August, 1537.

By his wife, Rosamond, Sir Richard had twelve children, who grew up and married with some of the best families of the county. The sons were Sir Thomas, the heir; Sir John, and Nicholas; Robert, George, and Christopher, who died young; Tristram, and Henry, who was the head of the family settled at Tong, near Bradford. The present owner of Tong, Sir Robert Tempest Tempest, (who inherited in a female line), is the son of Sir Cornwallis Ricketts, of Leicestershire, Bart., by a daughter of John Plumbe, of Tong, whose mother was one of the daughters and co-heirs of John Tempest—Mr. Plumbe having assumed in 1824 the name and arms of Tempest in addition to his own.

Sir Richard's daughters were Elizabeth, married to Sir Peter Frechville, of Staveley in Derbyshire; Jane, married to Sir Thomas Waterton, of Walton Hall, near Wakefield; Anne, the wife of John Lacy, of Cromwellbotham; and Beatrice, married to William Gascoigne, of Shipley, and was the great grandmother of the celebrated Thomas Wentworth, Earl of Strafford.

The first Tempest of Bolling Hall was a Richard, so also was the last; but while the former made the family renowned, the latter brought it into disgrace. The last-named Richard was for a time an ardent Royalist and aided that cause at both the sieges of Bradford, and it is not unlikely that he acted as host to the Earl of Newcastle when staying at Bolling Hall in June 1643. What caused him to change sides must remain a mystery, for his wife's relations were staunch Royalists, but his near neighbour, Henry Tempest, of Tong, was a Parliamentarian and commander of a Train Band, and it is possible he may have had something to do with his conversion. At anyrate he submitted himself to Lord Fairfax and took the oath of allegiance to the Parliament before a committee at York. There is a tradition that he staked and lost the manor of Bolling at the gambling table, but there is no truth in this as he sold it (in 1649) for £7,100 to Henry Savile, of Thornhill Green, thereby ending the Tempest connection with Bolling. Having recklessly spent his money and got into debt, he was arrested and lodged in the King's Bench. He ended his wretched career within the Rules of the Fleet Prison on the 30th November, 1657.

From the Saviles, Bolling Hall passed into the hands of Francis, son of William Lindley, of Hull; and a descendant of his, Francis Lindley Wood, disposed of the manor and estate in 1816 to Messrs. John Sturges, Thomas Mason, and John Green Paley for £20,000, having previously disposed of the minerals to the proprietors of the Bowling Ironworks for a still larger sum. By deed of 31st January, 1834, Mr. Mason conveyed the manor, the hall, and his share of the Bolling estate to Mr. Paley for £12,000, in whose family the property still remains.

Bierley Hall has always been an interesting spot to Bradford people —an interest considerably heightened by the fact of its having been the residence of that learned and good man, Dr. Richardson, who was born here on September 6th, 1663. He was educated at Bradford Grammar School, from whence he proceeded to Oxford, and afterwards to Leyden where he studied for the medical profession. Returning to his home at Bierley to which he seems to have been greatly attached, he began that long career of study and research in scientific and other subjects that gained him such a distinguished position among the learned men of his time. Among others, scarcely less eminent, he enjoyed the friendship of Dillenius, Ray, Hearne, Thoresby, Marmaduke Fothergill, and Drake.

The hall was built about 1690, but it has undergone considerable alteration at various times. The cedar of Lebanon was, when a seedling, sent with some others to Dr. Richardson as a present by his friend, Sir Hans Sloane. It is now rapidly falling to decay. The beautiful drawing of it by Mr. Charles Cousen, and engraved by Mr. J. C. Bentley, of Bradford, (see frontispiece,) will give the reader a good impression of its noble appearance some forty years ago.

Broadstones.

CHAPTER X.

Some Old "Nooks and Corners."

BRADFORD may not perhaps at any time have been so rich in historic relics and associations as some other towns in Yorkshire that might be named, nor yet is it quite so barren in this respect as many are disposed to imagine. The stranger on the look out for antiquities might fail to meet with the quaint old gables, and the over-hanging houses with diamond-paned windows that tell at a glance of town life of the fifteenth and sixteenth centuries; but till within recent years it was by no means lacking in interesting mementos of bygone times, and it was next to impossible to ramble through its old thoroughfares without stumbling upon some old "nooks and corners" full of historic interest, and very closely intertwined with periods of its existence belonging to a very remote past. Some of these have been already noticed in preceding chapters, but there are others that call for special mention.

One of the quaintest bits of old Bradford was the narrow thoroughfare called "Broadstones," which was swept out of existence shortly before the visit of the Prince and Princess of Wales in June 1882. A glance at Mr. Cragg's admirable sketch renders any description of this piece of antiquity unnecessary. One feels all the more reconciled to the loss of such an old landmark as this when it is borne in mind that its removal was to give way to so important a place as the Forster Square of to-day, which affords so striking a contrast that it is almost impossible to realise that such a shabby old street could possibly have existed here so recently.

It is only within the past twenty years or so that Bradford has redeemed its character as a town for good shops. Formerly a shop was little else than a portion of the tenement in which resided its proprieter and his family. Now-a-days, however, the shopkeeper locks, bolts, and bars his premises at night and sleeps in the suburbs, and a *bona-fide* lock-up shop is no longer the exception but the rule. Although Kirkgate was the principal street in Bradford, and must have been so from the time that it took its name from the "Kirk" at the bottom, it was not noted by any means as a thoroughfare for shops. Down to the end of last century it was little more than a country lane in which the Bradford gentry built their houses, and cultivated their gardens. Before Market Street was constructed, the coaches running from Leeds to Halifax by way of Bradford came by the old Leeds Road down Barkerend and Church Bank, up Kirkgate, down steep Ivegate and then away by Great Horton and Queensbury, a rough and tumble journey not at all to the liking of those who travelled upon it.

Kirkgate in 1827.

The opening of the Canal in 1774 had the effect of rousing Kirkgate from its former quiet. Quite a colony of shops and houses sprang up in the neighbourhood of Broadstones. Opposite the present Midland Station were some old shops that seemed to be built very deep down considering their close proximity to the "flood gates" of the town. There was a noted huckster's shop where the late Mr. Brear's shop now stands kept by a woman familiarly known as "Mally," a sort of emporium for all sorts of dry goods. This shop had always a crowded out appearance, not so much of customers as of the multifarious commodities sold by Mally. Even the stone "bank" at the door was always piled up with the wares she had for sale. A little shop next door, was occupied by a barber who went by the name of "Dumb John." He rarely spoke to his customers unless in reply to some question put to him, and even then only in monosyllables. John's shop was afterwards occupied by the Cousens, who at one time, it is said, shaved half the population in Bradford. By the way, Dumb John's charge for hair-cutting was a penny, and for shaving, a half-penny.

OLD SHOPS—BOTTOM OF KIRKGATE.

Over the way was, in more recent times, the well known shop of Messrs. Watson, known as the "Brown Cow Shop" from its close proximity to the Brown Cow Inn. It was afterwards occupied by Messrs. Bailey and Holdsworth, tobacconists, who had to vacate it, as the site of that and adjoining shops was wanted for the new Station Hotel.

It would doubtless be refreshing to the memories of old Bradfordians to be reminded of all the shops and shopkeepers that were in existence in their younger days, but a generation has arisen to whom a mere record of the names and localities of these would be of little interest. Among the best known shops in Kirkgate were those of Mr. Brumfit, tailor and pawnbroker, Mr. Longfield, Mr. Peter Rnssell, Mr. Thomas Hunter, tailor, Mr. Bailey Blackburn, druggist, Mr. Wilson, silversmith, Mr. Outhwaite, chemist, Mr. Farrar, tailor, Mr. Keys, druggist, and Mr. Hargreaves, confectioner. At the corner of Chapel Court, now occupied by Messrs. Brooke, Bond & Co., was the printing and bookselling shop of Edward Keighley, but in 1839 this place was occupied by the brothers William and Henry Byles. The shop of Mr. Tordoff, tea dealer, is yet flourishing, and so also is that of Mr. Ben Johnson across the street.

One of the best known of the shops in Westgate was that of the late Mr. Manoah Rhodes, watchmaker and silversmith, which stood at the corner now occupied by the Central Coffee Tavern. It is sixty-seven years since Mr. Rhodes, then a mere stripling, journeyed on foot from Morley, his native place, to Bradford, and entered the service of Mr. Allott, in Kirkgate, to learn the business of watchmaker, &c. In 1836 he commenced business for himself at the bottom of Westgate, but in a very much smaller building than the one occupied by him before removing to the splendid shop in Kirkgate.

Mr. Manoah Rhodes' Old Shop.

Next above Mr. Rhodes' old shop was that of Mr. Wyrill, the ironmonger, and a little higher up was "Tommy" Cure's, in which he carried on his business of grocer and tallow chandler. At the corner of Godwin Street was, and still is the little druggist's shop, which from the familiar name of its proprietor, came to be known as "Cockshott's Corner." Smithson, the tobacconist, still carries on his business in one of the quaintest and most ancient of the very few old buildings that now exist in Bradford. A little above the Pack Horse Inn was

Old Shops in Westgate.

the shop of Mr. John Illingworth, the draper, now represented by the large establishment on the opposite side of the street, of Messrs. Illingworth & Newboult. Facing the old Court House was Judy Barrett's spice shop, the speciality of which was her world-famed humbugs. A few doors higher up was Mr. Lund's periodical and book shop, which was one of the best and most popular of its kind in Bradford.

Crossing over and coming down the other side of Westgate, we notice a few old shops that are all but forgotten now, namely those of Charles Rhodes the printer, Muff the milliner, Penny the tailor, and Sewell the watchmaker. Mr. Rich, the tea dealer, was located near the Bull's Head, and close by William Maud (Maud and Wilson) commenced business as a surgeon. Below the Bull's Head was the shop where Mr. Charles Stanfield carried on the businesses of bookseller, printer, stationer, commissioner for taking special bail, vendor of patent medicines, and distributor of stamps! It was but a small place for so many callings, but Mr. Stanfield was a shrewd man of business and he "made money" out of it. He was succeeded by Mr. Henry Gaskarth. In old John Stanfield's day, the next door neighbour was Richard Sedgwick the printer.

Ivegate is but a sorry sample of a street for central Bradford of to-day. The reconstruction of so busy and important a thoroughfare cannot however be far distant. But indeed, we like it as it is, for it is now one of the few remaining bits of old Bradford that serve to link the present with the far away past. It was however, shorn of its best and most antiquated ornament when the old Hall of Pleas and Toll Booth, and the shops below, were pulled down some years ago.

Of the old shops in Ivegate, the most noteworthy were those of Mr. Crossley, the Quaker tea-dealer; Smith, the pork butcher; Bilton and Maud, the grocers; Brumfit and Simpson, the tallow chandlers; Cussons, the bookseller; John Wilton, the clothes broker, and Chatterton, the spice merchant, who gloried in the excellent quality of his "parkin pigs," and who had an exhibition upstairs of his spicy handiwork, consisting of all the illustrious characters of the day, occasionally varied by a most dazzling representation of Daniel in the den of lions, also in spice.

Old Ivegate.

We must not omit to mention that Mr. John Dale commenced business as a printer and stationer at No. 4, Ivegate, the shop now occupied by Mr. Kendrew. Underneath was a well-known circulating library kept by one Tranter. This was one of the earliest of its kind in Bradford. Tranter was himself a veritable bookworm, but he could always find time to bind his own shabby volumes, as well as those of other people who were not over fastidious in the matter of style and elegance. Next door below the Unicorn Inn was Mrs. Cousen's shop of drapery goods, which has since developed into Mr. George Thorpe's immense establishment.

Market Street was not opened out as a public thoroughfare until near the close of last century. It went by the name of New Street before, and long after, the erection of the Market building from which it took its present name. Once fairly started as a street it made steady progress, and filled up gradually on both sides with buildings of various kinds. Shopkeepers, however, fought shy of it for a while, but even their prejudices eventually gave way, and in course of time several respectable shops were erected. Near to the White Swan Inn was the abode of a rhyming shoemaker named William Feather, who generously treated the public to a specimen of his muse, on the sign-board of his shop.

Within this house a poor man dwells,
In spite of wind and weather;
Boots and shoes he makes and mends,
And his name is—William Feather.

The shops on the White Swan side of Market Street that will be best remembered were those of the Brothers Neesom, grocers and hop merchants; W. H. Blackburn, music dealer; Allison, the bootmaker; Benjamin Read, tinner and brazier; George Dale, hairdresser; Joseph Hill, tea dealer; Franks, the optician; Clemesha and Chantry, confectioners; and John Dale, printer and stationer. On the other side of the street, were the shops of Mark Oddy, rope maker; William Brooksbank, silversmith; Walmsley, the boot maker; and, near the Hope and Anchor Inn, the once familiar shop of the late Alderman Henry Brown,—an establishment that has kept good pace with the commercial progress of Bradford.

Ald. Henry Brown.

Mrs. Brown, the mother, began business in 1817 in a very small way indeed, her stock-in-trade consisting chiefly of fustian goods, and ready-made underclothing; but she worked on sound principles, and by industry and perseverance succeeded in forming a business, which, on her retirement in 1834, was a large and profitable one. The good lady followed a code of rules well worth remembering even in these advanced times. She resolved to sell for cash only; to give her customers their money's worth, and never to attempt to extend her business except in accordance with her means.

Brown and Muff's Old Shop.

Since the year 1817 the shop has passed through various stages of enlargement. Our illustration represents, we believe, the second stage. In 1845, Mr. Henry Brown took into partnership his brother-in-law, Mr. Muff, and since then the concern has grown into its present large proportions.

Few men were more sincerely respected than the late Alderman Brown; and he deserved to be, for he was indeed a useful and worthy member of society. No man ever took a more genuine interest than he did in all that concerned the general well-being of the town. His name was a "household word" throughout Bradford and the district, and his memory cannot but be held in esteem and veneration for generations to come.

Crossing the end of Bank Street from the Hope and Anchor, we come upon the old Market building. The side of it fronting to Market Street presented a dark and dingy appearance, and the shops underneath were of a shabby and inferior order. Among the occupiers of these were Abraham Bentley, town crier and newsagent; Taylor, the cooper; Hall, the cutler; Timothy Ingham, auctioneer and sheriff's officer, and Bartle, the confectioner. Passing Mr. Parkinson's tobacco and snuff establishment and the Boar's Head, we encounter a few well-known old shops that always looked thrifty and respectable, namely, those of Mr. Deighton, dealer in fishing tackle; Mr. Holgate, barber and toy dealer, and Mr. (afterwards Ald:) Joseph Farrar, the hatter.

There were several old shops in Tyrrel Street, Sun Bridge, and Bridge Street, but we cannot attempt to notice them separately.

Horse Fair in Bridge Street.

Those in front of the Bowling Green are shown in the above illustration, which is from a photograph kindly lent us by Mr. Robert Parkinson, chemist, of this town. Twice a year, this part of Bridge Street was the favourite arena for the horse and cattle dealers who came to Bradford at fair times, and exhibited their "live stock" in a manner greatly to the discomfort, and sometimes to the danger of passers by. It was felt to be a vast improvement and relief when in 1866 the Corporation purchased the manorial rights and put an end to this state of things. The marvel was that so glaring a nuisance had been allowed to exist so long.

The "pleasure" fair began with the cattle fair, and continued for two or three days after. Along both sides of the streets were stalls of an endless variety, at which nuts and brandy-snap, children's toys, or indeed almost anything might be purchased. Interspersed among these were loud-mouthed quack-doctors and "cheap-jacks." The fair proper was, however, held in the open space adjoining the old Christ Church at the top of Darley Street, and in the Market place behind the Manor Hall. There was no difficulty in discovering either of these places, for the beating of drums, the clashing of cymbals, and the bawling of showmen announced their whereabouts long before they were reached. Here were gathered in one glorious medley the wild beast shows, waxwork exhibitions, and the booths of wandering

Thespians where tragedy was given out thick and fast, and five-act dramas were rattled off in almost as many minutes. Here also were to be seen conjuring ponies, fortune-telling pigs, sea monsters, and all the wonderful things that went to make up the "fun of the fair."

No part of old Bradford has undergone a greater change than that now represented by New Market Street, the Town Hall, the Mechanics' Institute and the block of adjoining shops. When Mr. M. W. Thompson laid the foundation stone of the Town Hall in 1870, he remarked, in the course of his address, that when his grandfather and grandmother were married eighty years before, the property on which the Town Hall was about to be erected formed part of their marriage settlement. His grandfather, the Rev. W. Atkinson, lived within a few yards of the place on which he (Mr. Thompson) then stood, and in this house his mother, Mrs. Thompson, was born.

The "lines where beauty lingers" were, however, completely rubbed out when the Old Foundry came into full blow on this very site, and no pleasanter objects met the eye than the roofless walls of old dismantled dwellings, like ruined cloisters blackened by age; chimney-stalks belching out perpetual clouds of dingy smoke, and blast furnaces with fire leaping from their summit and glowing at their base, keeping up one ceaseless, deafening roar, by day and night.

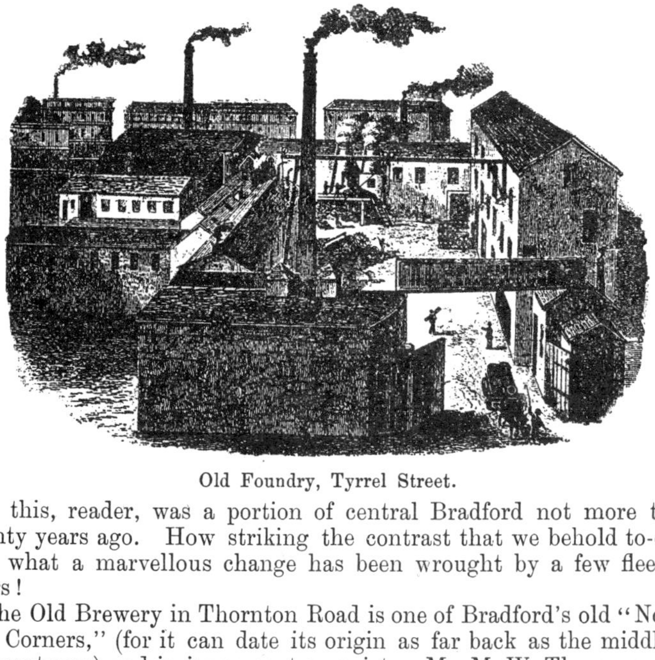

Old Foundry, Tyrrel Street.

And this, reader, was a portion of central Bradford not more than twenty years ago. How striking the contrast that we behold to-day, and what a marvellous change has been wrought by a few fleeting years!

The Old Brewery in Thornton Road is one of Bradford's old "Nooks and Corners," (for it can date its origin as far back as the middle of last century;) and in its present proprietor, Mr. M. W. Thompson, we have the representative of one of its oldest and most respected families. His father, Mr. Matthew Thompson, came to this town with his younger brother, Benjamin, when both were boys. Matthew's first start in life was made when under the charge of his uncle, Mr. Benjamin Peile, who then carried on the business of a dyer. Benjamin, his brother, was apprenticed with Mr. Richard Fawcett, to learn the worsted business. Afterwards, the two went into partnership in the latter branch of industry, and carried on business at the mill in Tetley Street, Thornton Road, still called "Thompson's mill," which their uncle had built for them. This place, which was reared in 1803, was the third factory erected in Bradford.

Mr. Matthew Thompson figures in local history as one of the most prominent and useful men of his time. It would, indeed, require a chapter to itself to set forth the various movements with which his name was associated. He married the eldest daughter of the Rev. W. Atkinson, and Mr. M. W. Thompson was their eldest son. Mr. Benjamin Thompson married Elizabeth, daughter of Mr. William Whitaker, then a partner in, but formerly sole proprietor of the Old Brewery.

Mr. William Whitaker had a son, Richard, who distinguished himself in the army, and was in the famous retreat to Corunna with Sir John Moore. Richard's sister, Elizabeth, became the wife of Mr. Benjamin Thompson, and by the marriage of Mr. M. W. Thompson with their only surviving child, that gentleman became the owner and sole representative of the old established firm of William Whitaker & Co.

Although known by the modest title of the *Old* Brewery, it may fairly lay claim to the superlative *oldest*, for it was the first industry of its kind in Bradford. In 1830, it was the property of Benjamin Thompson, Henry William Oates, James Marshall, Henry Leah, and Thomas Pullan. In that year Thomas Pullan went out of the concern, the other partners taking his share. Mr. Benjamin Thompson and Mr. Leah purchased the shares of Mr. Marshall and Mr. Oates in 1833, and on the death of Mr. Leah in 1846, Mr. B. Thompson purchased his share and thus became sole owner.

The recent construction of Sunbridge Road necessitated the complete demolition of the old Soke Mill, at the bottom of Miller-gate, and the wiping out thereby of every trace of one of Bradford's ancient relics. Latterly the place had been known as the Queen's Flour Mills, and for some years had been tenanted by James Ellis and John Priestman, who paid a rent amounting to £1,250 per annum. The blackened walls of the old mill were hardly in keeping with the changing aspect of this part of the town, and though a familiar and interesting object to old Bradfordians, the pulling down of this ancient landmark was an event that happened none too soon.

The old stream or goit, we need scarcely add, has shared the fate of the mills to which it had long been a necessary adjunct. For some

Doorway of Old Corn (Soke) Mill.

years back the filthy and putrid state of its waters had been nothing less than an open disgrace to the town, and its abolishment was hailed as a positive blessing.

CHAPTER XI.

Early Bradford Literature & Art.

WHATEVER may be in store for the future, Bradford has not certainly distinguished itself in the past either for its literature or its literary characters. We could name some local authors who have complained bitterly of the lack of appreciation and encouragement on the part of their townsmen, but it will suffice to instance the case of Mr. John James who keenly felt the soreness of neglect and absence of sympathy in his literary struggles. Remembering that his own most valuable work the "History of Bradford and its Parish"—the labour of nearly half a lifetime—was published at a loss, we can hardly wonder that he should have placed on record this humiliating confession. "The people of Bradford," he says, "are not remarkable for their encouragement of literary effort; especially as the emanation of a townsman. Political orators are chiefly patronised, and political speeches afford the easiest access to local fame. Literary merit is unrecognised in the competition. *It must look abroad for encouragement.*"

The date of the first book printed in Bradford is, we believe, 1785, and the printer of it was John Nicholson, of Kirkgate. He and his sons Samuel and George were located here as early as 1781, and they were undoubtedly the pioneers of the printing press in Bradford. Before they commenced business nearly all the printing for this town was done in Leeds. York printed its first book in 1509; Leeds, 1710; Halifax, 1760; Pontefract, 1777; Sheffield, 1780; Huddersfield, 1786; Barnsley, 1809; and Otley, 1813. It will thus be seen that Bradford was far from being the earliest in the field. It could not, of course, be expected to compete with York or Leeds, but considering its population during the whole of last century, it should have kept pace with such towns as Doncaster, Wakefield and Halifax.

In the year 1800, Bradford could only boast of two printers. These were the Nicholsons in Kirkgate, and Richard Sedgwick in Westgate, who was both printer and bookseller. The Nicholsons were related to John Nicholson, the "Airedale Poet," and printed his earlier poems. On one occasion their stock-in-trade was under distraint for debt, and was being knocked down by the auctioneer's hammer; but as the poet was entitled to a half-share in the sale of his poems, he objected to the disposal of the books in this summary fashion. He forbade the sale going on, and when the auctioneer ignored his right to interfere, the stalwart poet laid hands upon him, dragged him down from his elevated position, and left him sprawling in the street. We are unable to say how matters were finally adjusted.

To the firm of John Blackburn & Son (afterwards William Howgill Blackburn,) belonged the honour of bringing out the first Bradford periodical. It was a small monthly issue of twenty pages, price threepence, and at this day would doubtless be regarded as but an insignificant production. Its chief interest lay in the fact of its being the first venture in the way of supplying the town with a periodical of its own,—not a successful venture it would seem, for only twelve monthly parts were issued. It bore the title—"The Bradford Instructive and Entertaining Miscellany," and began and terminated its career in the year 1818.

Mr. John Stanfield's printing office and stationer's shop were at the bottom of Westgate, which was then, (fifty years ago,) regarded as the very centre of Bradford. What Thomas Gent had been to Yorkshire, John Stanfield was to Bradford. As a typographer, he long held the foremost place here. The concern was established by Mr. John Smith, who died in 1793. John Stanfield was his nephew, and learnt his business with him, and after his death, carried it on until 1835, when his son, Charles Stanfield, succeeded him. Charles will be best remembered as the publisher of Mr. James's "History of Bradford;" the first collected edition of John Nicholson's poems, and other local works. Mr. Henry Gaskarth, now of Sunbridge Road, is the present representative of this old established business.

Thomas Inkersley, printer, publisher, bookseller, and postmaster, was in his time one of Bradford's most useful citizens. Truly marvellous must have been his energy and industry. To enumerate the books, pamphlets, &c. that emanated from his printing press would be to compile a long and interesting catalogue of local and general literature. In local bibliography he takes the first place, and bids fair to do so for some time to come. It was to Mr. Inkersley that the Rev. Patrick Brontë was attracted to have his works printed. These were "The Maid of Killarney," and "The Cottage in the Wood," both of which appeared in 1818, when Mr. Brontë was living at Thornton, and when Charlotte was a child of but two years old.

Mr. Henry Wardman, printer, of No. 6, Chapel Lane, was an old Bradford worthy whose speciality was the printing of children's books. Choice little things they were too, notwithstanding that they were sold at the very modest figure of twenty for sixpence! To Sunday-school children they were always welcome gifts, for the prodigal age of children's literature was not yet. Mr. Wardman was a Wesleyan, and a truly good man.

Of Mr. Spencer, the printer, in Broadstones, we are not able to say much. Beyond a few pamphlets and broadsides, we have not met with anything printed by him. These broadsides were such as were formerly sold at feasts and fairs—hung out in long lines like so many clothes put out to dry. Very quaint and curious many of them were: songs and ballads that were popular with a bygone generation, and

Old Shops in Westgate.

sung by lusty, if not musical voices, in the streets or the tap-rooms of market towns and villages. But of all the tap-room songs in use some fifty years ago, there was not one more popular throughout the West Riding than that from Nicholson's "Poacher," beginning with the words "Come all ye brethren of the night." It had its day, but is now never heard.

A well-known Bradford printer of some forty years ago was James Ibbetson, who first had his shop in the New Market Place, Kirkgate, and then near to the Bowling Green Inn, where in 1845 he published the first Bradford Directory. John Wood, the schoolmaster, makes the following reference in his "Autobiography" to this project. "Mr. James Ibbetson, having for some time witnessed the rapid increase of the population of the borough, at length decided to publish a Directory, and I was engaged to compile, superintend, and manage the whole affair. This took up the whole of my time for at least twelve months, and I was paid good wages for my work."

Mr. Squire Auty, in 1848, published what he called the "Blue Book of British Manufactures" which was intended as a sort of set-off to the "Black Book of Sinecures and Pensions of British Government." He also issued the "Orange and Protestant Minstrel" in 1852.

There has been nothing more wonderful in the whole annals of English literature than the rapid growth of the newspaper press. At the commencement of the present century, nine weekly journals constituted the entire number of newspapers for the broad county of York. To-day it can boast the existence of one hundred and thirty publications that may be classed as newspapers, of which not fewer than twenty are issued daily.

The first impression of Bradford's first newspaper was issued on Thursday, July 14th, 1825, and it bore the title of *The Bradford Courier and West Riding Advertiser*. It was a Tory organ and was floated by a company of shareholders. Its printer and publisher was the Thomas Inkersley already mentioned. The general dimensions of the *Courier* were very similar to the *Bradford Daily Telegraph* of to-day. Its price, however, was not a half-penny but *sevenpence*, and not a dear paper either when a few facts are taken into consideration. First there was a four-penny stamp duty upon every copy; then there was a nice little duty of 3s. 6d. upon every advertisement inserted, and last, there was a duty of three-pence per pound upon the paper used for printing. The "canker-mark," or four-penny stamp, was not abolished until 1836, when it was reduced to a penny, and remained so till finally abolished in June, 1855. The advertisement duty was reduced to 1s. 6d. in 1833, and entirely abandoned in 1853.

These facts will serve to show the difficulties that formerly stood in the way of newspaper enterprise. But there were other obstacles besides these against which local journalism had to contend. Comparatively few of the working classes could afford the luxury of a weekly paper in their own homes; hence was begun the system of "clubbing up" by several families, in order to purchase and make one paper suffice for a tolerably large circle of readers. It was, indeed, no unusual thing for a single paper to be made to answer the requirements of an entire village. However commendable this might be on the score of economy, it was a practice not very well calculated to enlarge the circulation of the local newspaper.

Notwithstanding all these hindrances to its progress, the *Bradford Courier* held on its course till April, 1828, having had an existence of nearly three years. But what an existence! In its own columns it confesses to a loss to its proprietors of not less than £500 per annum. As a political organ it perhaps served its day and generation. As a financial venture it was a failure.

In spite of the overwhelming difficulties in the way of provincial journalism at this period, it may seem strange that the *Bradford Courier* found a rival in the field within the space of nine days of its own birth. This was the *Bradford and Wakefield Chronicle*, the first issue of which bore date July 23rd, 1825. It was similar to the *Courier* in size and price, but in politics it described itself as "moderate Conservative." In reality it was Whig. Its printers and publishers were Messrs. Stanfield, Sons & Co., of Westgate. During the heat of the great strike of 1825, there was a pretty brisk demand for both the papers, but afterwards it became apparent that one or the other would have to succumb. The *Chronicle* was the first to give in, after a brief existence of nine months and one week.

After the demise of the *Bradford Courier* in 1828, there was an interval of six years before another attempt was made at journalism here. Newspaper readers were, however, meanwhile kept well supplied with the Leeds papers, which were brought to Bradford by a mounted messenger who had a large bag swinging on each side, in one of which were copies of the *Mercury*, and in the other the *Intelligencer*.

On the 6th of February, 1834, appeared the first number of the *Bradford Observer*. It was issued from the quaint-looking building in Piccadilly next door above the present *Observer* Office, and the price of it was sevenpence, fourpence of which was stamp duty. The entire staff engaged in its production was not more than ten. When its Jubilee was celebrated on February 6th, 1884, not less than 130 persons were employed upon it.

This, the leading journal of Bradford, was founded by a number of gentlemen who thought the town had developed sufficiently in size and character to have a newspaper of its own. Amongst their names were those of Mr. Robert Milligan, Mr. James Garnett, Mr. Henry Forbes, Mr. Thomas Aked, Mr. Samuel Laycock, Mr. Miles Illingworth, Mr. John Rawson, solicitor, and Dr. Godwin. The capital for the new venture was raised in shares of £25 by about ninety shareholders. The present senior partner of the firm, Mr. William Byles, was called to Bradford from the *Athenæum* to undertake the duties of printing and publishing the paper, and to his steady perseverance and ability is due the credit of having steered it safely through many

W. BYLES, Esq.

vicissitudes, and brought it to its present position as one of the leading journals of the West Riding. If it has grown with the growth of Bradford it has also shared its adversities, for, notwithstanding a large increase in population and a considerable diminution of the stamp duty, the *Observer* was doomed to pass through long and peculiar trials before it came to be regarded as a successful undertaking. It was first issued as a daily morning paper on the 5th October, 1868.

More than sixty years have elapsed since the appearance of Bradford's first newspaper. Since then many other journals have sprung into being, and catered for a time for public patronage, but the span of life accorded to some of these was but brief and fitful. The *Bradford Daily Telegraph*, now a flourishing evening paper, issued its first impression on July 16th, 1868. The late Mr. Thomas Shields was its founder and proprietor.

In bygone times, the Bradford Grammar School produced men who rose to eminence, and of whom the town was justly proud. The present century has not, so far, beyond one or two exceptions, produced any distinguished literary characters. The most striking of these exceptions were the Brontë sisters, whom Bradford may fairly claim by virtue of having been born and having spent their lives within its parish. The three sisters often visited this town, and an old Bradfordian yet living, who knew them well both before they became famous and after, writes thus:—"I have seen the Brontë sisters many, many times. They were the most timid and sensitive creatures it was possible to gaze upon. They generally dressed in old-fashioned gowns of faded black silk, whilst their feet were encased in strong low-fitting shoes, and various-hued stockings. If you met them in Kirkgate or any other narrow street on a Thursday or Saturday, when throngs of people were about, they invariably clung to the wall fast hold of each other, as if afraid of being noticed. They were the shyest ladies, too, I ever knew, principally accounted for, no doubt, by their short-sightedness, their not intermixing with general society, and by their living in such an outlandish place as Haworth. Little did the people of Bradford, who gazed with such curiosity upon Patrick Brontë's daughters, imagine that they were to play so prominent a part in the literary world."

Another literary character whom we may claim for Bradford, by reason of his long connection with it, although he was born at Weardley, near Harewood, was John Nicholson, the "Airedale Poet." John was a genuine Yorkshireman, and an intense lover of its charming scenery, and he may be best described as belonging to the broad county. His life, his poetry, and his whole instinct were thoroughly Yorkshire, and Yorkshiremen were proud of him. The story of his chequered life and lamentable end is one that is well known to readers of Yorkshire literature. We have all the more pleasure in giving an illustration of the little rustic cottage at Weardley in which Nicholson was born on 29th November, 1790, because it is doomed ere long to be pulled down, a step which every lover of the Yorkshire poet must sincerely regret.

Birthplace of John Nicholson.

Some forty years ago, a little shop was opened at the top of Westgate, where books, newspapers, magazines, &c. were to be had. It was a very modest and unassuming shop, but its worthy proprietor was evidently an object of attraction, for the small establishment was the favourite resort of a circle of friends who might then be justly termed the *literati* of Bradford and the district. We, of course, allude to the late Mr. Abraham Holroyd, the poet and antiquary. Mr. Holroyd has written, compiled and published much that is truly excellent since he began business in Westgate, but to our mind he has brought forth nothing more choice or valuable than his little magazine, entitled—"The Bradfordian," the bringing out of which he said, "gave me the most pleasure of anything I ever did in my life. It was truly 'a labour of love,' and it brought me into contact with the best men and women of the time in Bradford and the vicinity."

Glancing to-day over the pages of this periodical, what memories are awakened of those who contributed to them of their best—some indeed, who were then only trying their "'prentice-hands" at literature, but whose names became afterwards widely known. First and foremost is the author of "Natterin' Nan,"—kind, genial Ben Preston, of whom Edwin Waugh said that "nature and he had evidently formed a partnership, and it would be a great shame if the firm did not produce something worthy of being handed down to posterity." Then follow John James, the sage historian, whose profound and logical essays form a striking contrast to Ben's "Creakin' Gate," and "Spicey Man;" Stephen Fawcett, author of "Bradford Legends and other Poems;" James Hird, author of "A Voice from the Muse," etc.; Edward Sloane, the humourist, and others. The "Bradfordian," too, was the repository of the earliest, and in some instances, the best effusions of such poets as James Waddington, ("Ralph Goodwin") of Saltaire; John Le Gay Brereton, "Jenny Wren," Eliza Craven Green, Robert Storey, Tom Nicholson, (brother of John), Robert Carrick Wildon, (the Tailor-poet of Tong); J. H. Eccles, Ben Hardacre, Sarah Annie Carey, John North, Abraham Wildman, and several others, whose contributions were interspersed by pleasing stories or chapters of local history from the versatile pen of Mr. Holroyd and others, who excelled as prose writers.

In Mr. Holroyd's work "A Garland of Poetry by Yorkshire Authors," we are introduced to several local poets whose names do not occur in the "Bradfordian." Among these are George Ackroyd, to whom the book is dedicated, William Dearden, William Heaton, John Illingworth, John Ackroyd (Thornton), and others.

Abraham Holroyd.

But even this does not complete the list of Bradford's past literary worthies. Dr. Scoresby, formerly the Vicar of Bradford, was an able and prolific writer on scientific and other subjects. The Rev. James G. Miall, for forty years the esteemed pastor of the Salem Congregation, compiled the "History of Congregationalism in Yorkshire," and three charming books entitled, respectively, "Memorials of Early Christianity;" "Footsteps of our Forefathers," and "Yorkshire Illustrations." Thomas Rawson Taylor, son of the Rev. Thomas Taylor, of Horton Lane Chapel, was a sweet singer of pure, devotional melody, but, after giving unmistakable indications of a rare poetic genius, was cut down by death at the early age of twenty-eight.

The late Mrs. Hanson was the author of two interesting books, entitled, "Fanny Lee's Testimony," and "Poems and Social Tales." Her husband, Mr. James Hanson, was proprietor and editor of the *Bradford Review*, and since the demise of that journal, has been an indefatigable worker in the cause of education, and at the present moment holds the office of Chairman of the Bradford School Board. Mr. Henry D. Inglis, editor of the *Bradford Courier*, established a wide reputation as an author under the *nom-de-plume* of "Derwent Conway."

If Bradford has not produced many distinguished literary characters in the past, neither has it been productive of many men who have attained positions of eminence in the walks of Art. It may have been that employers were either too busy or too sordid to care for such things, while the employed were too ignorant or too poor to feel any interest in (to them) such trifling things as pictures. But, indeed, there are those who believe that even in these days of boasted achievement in art culture, local talent, no matter how meritorious, still goes unrecognised and unencouraged, and that although the wealthy tradesman of to-day is a lavish picture-buyer, and is proud to have the walls of his palace adorned by costly works of art, yet in his choice of a picture he is far more influenced by the distinguished name of the artist than by a rightful appreciation of its merits. Whether this be so or not will be best known to the promoters of our local art societies, and with them we leave it.

Sixty years ago, a society calling itself "The Bradford Artists' Society of Painting and Sculpture," was established here by a few young and enterprising artists. With very high hopes they engaged a room in Darley Street, and started an exhibition which consisted of a few choice specimens of sculpture, and a hundred and fifty pictures of various degrees of merit. Some were works of the old masters which had been kindly lent for the occasion, others were the productions of artists from neighbouring towns, while the remainder were exclusively the work of Bradford artists. The *Bradford Courier* did its utmost to induce public patronage to this praiseworthy effort. "There are three or four young artists in Bradford," it stated, "of considerable talent, whose works are little known to the public. By this means their productions will be brought into notice. Mr. T. M. Richardson will exhibit a view of Edinburgh Castle; Mr. J. Wilson Anderson, two sea views; Mr. J. Clayton Bentley, an excellent portrait of his father (Lawyer Bentley); and Mr. Geller has several pictures which do him credit as a self-taught artist."

This attempt to encourage a taste for art in a town numbering its forty thousand inhabitants proved a complete failure, and to its projectors a serious financial loss. One gentleman, indeed, who sympathised with the movement gave them half-a-sovereign, but alas, it proved to be a bad one! a fact, however, of which the generous donor was doubtless in ignorance.

Some of these young artists lived to attain a celebrity something more than local. As they appeared to be before their time in Bradford, they sought for themselves "fresh fields and pastures new." One of these was William Overend Geller, the eminent engraver, who was a native of Bradford. Marvellous, indeed, must have been his

WILLIAM OVEREND GELLER.

Drawn by MISS A. GELLER.

industry, for while very young he taught himself both steel and wood engraving, and became so proficient as to be able to impart instruction to others. To him his brother James, who afterwards became a well-known engraver in London, was indebted for his first lessons.

It was in May, 1833, that Mr. Geller removed to London, and in the autumn of that year he painted the copy of "Cymon and Iphigenia," at the British Institution, from the celebrated picture of Sir Joshua Reynolds, then in the possession of William the Fourth. While in London, he enjoyed the friendship of John Martin, of the "Plains of Heaven" reputation, though he was never a pupil of his as some believe. Mr. Geller possessed originality in an eminent degree, and there can be no doubt that had his pecuniary means allowed him to follow the natural bent of his mind, his genius as a painter would have placed him on a much higher pinnacle than that which he ultimately reached. He had a fertile imagination, a dexterous hand, a quick perception for picturesque effect, great skill in grouping and composing, while his industry and application, judging by the amount of work he did, must have been immense. But it is as a first-class engraver that he takes high rank. Among the best of his works in this art may be mentioned the "Deathbed of Calvin;" the "Deathbed of Wesley" after Marshall Claxton, and the portrait of Thomas Campbell, the poet, of which the London press was unstinted in its admiration and praise. One of his most successful efforts was an engraving for an American firm of publishers, entitled, "Franklin at the Court of France." This work was, alas! for ever linked with the most painful associations to Mr. Geller and his family. The plate was finished and safely sent to its destination, but Mr. Geller had afterwards to send over six artists to colour impressions, and among these was his son William Henry, who sailed in the *City of Glasgow*, which left Liverpool in March, 1854, but was never heard of again.

The pictures by Mr. Geller with which Bradford people are most familiar are the portraits of John Nicholson (painted and engraved), Dr. Richardson, and the Revs. Henry Heap, N. T. Heineken, W. Atkinson, Thomas Taylor, Dr. Steadman, Jonathan Glyde, Henry Dowson, and Dr. Fawcett. Many will be interested to know that he painted the fine portrait of Dr. Steadman which still adorns the walls of the Bradford Mechanics' Institute. Of the excellence of Mr. Geller's portraits and their faithful likeness to the originals it is needless to speak. In how many homes in Bradford and the district, the engraved portraits of the local worthies just named may yet be found, treasured up as family relics from year to year?

Joseph Clayton Bentley, a friend and colleague of Mr. Geller, was born at Bradford in 1809, and was the youngest son of Mr. Greenwood Bentley, solicitor. He was first taught landscape painting, in which he made great progress, but in 1832 went to London in order to learn the art of engraving, under the tuition of Mr. Brandard. In this he made such rapid headway that his name soon appeared in many of the illustrated serial publications then published by Messrs. Fisher & Co. and Mr. Virtue. His previous knowledge of painting greatly assisted his progress, and it is certain that it contributed very largely to the spirit, breadth, and variety of colour which distinguished his engravings, and enhanced their value far beyond that of mere dry mechanical copying. His paintings appeared in the various exhibitions in London, and many of the provincial towns. They consisted chiefly of views in Yorkshire, painted with great freedom of hand, and with a nice feeling for colour.

Mr. Bentley was for a time engaged by Mr. Virtue to copy and then engrave several high-class paintings for a costly work published by that gentleman, entitled "Gems of European Art." Among these were "The Fountain," after Zuccareth; and "The Sunny Day," after Cuyp, which were fine examples of the artistic taste which Bentley threw into his work. So also were those which he executed from the Vernon Gallery for the *Art Journal*, viz. "The Wooden Bridge," after Callcott; "The Brook by the Way," after Gainsborough; "The Valley Farm," after Constable; "The Way to Church," after Creswick; and "The Windmill," after Linnell.

At the time of his death, Mr. Bentley was engaged on other plates for the *Art Journal*, and his loss was felt to be one which it would be very difficult to supply. He was a man of quiet unobtrusive habits, and greatly esteemed by all who knew him for his amiable and obliging disposition. He died on the 9th October, 1851; aged 42.

John Cousen was an artist and engraver of whom Bradford might justly feel proud. He was born here in 1804, and when about fifteen years old was articled to the celebrated John Scott, the animal engraver. The taste and refined artistic feeling of Cousen were not exceeded, if equalled, by any other engraver of his time. His larger plates, "Mercury and Herse," after Turner; "Towing the Victory into Gibraltar," and "The Morning after the Wreck," both after Stanfield, were of great excellence; but perhaps his exquisite taste was best displayed in his smaller book-plates after Turner, which are full of artistic feeling, and playful execution.

"Mr. Cousen," said the *Times*, in its obituary notice of this artist, "was of a somewhat reserved and retiring disposition, but the few with whom he associated, loved him for the kindness of his heart, his genial humour, and the unaffected simplicity of his character. He was a native of Bradford, and died at his residence at South Norwood in January, 1881, in his 77th year."

Charles Cousen, a brother and pupil of John Cousen just noticed, was born at Bradford in 1813. The view of Bierley Hall (frontispiece to this work,) was drawn by him, and engraved by Mr. J. C. Bentley. The frontispiece to Mr. James' "History of Bradford" was also drawn by him, and engraved by his brother John. He excelled in combining figure with landscape drawing.

Henry William Topham, of Bradford, was apprenticed as an engraver with his uncle, Samuel Topham, the well-known engraver of Leeds. He engraved three of the plates for the "History of Bradford."

F. W. Topham, the eminent artist, was cousin to Henry William, and was apprenticed with him at the same time to learn engraving under their uncle Samuel. His son, F. W. W. Topham, is an artist now rapidly rising to distinction.

Mr. J. Wilson Anderson was a local artist of considerable merit. We have already referred to his taste and ability as scene-painter for some of the early Bradford theatres. His fine painting of the "Royal Oak" was for many years a familiar object in Kirkgate, and was regarded in the light of a companion picture to the "Bull's Head," near by, painted by his old friend Mr. Geller. Both were genuine Bradford relics, and it is gratifying to know that the latter is carefully treasured by Mr. Waterhouse, formerly the kind and genial host of the Bull's Head Inn, and now of Armstrong's Hotel, Horton Lane.

That "luckless lad," of Haworth, Patrick Branwell Brontë, was ambitious to become a portrait-painter, and his father, yielding to his wishes, allowed him to receive instruction in that art. After being in the hands of a Leeds artist for some time, he came to Bradford with the intention of starting business on his own account. He engaged "private apartments," and, under the protecting wing of his relative the Rev. W. Morgan, of Christ Church, he began life as a portrait painter. Among others he painted the portrait of that reverend gentleman, and also that of Mr. Heap, the Vicar. This project, however, like many another of this ill-fated youth, came to nothing. If artists of such talent and experience as Geller and Bentley could not succeed in Bradford, there was small chance for one so young and inexperienced as Branwell Brontë. During his brief residence here he made the acquaintance of Mr. J. H. Thompson the portrait-painter, and a close friendship existed between them.

CHAPTER XII.

Some Notable and Odd Characters.

BRADFORD has not been unprolific in the production of strange and eccentric characters, although it may not boast of so great a prophet as Mother Shipton, so notorious a witch as Mary Bateman, or so determined a fanatic as Jonathan Martin.

In bygone years astrologers and fortune-tellers appear to have been plentiful enough, and to have made it a "paying business" too. Writing in 1842, Mr. James says—"The tribe of these imposters ('Wisemen' and astrologers), notwithstanding the spread of general intelligence, and the progress of civilisation, is still numerous, and continues to thrive on the credulity of the lower class of inhabitants. So lucrative has the profession of fortune-telling in this neighbourhood been, that many of the adepts in it have died worth considerable sums of money." He then cites the case of a poor aged weaver named Sutcliffe who having been frequently injured by his neighbours, imagined that his house was haunted by an evil spirit, and in order to "lay" it, had recourse to one John Hepworth, a notorious Bradford fortune teller, who, after pouring human blood mixed with hair into a large bottle, corked it up tightly, and put it into the fire, when it soon after exploded and killed the old weaver on the spot.

But even in these days of enlightenment we have not quite got rid of the folly and credulity, the existence of which Mr. James lamented a quarter of a century ago. We have but recently met with a man in the full possession of his senses who verily believed that the carrying of a hard potato in each of his trousers' pockets was an infallible cure for rheumatism; and that to this simple remedy he was indebted, in his own case, for a complete cure of that distressing complaint. It has also been our experience to meet with a noted "planet ruler" who has so much faith in astrology as a means of foretelling future events, that he feels quite assured it will ere long become an important branch of Board School education.

Those Bradfordians whose memories can stretch back to sixty years ago will doubtless remember the crowds that used to gather on Sundays, in the neighbourhood of Tyrrel Street and Bridge Street, in order to witness one of the most extraordinary spectacles that ever passed through the streets of Bradford. Every Sunday afternoon the notorious character known as "Prophet Wroe" held a sort of service in the upper room of the old Cock-pit, and to this place he walked from Dudley Hill in procession with twelve (not the scriptural ten) virgins dressed in white and with long white falls. The prophet himself was conspicuous by the flowing beard and brown hat worn by the "faithful." The large crowds that assembled to witness this novel procession were generally of a peaceful sort, and did nothing more than indulge in a bit of pleasant banter; but it was when the the prophet challenged his audience within the walls of the Cock-pit to a discussion on the merits of Southcottianism that the peace was broken, and the temperature suddenly changed from "calm" to "stormy." On one of these occasions matters became so serious that he was glad to beat a retreat from his sanctuary, and was only saved from very rough handling with the crowd outside, by seeking protection in some premises at hand.

John Wroe was a native of Bowling, and was baptised at the Bradford Parish Church in 1782. The house in which he was born is yet standing and a view of it will be found on the title page of this work. John's father was a worsted manufacturer, coal proprietor and farmer at Bowling, but John himself did not take kindly to business habits. Probably he felt cut out for a higher and holier career. Not long after his marriage he was struck down with a fever, from which he but slowly recovered. From this point he began to "see visions, and dream dreams." He was often seized with epileptic fits, after which he would lie in a state of trance for many hours at a stretch, and angels appeared to him, and told of strange things that would happen to him. Little wonder that he should conceive the idea that he was singled out by God for the purpose of carrying on some great mission upon the earth. Under this belief he did not hesitate to make known his Divine calling, and boldly declared himself to be a veritable prophet of the Lord. He prophesied, and some of his prophecies were so strangely fulfilled that many were induced to believe in him, and to regard him as possessed of supernatural powers.

Prophet Wroe.

There was something about the Southcottian sect that was just to John's fancy. He made himself acquainted with its doctrines, and not very long after the death of the great prophetess Joanna, he aspired to the high honour of donning her prophetic mantle. The disciples of that religious impostor were, however, shy of John's approaches, especially in view of his great pretensions, but he eventually succeeded in winning them over, and ere long became, in Bradford, their acknowledged leader.

Those who are acquainted with the singular history of Joanna Southcott will remember that she had died without fulfilling her own prophecy that she would give birth to the long-promised Shiloh, and that she herself would live forever. And yet her simple-minded followers clung to the belief that she would one day rise again and be the mother of Shiloh. "Such," says a recent writer on this subject, "it may be presumed, is the dream of the small remnant of Southcottians which still holds together and worships in peaceful seclusion, some in the mansion erected for Prophet Wroe, near Wakefield, some in Rossendale, and some in other remote places. But the sect is dying out it would appear, for they have now no prophet or prophetess who is bold enough to go forth amongst the people and declare the gospel according to Joanna."

One of the most formidable opponents the Southcottians had in Bradford was John Rushton, a well-known and worthy character in his day. John was a glib versifier, but we can hardly rank him as a poet. For himself, however, he claimed nothing short of Divine inspiration, for he unblushingly asserts—

> It pleased the Lord so to furnish my head,
> That I need not enquire what is next to be said.

John Rushton could certainly say some sharp and stinging things, and his rhymes (issued in broadsides, printed by Nicholson) were a great source of annoyance to the followers of Joanna. Not less than seventeen of these sheets appeared, but the verses were sad doggerel, and surely incapable of doing either good or harm. A few lines from a sheet entitled—"The Southcottians Dissected, or Enthusiasm Exposed," will serve as a fair sample of the rest,—

> Have you been at the Theatre at Darley Street top?
> Which wise men all pass by; where fools love to stop;
> Where zealots hold forth, and make whimsical speeches
> About some old woman that makes up old breeches.
>
> When she (Joanna) shall bring forth her wonderful son,
> The play will be ended, the farce just begun;
> Then all her admirers, who vauntingly sit
> In the gallery so high, will fall into the pit.

One almost regrets that Rushton should have harped so much upon one string. He might very well have told us, in his circumstantial style of verse-making, of other matters of local interest that were going on in his day. He was not evidently "the poet of the future," nor did he write "for all time," as his effusions are now all but forgotten. He will be best remembered for his long and useful career in connection with various religious institutions in Bradford. To his varied accomplishments he added those of a singer, bass player, and musical composer, and his services were in great demand on anniversary and other special occasions. For several years he was leading singer at Westgate Baptist Chapel, then at Kirkgate Chapel, and afterwards at Horton Lane Chapel, where his daughters, Sarah and Mary Ann, were in the choir.

Another popular rhymester of fifty years ago, was Reuben Holder. Like that of many another genius, Reuben's life was an eventful one. He himself has recorded the fact that he was born at Hunslet in 1797, and that he was brought up a collier. When but five years old he drove a gin-horse at the pit mouth, and at eight was sent to work in the pit. Afterwards he became a brickmaker, but the later years of his life were spent in the joint occupation of hawking fish, and his poems. His verses were printed on broadsides, and sold by him in the Bradford market on Saturday nights. When teetotal advocates were not so plentiful as now, Reuben made a bold stand for total abstinence principles, and thus became one of the pioneers of the Temperance movement. One of his most familiar attitudes was that of standing with a long rod in his hand, at the top of which was a barrel with the ends knocked out, while he recited to the gaping onlookers his own immortal verses, entitled "Lines on the Teetotal Barrel" of which the first verse ran thus :—

You drunken fond fuddlers give ear to my story,
Of drinking its time you began to be weary;
The way to be sober, I'd have you to know it,
Don't drink from a barrel till you can see through it.

Like all men of celebrity, Reuben Holder had his calumniators. Contemporary poets, too, were wont to make fun at his expense, but this was no doubt to be ascribed to jealousy. John Nicholson struck off the following impromptu while listening to Reuben's recitals :—

Here sits Reuben Holder
  At his old scheming tricks;
Too idle to get clay,
  And too lazy to make bricks.

Even Stephen Fawcett, of "Bradford Legends" fame, must needs have a fling at him in some humourous lines that he threw off. But Reuben cared nought for scoffers, and stuck to his muse. If his poetry lacked elegance and rhythm, it certainly was not wanting in versatility. We have before us many of his broadsheets and they cover a wonderful variety of subjects. He has "Lines on the Florentine Venus" and on "Her Majesty the Queen," the same portrait (a rude woodcut,) doing service for both. "Lines on the Distressed State of Trade;" "A Cry for Bread;" "Joseph Barker and the Socialists," and many others of pretty much the same merit.

Poor Reuben! his was truly a hard, bitter struggle for existence, and infinitely more deserving of sympathy than scorn. His poetic fame brought him little gain, and he had always the appearance of a poor, down-trodden man. Although his verse was but sorry stuff, yet he had his admirers, some of whom believed he was all but inspired. What he might have been, had his lot been cast in more favoured times, it is of course difficult to say. He was certainly one of the best known characters of his day. He made the best use of the gifts that he had and left a mark behind him. What more can be said of any man?

A very different type of character to Reuben Holder, was Jonas Tasker, the old sexton and verger of the Parish Church. Jonas was certainly an oddity, but by no means a favourite with his fellows. Gruff and churlish in speech, and not over courteous in manner, he was more feared and avoided than otherwise. Many stories are yet current of some of Jonas's peculiarities, but they are of too grim and ghastly a character to be repeated to refined and sensitive ears. His duties as sexton were, of course, hardly of a kind to inspire cheerfulness or pleasantry, for during his long term of office it devolved upon him to put the sod over many an old Bradfordian with whom, in life, he had been on the most intimate terms.

Thomas (or "Tommy") Ramsden was an interesting old Bradford character. When he kept his bookstall in Kirkgate more than a quarter of a century ago, it was regarded as a pleasure and a privilege to pull up in front of it in order to listen to his quaint lectures and dry humour,—often bestowed, we fear, upon an audience more disposed to hear his talk than buy his books. Ramsden had been an auctioneer in a good way of business before lapsing into the book trade. His last estate was not an improvement upon his first, for he became very poor, and eventually that useful institution, the Bradford Tradesmen's Benevolent Society, selected him for an annuitant, but he died soon after.

Thomas Ramsden.

A still familiar name in Bradford is that of "Old Judy Barrett," whose spice shop, in Westgate, was perhaps the best known of its kind in the town. "Humbugs" were her speciality, and it is not

Blind Jimmy.

too much to say that the very superior quality of these succulent sweets contributed much to her fame. It is said of Judy that in her young days she knew everybody who lived in Bradford. Her early life was one of great hardship. She might often have been seen going all the way to Low Moor with a donkey and cart which she loaded with coal, and frequently carried a sackful on her own back all the way to Bradford.

James Mortimer or "Blind Jimmy," of Heaton, was a genuine old Bradford oddity. Although dependent upon charity for his subsistence, he was in no sense of the word a beggar. His quaint figure, dressed in long drab top-coat and hat slung in front, and playing in a quiet devotional style some old-fashioned psalm tune on his clarionet, will yet be remembered by many. He had certain stands for certain times of the day which he kept with wonderful punctuality. The steps of old Zoar Chapel; the bottom of Eldon Place; Mr. Hailstone's lodge-gates in Horton Lane, and the entrance to the Market in Kirkgate were his favourite positions. He led a respectable and orderly life, and on his death his remains were interred in the burial ground of St. Paul's Church, Manningham.

That a good many stories, humorous and other, should have been handed down concerning the eccentricities of local preachers can hardly be a matter of surprise. If the system begun by John Wesley more than a century ago, of itinerate preaching, and the drafting in of lay workers had done nothing else, it certainly did much for the development of character. For evidence of this it is enough to point to such remarkable men as John Nelson the Birstall stone-mason, Dickey Burdsall, Billy Dawson, Sammy Hick, and others.

The day of the old style of local preacher has however gone by. Except in country villages, and out-of-the-way corners, his influence has all but waned, and he is become "a thing of the past." He flourished best in the days of the hand-loom and the comb-pot, and when these went out, he went with them.

There was a rugged earnestness about the genuine local preacher that was always acceptable, especially to those of his hearers (and there were many such,) who did not think a preacher was sincere unless he gesticulated till he positively perspired. Some "locals," too, had a happy knack of imitating the styles of the popular preachers of the day. There was one such in Bradford about fifty years ago, named Saul—a man of stentorian lungs—who copied the style of the Rev. Robert Newton. He procured the grandest sermons he could from the "Penny Pulpit," and delivered them, word for word, with a gusto and vehemence almost alarming.

But a very different character to this was good old Abraham England, of Eastbrook Chapel, a truly worthy man. There was no sham about his piety. He was a man of intelligence withal, given to study, and possessing a library, poor though he was, of more than a thousand volumes! He was a character too, and had his own peculiar way of "inculcating truth." His mind had a "legal turn" to it, and he was fond of splitting theological hairs, but he generally split them to some purpose.

Then there was "Brother" Pickard, not so well known as old Abraham, but a good and useful man none the less. Quaint of speech he was, yet logical in argument beyond all question. Speaking of the Parable of the Prodigal Son, he would elucidate the subject something after this homely fashion: "Ye mayn't knaw what husks means: they are just potato peelings and such stuff as that; it wur all he hed to eyt, poor fellow, husks."

Speaking of the earnest, well-meaning type of local preacher, we have an impression that he has had but scant justice done to him. With all his eccentricities and peculiarities he was a power for good in his day and generation, and his memory is deserving of being held in reverence and honour.

The strides of progress that have been made during the past fifty years have not been brought about without the sacrifice of some time-honoured customs that were dear to old Bradfordians. Several years have now passed since the old Christmas Waits were last heard in the streets, and when a few more years have rolled away, the fact they were ever heard at all will be spoken of as a thing belonging to the bygone time.

The oldest company of Waits in Bradford was formed about ten years before the passing of the Reform Bill in 1832. In the year 1829, Mr. E. C. Lister and Mr. Matthew Thompson, who sat as magistrates at the "Spotted House," Manningham Lane, gave permission to one Samuel Smith, otherwise "Blind Sam," to form a company of Waits for the town. Sam was not long in finding three other associates (all blind) who were willing to join in the enterprise, and another (who was not blind) to act as guide. The names of Sam's blind companions were, Jim Fletcher, Billy Blazeby and Jack Dodge. Furnished with musical instruments, and all tied to a pole, except the guide, they began their nightly perambulations, making music that could hardly be called sweet, but which linked with the festive season of Christmas and other interesting associations, was always welcome, especially to the young, who liked nothing better than to tumble out of bed to have "just one peep". at the odd procession as it passed along the street.

But alas for the uncertainty of human plans and schemes! In 1862 a rival band of Waits which had the presumption to call itself "The New Borough Waits" sprung into existence, and from this point began a long course of mutual jealousies, bickerings and retaliations. Whether it was that the inhabitants did not care to patronise the two sets, or that so old-fashioned an institution could not adapt itself to new streets and new modes of life, we will not venture to say. Certain it is, that the Bradford Waits, both the old set and the new, have ceased to exist, and in course of time will pass into the limbo of "forgotten things."

List of Subscribers.

LARGE PAPER COPIES.

ACKROYD, GEORGE, J.P., 5, North Park Villas, Manningham.
Anderton, Herbert F., Bolton Royd, Manningham.
Akam, Benjamin, 35, Cecil Avenue, Horton.

BRIGGS, EDWARD, Briggella Mills, Horton.
Briggs, Arthur, J.P., Rawdon, near Leeds.
Burnley, James, J.P., 10, North Park Road, Manningham.
Brown, Thomas, Mount Cross, Bramley.
Bradford Subscription Library, (per John Dale & Co.)
Bolton, George, 28, St. Paul's Road, Manningham.

CRANBROOK, RIGHT HON. THE VISCOUNT, G.C.S I., Hemsted Park, Staplehurst.
Colefax, J. S., J.P., 2, Aldermanbury, Bradford.
Cass, John, J.P., Claremont, Bradford.
Cole, Jabez, West Bowling, Bradford.
Crabtree, Amos, Greaves Street, Little Horton.
Carter, F. R., Savile House, Potternewton, Leeds.
Clarkson, Matthew, New York, U.S.A.
Cudworth, William, Bradford.

DEVONSHIRE, MOST NOBLE THE DUKE OF, K.G., D.C.L , Devonshire House, London.
Dickons, J. Norton, 12, Oak Villas, Manningham.

EMPSALL, T. T., Ashgrove, Bradford.
England, J. J., Upper Wortley, near Leeds.

GARDINER, WALTER, Solicitor, Bradford.
Galloway, Councillor Jesse, West Bowling, Bradford.
Galloway, Fred C., 493, Manchester Road, Bradford.

HAINSWORTH, LEWIS, 120, Bowling Old Lane, Bradford.
Holden, Alderman Angus, Woodlands, Manningham.
Harris, Alfred, J.P., Lunefield, Kirkby Lonsdale.
Hardcastle, Frederick, Solicitor, Bradford.
Hollingworth, William, 281, Little Horton Lane, Bradford.

ILLINGWORTH, HENRY, Ladye Royde House, Bradford.
Illingworth, William, Cambridge House, Bradford.

JEFFERY, H. J., Solicitor, Bradford.

LISTER, S. CUNLIFFE, J.P., D.L., Swinton, Masham.
Lupton, W. C., 9, Cheapside, Bradford.
Lincey, J. H., Beckett's Bank, Bradford.
Lockwood, Thomas, Bilton House, Harrogate.

MILNE-MILNE, S., Calverley House, near Leeds.
Myers, S. P., J.P., 5, Colliergate, Bradford.
Margerison, S., Calverley, near Leeds.
Mechanics' Institute, Bradford, (J. Holbrey, Librarian).
Moulson, Ald: William, Ex-Mayor of Bradford, Little Horton.
Milnes, Eli, 99, Swan Arcade, Bradford.
Mason, Henry, Bankfield, Bingley.

PIKE, GENERAL ALBERT, Washington, D.C., U.S.A.
Priestman, Walter, Ellerburn, Park Drive, Manningham.
Pearson, W. H., West Bowling.
Power, Robert, 28, Moorhead Villas, Shipley.
Parkinson, Joseph, Duckworth Lane, Bradford.

RIDEHALGH, RICHARD, Ripponden, near Halifax.
Rabagliati, Andrea, M.A., M.D., 9, Walmer Villas, Bradford.

SCORAH, JOHN B., AND THOMAS, 31, Horton Lane, Bradford.
Stansfeld, John, Daisy Bank, Meanwood, Leeds.
Sowden. John, A.M., 1, Blenheim Road, Manningham.
Smith, Wheater, 17, Hampton Place, Bradford.
Skidmore, Charles, Stipendiary, Selborne Villas, Manningham.

TEMPEST, BART., SIR ROBERT TEMPEST, Tong Hall, Drighlington.
Thompson, M. W., Park Gate, Guiseley.
Thackwray, William, Peel Square, Bradford.
Turner, J. Horsfall, Idle, near Bradford.
Tordoff, Alderman T. D., Carlton Villas, Heaton.
Thornton, Joseph, 138, Bowling Old Lane, Bradford.
Tolson, Henry, Queensbury, near Halifax.
Thornton, John, Bradford.

WALLER, THOMAS W., Selborne Villas, Manningham.
Whitehead, Francis, Briggella Mills, Horton.
Wurtzburg, John H., Leeds.
Wright, N. W., Blake House, Undercliffe.
Woodhead, Joseph, Longdenhead Lane, Huddersfield.
Waterhouse, David, Hillside House, Coleridge Place, Bradford.

SMALL PAPER COPIES.

ATTREE, R. E., CAPTAIN F. W. T., 11, Kingswood Villas, New Brompton, Kent.
Armitage, Captain Godfrey, J.P., The Court, Ackworth.
Anderton, Herbert F., Bolton Royd, Manningham.
Ambler, John, 6, North Park Road, Manningham.
Ackroyd, George, J.P., 5, North Park Villas, Manningham. (2 copies)
Ackroyd, Samuel, J.P., Little Horton.
Atkinson, W. F., Solicitor, Bradford. (4 copies)
Atkinson, C. J., Solicitor, Bradford.
Andrews, William, F.R.H.S., President Hull Literary Club.
Aykroyd, Alfred, J.P., Oakwood Villa, Toller Lane, Manningham.
Atkinson, Charles Law, Solicitor, Bradford.
Atkinson Charles, 210, Manchester Road, Bradford.
Appleyard, John, M.D., 1, Clifton Villas, Manningham.
Armitage, J., 14, Victoria Road, Saltaire.

BRADFORD HISTORICAL and Antiquarian Society.
Bradford Free Library, (Butler Wood, Librarian.) (10 copies)
Busfeild, W., J.P., St. Ives, Bingley.
Balme, E. B. W., M.A., J.P., Cotewall, Mirfield.
Baildon, W. Paley, 5, Stone Buildings, Lincolns Inn.
Binns, J. Arthur, Official Receiver, Bradford.
Briggs, Arthur, J.P., Rawdon, near Leeds.
Briggs, Charles, Briggella Mills, Horton.
Bottomley, Joseph, 11, Ashgrove, Bradford.
Bell, J. H., M.D., 20, Lumb Lane, Bradford.
Barrans, F. C., Bradford.
Barker, Mrs., Bradford.
Beanland, Frederick, Bradford.
Byles, W. Pollard, 1, Selborne Terrace, Manningham.
Brunton, J. W., Gaythorne Road, West Bowling.
Bailey, Samuel A., Victor Road, Manningham.
Bromley, Charles, Belle Vue House, Goole.
Briggs, S. T., 18, Southfield Square, Manningham.

Beecroft, Mrs., 46, Caroline Street, Saltaire.
Blackburn, G. B., 45, Blenheim Road, Bradford. (2 copies)
Brookes, W. M., School House, Bolton.
Braithwaite, John, 262, Lumb Lane, Bradford.
Burnley, James, J.P., 10, North Park Road, Manningham.
Bramham, G., 194, Undercliffe Street, Bradford.
Bradberry, A., 51, Victoria Road, Saltaire.
Boyes, William, 8, Spring Gardens, Bradford.
Barros, John T., 27, Cecil Avenue, Bradford.
Bools, W. E., 7, Cornhill, E.C.
Braithwaite, H. W., Britannia Mills, Bradford.
Brown, Thomas, Mount Cross, Bramley.
Boys, W. M., 9, Merton Road, Bradford. (2 copies)
Bentley, Joseph, Secretary Bradford Coffee Tavern Co.
Behrens, Frederick, Springfield House, Bradford.
Behrens, H., Springfield House, Bradford.
Barker, Alfred, Fryston Place, Undercliffe Street.
Binns, Joseph, 24, Kingswood Terrace, Great Horton.
Barraclough, Aquila, 3, Faxfleet Street, Bradford.
Bastow, Fred, 13, Little Cross Street, Bradford.
Bilsborough, Thomas, 11, Neal Street, Bradford.
Bray, George, 86, Otley Road, Bradford.
Booth, William, Idle, near Bradford.

Collyer, Rev. Robert, D.D., The Strathmore, New York, U.S.A.
Chettle, D. W., 658, St. Mary's Terrace, Manningham.
Cordingley, J. R., 10, Melbourne Place, Bradford.
Clapham, J. Arthur, 16, Apsley Crescent, Bradford.
Craven, Frederick, 33, Kirkgate, Bradford.
Cotton, John, M.I.M.E., Vere Street, Bradford.
Claridge, W., M.A., Farcliffe Terrace, Bradford.
Chadwick, S. J., Lyndhurst, Oxford Road, Dewsbury.
Craven, Percy L., Rock Bank, Peel Park.
Craven, S. K., 41, Carlisle Street, Manningham.
Clough, J. H., 15, Easby Road, Bradford.
Cooper, Samuel Joshua, Mount Vernon, Barnsley. (2 copies)
Cliff, John, F.G.S., F.R.S., Nisbet Hall, Fulneck.
Carter, Bennett, 12, Spring Place, Shearbridge, Bradford.
Carter, Sydney H., ,, ,, ,,
Clay, J. W., F.S.A., Raistrick House, near Brighouse.
Crabtree, Charles, 32, Greaves Street, Little Horton. (3 copies)
Cryer, B. G., 24, Grantham Road, Bradford. (2 copies)
Collins, John, 4, Buxton Street, Manningham.
Clough Lee, 3, Blenheim Road, Bradford.
Camidge, William, Savings' Bank, York.
Chatburn, William, Clough Street, West Bowling.
Croft, Joseph, (Bradford Banking Co., Limited).
Cousen, James, 22, Springswood Terrace, Shipley.
Cockerham, J. W., Heatherbank, Bingley.
Cure, John, 305, Bowling Old Lane, Bradford.
Carter, J. W., 30, Lincoln Terrace, Lincoln Road, Bradford.

Duggan, Ald: E. P., 69, Ashgrove, Bradford.
Davis, J. W., F.G.S., F.S.A., F.L.S., Chevinedge, Halifax.
Dawson, G. F., J.P., Lightcliffe, near Halifax.
Dickinson, Walter, (Messrs. Stein & Co., Currer Street, Bradford).
Darlow, Stephen, Bingley.
Draper, William, Manchester Road, Bradford. (2 copies)
Dawson, John E., Eldwick Grange, near Bingley.
Dale, Mrs. Hannah, 34, Park Crescent, Otley Road, Bradford.
Drane, William, 12, Northfield Place, Manningham.

Denison, R. W., (Fred Butterfield & Co., 9, Piccadilly, Bradford). (2 copies)
Denby, Walter, M.D., The Infirmary, Bradford.
Dale & Co., John, 17, Bridge Street, Bradford.
Dean, S. E., 41, Parsonage Road, West Bowling.
Dean, John, 29, Marshall Street, Bradford.
Downing, William, 3, East Parade, Bradford.
Dunlop, James, 49, Marshall Street, Bradford.

England, J. J., Wortley, near Leeds.
Eshelby, H. D., F.S.A., 24, Park Road South, Birkenhead.
Eccles, Charles, Bradford.
Ellis, Arthur, c/o W. Ellis, Bolling Hall, Bradford.
Emsley, Robert, 28, Kaye Street, Bradford.
Edmondson, Henry, 5, Marlboro' Road, Manningham.
Earnshaw, Rev. John, 2, Sedgefield Terrace, Bradford.
Eddowes, Rev. John, Eastgate Vicarage, Darlington.
Ellis, George, Castlefield, Bingley.

Fitzgerald, Major, Hardwick House, Richmond, Surrey.
Forster, Mrs. W. E., Wharfeside, Burley-in-Wharfedale.
Federer, Charles A., L.C.P., 8, Hallfield Road, Bradford.
Fox, William, 71, Longside Lane, Bradford.
Foljambe, Cecil G. Savile, Cockglode, Ollerton, Newark.
Fawcett, J. E., 19, Dale Street, Bradford.
Flather, Thomas, Borough Accountant, Bradford.
Ferrand, W. E., 65, Southfield Square, Bradford.
Firth, William, 17, Trinity Terrace, Bradford. (2 copies)
Fieldhouse, Isaac, 297, Manchester Road, Bradford.
Fawthrop, Joseph, 59, Round Street, West Bowling.
Fyfe, James, 1, Sunny bank, Shipley.
Fulda, L., 62, Leeds Road, Bradford. (2 copies)
Fell, J. A., 42, Victoria Road, Saltaire.
Fell, Timothy, West Bowling.
Farrar, George Henry, 13, Kirkgate, Bradford.
Fleming, F. G., Halifax.
Forshaw, Charles F., M.A., LLD., Westgate, Bradford.
Field, Samuel, 6, Turner Place, Bradford.
Foster & Sons, John, Queensbury.
Fawthrop, John, 412, Bowling Old Lane.
Friend, A
Friend, A

Glossop, William, 33, Kirkgate, Bradford.
Galloway, Fred C., 493, Manchester Road, Bradford.
Green, Joseph J., Stanstead, Montfitchett, Essex.
Gunston, J., North Parade, Bradford.
Gaunt, J. E., Solicitor, Bradford. (2 copies)
Grainge, William, Harrogate. (2 copies)
Greaves, William, Solicitor, Bradford.
Garnett, Robert, 18, Grantham Road, Bradford.
Gidley, William, Ovenden, Halifax.
Goyder, David, M.D., 88, Great Horton Road, Bradford.
Greenbury, F., M.B., 733, Manchester Road, Bradford.
Gledhill, Alfred, 12, Merton Road, Bradford.
Godwin, John V., J.P., Rawdon.
Gaukroger, Walter, 6, Merton Road, Bradford.
Greening, Charles, Albion Court, Bradford.
Greenwood, Thomas, 2, Cliffe Villas, Manningham.
Gaskell, G. A., Ebridge House, Bingley.
Greaves, Hanson, West Bowling.

Hailstone, Edward, F.S.A., Walton Hall, near Wakefield.
Holden, Ald: Angus, Woodlands, Manningham. (6 copies)

Harris, Alfred, J.P., Lunefield, Kirkby Lonsdale.
Hirst, Col: Henry S., C.B., Clayton, near Bradford.
Hardy, Lawrence, J.P., Royds Hall, near Bradford.
Harrison, John, Solicitor, Leeds.
Holdsworth, Ald: William, West Bowling.
Hardaker, Ald: John, 3, Ashburnham Grove, Manningham. (2 copies)
Hill, Ald: Thomas, J.P., Royds House, Manningham.
Hammond, Councillor E. W., Horton Hall.
Hart, Joshua, 2, Selborne Grove, Manningham.
Head, John, C.E., F.G.S., 122, Clapham Park Road, London, S.W.
Hainsworth, Lewis, 120, Bowling Old Lane, Bradford.
Hainsworth, Albert, Fernsholme, Bury.
Haley, Francis, Vere Street, Bowling.
Hoyle, William, 16, Oakroyd Terrace, Manningham.
Hodgson, J., 9, St. Andrews Place, Bradford.
Hitchin, Councillor John, 10, Westgrove Street, Bradford.
Hanson, B., 28, Southfield Square, Bradford.
Hall, Albert Victor, 25, Spring Cliffe, Manningham.
Hall, Benjamin J., 15, Spring Cliffe, Manningham.
Harris, Henry, 54, St. Paul's Road, Manningham.
Hardaker, J. H., Bradford. (2 copies)
Holbrey, Joseph, (Bradford Mechanics' Institute).
Harrison, Henry, 29, Primrose Terrace, Bradford.
Holdsworth, Ralph, 23, Kirkgate, Bradford. (2 copies)
Hartley, John, 28, Cowper Place, Bradford.
Hustler, Edwin, Spring Mount, Horton Road. (2 copies)
Hemingway, Samuel, Walmer Villas, Bradford.
Holdsworth, Albert, 236, Lower Rushton Road, Leeds Road.
Holdsworth, Mrs. Selina, ,, ,, ,,
Hertz, William M., 3, Oak Mount, Manningham.
Hardy, Sylvester, Roundhill Street, Little Horton.
Hayward, Tom, Bradford.
Hanson, William, Saltaire.
Holiday, Alfred J., 12, Whetley Grove, Bradford.
Harrison, Parkinson & Co., Sun bridge, Bradford. (3 copies)
Hall, Norman, 127, Horton Lane.
Halford, Ezra, Bradford.
Holgate, James, 6, Milton Street, Halifax.
Hepworth, George, Brighouse.
Haigh, Mrs., Ashton Road, Morecambe.

Iveson, Joseph, West Bowling.
Illingworth, Thomas, 6, Ashburnham Grove, Bradford.
Illingworth, Thomas, Ivy House, Salterhebble.

Jackson, William H., Undercliffe.
Johnson, Ben, Kirkgate, Bradford.
Jackson, Richard, Commercial Street, Leeds. (2 copies)
Jowett, John, 224, Manchester Road, Bradford.
Jowett, Henry, 214, ,, ,, ,,
Jarvis, J. J., 26, ,, ,, ,,
Jowett, J. S., *Brighouse News*, Brighouse.

Kay, Councillor James, West Bowling.
Knight, J. W., 7, Miall Street, Bradford. (2 copies)
Kelsal, J. C., Sydenham Place, Bradford.

Lee, Edmund, The Registrar, Bradford.
Lincey, J. H., (Beckett's Bank), Bradford. (2 copies)
Lund, Charles, Ilkley. (4 copies)
Lancaster, Seth, 48, Wakefield Road, Bradford.
Last, J. T., Solicitor, Bradford.

Lund, Miss, Eldermere, Ilkley.
Longfellow, T., 5, Harold Place, Saltaire.
Loughnan, Mr., Newton Street, Bradford.
Library, British Museum, Russell Street, Bloomsbury, London.
Library, The Bodleian, Oxford.
Library, The University, Cambridge.
Library, Trinity College, Dublin.
Library, Faculty of Advocates, Edinburgh.
Libraries, Public, Leeds, (James Yates, Librarian).

MECHANICS' INSTITUTE, BRADFORD, (J. Holbrey, Librarian).
Milne-Milne, S., Calverley House, near Leeds.
Mitton, E. W., 8, Eldon Road, Hampstead, London.
Mason, Henry, Bankfield, Bingley.
Maddocks, Councillor John, Park Drive, Heaton.
Musgrave, Edgar, Bradford.
Monckman, J. W., 19, Charles Street, Bradford.
Marshall, A. G., 11, Oak Villas, Bradford.
Mitchell, J. H., J.P., Horton Villa.
Mann, S. B., 3, Park Terrace, Halifax.
Moulson, Angus, 28, Merton Road, Bradford.
Muff, Henry, 18, Claremont.
Myers, F., Bentley Street, Bradford.
Matthews & Brook, Messrs., Sun bridge, Bradford. (13 copies)
Maw, William, (Bradford Infirmary).
Murgatroyd, J. J., 10, Granville Terrace, Frizinghall.
Murgatroyd, Benjamin, ,, ,, ,,
Muff, T. P., 26, Market Street, Bradford.
Middlemiss, William, 53, Southfield Square, Bradford.
Megson, W. B., 32, Fairfield Road, Manningham.
Miles, J., Sunbridge Road, Bradford. (4 copies)
McLandsborough, John, 5, Lindum Terrace, Bradford.
Mitchell, H. B., York Villas, Norfolk Road, Sheffield.
Middlebrook, Joseph, 12, Coleridge Place, Bradford.
Moody, Mr. Charles, West Bowling.
Metcalfe, Thomas, 4, Sawrey Place, Horton Lane.
Megson, Alfred, Swan Arcade, Bradford.
Mosse, Rev. C. W., Huish Rectory, Beaford, N. Devon.
M'Cormick, Rev. F. H. J., Whitehaven, Cumberland.
Margerison, Joseph, Calverley, near Leeds.

NEWTON, OLIVER, Solicitor, Bradford.
Newton, William, 17 & 19, Kirkgate, Bradford.
Newboult, George, (Illingworth Newboult & Co.), Bradford. (2 copies)
Newboult, Alfred, 175, Hollings Mount, Manningham.
Newboult, F. W. T., Aldermanbury, Bradford.
Nicholl, Samuel H., West Bowling. (2 copies)
Nichols, Richard, 12, Edmund Street, Bradford.
Naylor, E., 48, Market Street, Bradford.

ODDY, WILLIAM, 55, Market Street, Bradford.
Oddy, John Charles, Kensington House, Girlington.
Oddy, Joseph H., Aquila House, Liversedge.
Oddy, John G., Hallcroft Hall, Addingham.

POWELL, FRANCIS SHARP, M.P., Horton Old Hall.
Pollard, Captain W., Springfield, Ripon.
Peterson, E. P., Architect, Bradford.
Priestley, Mr. John, Bradford.
Pearson, W. H., New Cross Street, West Bowling. (4 copies)
Pearson, Thomas H., ,, ,,
Peel, Frank, Heckmondwike.

Peacock, Frederick G., Solicitor, Bradford.
Poole, Richard, 78, Great Horton Road.
Patchett, Arthur, 274, Undercliffe Street.
Parkinson, M. A., 2, Lansdowne Place.
Pearson, George, Parkfield Road, Manningham. (2 copies)
Power, Robert, 28, Moorhead Villas, Shipley.
Power, John, Eldon Lane, near Bishop Auckland.
Patchett, John, Mildred House, Undercliffe.
Pepper, George, 1, Devonshire Terrace, Manningham.
Platts, Alfred, Solicitor, Bingley.
Pickles, Benjamin, 69, Whetley Lane, Bradford.
Pickard, William, 34, Grove Terrace, Bradford.
Pickles, Mr., Manchester Road, Bradford.
Preston, John Emanuel, Gilstead, near Bingley.

Ryan, Rev. Vincent J., Manfield, near Darlington.
Redhead, Rev. G. E., 7, White's View, Bradford.
Richardson, Thomas, 8, Lumby Street, Bradford.
Reynard, Mrs., The Wick, Scarborough. (2 copies)
Rigg, Joseph, 10, Swaine Street, Bradford.
Rawson, Benjamin Currer, Solicitor, Bradford.
Robson, E., Wakefield Road, Bradford.
Robson, J. A. L., Mechanics' Institute, Keighley.
Reacher, Rev. John, Wesley House, East Molesey, Surrey.
Riley, William, 66, Shearbridge Road, Bradford.
Rawson, Joseph, Deputy Town Clerk, Bradford.
Rawson, Mrs., Clough Street, West Bowling.
Rhodes, William Venables, Oldfield House, Heckmondwike.
Richardson, G. B., 19, Thornton Road, Bradford.
Roberts, George, Lofthouse, Wakefield.
Ramsden, A. W., Bingley.
Rawson, Isaac, Sawrey House, Bradford.
Rayner, John, 26a, York Street, Manchester.
Randall, Joseph, Bank Chambers, George Street, Sheffield.
Ridehalgh, Richard, Ripponden, Halifax.
Rawnsley & Ellershaw, Messrs., New Cross Street, West Bowling. (2 copies)
Robinson, Samuel, Solicitor, Bradford.
Rawlings, Mr. (W. Firth & Sons, Bradford).
Rayner, Mrs., Pudsey.
Reynolds, Miss, West Bowling.

Salt, Edward, J.P., Ferniehurst, Baildon.
Swallow, David, 7, Drewton Street, Bradford. (2 copies)
Seebohm, Benjamin, 1, Dynevor Road, Bedford.
Stuart, J. A. Erskine, L.R.C.S., Edin. Staincliffe, Dewsbury.
Sewell, A. B., Parish Clerk, Bradford.
Stamford, Mr., Solicitor, Bradford.
Stead, John James, Heckmondwike.
Smith, William, F.S.A.S., Morley, near Leeds. (2 copies)
Speight, Harry, West Bowling. (2 copies)
Scorah, Messrs. John B. and Thomas, Horton Lane.
Sutcliffe, Frederick J. R., A.I.C.E., etc., etc., Low Moor Iron Works.
Schofield, John, 5, George Street, Bradford.
Sowden, Thomas, Grange Cottage, Allerton. (2 copies)
Smith & Son, G. B., Exchange, Bradford. (2 copies)
Sanctuary, Isaac, Saltaire. (2 copies)
Smith, John, 27, Alexandra Road, Shipley.
Smith, William, 113, Fitzgerald Street, Bradford.
Seymour, Charles Henry, Bowling.
Sykes, Arthur F., 14, Neal Street, Horton Lane.
Sutton, R. H., 25, Princess Street, Manchester.

Schofield, Edward, Kingsley House, Victor Road.
Silcock, J. R., 52, Peel Square, Bradford.
Suddards, Thomas, 172, New Cross Street, West Bowling.
Shaw, Walter T., Manningham.
Scott, Silas, J.P., Shipley.
Suddards, William, Darley Street, Bradford.
Sugden, Edward, 48, Elizabeth Street, Bradford. (2 copies)
Seymour, William Edward, 73, Rufford Street, Leeds Road.
Shaw, William, 17, Spring Place, Horton.
Smith, Thomas W., 297, Bowling Old Lane.
Skevington, Thomas William, Shipley.
Shaw, Henry, 67, Girlington Road, Bradford. (2 copies)
Spencer, Miles, 10, St. James' Square, Bradford.
Stowell, Christopher, 426, Manchester Road.
Smith, John, Crescent Hotel, Ebor Street, Horton Lane.
Smith, Councillor John, 5, Sawrey Place, Horton Lane.
Soppitt, H. T., Rosemount, Bolton.
Steel, George, 24, Swaine Street, Bradford.
Smith, Sydney, (Bradford District Bank).
Smith, George, 80, Little Horton Lane.
Shepherd, H. W., 35, Elizabeth Street, Bradford.
Staunton, W., Bradford.
Snow, George Francis, 16, Southey Place, Bradford. (2 copies)
Sutcliffe, Frank, 3, Heaton Grove.
Sutcliffe, Benjamin, 647, Leeds Road.
Shaw, Giles, 72, Manchester Street, Oldham.

Thompson, M. W., Park Gate, Guiseley. (4 copies)
Taylor, Rev. R. V., B.A., Melbecks Vicarage, Richmond.
Taylor, John, 79, Gloucester Place, Portman Square, London, W. (2 copies)
Tempest, Mrs. Arthur, Coleby Hall, Lincoln.
Turner, Samuel, West Bowling.
Turner, J. Horsfall, Idle.
Thackeray, Charles W., 1, Mannheim Road, Toller Lane.
Thornton, Joseph, West Bowling. (3 copies)
Turner, John W., 27, Water Street, Huddersfield.
Turner, J. W., Bradford.
Tetley, Samuel, West Bowling.
Thornton, Mrs. W., Alexandra Road, Shipley.

Topham, Edward W., 10, Springwood Terrace, Shipley.
Townend, Edmund, 17, Cliff Villas, Toller Lane.
Tacey, W. G., M.D., 6, Manningham Lane.
Thompson, John, (Bradford Banking Co., Limited).
Turner, Isaac, 108, New Cross Street, West Bowling.
Terry, Percival, B.A., Oxon., High Street, Bradford.
Telford, H., (Parker Hodgson & Co., Bradford).
Townend, W. H., Heaton Hall, Bradford.
Tempest, William, 130, New Cross Street, West Bowling.
Thornton, S., 37, Titus Street, Saltaire.
Thornton, Mrs. Hannah, 406, Bowling Old Lane.

Waugh, Edwin, The Hollies, New Brighton, Cheshire.
Walmsley, John, Ashgrove, Bradford.
White, J., Daisy Hill, Rawdon.
Wilcockson, Charles, West Bowling.
Wells, Isaac, 65, Roundhill Street, Little Horton.
Waterhouse, J., Sunfield, Allerton.
Watmough, Ephraim, 149, High Street, Great Horton.
Waterhouse, David, Hillside House, Coleridge Place. (2 copies)
Wade, J. H., Solicitor, Bradford.

Ward, Samson, West Bowling.
Ward, Jane, (Mr. Halford, Bradford).
Widdop, Arthur, 17, Fairbank Road, Whetley Lane.
Wood, Ald: W. Willis, Greenhill House, Leeds Road.
Wright, J. C., Market Street Chambers.
Wright, Councillor James, West Bowling. (2 copies)
Whitaker Thorp, F.C.S etc., 46, Smiddles Lane, Bradford.
Ward, H. H., 62, Southfield Square.
Whitehead, R. 46., Well Street, Bradford.
Walker, J. W., 127, Horton Road.
Wroe, William, 41, Southfield Square
Whaley, Thomas, Oakleigh Road, Clayton.
Wright, Samuel, Solicitor, Bradford
Whiteley, John M., 70, Salt Street, Bradford.
White, Joseph, 4, Mornington Villas, Bradford.
Woodd, Charles, H.L, J.P , Roslyn House, Hampstead, London, N.W.
Wood, Butler, (Bradford Free Library).
Waud, Horace, C., 14, Apsley Villas.
Weber, A., 36, St. Paul's Road.
Williams, W.E., Free Library, Doncaster.
Watson, Hustler, White Bear Inn, Bradford Moor.
Woolly, Alfred, Burlington Terrace.
Waterhouse, Thomas, Armstrong's Hotel, Bradford.
Wright, N.W., Undercliffe.
Worsnop, J. M. D., (per Mr. J. Schofield).
Webster, John, 32, Drewton Street.
Whaley, S. W., Church Bank, Bradford.
Wilcock, John W., Idle.
Whitehead, Oliver, 49, Little Horton Green.
Wright, George, West Bowling.
Wilkinson, J., 348, Wakefield Road.

YEWDALL, HENRY, Solicitor, Bradford.

Subscribers to the Second Edition.

Armitage, Lady, Kirklees, Brighouse.
Armitage, W. H. Wotton under Edge, Gloucestershire.
Akeroyd, Zaccheus, 105, St. Stephen's Road, West Bowling.
Ambler, Mrs. Jeremiah, 10, Selborne Villas, Manningham.

Bromley, Charles, Belle Vue House, Goole.
Bilbrough, W. R. 15, Beech Grove Terrace, Leeds.
Briggs, T. General Post Office, London, E.C.
Burnley, James, 12, St. Alban's Villas, Highgate Road, N.W.
Binns, Æthelbert, Wilsden.
Brigg, Benj. S., J.P., Burlington House, Keighley.
Brear & Co , Limited, Kirkgate, Bradford. (25 copies)
Beldon, Mrs., 14, Rushton Road, Thornbury, Bradford.
Bankart, John, H., Bolton Grange, Bradford.
Baxter, William, 6, White's View, Bradford.
Booth, W. E. 21, St. James Market, Bradford.
Barker, Herbert, 88, Toller Lane, Manningham.
Butterfield, E. P. Wilsden.

Cranbrook, Right Hon. the Viscount G.C.S.I., Hemsted Park, Staplehurst.
Caine, W. S. 33, North Side, Clapham Common, S.W.
Craven, C. W. 16, Lawkholme Lane, Keighley.
Craven, John E. Mulcture Hall, near Todmorden.
Clarkson, Henry, (Author of "Memories of Merry Wakefield,") Alverthorpe Hall, Wakefield.
Cawthra, Wm., Eldwick, Bingley.
Carter, F. R. Savile House, Potternewton, Leeds.
Charnley, Will, 2, Poplar Bank, Rochdale.
Campbell, J. Upper Castle Street, Bradford.
Croft, William, Street House, Dudley Hill.
Cockcroft, Wm. Henry, Leefield House, Allerton.

Duff, Rev. Archibald, LLD. 51, St. Mary's Road, Bradford.
Dobson, Benjamin, 75, Leeds Road, Bradford.
Dobson, Edward, 17, Oak Lane, Bradford.
Dobson, A., 10, Highfield, Manningham.
Denison, S., M.I.M.E., 32, Clarendon Road, Leeds.

Emberton, Thomas, M., The Cedars, Methley, Leeds.
Edhouse, Henry, 649, Leeds Road, Bradford.

Farrah, John, Harrogate.
Fairbank Mrs., Long Preston, near Skipton.
Fairbank, John, Wrosehill, Windhill, Shipley.
Firth, John, 10, Merton Road, Bradford.
Forshaw, Dr., North Parade, Bradford.
Free Library, Bradford, (Butler Wood, Librarian.)

Glossop, William, Bradford.
Galloway, F. C., Bradford,
Graham, William, 40, Parkgate, Bradford.
Guest, W. H., Arlington Place, 263, Oxford Road, Manchester.
Grant, Rev Alexander, T., Leven Parsonage, Fife.
Gidley, Herbert, Talbot Street, Bradford.

Hollywood, Rev. John, M. A., the Vicarage, Bankfoot, Bradford,
Hainsworth, Lewis, 320, Bowling Old Lane, Bradford.
Howarth, John, 53, Whetley Lane, Bradford. (2 copies)
Hardaker, John, 23, St. John's Terrace, Leeds.
Hippisley, J. E., 483, Little Horton Lane, Bradford.
Hutton, (senr.) Chas., Eccleshill, Bradford.
Howson, J. M., 12, Ashfield, Bradford.
Hall, Harry H., 25, Spring Cliffe, Manningham.
Hollingworth, G. F., 381, Little Horton Lane, Bradford.
Horsfall, Edward, 86, Toller Lane, Manningham,
Hamilton, Robert, 112, Manningham Lane.

Illingworth, Joshua, 97, Trinity Street, Spring Bank, Hull.

Jackson, Wm. H., Belvoir House, Heaton
Jowett, J. Atkinson, Clock House, Manningham.

Killingbeck, John, Kidderminster.
Kaye, Walter J., M.A., Ilkley College, Ilkley.
Knowles, C. H., 16, Parliament Street, Harrogate.

Lorne, the most Noble the Marquis of; Kensington Palace, Kensington, London, W.
Lössel, A. C., 42, Vicar Lane, Bradford. (2 copies)
Lacey, William, Methley Farm, Leeds.
Lockwood, Thomas, 79, Sterling Street, Bradford.
Langdale, Thomas, 79, Napier Street, Laisterdyke, Bradford.

Masham, the Right Hon. Lord, Swinton.
Middlebrook, J. A., 2, Piccadilly, Bradford
Moorhouse, J. B., Cecil Mount, Horton Park
Mortimer, Charles, Franklin Street, Milwaukee, Wisconsin.
Matthews & Brooke, Market Hall and Sunbridge Road, Bradford. (25 copies)
Miles, Thomas, 13, Sunbridge Road, Bradford. (7 copies)

Norcliffe, Rev. C. B., M A., Langton Hall, Malton.
Nussey, Samuel L., Potternewton Hall, near Leeds.

Ormerod, Hanson, Boothroyde, Rastrick, Brighouse.
Ogden, J. M., Ellescope House, Sunderland.

Pollard, Collingwood, 5, Cheapside, Bradford. (2 copies)
Pawson, Henry, 1, High Street, Sheffield.
Pickard, Alfred, 5, Albion Street, Wakefield.
Proctor, Richard, Oak Mount, Burnley.
Pearson, W. H., 11, Raglan Street, Bingley.

Ross, Percival, A.M., I.C.E., North Bierley, Bradford.
Richardson, Wm. R., M.A., Alwyn House, Shortlands, Kent.

Sowden, W. M., 61, St. Mary's Road, Manningham.
Stansfield, W. G., Darley Street, Bradford. (2 copies)
Singleton, James, 43, Delph Mount, Hyde Park, Leeds.
Smith, Colonel Rowland, Red Hall, Lincoln.
Smith, Tom C., F.R.H.S., Green Nook, Longridge near Preston.
Stockdale, Albert, Woodhouse Hill, Huddersfield.
Speight, Mrs., Thornville, 226, Manningham Lane.

Turner, J. Horsfall, F.R.H.S., Idle, Bradford.
Tetley, Herbert, H., 16, St. Andrew's Place, Bradford.

Whitley, Jonas, Ellercroft, Allerton, Bradford.
Walker, Thomas, 1, Thorncliffe Square, Bradford.
Wilson, Chas. Macro, Waldershaigh, Bolterstone, Sheffield.
Wright, Miss, Ling Bob, Wilsden.
Waterhouse, Charles, Market Hall, Bradford. (7 copies)